b Bristol
Polytechnic

Author:

Title:

BRISTOL POLYTECHNIC
REDLAND LIBRARY
REDLAND HILL
BRISTOL BS6 6UZ

This book should be returned by the last date
stamped below. The period of loan may be extended
if no other reader wishes to use the book.

-9. NOV. 1987 REFCL			
CL 3. MAR 1992			
07. NOV 2003			
28. NOV 2003			
			B38/4/84

Between class and elite

To my parents

Zygmunt Bauman

Between class and elite

The evolution of the British labour movement
A sociological study

Translated by Sheila Patterson

Manchester University Press

Klasa – ruch – elita
© 1960 Państwowe Wydawnictwo Naukowe, Warsaw
This translation © 1972 Manchester University Press
Published by the University of Manchester
at the University Press
316–324 Oxford Road, Manchester MI3 9NR
ISBN 0 7190 0502 7

Distributed in the USA by
Humanities Press Inc
450 Park Avenue South, New York, N.Y. 10016

Made and printed in Great Britain by
William Clowes & Sons, Limited
London, Beccles and Colchester

Contents

List of tables

Preface

to the English edition

Over fifteen years have passed since I began work on this book, stimulated by the lively atmosphere of Robert McKenzie's seminars, and with access to the wonderful collections in the LSE library. Fifteen years mean a great deal in the life of modern science, since, according to Professor de Solla Price, roughly half of all the papers so far published have been written during the last decade, while seven in every eight scientists who have been active in the history of mankind are alive and working today. The history of the British labour movement is by no means an exception, though scholarly interest in this field has visibly subsided since the 1950s, when Labour's new, national political role ceased to be regarded as something out of the ordinary, requiring a special explanation, and became a matter of everyday routine. Nevertheless, hundreds of new monographs and case studies were prepared and a portion of them made available to the public, while thousands of entries in archives were transferred from a purely physical into a cultural existence, i.e. tranformed into 'historical facts'. In view of all this, I owe my readers what is called in sociological jargon a 'rationale'. Why should I have decided to add this book to the dozens circulating among scholars, almost fifteen years after it was written and with no serious attempt to incorporate the sources which have been made into 'facts' by the studies published since then?

The rationale is relatively simple. This is not a study which should be judged by the standards of historiography. Its value—if it has any—consists not in 'discovering'—or, more correctly, creating—new, hitherto unknown facts. Even at the time it was written the book was based mainly on a secondary analysis of data already gathered and processed by others, and contributed little on the level of purely empirical statements. Its contribution was configurational, not substantive: it was the result of applying a new approach and reorganising the known empirical material in a new analytical perspective. To the best of my knowledge, this approach has not yet become obsolete and may still prove its fruitfulness in the study of the dynamics of social movements. The analytical framework applied in this study retains its relative independence towards the empirical field to which it was applied—in so far as nothing has been discovered on the empirical level which would make the theoretical model unworkable. In other words, this is a sociological, not a historiographic study, and I should like it to be judged in terms of:

(a) the exhaustiveness or inadequacy of the inventory of items extracted from the social totality to be included in the system under analysis;
(b) the heuristic value of the basic distinctions made within the system being analysed;
(c) the resulting contribution to our understanding of the dynamics of social movements in general and movements emerging in the working class in particular.

Here I must confess that I intended to arrive at a relatively coherent theory of labour movements, this being an analytical starting point to a more general theory of social movements as a whole. This intention stemmed from my dissatisfaction with most of the influential theories on the subject in current circulation.

Social movements usually content themselves with an ideological rationale of their aims and stop short of involvement in theoretical considerations of a more detached character. Theories of social movements and labour movements which stand closer than others to this rule are the creation of intellectuals. One can hardly assume that it is easy for intellectuals to put aside their own expectations and desires even when dealing with seemingly indifferent social phenomena; but they have seldom, if ever, succeeded in preserving anything like a detached attitude towards the prodigy of labour's emancipation. Changing fashions in theories of labour movements reflect the changing moods and fads of the social sciences, but they are no less indicative of the discontinuities, deviations and divisions in the intellectuals' own political history.

The joint operation of the two factors is rarely so conspicuous as in the case of messianic theories. A sense of their own powerlessness was—possibly until the dawn of the scientific era—by far the most painful and potent sentiment felt among intellectuals. Hence the search for an omnipotent elemental force and the continuous dream of a salutary union of 'the thinking minority and the suffering majority', the modern version of the millenarian mystics of a reinstated primeval unity. Hence, in slightly different variations of a similar motif, the image of a still unpolluted reserve of pure morality and fresh cultural creativity, called in to cleanse the defiled and decadent world. Hence—in still another, somewhat stronger version—the obstinate persistence of the old death-wish for a 'great purification', a new incursion of Huns savage enough to resist all 'civilised' temptations and remorseless enough not to calculate the costs of total destruction. One way or another, whenever these chiliastic expectations and dreams were focused on the labour movement, its endeavours were never approached in a neutral manner. Studies of actual labour movements became exercises in censuring their closeness to or deviations from the assumed ideal. Instead of analysing the genuine trends in the dynamics of labour movements, the adherents of messianistic theories had—by the sheer logic of their approach—to assess the extent of 'loyalty' or 'treason' toward the vocation, the historical mission, the objective aim. More often than not these evaluations and the consequent harsh verdicts had little in common with the inherent dynamics of the labour movement itself.

In the academic scientific literature on the subject it is fashionable to disparage or dismiss these messianistic hopes as proto-scientific, ideological projections. It is tacitly or explicitly assumed that the accepted theories are free from similar shortcomings. But a lot of goodwill is required to believe that the scientific and empirical purity of these other theoretical approaches will stand an authentic test. One does not need much imagination to discern the Benthamite–Spencerian–Hobsonian liberalistic theme behind the Webbs' concept of trade unions as vehicles of industrial democracy; or the 'free market' bogey behind Selig Perlman's image of labour organisations as devices of economic bargaining; or the American neo-romantic interest in 'belongingness' and 'togetherness' behind Frank Tannenbaum's thesis that the trade unions emerged to compensate for the lack of human warmth in the depersonalised modern workplace. In fact one begins to doubt whether any single-factorial theoretical explanatory system of the labour movement can do much more than reflect the politically loaded cognitive formulae of their authors.

In this study I have done my best (with what success I am not sure) to avoid the teleological trap in both its strong and its weak version, i.e. the assumption that there is a final goal state to which the labour movement is drawing nearer by fits and starts; that this state can be determined independently of the movement's actual history and that, once determined, it provides the proper scale to measure the 'maturity'—or even the 'rightness'—of its particular forms and to establish the evolutionary—as distinguished from the simply historical—location of those forms; or that, apart from 'what the movement actually is', there is also something which the movements 'should be' in some objective sense, e.g. not just from the point of view of one or another political party. I have assumed, on the contrary, that no goal, final form or measuring standard is set for the labour movement, once and for all, in any form, whether quasi-empirical or openly transcendental, and that the tasks which the movement itself sets for its activity are dependent variables of the complex system to no less an extent than its other attributes.

I have tried to look at the labour movement as an active, adaptive and self-regulating system, 'assimilating' its 'outer' environment by trying to impress on it the desired structural changes and 'accommodating' its own structure to the changing requirements of the successful assimilation. It is my contention that little cognitive profit can be gained by singling out a unidirectional chain of 'causes' and 'effects' and ordering systemic parameters according to their assumed deterministic significance. The 'structure of the class', 'structure of the organisation' and 'structure of the elite' having been isolated as heuristically useful 'sub-systems', their actual interaction and reciprocal impact are the matter of empirical historical study. The 'morpho-generic' and 'thelos-generic' capacity of the system is synonymous with the notion of a 'viable' or 'living' system as such. In this I side with Walter Buckley in his pertinent critique of the limitations of the organic metaphor. To realise just how disastrous such metaphors can be when applied to a social system, it is enough to take a closer look at the sterile sophistication of the Parsonian theoretical model.

It was a consciously adopted premise of this study that organised social phenomena in general, and labour movements in particular, are not strongly enough 'pre-conditioned'—in either the genetical or the teleological sense—to not being able to produce new structures, patterns and standards. In fact, this continuous 'production' constitutes the only meaning of their 'action'. To explain this creative dynamics one should not point to 'outer' forces, which are inexplicable because left outside the analytical system, nor should one relegate the change to the margin of deviations borne by the system's inefficiency. The system is not entirely deterministic in relation to its environment. Every state of the system is a gamut of options and no state is 'complete' or 'total' until the element of active choice, resulting always from the flexible interaction of partly autonomous sub-systems, is added to the 'objective structure' of the situation.

It was also a premise of this study that the 'prerequisites' of the class are by no means more influential deterministically on, say, the structure of its organisations than these organisations are on the situation of the class itself. In other words, the labour movement as a system—and, above all, its historical dynamics—can be comprehended only in their spatial and temporal totality; as a historical process of creative and active adaptation, both constrained by its own past and free to create new forms and set forth new aims, continuous and discontinuous, self-stabilising and self-dynamising.

To those who feel more at home when dealing with labels instead of phenomena, I must confess that, in my opinion, this understanding of social reality is what Marxism in its activist, uninstitutionalised version is all about.

It is a matter of routine to remind readers that the responsibility for the numerous obscurities as well as for such illumination as may be found in this study is mine. But I owe a debt which is far from routine to the inspiration of two great Polish thinkers and social scientists, from whom the post-war generation of Polish sociologists were fortunate enough to learn their craft.

My teacher was the late Professor Julian Hochfeld, the pioneer of creative Marxian sociology in post-war Polish academic life. In him was admirably combined a sharp and modern analytical mind with a profound and unmatched knowledge of the humanistic tradition. I have drawn lavishly on his vast learning and stimulating ideas. It is greatly to be regretted that one of the many studies carried out by Professor Hochfeld's disciples should now be made available to Western readers before the original works of their teacher have been translated.

I was also fortunate in having the opportunity of studying under the guidance of the late Professor Stanislaw Ossowski, who was kind enough to read the first draft of this study and from whose comments I drew invaluable guidance as well as confirmation of the rightness of the method I had hesitantly chosen. That was in the happy years of unconstrained intellectual creativeness, when the fertile stimuli of the great socialist experiment were still uncurbed by administrative checks, when the Polish universities made the most of the freedom won in the battles of the Polish October. It was the good fortune of Polish sociologists that they were guided into their brief but fruitful Golden Age by two men of such outstanding intellectual and moral integrity.

Professor Robert McKenzie introduced me into the vast domain of the British political scene and its history. I could not even begin to try to enumerate the things I learnt from him during my period of study at the London School of Economics. He has contributed immensely to whatever conclusions may have been reached in this book, and even more to the fact that it contains far fewer immature and false ones than would otherwise have been the case.

And there is Mrs Sheila Patterson, who has invested immense effort in the English translation and also (with the able assistance of Mrs Betty Bradbury) in the correction of the many typographical and editorial shortcomings of the original Polish edition. I only wish that the value of the study could match the merits of her editorial abilities and dedication.

Z.B.

I

The embryonic period of the labour movement
1750–1850

Part I is concerned with the working class during the process of its creation, i.e. with the prehistory of the working class. In it I have set myself certain tasks which, basically, involve the analysis of two sets of problems. The first consists of a reassessment of the history of the genesis of the working class from the perspective of the mid-twentieth century. This takes into account, on the one hand, therefore, those elements in its structure and its movement which were, as later developments showed, to prove lasting and to remain in its list of attributes to the present day. On the other hand, it is concerned with ascertaining to what extent the principal attributes of the English working class and labour movement of today were characteristic of them in the 'pre-historic' period; when they made their appearance; and what factors influenced their emergence.

The second set of problems consists of a sociological analysis of the structure of the working class, the labour movement and the elite of this movement, an analysis that should assist the main purpose of this study—the establishing of correlations and interdependences between these three extremely important elements in the social history of the working class.

A consideration of the first set of problems indicates that to apply the terms 'prehistory' or 'embryonic period' to the working class of the hundred years between 1750 and 1850 is entirely justified. It was only around 1850 that the labouring population of Britain began to show the characteristics which we associate with the designata of the concept of 'class', if these are held to include both separateness and a measure of social cohesiveness deriving from the long-term holding of a particular position in the social process of production. What existed before was rather the raw human material from which the future working class was to be created than the class itself.

The industrial revolution created the working class. During the course of that revolution, however, particularly in its first phase, which was centred on textiles and steam, there was only an undifferentiated mass of human beings, from which a stratified and articulated class was to develop. The working class was the product of the industrial revolution, but the process of its evolution was delayed in relation to the evolution of those factors that called it to life. Although a modern engineering industry came into existence during the period covered in this chapter, the British working class, by comparison with its later development, remained in a fluid and undefined state, creating hardly any lasting forms to become its permanent characteristics.

An epoch is seldom far-sighted enough to see beyond its own mental boundaries and to make the finest distinction of all—that between its own illusions and its own reality. Even Karl Marx shared the nineteenth century's misconceptions about the real nature of the transition to an industrial society. Unaware of the cultural dimension of the problem, he regarded the separation of manpower from the means of production, defined as the 'primary accumulation of capital', as an indispensable and adequate condition for transforming post-feudal agriculture into capitalist industry and the peasants and artisans of yesterday into the industrial workers of contemporary times. No place was left for cultural shock and its side effects, nor in fact for any intermediate period with its own socio-logical profile and specific issues. In an age of unshaken faith in the clearly superior rationality of industrial modernity—as well as the innate ration-ality of human choice—it was taken for granted that, given the chance, people would opt without hesitation for the type of living heralded by the new system. Because of this belief, no compunction was felt about advocat-ing the harshest measures to force people to accept the new happiness. Marx wished to base the new industrial system on a decent and humane organisation of society. At both ends of the scale the great leap forward was seen as irreversible and beyond discussion.[1]

It was not until the publication of Max Weber's *Die Protestantische Ethik und der Geist der Kapitalismus* that the attention of scholars was drawn to the fact that the impoverished peasants and artisans were not being auto-matically reborn in the new industrial roles.

> Raising piece-rates has often had the result that not more but less has been accomplished in the same time, because the worker reacted to the increase not by increasing but by decreasing the amount of his work . . . The oppor-tunity of earning more was less attractive than that of working less. We did not ask 'How much can I earn in a day if I do as much work as possible?' but 'How much must I work in order to earn the wage . . . which I earned before and which takes care of my traditional needs?' . . . A man does not 'by nature' wish to earn more and more money, but simply to live as he is accustomed to live and to earn as much as is necessary for that purpose. Whenever modern capitalism has begun its work of increasing the pro-ductivity of human labour by increasing its intensity, it has encountered the immensely stubborn resistance of this leading trait of pre-capitalistic

---

1 If there was anything to impede the natural process of transforming human beings into industrialists, it was only the misconceptions of those responsible for society. The paradox of Spencer's ruthless integrity was fairly typical of the epoch's beliefs: 'The poverty of the incapable, the distresses that come upon the imprudent, the starvation of the idle, and those shoulderings aside of the weak by the strong, which leave so many 'in shallows and in miseries', are the decrees of a large, far-seeing benevolence . . . When regarded, not separately, but in connection with the in-terests of universal humanity, these harsh fatalities are seen to be full of the highest beneficence.' (*Social statics*, London, 1851, p. 323.) They were being given the chance, and they would make the best of it, if they were not hampered by ill-judged saviours. It was not very easy to understand why they should not do so, as 'every

labour.[1]

In his search for a factor strong enough to overcome this 'nature', as reinforced by traditional or bureaucratic routine, Weber tended to reduce the issue to the charismatic power of religious ideology. Troeltsch, Sombart, Tawney, Fullerton, Robertson, See and many others have tried hard to check Weber's thesis and to discover to just what extent it provides a satisfactory explanation for the institutionalisation of a rough-and-tumble adventurous greed into the 'rational organisation of the profit-seeking activity'. There is, however, little doubt that no feeling of mission inculculated by any religion can account plausibly for the tortuous path which the homeless and uprooted crowd had to follow to arrive at its new, capitalistic 'routinisation'. Ruthless discipline was necessary to extirpate the 'restless and migratory spirit' (as Arthur Redford called it) of those suspended in the void between two contradictory cultural systems. That there was no effective ideological substitute for this measure has been convincingly proved by the history of socialist regimes which undertook the task of industrialisation unfulfilled by the capitalists.

Seen from this perspective, Part I depicts the circuitous roads which led to the rise of the British working class of today—a typical enough story only too well known by the rest of the industrialised world, and one which is now being painfully learned by the latest arrivals on the industrial scene.

The labour movement and the elite of that movement were tailored to the measure of the preliminary stage of the development of the working class.

individual endeavours as much as he can both to employ his capital in the support of domestic industry . . . and by directing this industry in such a manner as its produce may be of the greatest value, he intends only his own gain, and he is in this, as in many other cases, led by an invisible hand to promote an end which of his intention'. (Adam Smith, *An inquiry into the nature and causes of the wealth of nations*, 1776, ed. E. Cannan, Dent, London, 1930, I, p. 421.)

1   Max Weber, *The Protestant ethic and the spirit of capitalism*, trans. T. Parsons, Allen & Unwin, London, 1930, pp. 59–60.

I

The structure of
the working class

The technological and economic aspects of the industrial revolution have produced such a wealth of literature that it seems superfluous to attempt to go over them yet again. I therefore propose to concentrate exclusively on the problems arising out of the social consequences of the industrial revolution in Britain, with particular reference to the structure of the working class. This account will also be concerned solely with classifying some questions which have been frequently raised in various contexts in the existing literature.

The main social consequence of the industrial revolution in England was the acceleration of social change, in contrast to the state of virtual stagnation hitherto prevailing in English society. All the components of social life were set in violent motion: social stratification, inter-class relations, *mores*, social ideals, hierarchies of values, and scales of prestige. A society which until then had been characterised by clear and stable divisions of classes and strata—explicitly expressed not only in objective form in the social structure but also in the sphere of social consciousness in all its manifold aspects—was brought into a state of confusion in which the old boundaries were crumbling while the new ones had not yet become set. Few traditional elements had survived the revolution in *mores*, while few new customs had succeeded in becoming traditions. The shattering of established structures gave society an exceptional internal dynamism and pliability. The gradual demise of the old structure and the maturation of the new both took place in a period of unusual flexibility. New classes arose not from the old classes but as if from a pliable mass of humanity, created out of the traditional social strata as a result of the industrial revolution.

The turn of the eighteenth and nineteenth centuries saw an unprecedentedly rapid increase of population and population density in Great Britain. In 1700 the population of England and Wales was 5·8 millions and in 1750 6·32 millions; by 1800 it had jumped to 8·8 millions.[1]

The population increase was even more rapid in the urban areas, the effects of the higher birth rate being augmented by migration from the rural areas. In 1725 Manchester was a little town with a population of only eight to ten thousand. By 1790 it had 50,000 inhabitants and by 1801

1 E. C. K. Gonner, 'The population of England in the eighteenth century', *Journal of the Royal Statistical Society*, LXXVI, 1913, p. 285.

95,000.[1] The increase in the number of people employed in industry was particularly rapid. In 1787 about 162,000 people were employed in the cotton industry, but by 1831 the total had risen to 833,000.[2] This was a genuine revolution in the demographic history of the British Isles, and one which in itself was bound to shake the foundations of the structure of established social forms.[3]

The population increase was not, of course, in itself the reason for the changes in English society—it was just one of the factors behind them. None the less it would be difficult to over-estimate the part played by the change in population. The sheer pressure of numbers shattered the established forms of social life, especially in the countryside, where they were geared to relatively sparse numbers with little tendency to expansion. The traditional forms of household management and ways of earning a livelihood failed to resist the pressure of the rocketing population—they simply could not assimilate such great masses of people. In the wake of this, the traditional ideals, social values, and rank orders of prestige between strata lost their value. Thus the rapid tempo of population growth was closely linked almost from the outset with the process of urbanisation, based on the development of capitalistic industry. The population which, in relation to the mechanism of a rural, cottage industry economy, constituted a 'surplus' or 'excess', could not be fitted into the cramped compartments of rural class divisions. At first, therefore, it was 'outside the class structure' and outside society in the form inherited from past centuries. For the time being it was a pliable, amorphous substance to which further evolution would ultimately give the form of a stable structure.

The process of expansion outwards from the extensive rural communities which provided the human material for urbanisation was in no case as simple and straightforward as the literature has sometimes presented it. The newly formed industrial areas were concentrated in the north-west of England and the south of Wales, while south and east England and

1 P. Mantoux, *The industrial revolution in the eighteenth century*, Cape, London, 1947, p. 366.
2 J. L. and B. Hammond, *The skilled labourer*, Longmans, London, 1919, p. 47.
3 The great contrast between this lightning population increase and the former state of affairs in England is illustrated in the following comment by Gregory King, writing at the end of the eighteenth century: 'In all Probability the next doubling of the people of England will be in about 600 years to come, or by the Year of our Lord 2300. At which time it will have 11 Mill. of People; But that the next doubling after that, will not be (in all probability) in lesse than 12 Or 1300 Years more or by the Year of our Lord 3500 or 3600. At which time the Kingdome will have 22 Mill. of Souls . . . in case the World should last so long.' ('Natural and Political Observations and conclusions upon the state and condition of England' 1696, British Museum, Harleian mss, No. 1898, p. 14; first published in G. Chalmers, *An estimate of the comparative strength of Great Britain*, Dilly & Bowen, London, 1782.)

north Wales remained almost entirely agricultural for a relatively long period. Yet there is no record of any large-scale direct migrations from the rural to the urban areas. In fact, those who lived in the countryside were tied to their immediate neighbourhood by the prevailing agricultural conditions and the generally poor communications. A journey to a county town was the undertaking of a lifetime, while London was a mythical city, known from folk tales rather than at first hand. The migration from country to town usually took place stage by stage. The swiftly growing urban organism would absorb the surpluses of population from its immediate neighbourhood; their place would then be taken by surplus people from districts further off, who would themselves in turn be absorbed in the urban areas.[1]

Urbanisation was a gradual process in more than the territorial sense. Those who worked on the land and in cottage industries never became stratified into two groups, one which remained in the classic rural economy, and one which was linked exclusively with capitalist industry. This kind of stratification was the outcome of, not the grounds for, the social changes of the period of the industrial revolution. For many decades ties with both capitalist industry and the rural economy were interwoven in the lives of the same people and social strata. In a later period these ties, which were of varying strength, became severed; this led to a separation into two distinct social strata. But, in the period when the industrial cities were being born, it would have been difficult to find in their sphere of influence either industrial workers pure and simple who had lost all ties linking them with the rural economy, or agricultural workers who did not also add to their earnings by co-operating in some way or another with capitalist employers. About the year 1770, according to William Radcliffe, only six or seven out of the fifty to sixty farmers in the village of Mellor, near Stockport, derived their living entirely from the land; all the rest made up their earnings from cottage spinning or weaving for local employers. On the other hand, the majority of workers in the industrial areas lived in the country and augmented their factory wages by working on the land.[2] These two groups were nearly on the residential and occupational frontier between town and country, industry and farming, though they were on different sides of it. The frontier itself was almost invisible.

This fact is worth emphasising, because it affords yet another indication of the overlapping of two different socio-economic systems in the period under discussion. The superimposition of one era onto a quite different one was a basic reason for the dynamism and plasticity of social structures.

1 Cf, for instance, A. Redford, *Labour migration in England*, Manchester University Press, 1926, pp. 15–16.
2 Mantoux, *The industrial revolution*, p. 63.

The working population had not yet cast off its rural shell. On the other hand, urban capitalism had not left the rigid traditions of the rural hierarchy untouched but was reaching out even in that direction in its creative expansiveness. The industrial revolution was transforming even that part of the rural population whose livelihood and way of life and earning a living were not directly influenced by the technological revolution. The decisive factor here was the revolutionary changes in inter-personal relations, not just the changes in techniques and technology, although the latter were in fact the cause of the whole metamorphosis.[1]

The social down-grading of small producers and craftsmen who had formerly been independent lay at the roots of the changes which were taking place in inter-personal relations. The process has received classic treatment both in Marx's *Das Kapital* and in Engels' *Condition of the working class in England*, that matchless sociological document of the period. While referring readers to these two works in general, I should like here merely to draw attention to the basic characteristics of that down-grading, leaving aside such significant phenomena as the replacement of the work of qualified craftsmen by machines operated by women and children, and the ruin of small workshops.

The most comprehensible and measurable determinant of such down-grading is to be found in the movement of wage rates. Unfortunately, few documents of indisputable scholarly worth have come down to us from this particular period, and later estimates have been made on the basis of rather fragmentary contemporary evidence. Yet the far-reaching consensus between different estimates is an indication, if not that they are accurate, at least that they give a correct picture of the basic movements of wages.

According to the contemporary testimony of F. M. Eden,[2] the mean wage increase for ninety-seven categories of male occupations examined over the second half of the eighteenth century was forty-seven per cent; the mean fall in wage rates in twenty-nine categories of female occupations was 10 per

1   The Hammonds' assessment of this situation is very apt: 'There were a number of persons who suffered when machinery superseded hand labour, or one machine superseded another; there were more who expected to suffer; but the incidence of the new power was not local or particular but universal. The whole working class world came under it. The miner, who had never been a domestic worker, and the handloom weaver, who remained a domestic worker, were just as sensible of this power as the spinner who went into the factory to watch a machine do the work that had been done in the cottage or the shearman who tried unavailingly to keep out of the gig-mill.' (J. L. and B. Hammond, *The town labourer*, Longmans, London, 1966 edn., p. 28.)
2   *The state of the poor*, 1797, quoted by G. H. Wood, *A glance at wages and prices since the industrial revolution*, Manchester, 1900, p. 56.

cent while that for fifteen categories of children's occupations was 13 per cent. Over the same period the proportion of women and children in the labour force increased considerably, while the prices of basic foodstuffs rose by 75 per cent.

When one comes to consider the first half of the nineteenth century, one is struck by the strong similarities between three independent *post factum* estimates (tables 1–3). Leaving aside the question of discrepancies, which

Table 1

The fluctuation of mean weekly wages in four industrial regions of England, 1797–1838

Year	Bolton		Glasgow		Cumberland		Manchester	
	s	d	s	d	s	d	s	d
1797	30		–		13★		–	
1800	25		13	1	15		–	
1805	25		15	4	23		–	
1810	19		11	6	10	10	16	3
1816	12		5	6	7	7	13	2
1820	9		5		6	6	11	
1824	8	6	–		7†		–	
1830	5	6	–		–		9	
1838	5	6	–		–		–	

★ 1798.   † 1823.

Source   F. M. Eden, *The state of the poor*, 1797, quoted by G. H. Wood, *A glance at wages and prices since the industrial revolution*, Manchester, 1900, p. 56.

could easily have crept in through the use of imperfect methods of calculation, a comparison of these three tables shows an identical trend. The accelerating expansion of the engineering industry in the period under discussion brought ever-increasing poverty to the population that had been drawn into the factory orbit.

The social consequences of the relentless downward movement of wages were described in detail by Engels.[1] The workers were reduced to such a low

1   It would be difficult to add anything to the wealth of material assembled by Engels on this subject. I shall therefore cite only a few significant features of the existence of the working class of this period. 'That an education worthy of the name was impossible for a population under such conditions results avowedly from the statements of the Commissioners of 1832. Factory workers were in those early days for the most part grossly ignorant. Even the fine spinners, who were the best paid,

level of existence that any sort of social action became impossible. Below a
certain minimum level, inter-personal ties of all kinds are broken. A community then becomes an arithmetical total of isolated individuals whose
biological needs become stripped of social coverings. This in turn makes it
impossible to set up more lasting associations which would be an expres-

Table 2
The fluctuation of weekly wage rates for cotton weavers, 1795–1834

Period	Mean weekly wage	
	s	*d*
1795–1804	26	8
1804–11	20	
1811–18	14	7
1818–25	8	9
1825–32	6	4
1832–34	5	6

Source   A table submitted by Bolton weavers to a House of Commons committee in 1834; cited by C. R. Fay, *Life and labour in the nineteenth century*,
Cambridge University Press, 1920, p. 215.

were only distinguished from the rest by their extravagant riotousness. Topics of
conversation were limited; power to converse rationally was possessed by few;
the noise of the factory was unfavourable to the exchange of ideas. Ignorant themselves, what wonder if they cared little to educate their children?' (J. M. Ludlow
and L. Jones, *Progress of the working class*, Strahan, London, 1867, pp. 13–14.) 'Too
often, the dwelling of the factory family is no home; it sometimes is a cellar,
which includes no cookery, no washing, no making, no mending, no decencies of
life, no invitation to the fireside.' This information refers to conditions in Lancashire
(Factory Commission, second report, 1833: Dr Hawkins, p. 5). 'The people employed
in the different manufactures are early introduced into them, many at five and six
years old, both girls and boys, so that when the former become Women they have
not had any opportunity of acquiring any habits of Domestic economy or the management of a family . . . The greater part of the Working and lower class of people
have not wives that can dress a joint of meat if they were to have it given them.
The consequence is that such articles become their food that are the most easily
acquired, consequently their general food now consists of bread and cheese.' (Home
Office, 42, 53, *Manchester Correspondent*, 1800.) The following table also gives the
consumption of gin and whisky (in gallons) in England and Scotland in the years
1821–33. It is taken from P. Gaskell, *Artisans amd machinery*, Parker, London, 1836,
p. 398:

Period	England	Scotland	Total
1821–23	11,687,984	6,541,719	18,229,603
1831–33	22,410,637	16,550,760	38,961,397

Table 3
The fluctuation of weekly wage rates for workers in the Scottish textile industry,
1797–1838

Year	Mean weekly wages	
	s	d
1797	18	9
1805	23	
1811	12	3
1814	18	6
1817	8	9
1813	6	
1838	6	3

Source   G. H. Wood, The history of wages in the cotton trade during the past
hundred years, Sherrat & Hughes, London, 1910, p. 112.

sion of common social interests and therefore an expression of mutual
concern. Below this minimum a change in social position occurs not in
quantitative but in qualitative terms. The worker who has been pushed
down to the depths of poverty is outside the periphery of society. In fact
his position is fundamentally hostile to that society, and he has no sense of
playing any role in it.

The disruption of almost all social bonds was a basic cause of the alienation of the working population. Once they were forced out of the stable
village community these people lost the social position assigned to them
by the traditional structure of that primary group. The formation of new
primary groups in centres of rapid urbanisation took place extremely
slowly by comparison with the tempo of urban expansion. The basic new
primary group, the family, did not in practice exist, or existed only in
vestigial form.[1] In so far as the position of the individual in society is
assigned by the position of his primary group and his relationship to
society by the value system that has been evolved by the group as a rationalisation of its interests, the factory worker of that period had no defined

1   'The greatest misfortune—the most unfortunate change which has resulted from
    factory labour, is the breaking up of these family ties; the consequent abolition of
    the domestic circle, and the perversion of all the social obligations which should
    exist between parent and child on the one hand, and between the children them-
    selves on the other.' (P. Gaskell, The manufacturing population of England, Baldwin &
    Cradock, London, 1833, p. 89.)

position within society, its machinery or its social hierarchy. The single, dominating feature of his relationship to society was a feeling of estrangement, of being cast out beyond the frontiers of all social groups.

In addition to the disintegration of the village community and family community, a third element was involved in the alienation of the working population: the disintegration of the traditional occupational hierarchy. The masses of humanity that filled the first factories were not differentiated occupationally.[1] Machines had reduced to simple operations tasks which had hitherto required craft skills, knowledge and experience that conferred great prestige both within the manufacturing community and beyond. The workers became merely the possessors of manpower in an almost pure form. Craft qualifications ceased to serve as a basis for individual differentiation, as an outlet for the upwardly mobile, or as a means of raising one's own social standing. In the early factories people of unknown antecedents mingled with the descendants of worthy artisans. Men with centuries of vagrancy behind them mixed with those who had lived a settled life following craft traditions; and persons totally unaccustomed to regular work and lacking any occupational skills found themselves together with the master craftsmen of yesterday, men who were accustomed to associate high social values with their craft and to guard its mysteries jealously. The prestige of a craft, of skilled work, of creative endeavour bordering on artistry—all these were suddenly depreciated. The products of his work ceased to satisfy the creative needs of the worker not only because he did not feel himself to be their creator but also because their production made no demands on him other than an expenditure of muscular energy. On the factory floor all differences in degree of craftsmanship, diligence and creative zeal were flattened out.[2]

If there was still room for any sort of grading at this underprivileged level, then one could say that the greatest pariahs in this pariah section of society at the turn of the century were the 'navvies', who were employed on the construction of the first railways, and the farm labourers, recruited

---

1   G. D. H. Cole, *Studies in class structure*, Routledge & Kegan Paul, London, 1955, pp. 37, *et seq.*

2   'In the early days factory labour consisted of the most ill-assorted elements: country people driven from their villages by the growth of large estates, disbanded soldiers, paupers, the scum of every class and of every occupation.' (Mantoux, *The industrial revolution*, p. 384.) 'Factory work in that early period might almost [indeed,] be described as a casual employment for unskilled labour; the millworkers were without any craft tradition or pride in efficient workmanship.' (Redford, *Labour migration*, p. 24.) 'The workers had become an incoherent, almost undifferentiated mass of suffering . . . The factory workers [were] an amorphous mass of men, women and children drawn from every county and every trade.' (R. W. Postgate, *The builders' history*, Labour Publishing Co., London, 1923, p. 30.)

from among the former smallholders, who also had already been transformed into an undifferentiated mass.[1]

After the sudden loss of their individuality and any possibility of keeping
their own existence separate from that of the fragmented masses, the
workers of the time were also abruptly confronted with a sharp increase
in social distance between themselves and the owners and managers of the
factories where they worked. Admittedly, social mobility within the
majority of craft occupations had long been only residual, despite the continued pretence that there was equality of opportunity and social parity,
as between journeymen and masters. The long-drawn-out process of
stratification that had taken place within the craft guilds had made it
increasingly difficult for the majority of craft apprentices to reach the
highest ranks of the guild hierarchy. Nevertheless, so long as a craft or trade
retained the characteristics of small-scale production, the social distance
between the master and his journeyman remained small enough not to
appear impassable. In consequence, the desire for advancement was
fostered, and the feeling that this desire might be gratified was reinforced.
The master craftsman was a figure from the same dimension of social
reality; his activities were comprehensible and fell within the boundaries
of the journeyman's experience. His position was only on the next rung of
a working career, not on some pedestal concealed in the clouds of an in-
accessible and alien reality.[2]

1 'The men who dug earth, blasted tunnels, and laid rails formed a class new to the
   country. Coming chiefly from the hills of Lancashire and Yorkshire (with an infil-
   tration of Irish) and the fens of Lincolnshire, they were physically hardy but were
   ignorant and brutalised. They formed a clan of their own, living in filthy hovels
   along the right of way. They were depraved and reckless. In a report made to
   Parliament in 1846 by Edwin Chadwick they were described as drunken and dis-
   solute, afflicted universally by loathsome forms of disease. They drank whisky by
   the tumbler, calling it "white beer".' (J. W. Dodds, *The age of paradox*, Gollancz,
   London, 1953, p. 245.) 'It became customary for men and women and children to
   work in gangs, tramping from place to place in charge of gang-masters, who entered
   into contracts with firms for the performance of field work.' (E. Selley, *Village
   trade unions in two centuries*, Allen & Unwin, London, 1920, p. 26.) 'The English
   agricultural labourer and an English pauper—these words are synonymous. His
   father was a pauper and his mother's milk contained no nourishment. From his
   earliest childhood he had bad food, and only half enough to still his hunger, and even
   yet he undergoes the pangs of unsatisfied hunger almost all the time that he is not
   asleep . . . His wretched existence is brief; rheumatism and asthma bring him to the
   workhouse, where he will draw his last breath without a single pleasant recollection
   and will make room for another luckless wretch to live and die as he has done.'
   (E. G. Wakefield, *Swing unmasked*, cited by Selley, *Village trade unions*, p. 13.)
2 'About 1720, an "eminent manufacturer" of Manchester would go down to his
   workshop at six o'clock in the morning, breakfast with his apprentices on oatmeal
   porridge, and then set to work with them. Having gone into business without

With the coming of the industrial revolution this state of affairs underwent a radical change. The semi-patriarchal relationship, with the master's wife preparing meals for her husband's journeymen, and both parties linked by common tastes and socio-cultural ideals, was replaced within the space of a generation or two by complete social separation between the employer and his employees.[1] For a certain time the factory owner might continue the master's tradition in the sense that he remained 'on the job', frequently visiting the factory and sometimes personally supervising his workers. In every respect, however, the relationship between manufacturers and workers was a complete contrast to that between masters and journeymen. The manufacturer's style of life, entirely different from that of his workers, his geographical, social and cultural isolation—all these were only the outer sign of the final and complete destruction of bridges between the upper and lower ranks in the production process.

The process by which strata were transformed into classes was swift and radical—though for the time being it took the form of a feeling of antagonism; not, yet, that of internal cohesion. This process took place on all fronts simultaneously, if not always with the same speed. In the traditional situation of the craft journeyman, movement up the occupational ladder had been inseparably linked with advancement to a higher stratum in society, and vice versa. For the factory worker the two ladders led in different directions. To be more precise, the rungs of the first, occupational, ladder had been removed, while the second ladder, that of class, did not, in fact, exist. The gulf between the classes was total. The workers were relegated to the extremes of poverty, and the new social system that was coming into being did not make provision for any mechanisms that would allow the living conditions of the working masses to be improved or that would provide an opportunity for more talented and energetic individuals within those masses to make a different life for themselves.

The manufacturers of that period of the industrial revolution were described by a contemporary writer as 'uneducated, of coarse habits, sensual in their enjoyments, partaking of the rude revelry of their dependants—overwhelmed by success . . .'[2] They seized with eagerness on every opportunity of widening the gulf that separated them from those who

capital, he earned his living from day to day, and if, after years of hard work, he managed to save a little money, he put it by and made no change in his daily habits. He rarely left his workshop or his shop and only drank wine once a year, at Christmas time. His favourite pastime was to go of an evening, in company with others like himself, to an alehouse, where the custom was to spend fourpence on ale and a halfpenny on tobacco.' (Mantoux, *The industrial revolution*, p. 375.)

1   G. M. Trevelyan, *Illustrated English social history*, IV, Longmans, London, 1952, pp. 13 et seq.
2   Gaskell, *The manufacturing population of England*, p. 55.

were subordinate to them. The technology of their factories required only an unskilled labour force, and such labour was available in quantity. Thus they had no difficulty in imposing on their workers such working conditions as they saw fit. The only limit was that set by the physical endurance of the workers. Deprived of the support conferred by the possession of a craft, the workers could put up no counter-force to their employers. Attempts at resistance meant at best the loss of one's job. The workers were reduced to atoms and, like atoms, became nearly enough identical to be moved about and replaced at will.

As a consequence of their unequal position in the economic struggle, the workers' 'acceptance' of the terms of a working agreement which, after all, involved two parties became more and more of a formality. In the mining industry, for instance, the custom was introduced by which the miners once a year signed an agreement, or bond, binding them to the mine for the entire year to come; the bilateral character of such an agreement was an obvious fiction.[1] Moreover, the coal owners of the Tyne and Wear had an agreement among themselves not to take on any miner unless he presented a certificate from his previous employer. Capitalist relationships during the period of the industrial revolution contained many elements of serfdom, and the freedom to hire out one's labour was in many cases still a fiction.

The feeling of estrangement from society was deepened by the unprecedented cruelty which characterised the everyday behaviour of many factory owners and supervisors towards their workmen.[2] The victims of such cruelty were in effect deprived of any sort of legal assistance from the society in which they lived and the State which was the representative of

1 'On the Binding day the Bond was hurriedly read out by the manager in the open air, before a crowd of men of all grades . . . few of whom could follow what he was reading, or even hear his words. Then and there the men had to put their marks— very few could sign their names—to the document which was to bind them to involuntary servitude for a whole year.' (S. Webb, *The story of the Durham miners*, Labour Publishing Co., London, 1921, p. 10.)

2 An extreme example of this kind of relationship may be found in the story of one Robert Blincoe, reported in 1828 in *The Lion*, edited by R. Carlile: 'The employer, one Ellice Needham, hit the children with his fists and with a riding whip, he kicked them, and one of his little attentions was to pinch their ears until his nails met through the flesh. The foremen were even worse, and one of them, Robert Woodward, used to devise the most ingenious tortures. It was he who was responsible for such inventions as hanging Blincoe up by his wrists over a machine at work, so that he was obliged to keep his knees bent up making him work almost naked in winter, with heavy weights on his shoulders, and filing down his teeth. The wretched child had been so knocked about that his scalp was one sore all over. By way of curing him, his hair was torn out by mean of a cap of pitch. If the victims of these horrors tried to escape, their feet were put in irons. Many tried to commit suicide . . .' (Cited by Mantoux, *The industrial revolution*, p. 424.)

that society. The law was not for them; the law courts, Parliament, the civil servants, the magistrates were all on the opposite side, the side from which the workers had been excluded.

Not only the law but legal opinion was against the factory workers. The ruling classes—which included not only the aristocracy that had usurped political power but also the middle class that aspired to exercise such power—were afraid of the restless and inflammable mass of humanity that was being herded together in hitherto unheard of concentrations around the new urban centres. This fear produced two sorts of reaction. On the one hand, the screws of legal bondage were tightened and even the faintest trace of rebellion met with the most severe counter-measures—as in the case of the Peterloo massacre. On the other hand, there was a desire to relieve the situation by means of charitable activities, some organised by individuals, others through the parish system. Whatever the method, it was generally accepted without question that the condition of the workers was in accordance with the laws of nature, and the possibility of change in any direction was not taken into consideration.[1] For the most part, society accepted the alienation of the masses of factory and farm workers, whose numbers continued to increase and whose poverty grew steadily greater.

The object of this brief account of the position of the working population in the first phase of the industrial revolution has been to underline three basic aspects of the social situation of this group—its amorphousness, its fragmentation and its alienation. The working population was amorphous because it was not differentiated in terms of occupation or craft qualifications; instead it had been reduced to a common denominator as an unspecialised labour force. It was fragmented because it had been torn away from its established primary groups and deprived, in its new environment, of the social bonds deriving from an occupational hierarchy, a family community or even a community based on local traditions. Finally, it was alienated from society because it had been precipitated into an abyss of ruthless poverty, deprived of both the right to defend itself and the possibility of taking the offensive, and refused any chance of advancing up the social ladder—whether as a class or individually.

The characteristics just underlined were applicable to the greater part of the working population in the period under consideration. Moreover, they applied to a sector that was steadily increasing in both absolute and relative terms. Outside it, however, there still remained a considerable

---

1   The *Mendip annals* of Hannah and Martha More are a good example of this approach. The two sisters, whose work was fairly representative of the charitable enterprises of that time, describe the appalling human misery and degradation encountered during their charitable excursions without ever displaying the slightest suspicion that the state of affairs disclosed was unjust and ought to be changed.

group that was later to be assimilated by the working class when it ultimately began to evolve; but for the time being this group was evolving
along different lines from the amorphous and fragmented masses herded
together on the factory floor.

This second group comprised two categories of workers. The first included what was left of the stratum of small-scale independent producers
in trades which already came within the sphere of the industrial revolution
from a technological angle but had not yet been organised on a factory
basis; thus their practitioners still retained their own workshops and a
semblance of their one-time independence. In fact, their independence
was an illusion. Both the raw materials and the selling outlets on which
they depended were entirely dependent on the capitalist entrepreneur.
Their economic position was determined by their relationship to the
latter, not by their relationship to the consumer.

Work in familiar conditions, a separate dwelling place outside the factory
concentration, frequently the ownership of a tiny plot of land, and finally
the ownership of a workshop inherited from one's forbears—these were
the factors that created the appearance of a continuity of social status and
provided a tradition which allowed those who were in reality hirelings to
go on believing in the value systems of their milieu and their established
social bonds. As long as the once independent producer remained within
the framework of his native groupings he was safeguarded against the processes of homogenisation and fragmentation which faced those of his
countrymen who had been uprooted from similar groups. The preroga-
tives that were associated with his former social position were in reality a
product of the past, but they gave him a feeling of being firmly rooted and
of being at home in society; they encouraged him to link his personal lot
with the workings of that society. However lowly the former status of
the small producer, it was none the less precisely defined, clearly located
in relation to the status levels of other social strata and joined to them by
well defined links; as such it was something that needed defending and
lent itself to such defence. Thus in the first phase of the industrial revolution the remnants of the small-scale producers constituted a conservative
group, a group on the defensive, which still accepted the values established
by a vanished hierarchy.

This group managed to survive through the whole period under discussion. What is more, in some years it increased in numbers because of
capitalist industry's need for auxiliary labour (for example, for the preliminary treatment of raw materials, for finishing or for tool making),
although it obviously never increased at the same tempo as the factory
work force. For instance, in 1820 there were still about 240,000 hand loom
weavers in England, and even in 1833 the number was estimated as high

as 213,000. By 1862, however, barely 3,000 were left.[1] According to contemporary evidence, as important a centre of the mechanised textile industry as Leeds still had over 3,500 small businesses in 1806, often with no more than one or two journeymen. By means of their methods of production and the kind of inter-personal relationships in them, these small shops kept up the guild traditions founded on occupational prestige, social proximity between master and journeyman, and opportunities for occupational advancement. Although they were decreasing, such opportunities still existed. An able young journeyman who was regarded as honest and industrious could get credit for the purchase of enough yarn to enable him to set up his own workshop.[2] Such a prospect in itself drew a clear demarcation line between factory workers and artisans in small-scale workshops.

This particular category of the non-assimilated groups of workers showed a definite tendency to disappear; its numbers and its social role grew steadily smaller. On the other hand, the second category in the group was to have a considerably longer run, although it eventually met the same fate as the first. Because of its longer survival, however, it was to exert a more powerful influence on the history of the English labour movement and the shaping of its structure, aspirations and programme.

This second category included the artisans in those trades which were not directly influenced by the industrial revolution until the second half of the nineteenth century, or in some cases even until the twentieth century. This was because their products began to be mass-produced only at a later stage. For the time being the situation of these artisans was influenced by the industrial revolution only in that it enlarged the demand for fine craft products by creating a large middle class which was eager to acquire these symbols of its newly won power. This strengthened the economic position of the craft workshops and even led to a temporary expansion in certain skilled trades, shoemakers, saddlers, cabinet-makers, braziers, pewterers and others[3]. Thus such skilled workers as printers, tailors, were favourably affected by the first phase of the industrial revolution, that great enemy of the skilled trades: the unexpected boom which it produced permitted the mastermen of these and many other crafts not only to keep their own workshops in operation without running the risk of losing them but also to cultivate the whole complex of guild

---

1 G. H. Wood, *The history of wages in the cotton trade during the past hundred years*, Sherratt & Hughes, London, 1910, p. 125.
2 Report from the Select Committee on Woollen Manufacture, 1806, cited by Mantoux, *The industrial revolution*, p. 60.
3 Cf, for instance, G. D. H. Cole and A. W. Filson, *British working class movements*, Macmillan, London, 1951, pp. 19–20.

procedure and customs and the type of human relations expressed in these procedures and associated with craft production.

To take the printing trade as an example: even in the second half of the eighteenth century it retained relationships inherited from the medieval guilds. Printing shops generally employed one or two journeymen, but the regulations of the Stationers' Company, the printers' guild, did not differentiate between the position of a master and a journeyman. A thrifty journeyman could easily start up his own printing shop.[1] In 1818, of the twelve largest printing houses in London, only four had more than ten journeymen.[2] The first half of the nineteenth century saw a multiplication of master printers, like mushrooms after rain, as a contemporary account described it. The more energetic journeymen usually began by buying a printing press and a set of type, and carrying out small orders on their own account after working hours. After a certain time the money thus accumulated enabled them to open their own printing shops[3]

In the brush-making trade, again, twenty-one out of the twenty-three workshops in London in 1835 employed no more than one or two journeymen. In every workshop the work process followed the old methods, with the master sitting at the same table with his journeymen.[4] A very similar structure and set of relationships were found in the manufacture of cutlery, where the essential tools were easy to come by,[5] in pottery[6] and in many other occupations. A Royal Commission of 1824 was struck by the feeling of mutual solidarity and community of interests between master hatters and their journeymen which emerged from the depositions submitted to the commission.[7]

The actual situation of the crafts mentioned above was reflected by masters and journeymen alike in their feeling of occupational distinctiveness, a feeling which was preserved with as much solicitude as their consciousness of the dignity of craft status. During the period when the storm of history was ripping traditional human relationships into tatters, the journeymen compositors issued a demand that their traditional right to wear a sword and a top hat should continue to be respected, with a re-

1   A. E. Musson, *The Typographical Association*, Oxford University Press, London, 1954, p. 14.
2   E. Howe and H. E. Waite, *The London Society of Compositors*, Cassell, London, 1948, p. 82.
3   Musson, *The Typographical Association*, p. 19.
4   W. Kiddier, *The old trade unions*, Allen & Unwin, London, 1930, p. 66.
5   G. C. Holland, *The vital statistics of Sheffield*, Greaves, Sheffield, 1843, pp. 182–3.
6   W. H. Warburton, *The history of trade union organisation in the north Staffordshire potteries*, Allen & Unwin, London, 1931, pp. 11–12.
7   G. Unwin, *Industrial organisation in the sixteenth and seventeenth centuries*, Oxford University Press, 1904, pp. 214 *et seq.*

minder that an Act of Parliament had accorded the status of 'gentlemen' to members of their craft.[1] They also protested vehemently when a statement published by the booksellers classified them in the same category as other printing workers in the press room.[2]

This category of the working population did not feel aware of any links between themselves and workers in factories, agriculture or the mines. In fact their fortunes and their social position at this time *were* still basically different. The labour force in the factories had not yet reached a stage where its members could begin to fight for a defined status in the society in which they lived but of which they were in effect not members with full rights. Since the chief aim of journeymen belonging to crafts which had so far resisted the wind of technical change was to defend the *status quo*, fenced round with regulations and privileges and hallowed by tradition dating as far back as Elizabethan days, they were conscious of ties not with the working population but with the lower strata of the middle class. It was in these circles that they carried on their social life; their ideals of life were formed in the bourgeois image and their goals were set according to its scale of values.[3]

To sum up, therefore, there were, among the population from which the working class was later to evolve, two fundamentally different groups at this time: one was amorphous, while the other had an occupational structure that was finely shaped and strong in traditions; one was fragmented, the other firmly embedded in its occupational groups, immobilised in its inherited systems of social values and moral norms, and welded into cohesive social groups. Again, the one was alienated from society, while the other was strongly rooted in it; the one was totally antagonistic in attitude to that society, the other was eager for society to recognise the privileges it had already gained, and hoped for new ones.

In conclusion, however, it should be observed that a process of stratification was beginning to gain momentum within the first, amorphous group even during this period. The process was still feeble and slow-moving, gaining strength and impetus only during the period that followed. An instance of it occurred in the cotton and wool textile mills,[4] where the male spinners who had formerly been independent producers took over the supervision of female spinners and children. This was more a sign of their greater organisational talents than a new social position such as was created

1 *Compositors' Chronicle*, 1841, Nos. 6 and 7.
2 Howe and Waite, *The London Society of Compositors*, p. 53.
3 Cf, for instance, D. Marshall, *English people in the eighteenth century*, Longmans, London, 1956, p. 61; E. J. Hobsbawm, 'The labour aristocracy in nineteenth century Britain' in *Democracy and the labour movement*, ed. J. Saville, Lawrence & Wishart, London, 1954, p. 205.
4 J. L. and B. Hammond, *The skilled labourer*, p. 154.

by the stratificatory mechanisms of the engineering industry. On the other hand, rather different relationships evolved in the iron and steel and engineering industries, which began to develop in earnest only towards the end of the period under discussion. Almost from the outset, the type of production in these industries required a considerable number of persons with high qualifications, more akin to the skills of master craftsmen than to the ordinary manual labour of the unskilled masses of textile workers. These qualified workers were, however, in no case perpetuating the guild tradition. They were, like their occupations, the creation of the engineering industry and of capitalism, not a relic which capitalism had so far failed to wipe out.[1]

Looked at in perspective, the emancipated position of these people in the process of production meant that they were better placed for the coming economic struggle with the manufacturers. Since they commanded complicated skills which were often in short supply, they were no longer atoms which could easily be replaced by other identical atoms. Those employers who had expended considerable time and effort in training these new skilled workmen had an interest in keeping them in their own factories. Such specialised work also required a higher level of general culture, a certain amount of schooling, better food and more tolerable conditions for relaxation after work. All these were the privileges of the new skilled workers created by the engineering industry.

These new skilled workers were already moving towards a new socio-economic status higher than that of the unskilled; yet so far they differed very little, either in their objective position or in their awareness of difference, from the rest of the working population. Moreover, there were as yet only a few of them, and their position in industry had acquired no traditions. The real stratification of the factory labour force, which played so great a part in determining the direction in which the English labour movement was to develop, was to be completed only in the subsequent period of its history.

---

1 As Matthew Boulton, one of the most enterprising pioneer capitalists of the engineering industry in England, wrote 'I have trained up many, and am training up more, plain country lads into good workmen [sic], where ever I find indications of skill and ability I encourage them.' (Quoted from Marshall, *English people*, pp. 272–3. Cf also Trevelyan, *Illustrated English social history*, pp. 15 *et seq.*)

2

The structure of the labour movement

Manufacturers' associations existed in England long before the industrial revolution. In the Middle Ages craft methods of production had given rise to a complicated system of associations, which persisted up to the period that directly preceded the beginnings of capitalism; many aspects of this system even filtered through into a society that was almost entirely capitalistic in character.

There is historical evidence to show that the craft guilds, which were really manufacturers' associations, also drew in their beginnings on the experience and the historical forms evolved by earlier societies. One example of such societies was the frith guild, whose traditions went back very far in England. It was a type of friendly society, based on ties of religion and even of family; and its main concern was to protect its members against accident and misfortune, and to give aid not only during their life on earth but in the life to come. There were also the town guilds, organisations that protected townsmen from the encroachments of feudal landowners: these were thus chiefly focused on an external struggle, to emphasise the separateness and freedom of the burgher estate, and were also called burghers' guilds. The merchants' guilds were organisations of a higher order than the guilds, comprising all the producers. Their main concern was with the internal affairs of the town, and they dealt with questions of equal interest to all members of the society. The craft guilds or trade guilds proper were themselves the inheritors of the forms of organisation set up by these early associations which operated in the medieval towns.

The tasks which the craft guilds set themselves, and which were laid down in their statutes, were concentrated on two basic matters: the establishment of various regulations relating to conditions of production, and endeavours to assure a secure livelihood and eternal salvation for their members. (The guilds customarily organised burials and looked after cemeteries.) The performance of two sets of functions was characteristic of the craft guilds. It was maintained throughout the period of the guilds' existence, despite the far-reaching changes that occurred in their structure and more particularly in their social content.

These changes were indeed profound. In the early craft guilds the functions of a workman, a master and supervisor, an entrepreneur, a merchant and a shopkeeper were at first combined in a single individual. This consolidation of a variety of functions did not last long. Even during the feudal era the process of stratification within the cities was bringing about the 'specialisation' of various functions and the formation of distinct and increasingly hereditary social strata based on different activities. This process took place gradually and by phases. First came the splitting of the craftsmen into large-scale merchant-entrepreneurs and small-scale master-men. Later there arose the stratum of 'professional journeymen'. These were men who could no longer expect automatic elevation to the status of master, but had to face the fact that either such emancipation would never be theirs or, if it came, they would be unable to start an independent workshop for lack of capital. This social stratification among guild members was naturally reflected in the structure of the guilds. The craft guilds, which had formerly been homogeneous, still retained a federal-type unity but in the seventeenth century divided up into three 'classes': the livery— the inner circle of the larger-scale masters; the householders—the organisation of the rest of the masters; and the yeomanry or bachelors, sometimes called the freemen— a further section composed of journeymen who had every reason to expect that they would spend all their lives as such.[1]

The class significance of the transformations just outlined is well shown in the history of guild attitudes to the problem of the statutory limitation on the number of journeymen in a workshop. At the outset the guild as a whole was interested in such limitation; the journeyman was a potential master, and limiting the number of journeymen was equivalent in these conditions to relieving the master from excessive market competition. But when the situation changed, in that it became impossible for journeymen to gain emancipation (for example, in the trades that were moving over to large-scale production), the privileges derived from the institutions of journeyman status and apprenticeship ceased to perform any function for the journeyman. For the masters, on the other hand, they became a source of unexpected advantages. The new state of affairs allowed them to employ masses of ordinary workers without paying them the full rate, on the pretext that they had still to be taught the trade. Moreover, the masters, while defending the institution of apprenticeship, began to attack the principle of limiting the number of journeymen. The journeymen, on the other hand, began to put up an increasingly stiff defence of the principle of the *numerus clausus*. This problem became the superstructure of the class conflict within the guilds. Clashes over the issue became increasingly bitter, to a point where in many guilds it led to the liquidation of the

---

1   The information on the history of the English guilds has been drawn from Unwin, *Industrial organisation*, and *English gilds*, ed. Toulmin Smith, Early English Text Society, London, 1870.

journeymen's sections, or to their being deprived of any influence in guild affairs.[1]

These remarks on the craft guilds are simply by way of introduction to the key problem of this chapter: did a historical link exist between the guild system and the workers' trade unions and, if so, in what sense? Did the forms created by the guilds impose a certain organisational structure, definite functions and way of looking at social reality on the first trade unions of the era of the industrial revolution? If so, to what degree? Did guild tradition exert any influence on the direction in which the workers' organisations developed? If so, to what extent?

English trade unions were 'born, not made', as W. Milne-Bailey rightly observed.[2] They arose spontaneously and simultaneously, in many different places and social milieux, without any common guideline, let alone a common organisational centre. The pace of the unions' growth was such that it is of particular importance to examine not only the structural and class premises but also the ideologies and organisational conceptions on which they were based and which caused them to assume a fairly uniform shape despite the lack of a unifying medium.

The problem under discussion is one which has been an object of interest and controversy to historians of the British labour movement for at least a century. Two opposing schools of thought have developed on this matter, one linked with the name of Lujo Brentano, the other with that of the Webbs.

The first school took the view that there was a direct link between the craft unions and the contemporary trade unions. This interpretation flourished during the 1860s and 1870s. At that time it completely dominated British historiography, imposing its views on the thinkers of the trade union movement of the time and drawing support for its conceptions from their unfaltering conviction that their genealogy reached back into the remote depths of medieval times.[3] This school was convinced that there was no organisational break between the guilds and the early trade unions; the unions evolved from the guilds as a consequence either of the removal

---

1 R. H. Gretton, *The English middle class*, Porcupine Press, London, 1919, pp. 189–190.
2 *Trade union documents*, ed. W. Milne-Bailey, Bell, London, 1929, p. 1.
3 The most important theorist of trade unionism in the third quarter of the nineteenth century, George Howell, declared: 'Trade unionism is an outgrowth of, if not exactly an off-shoot from, the old guild system of the Middle Ages ... Trade unionism not only owes its origin to the old English guilds, but the earlier Trade Unions were in reality the legitimate successors of the Craft Guilds, which flourished in this country down to the time of the suppression of the monasteries and other fraternities by Henry the Eighth, in the thirty-seventh year of his reign.' (G. Howell, 'Trade unionism—new and old' in *Social questions of today*, ed. H. de B. Gibbins, Methuen, London, 1891, pp. 1–2.)

of the masters or of the gradual organisational separation of the journey-men sections. Even before Brentano, Ludlow was developing this interpre-tation;[1] it was built up rapidly, with a truly German methodicalness and attention to detail, in Brentano's comprehensive study.[2] The unchallenged sway of this conception ceased in the 1890s, with the appearance of the Webbs' inspiring study. Nevertheless, some writers, whose concern was with the history of the guilds or with tracing the genealogy of the first trade unions, continued to maintain that the unions were linked with the guilds not only by tradition but by material historical bonds. George Unwin was one such writer at the beginning of the twentieth century.[3] We also find traces of this conception in later studies, for instance in Postgate's history of the building unions,[4] and, in a more general context, those by M. Fothergill Robinson.[5] Reading these works, and others not cited here,

1 Ludlow argued that the first trade unions were born when the masters and capital-ists withdrew from the craft guilds, as a consequence of which the guilds were forced to change into trade unions, in that they were limited only to the class of journey-men . . . 'The trade society of our day is but the lopsided representative of the old guild, its dwarfed but lawful heir.' (J. M. Ludlow, 'Trade societies and the Social Science Association', *Macmillan's Magazine*, February–March, 1861, p. 316.) In this passage Ludlow was talking of the organisational link. Elsewhere he stressed the existence of a functional link as well: 'The guilds of the fourteenth century, under forms to a great extent religious, could fulfil the purposes, on the one hand, of a modern friendly society, in providing for sickness, old age and burial; and, on the other hand, of a modern trade society, by rules tending to fix the hours of labour, and to regulate competition. . .' (*Contemporary Review*, March 1873, p. 564.)

2 L. Brentano, 'On the history and development of gilds' in *English gilds*, ed. Toulmin Smith.

3 'In tracing backwards the spiritual ancestry of the organised skilled workmen of the present day, the first link is undoubtedly to be found in the small master of the seventeenth century. It is in his efforts after organisation, partly in their success, but quite as much in their failure, that the immediate antecedents of the modern trade union are to be sought. We have so far been following the history of these efforts along two main lines, the attempt to preserve an active share in the control of the older companies by means of the yeomanry organisation or other-wise, and the attempt to secure economic independence through separate incorpora-tion.' (*Industrial organisation*, p. 200.) Unwin went on to draw a genealogical tree (see diagram overleaf) of the trade union movement of his time, tracing its industrial pedigree back in an unbroken line to the early medieval guilds. (*Industrial organi-sation*, pp. 12 *et seq.*)

4 Postgate, *The builders' history*, pp. 6 *et seq.*

5 'It has now been established that some measure of authority was maintained in some instances by Gilds until the end of the eighteenth century. Friendly Societies made their first appearance during the seventeenth century, and Trade Unionism dates from the reign of Queen Anne. It is indeed apparent that there was no chrono-logical gap in organised manifestations of the ever-living principle of mutual aid . . . Though the dying Gilds . . . gave an ever-waning light and the new-born Friendly Societies emitted but a feeble gleam, the torch of associative effort still burnt on;

one can have no doubt that their conceptions were derived from German idealistic social philosophy of the nineteenth century, which sought to find in the history of social structures manifestations of the *Korper*, drawing conclusions of a correlated continuity in the stratum of social structures.

The Webbs applied the positivistic method to the problem, and this led them to adopt a diametrically opposed position. They took the hypothesis about historical continuity in its literal sense and were therefore prepared to recognise as the only criterion of its truth the discovery of documentary evidence that the early union structures were directly descended in the organisational sense from the guilds, or from the products of their disintegration. In the Webbs' view no such evidence existed. They therefore maintained firmly that no organisational link existed between the guilds and the trade unions, and that in the organisational sense the latter had sprung out of the void.[1]

  its fire was never extinguished.' (M. Fothergill Robinson, *The spirit of association*, Murray, London, 1913, p. 100.)
1 'The trade unions can be regarded as one of the fruits for good or evil of the industrial revolution ... Nothing like them can be found in any of the preceding centuries. The Gilds, the Trade Clubs and Societies existed earlier but the development of industrial activity in its contemporary sense and meaning created something entirely different—the Trade Unions ... The Trade Unions of the nineteenth

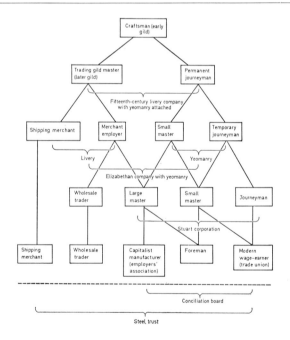

The authority of the Webbs among the historiographers of the labour movement was so absolute that this conclusion had a long and almost unshakeable influence on virtually all the studies dealing with the relationship between guilds and trade unions that have appeared since. The Webbs' conception has been interpreted both functionally and structurally, but in each case its absolute validity has gone unchallenged; that is to say, the existence of any genetic link between the trade union movement and the organisational machinery created by the guilds has been denied. The powerful influence of this view is found both in the works of such authoritative scholars as G. D. H. Cole and Sydney Chapman and also in those of lesser known writers such as Gilbert Stone, and many others.[1]

Such total divergence of viewpoints between historians as eminent as Brentano and the Webbs is baffling, particularly for non-historians. Nevertheless, contrary to Brentano's view, it would seem that the problem of continuity between the guilds and the unions is not exclusively a matter of spiritual community. On the other hand, the Webbs' interpretation notwithstanding, it is surely not just a matter of finding missing links in an organisational chain. Both elements are essential so long as they are not considered in isolation from each other and—most important—in isolation from the stratificatory changes that were taking place within the working population.

At this point we must revert to a question already considered—that of the division of the working population into two distinct groups in the first phase of the industrial revolution. Unless this is taken into account, it

century were not the child of the past, the heritage of history; the conditions of the era gave birth to them ...' 'The supposed descent of the Trade Unions from the medieval Craft Gild rests ... upon no evidence whatsoever. The historical proof is all the other way'. (Summarised from S. and B. Webb, *The history of trade unionism*, Longmans, London, 1894, revised edn. 1920, p. 13.)

1 '... Trade unions can be traced back beyond the eighteenth century, and analogies to them can be found, not, indeed, in the medieval Gilds but in many fraternities of journeymen which existed under the Gild system, and often in opposition to the Gild organisation controlled by the masters ... But Trade Unionism, in the sense in which we understand the term, was really born in the troublous days of the French Wars and the Industrial Revolution.' (G. D. H. Cole, *Organised labour*, Allen & Unwin, London, 1924, p. 1.) 'Trade Unionism, broadly conceived, emerged from the general economic restlessness which inaugurated the Industrial Revolution. Whether in all cases or not a gulf lay between the combinations of the old order and those of the new, trade unions marked a distinct break with tradition.' (Sir S. Chapman, quoted by G. Stone, *A history of labour*, Harrap, London, 1921, p. 217.) 'It should be fully understood that there is no historical connection between the medieval gild and the modern trade union ... The aims [of trade unions] were different, the modes of pressing these aims were different, even the needs for combination were different from the aims, modes and needs present to the gild brethren.' (Stone, *History of labour*, pp. 66 et seq.)

would seem virtually impossible to solve the problem with which we are concerned.

Later historians, who were uninfluenced by the German idealistic school's interpretation of history, have rejected the idea that there was no organisational continuity between guilds and unions. Their view seems convincing. None the less, it is equally a matter of fact that a tradition of defensive organisation existed among that part of the working class which was descended from the disintegrating guild communities. The inertia of this milieu, the snail-like tempo of change in its awareness of the world around it, the fossilisation of its moral norms, customs and relationships between superiors and inferiors—all these support the view that a feeling of the purposefulness of a defensive and restrictive kind of organisation continued to exist in this group.[1] What guaranteed the continuity of the tradition was the exclusiveness of the primary group, its lack of flexibility and its almost instinctive tendency to react collectively in a similar way to similar situations.

It seems almost certain that—quite apart from the chances of still un-covering evidence of organisational links which perhaps never existed—one can easily find in the first trade unions all the ideas that were typical of the guild concept of organisation. First and foremost, there was the idea of a community of occupational interests (occupational, not class) and of association for the defence of those interests. There were, in addition: the idea of establishing the conditions of production as the best way of defending occupational interests; the conceptions of various forms of mutual aid administered by the organisation; the idea of an organisation based on occupation combined with that of a socio-cultural society; and, lastly, the tradition of an organisation which was self-disciplining, and the whole semi-mystical ritual of initiation and procedure. As we shall see later, some of the early trade unions were slavish imitators of guild traditions in all these characteristics. Moreover, these were the same unions which were set up in the craft milieu as a reaction to the growing threat to the tradi-tional socio-economic *status quo*, and not those unions which arose amongst the unorganised mass of factory workers who had neither guild nor occu-pational traditions.

Thus it would seem most probable that the question of the historical continuity of the guilds must be considered separately for the two cate-gories of the working population that existed at this period. In the case of

1 Here one should note that George Unwin, who inclined to a Brentano-type approach, emphasised just this point, that of the continuity of tradition which began to act in a new way, a historical situation that was different but at the same time similar, so long as the community preserved its continuity as a group (*Industrial organisation*, pp. 8–9).

the crafts which for the time being remained outside the direct range of influence of the industrial revolution, the journeymen at a certain moment employed the same defensive measures as the small masters had earlier used against the guild magnates, and the whole fraternity of craftsmen had earlier still used against the large landowners. Continuity of tradition imposed the same forms of organisation, and the same conceptions of aims and methods of action. The habit of reacting in a defined way to defined situations made it unnecessary for people to wander about looking for the right course.[1]

On the other hand, when we turn to the first organisations that arose among those workers who were not a relic of the old economic structure but a product of a new one, we find no traces whatever of a guild tradition being directly inherited. The widely differing cultural backgrounds and diverse origins of the masses of factory workers made them plastic, receptive and ready to accept conceptions and structures from without; it did not, however, help to consolidate the traditions of the craftsmen, who formed only a section of the factory workers and who had in any case already been dislodged from the milieu which was the materialisation of their traditions. In the period that followed, one of the strata which were to emerge from the still undifferentiated mass of workers reached out once more towards guild traditions in building up its unions. The orientation was, however, no longer towards the original guild traditions but towards the versions cultivated by the journeymen of the nineteenth century.

To return to the earlier period, there were by the last quarter of the eighteenth century a considerable number of workers' organisations, generally called 'trade clubs', among the skilled workers in occupations

1 The existence of this kind of continuity is revealed in the works of sociologists and historians concerned with trade union traditions in other countries within a highly developed guild system. For instance, we read in a study of trade union history in Scandinavia: 'The journeyman–master ratio increased, particularly in the building trades (one in twenty in Copenhagen in 1840, one to thirty-five in Stockholm), and most journeymen had to resign themselves to a permanent status at that level. Consequently, special journeymen's associations developed within many of the gilds, primarily to provide sickness and death benefits and travel assistance, but also to some extent to represent the wage interests of the journeymen against the masters ... The Scandinavian gilds provided a direct organisational base for some employer associations and trade unions. Even in the absence of a direct link between the two sets of institutions, the gilds created a propensity to organise which considerably furthered the growth of the early employer associations and trade unions.' (*Comparative labor movements*, ed W. Galenson, Prentice-Hall, New York, 1952, pp. 108–109.) This monograph is of comparatively recent date, so there is less reason to suspect its writer of being influenced by the interpretations that were modish in the nineteenth century.

traditionally linked with guilds and as yet untouched by the influence of
the techniques of the industrial revolution. These were occupations which
had preserved the social status to which they had been entitled for centuries
and which guaranteed their practitioners a relatively high standard of
living and to some extent a social education. Trade clubs existed among silk
weavers, hosiers, goldsmiths, knife makers, hatters, tanners, printers,
brush makers, basket makers, calico printers, shipwrights, blacksmiths,
coach-builders, dyers, cabinet-makers, carpenters, bricklayers, rope
makers, bookbinders and others. All these were crafts in which the
methods of work were still those of the period before the industrial revolution, crafts which still retained their traditional intra-stratal relations.
Such bonds were not, however, apparent among the newly emerging
sections of the non-craft working population, as for instance the textile
workers. Nor were they found among the miners. Although the latter
constituted an early section of the manufacturing workers, with old-
established occupational traditions, they had no guild tradition nor a
crystallised occupational stratification; moreover, they were so discrimi-
nated against as to make organisation impossible.

Taft, following Brentano, holds that the first trade unions arose because
of interference, or the threat of interference, with established customs.
The first unions were set up with aims that were defensive, not offensive,
with the intention of maintaining the existing *status quo*, not of forcing
through any progressive changes.[1] This view seems entirely valid, but only
in relation to the category of workers described above. Defence of the
status quo can be a stimulus for organisation only if that *status quo* is solidly
established in both the institutions and the consciousness of its defenders,
and has values and advantages which make men wish to preserve it. Neither
of these factors was present in the case of the factory workers, who had
been uprooted from their traditional communities and deprived of their
own traditions.

Many writers have emphasised the obvious fact that membership of the
first trade unions was restricted to the category of semi-craftsmen. This
circumstance is most frequently attributed to the relatively greater degree
of social maturity found among such workers.[2] To arrive at a full under-

1   P. Taft, 'Theories of the labor movement' in Industrial Relations Research Associa-
     tion, *Interpreting the labor movement*, Harvard University Press, Cambridge, Mass.,
     1952, p. 2.
2   For instance, Lord Francis Williams made the following comments: 'The combina-
     tions of workers which first came into existence to seek protection against the
     attacks of the new mercantile capitalists of the eighteenth century were not enuncia-
     tors of a new economic or class doctrine but petitioners for the restoration of ancient
     rights.' (*Magnificent journey*, Odhams Press, London, 1954, p. 131.) The Webbs
     commented as follows: 'But it is not among the farm servants, miners or general

standing of this highly significant phenomenon in the history of the British labour movement one needs to bring together factors cited by different authors in different contexts, for example:

1 The existence of a status that needed to be defended.
2 A relatively high level of social maturity and living standards, which made it possible to set up reasonably permanent associations with long-term objectives.
3 The high degree of occupational articulation in the artisan communities, which made them the pioneers of the trade union movement.

This last fact is hardly ever brought out in the literature on the subject. The occupational hierarchies consolidated by the guilds created not only interests specific to the stratum but also habitual modes of expressing them. Consolidated in the group consciousness, the guild structures provided patterns for the institutionalisation of occupational interests. In this way the guilds prepared the ground for the trade union movement. The unions sprang up where the seed had been sown by the guilds.

The printing trade is one of those to which these observations are relevant, and the following sketch of the antecedents of the union movement among the printers may serve to illustrate our thesis.

The traditional organisation of printers' journeymen into chapels in every printer's shop dates back to the seventeenth century. The memoirs of Thomas Gent, a printer from York, written in 1746, contain an account

labourers, ill-paid and ill-treated as these often were, that the early Trade Unions arose . . . The formation of independent associations to resist the will of employers requires the possession of a certain degree of personal independence and strength of character. Thus we find the earliest Trade Unions arising among journeymen whose skill and standard of life has been for centuries encouraged and protected by legal or customary regulations as to apprenticeship . . .' (*The history of trade unionism*, p. 44.) 'It was the skilled workers, who traditionally had enjoyed not merely relatively high wages, but also protected wages, that immediately set up organisations when the new conditions, placing power in the hands of the employers, led to the abandonment of all pretence of fixing wages by custom . . . Thus, the aim of these early Trade Unions was to preserve the long-standing labour monopoly in their own trades, to restore the old conception of 'customary wages', and in short to stabilise conditions at the comparatively satisfactory level that had hitherto prevailed. Their method was to seek legislative protection, for that was how the standard had been regulated since Tudor times.' (Milne-Bailey, *Trade union documents*, p. 7.) 'These artisans' clubs, indeed, were not engaged in that life and death struggle which characterised later periods of Trade Unionism, for their members did not come from the most oppressed classes; they were, in fact, the aristocrats of the working-class world. Among the labourers, as distinct from the skilled craftsmen, there was no attempt at organisation.' (C. M. Lloyd, *Trade unionism*, Black, London, 1921, p. 3.)

of the writer's initiation as a member of the chapel in 1712.[1] The oldest
account of the structure of a chapel was given by Joseph Moxon in his
Mechanick exercises in 1683. Initially the chapel was like a guild branch. All
the freemen employed in a printing shop were automatically members.
At first the father of the chapel was the eldest of the freemen, but later this
position became elective. The immediate reason for setting up a chapel was
to promote production. Its task was to maintain working discipline and to
regulate the communal life of the freemen: the chapels backed up the
workshop's regulations with a system of rewards and penalties.[2]

The organisational form of the chapel survived into the nineteenth
century virtually unchanged, but its functions underwent profound changes
as the printing shops became transformed into capitalist printing businesses.
The main concern of the journeymen who were associated in the chapels
shifted from matters of discipline and living conditions to the increasingly
urgent problem of defending their occupational interests. In particular,
the chapels opposed the trend towards larger printing shops, a trend that
was combined with a sharply increasing ratio of journeymen to masters,
and consequently with decreasing opportunities for the journeyman to set
up on his own. At the same time the journeyman opposed the rise of
capitalist printing houses, thus defending those who were to become small
master printers from their competition. For both these reasons the chapels
concentrated their efforts on securing legal or customary restrictions on the
intake of young apprentices and on perpetuating a reasonably favourable
ratio of journeymen to masters. The emergence of this problem set the
chapels against the masters for the first time. From being auxiliary institutions of the master printers, they were gradually transformed into organisations to defend the distinctive occupational class interests of the journeymen against the masters—although the chapel members did not become
aware of this fact until much later. The same problem was basic to the

---

1   *The life of Thomas Gent, printer, of York, written by himself*, 1832, p. 16.
2   See the text of a statutory declaration by the chapel of the printing office of Neill &
    Co., Old Fishmarket Close, Edinburgh, dating back to 1785: 'Experience has fully
    evinced that without Laws and Regulations order can never be observed in any
    community. The observance of order and regularity is not more necessary in society
    than in a printing office, and the strict observance of rules becomes more neces-
    sary when members are somewhat numerous; therefore the journeymen and
    apprentices in Messrs. Neill's, observing with regret the little regard paid to order
    in the execution of the work of the house, and the train of evil consequences atten-
    dant thereon, both to masters and servants, with a view to prevent said conse-
    quences in future, resolved to erect themselves into a chapel . . . and they also
    agreed to sign, support and enforce the following rules and regulations.' One of these
    rules referred to laid down a fine of twopence for each offence. (Quoted from S. C.
    Gillespie, *A hundred years of progress*, Scottish Typographical Association, Glasgow,
    1953, p. 15.)

setting up of the first printers' trade union—the London Trade Society of Compositors—in 1816.

The activities of the chapels also helped to prepare the ground for the union. At the end of the eighteenth and the beginning of the nineteenth centuries it became customary for the senior members of all the chapels in a locality to assemble once a year in an alehouse for a sort of unofficial conference at which they discussed professional matters which were of equal interest to all the chapels. When the matters under discussion were of particular importance to journeymen, additional delegates were summoned from the chapels; there were even meetings that were something in the nature of general assemblies of journeymen. In the course of these conferences the organisational bond between the chapels became stronger from one year to another. A feeling grew up that the interests of journeymen extended beyond the walls of a single printing shop and that there was a need for them to co-ordinate their efforts. The question of restricting the intake of apprentices speeded this process immensely—for the argument made sense only when it was applied in relation to the printing trade as a whole.

In this way the first printers' trade unions simply reinforced the organisational links that had previously existed between the chapels as they were evolving out of the feudal tradition. The unions were to some extent a superstructure over the system of chapels, an institutionalisation— perhaps simply a more lasting form of institutionalisation—of social bonds already in existence and becoming stronger each year. In London, for instance, one can reconstruct an unbroken organisational chain between the annual consultations of the chapel elders and the London Trade Society of Compositors, the London General Society of Compositors (1826), which existed consecutively with the former body, the London Union of Compositors (1834), which resulted from the fusion of the two earlier associations, and, lastly, the London Society of Compositors, set up in 1845 —the final form of trade organisation for the compositors. The same sort of processes took place in other areas of England and Wales and also in Scotland, where the printing trade unions that evolved out of the chapels were set up between 1826 and 1836 but reached their final crystallisation in the 1840s.

The formation of the journeymen's unions was, as I have said, the result of the crystallising process which the interests of the journeymen became distinct from those of the master printers. Nevertheless, this note of class opposition did not for many years appear either in the programmes or in the practices of the printing unions. The journeymen still had some prospect of passing into the ranks of the master printers; moreover, they were still constrained by guild attitudes to life. Thus, although they were organised in unions, they were far from any intention of attacking the owners of their printing shops. It was not an awareness of social inferiority in relation to their masters, but an attitude of superiority in relation to the undifferentiated masses of labourers, that chiefly helped to cement the first unions. The journeymen printers had for long been distinguished among working men by their aristocratic exclusiveness, their high educational level, their clannish customs and their closed social circle. The appeal to restrict the recruitment of apprentices was understood not as an attack on the authority of the master printers but as a defensive measure, carried out in the joint interests of masters and journeymen; it was regarded as an attempt to protect their high status against the influx of the unorganised impoverished mass of unskilled workers that was making its tempestuous way into the newly established urban areas. The motivation of this campaign, as set out in many union documents of the period, leaves us in no doubt that the early trade unions put this interpretation on it.[1] The journeymen printers' unions directed their campaign downwards, not upwards, and this circumstance, together with many others, indicated a close genetic kinship between the unions and the guild system.[2]

The acceptance of a policy of restricting apprenticeships is not, however, sufficient in itself to establish the degree to which guild tradition influenced trade unions. Considerable difficulties arise, particularly over the fact that in the United States—as in some other areas of later European colonisation which had not experienced the feudal era with its guild system—the first trade unions also took up with equal energy the struggle to restrict entry to their particular trade to outsiders. The doubts to which this gives rise can, it is true, be partially dispelled when one considers that, although there were no guilds in the United States, there were guild traditions, brought in by immigrants from the Old World as part and parcel of their cultural baggage. This explanation is, however, inadequate if we take the view that the form of the union movement, like that of other social structures, was determined not just by the contemporary cultural climate but by the material characteristics of an evolving environment. In the last

1 See the following extract from the resolutions of the London Union of Compositors: 'It was also suggested that journeymen, in the future, should abstain from introducing more than one son to the business—"since such conduct is impolitic on the part of the parents, and unjust to the lads, who thus become introduced to a trade already overburdened with lads".' (Quoted by Howe and Waite, *The London Society of Compositors*, p. 94.) As can be seen, the journeymen's aim was to make their craft into a hereditary monopoly, with even an entail.

2 Unless particular references are given, the information on the emergence of trade unions among printers is drawn from Gillespie, *A hundred years of progress*, Howe and Waite, *The London Society of Compositors*, and Musson, *The Typographical Association*.

resort, one can find a very simple explanation for a union's acceptance of the policy of limiting the number of apprentices without having recourse to an investigation of guild traditions. For it was the easiest and most obvious remedy that could be devised to counteract the visible decline of craft status caused by the setting up of modern factories. Nevertheless, in my view, the fact that this remedy, and not another, was employed by the first trade unions which emerged among English workers of the particular category under discussion was only an element in a much wider process of transforming social structures which had been institutionalised into guilds, and that this element was determined by the whole. To prove this thesis, however, it is necessary to look for characteristics other than the tactical restriction of apprenticeship which would link the first trade unions with the craft guilds.

For instance, it may be noted that the first trade unions among the craft journeymen were, like the guilds, not only organisations to protect craft interests but also something in the nature of social and recreational clubs. The Society of Masons and two carpenters' unions in Newcastle laid it down that their members must each spend twopence for beer at every session meeting, while the first entry in the cash book of the joiners' union in Preston referred to moneys spent on beer provided at the members' meetings.[1] Union meetings generally took place in alehouses, and some individual houses became virtually union premises, combining the qualities of an office and a social club.[2] The unions regarded it as one of their chief tasks to foster close social links and to ensure correct and courteous relationships between practitioners of the same craft. The first unions expressed in their statutes a concern that members should be well behaved; licentious behaviour, swearing, quarrelling with fellow members and so on were frowned upon. Confirmation of this can be found in so many statutes of the period under discussion that it is pointless to cite them in detail.

The most significant proof of the validity of my hypothesis is, however, the highly developed feeling of a community of interests with the masters that prevailed in the first journeymen's trade unions.[3] These unions were

1 Postgate, *The builders' history*, pp. 20–21.
2 N. Wymer, *English town crafts*, Batsford, London, 1949, p. 8.
3 During the strike of 1820 the members of the hatters' union appealed to the masters as follows: 'For are not there among you those who have toiled in our ranks who have been raised by providence above their fellows? . . . We cannot suppose that the generosity of our masters, from the generous manner in which we have been treated by them, could have engendered such evil against us . . . Nothing can ultimately tend to beneficial purposes in long protracted warfare, as we consider the interests of the one connected with the interests of the other; but that the sacrificing ourselves to an additional number of apprentices would be entailing on our posterity misery and disgrace, and would in nowise be advantageous to you, as there has always been

the institutionalisation of a shared occupational interest, not of a class one. Until the final transformation of craft workshops into capitalistic enterprises this occupational interest continued to link journeymen and masters even after class interests had begun to divide them. The unions' defence of the *status quo* was an attempt to resuscitate and preserve the guild traditions and to recreate the craft communities together with their whole complex of social ties and customs. This is a special feature of the first unions which is not found where there were no craft guild traditions.

A second type of organisation, also derived from guild traditions, was evolving in the same social environment and at the same period—this was the friendly society.

All-embracing social welfare for members was one of the essential functions of the craft guilds. The principle of communally organised assistance for individual members was universally accepted and applied in the English guilds—in relation to all kinds of accidents and disasters, to old age and to old age pensions and death benefits; payments were made out of a fund built up from regular subscriptions paid in by members of that community. In their excellent study of the history of the craft guilds the Toulmin Smiths quote sections from many guild statutes regulating the social obligations of the guild community towards its members in various vicissitudes of life in which social assistance was needed.[1] These functions of guilds provided the individual with a substitute for social security and freed him from most of the anxieties due to unexpected misfortunes by making them a collective responsibility. In this way the guilds were an imposing

found by the ancient laws and customs a sufficient number of men for every purpose connected with the trade. We remain, Gentlemen, with respect, etc.' (British Museum, Add. MSS, 27799, 80.) Again, one can cite a passage from the 2 February 1835 report of the council of the London Union of Compositors: 'The masters are more at enmity with each other than with us;... in truth, our wages do not so much depend on the master printers of London, as on the opulent booksellers, who have contrived to throw the apple of discord among our employers, and have made them underwork each other to such an extent, as has excited a degree of hostility among them.' The reference here is to the competition between master printers, which hit journeymen's wages and was blamed on the wholesale booksellers. This report was calling for a common front of journeymen and master printers against the booksellers. (Quoted by Howe and Waite, *The London Society of Compositors*, p. 96.) It seems probable that this feeling of a mutual community of interests also stimulated the journeymen's dislike of the newly created small workshops, although they should have adopted a sympathetic attitude to them as a manifestation or process in which they themselves had a vital interest. Instead the journeymen denounced the small master printers who had emerged from their ranks, as men who possessed neither the qualifications essential for an employer of workers nor the capital needed to enter a respected occupation. (*Compositors' Chronicle*, April 1841.)

1 Toulmin Smith, *English gilds*.

element in maintaining the relatively high and durable socio-economic status of the craftsmen; moreover, they were an additional and important factor in welding together the various levels of the craft hierarchy into a single whole with common interests.

As the craft unions moved towards disintegration, their mutual aid functions retained the greatest liveliness. These functions were the earliest to be hived off from the whole complex of guild activities and be carried out by separate independent organisations, without regard to the further uncertain fortunes of the guilds. In the view of Ludlow,[1] a specialist in the history of the guilds, the hiving off of the guilds' mutual aid functions into separate fraternal societies began as early as the first half of the seventeenth century. The annual report of the 1883 commission (to enquire into the friendly societies) listed seventy-seven English friendly societies; of these the earliest gave the date of its setting-up as 1687, the latest as 1780. The oldest of the Scottish friendly societies, the Linlithgow Society of Dyers, was set up in 1679, long before the industrial revolution.[2]

The traditional continuity of the friendly societies was expressed in the societies' own version of their genealogies.[3] The Freemasons confined themselves to tracing their ancestry back to Solomon; the Druids, however, claimed Noah as their founder, while the Free Gardeners traced themselves back to Paradise, and the Oddfellows officially maintained that their first member was Adam. The Foresters were less demanding. Although their first members were said to have felled trees in the Garden of Eden their traditions laid most stress on Robin Hood, Little John, Friar Tuck and other characters of equal historical authenticity.

In any case the origins of the friendly societies can certainly be traced back to some period before the industrial revolution, and their roots lay deep down in the guild system. Nevertheless, there was no sudden increase in the number of friendly societies until the turn of the eighteenth and nineteenth centuries—in the same period in which the first craft trade unions began to emerge. The cause of this upsurge in numbers was probably the same as that which stimulated the birth of the trade unions: the threat to status and craft privileges posed by the onward march of capitalist methods of production. As those foundations of existence which had so far been stable began to totter, the social strata whose status was threatened were impelled to seek social means of combating a danger

---

1 *Contemporary Review*, March and April 1873.
2 J. M. Baernreither, *English associations of working men*, trans. A. Taylor, Swan Sonnenschein, London, 1893, pp. 160 et seq.
3 Here one should also take into account the widespread contemporary indifference in matters of historical accuracy and the powerful urges to mystical and religious rationalisations. (Fothergill Robinson, *The spirit of association*, p. 140.)

which no individual could face alone. Here again recourse was sought to a tradition handed down by the friendly societies, that of the welfare functions of the societies, that of the welfare functions of the guilds. Although it was by now ailing, this tradition provided a ready-made form for new social needs. In the outcome the friendly societies, which had until then been vegetating, burst suddenly into full bloom: the number of their members and branches increased almost in geometric progression,[1] and their role in the life of the journeymen steadily expanded. The qualified and better paid craftsmen of many traditional occupations gradually achieved, as an addition to their privileged social status, some sort of modest social security. The knowledge that the friendly society would look after them in the event of a loss of earnings, family misfortunes and even after death gave them self-assurance and a sense of their position in society; it paralysed any possible temptation to adopt a nonconformist attitude to the social order which had become the indispensable condition of protection for this life and the life hereafter.

Not surprisingly, the system of guaranteed security, built on a belief in the durability of what were in reality relics of post-feudal days, was to break up rapidly under the impetus of the capitalistic offensive. With the social devaluation of the skilled crafts, the friendly societies lost their financial bases. There were bankruptcies, massive decreases in membership and a loss of social authority. A similar fate also awaited the craft unions. For the time being, however, both institutions continued to function with a certain verve, as an institutionalised form of the conservative interests of the heirs of the guild craftsmen.

It was natural for such organised associations of the craft section of the working population to keep themselves aloof from the mainstream of the political conflicts of their time. The craft stratum had no tradition of engagement in everyday politics on a national level. For centuries politics had been the preserve of the aristocracy and even in the eighteenth century not only statesmen but also MPs from both the governing and opposition parties were still being recruited from its ranks. Until 1832 legal restrictions had denied even the middle class very much chance of reaching the highest levels of the political hierarchy and in practice this state of affairs continued for several more years. Craftsmen had even less chance of success. So the associations under discussion generally took an interest in the proceedings of Parliament only when they were appealing to society to guarantee their privileges on the model of the Elizabethan statutes.

---

1   For instance, in 1834 the Manchester Unity Society had only 781 branches and 47,638 members; two years later, however, it had 1,100 branches and over 70,000 members. (J. F. Wilkinson, *The friendly society movement*, Longmans, London, 1891, pp. 31–2.)

There were, however, three deviations from this general attitude. The first is to be found in the brief history of the London Corresponding Society, a political organisation founded at the end of the eighteenth century by a bookmaker, Thomas Hardy. The Society was an echo of the bourgeoisie's increasingly ardent struggle for a share in government, but it went further than the political demands put forward by that class by calling for the payment of members of Parliament: in class terms this was undoubtedly a demand for the admission of popular representatives to Parliament.[1] The London Corresponding Society recruited its members exclusively from craft circles, and more particularly from independent master craftsmen; it never displayed a nonconformist attitude towards the social system of the day and its policy programme expressed very bourgeois interests.[2]

The second deviation from the general attitude was the campaign of the wealthy London tailor, Francis Place, to secure the repeal of the Combination Act, which forbade the setting up of associations. This Act had been forced through Parliament because of fears that the French revolution, and particularly unions of the Jacobin type, would spread to the British Isles. Place's campaign was carried out with the support of the elders of the union movement, although he personally was an opponent of the unions; his view was that they had emerged as an expression of the drive to freedom and of protest when the fulfilment of this drive was prohibited, and that they would disappear immediately the prohibition was lifted. Incidentally, this view reflects in a very typical way the manner in which the craftsmen of that period viewed their reduced social status. Place succeeded in getting the Combination Act repealed by means of a procedural trick. After this his short-lived movement, which had only one concrete and sectional aim, languished and died a natural death.

Finally, the third exception to political apathy which prevailed in the craft sector was the contribution made by some of its component parts. These were congregated in the Chartist party of 'moral force', of which they formed the mainstay. Their viewpoint was expressed by William Lovett and by the London Working Men's Association, of which he was the leader. Lovett's group was impelled to action by the great revolutionary movement of the factory workers. It set itself much more modest goals

1 H. Collins, 'The London Corresponding Society' in *Democracy and the labour movement*, ed. J. Saville, Lawrence & Wishart, London, 1954, pp. 132–4.

2 Here are some characteristic extracts from the London Corresponding Society's 'Address to the Nation on the subject of a Thorough Parliamentary Reform': '... That no man shall be taxed, but by the consent of himself, or his representative freely chosen by himself.' 'Commerce is nearly stopped! Manufacturers are ruined! Artisans are starving! Provisions rise in price! The revenue decreases, and fresh taxes are wanting.' (Cole and Filson, *British working class movements*, p. 45.)

than did the more radical wing of the Chartist movement, which was campaigning not only for Parliamentary reform but for a social revolution. The revolutionary situation forced Lovett into the same camp as Feargus O'Connor, but their alliance was of necessity short-lived. The artisans were seeking to establish themselves on a better and surer basis in the society in which they lived, whereas the factory workers had been reduced to desperation and sought the total overthrow of a social system that was alien and inimical to them. In consequence, the history of the Chartist movement was one of constant friction between the two extremes of conformism and nonconformism. The artisans worked within the movement to defend and strengthen their social status.[1]

These are the only three known exceptions to the attitude of political indifference prevailing among the first craft trade unions, which in general expressed the specific interests of occupations and local communities, not those of a class.

The labour movement among the factory workers developed along entirely different lines. This section of the working population had a different internal structure and a different position in society; hence for a time its social movement took a dramatically different course.

The factory workers were rejected by society, plunged into an ever deepening abyss of destitution, deprived of civic rights and faced at every step by a wall of indifference, antipathy and fear erected by the politically privileged classes. In consequence, they adopted an attitude of total opposition to society and the complex of social relations that characterised it. They constituted an amorphous group which lacked any natural means by which its social interests could be crystallised, and any group interests which would modify its attitude of total nonconformism. The group was fragmented, and thus unable to demonstrate its real interests. In its spontaneous outbursts of protest it was governed by the law of the mob. It was deprived of any basic security or stable livelihood, and was helpless before the incomprehensible forces that governed social evolution and treated this group with increasing brutality. Its members lacked any awareness of distinctiveness, or of the strength and value of the individual, and sought all these essential elements of social existence outside their own milieu. For this reason they readily embraced mystical and messianic conceptions. Messianism constituted a spiritual compensation for the insta-

---

1   Cf the following excerpts from the 'Address and rules' put out by Lovett's organisation in 1836: 'Objects:— (1) to draw into one band of UNITY the *intelligent and useful* portion of the working class in town and country; (2) to seek by every legal means to place all classes of society in possession of their equal political and social rights.' (Cole and Filson, *British working class movements*, p. 347.)

bility and incomprehensibility of existence and the loss of the individual in the mass.

The hordes of factory workers were incapable of setting up stable organisations and rarely made an active appearance in the social arena. When they did occur, however, such manifestations, extremely violent, were potentially explosive and imbued with the threat of armed revolt and revolution. Each manifestation was in complete contrast to the controlled, mannerly and over-cautious operations of the craft unions.

The inflammable social masses which filled the first factories found a natural outlet for protest in expressions of hatred of their immediate environment. Their chronic frustration would erupt in an irresistible desire to destroy the machines and the gaunt factory buildings, which were the object of the same kind of hatred as that felt by the long term prisoner for his gaol. The second half of the eighteenth century and the early part of the nineteenth are filled with reports of the burning of factory buildings, warehouses containing raw materials or finished goods, and the destruction of machines. That this phenomenon had become widespread by the middle of the eighteenth century is shown by the fact that in 1769 Parliament passed a special law equating the wilful destruction of any building containing machinery, either by a single person or by an illegal and seditious mob, with the crime of arson and making this punishable, like arson, by death.[1] Nevertheless, this drastic measure did not deter the machine-breakers. Indeed, it could hardly do so, since the attacks on the factories were not carried out by any organised groups, nor were they the result of any planned action. In each particular case there was a sudden flare of revolt arising from a chance spark, and no more foreseen by those who took part than by the constables and judiciary.[2] It was only in the final phase of the machine-breaking that it assumed a semi-organised form.

When the labour movement began to pass into the organised phase of its development it found more rational targets for its demonstrations of nonconformism. But this did not mean that the violent forms which it assumed were moderated in the slightest. For several decades to come the factory

1 Mantoux, *The industrial revolution*, pp. 409 *et seq.*
2 Lloyd Jones was an eye-witness of a typical spontaneous outburst of desperate protest. He gives the following description of the destruction of a Manchester textile factory by a crowd of workmen: 'The burning building was surrounded by thousands of excited people, whose faces, reddened by the ascending flames, expressed a fierce and savage joy. As the fire forced its way from floor to floor, darting through the long rows of windows, cries of exultation were shouted by the crowd, and when, finally bursting through the roof, it went roaring into the heavens, the maddened multitude danced with delight, shouting and clapping their hands as in uncontrollable thankfulness for a great triumph.' (Ludlow and Jones, *Progress of the working class*, pp. 22–3.)

workers' movement remained in a state of total opposition to capitalist society and carried within it the seeds of revolt, if not of social revolution.

The ruling classes also viewed the movement in this way. The first unions of factory workers were seen as germs of revolt, a baleful and mysterious force which ought to be countered by harsh measures. The ruling classes, mindful of the example of the Jacobins, did not entertain the possibility of reaching an agreement with the rising wave of the labour movement. Their attitude to the unions was characterised by hatred and apprehension.[1]

In consequence, the young unions had to face an avalanche of repression which was quite as desperate and hysterical as their own activities. The most insignificant demonstrations of protest, even perfectly peaceful ones, were followed by punishments whose cruelty was quite unrelated to the degree to which social order had been undermined. The object was not to mete out a penalty appropriate to the offence but to spread fear and an almost irrational terror among the workers as a deterrent against further demonstrations of hostility to the social system. These punishments were intended to serve as a warning and an indication that a state of war existed between society and the factory rebels.[2]

This kind of reaction from the courts, constabulary and other agencies of the social order against the evolving labour movement helped to intensify the feeling of estrangement and social rejection among the factory workers; it also introduced the stimulus of martyrdom and self-sacrifice to the union movement. This movement frequently cut itself off within the narrow confines of conspiratorial action, introduced rules and regulations of a sectarian nature, and surrounded itself with a fog of mysticism. It was prone to weave messianistic dreams about a handful of saviours of society, dreams which owed much of their content to the apocalyptic visions which these desperate 'outcasts' found particularly attractive. The union movement was declaring war not so much on the capitalist class as on the whole of society, which it regarded as depraved to the marrow, corroded by moral decay and destructive of all human liberties. At this period hatred

1 Cf this passage in a letter from Dr Arnold of Rugby to the Chevalier Bunsen in
   1834: 'You have heard, I doubt not, of the trade unions; a fearful engine of mischief,
   ready to riot or assassinate; and I see no counteracting power.' (Quoted in C. R. Fay,
   Life and labour in the nineteenth century, Cambridge University Press, 1947 edition,
   p. 53.)
2 For example, in the winter of 1830 a crowd of starving agricultural workers from
   the country south of the Thames organised a hunger march to demand a rise in
   daily wage rates to half a crown. The reprisals were appalling. Three of those who
   took part in the march, after being chosen more or less at random, were hanged;
   another 420 were taken from their houses and families and deported to penal
   servitude in Australia. (Trevelyan, *Illustrated English social history*, IV, p. 9.)

of the employers was still only one facet of a general attitude towards society, the primary hatred being concentrated on the most accessible and obvious targets, the machines and buildings of the factory system.

The records of that period are full of first-hand reports concerning secret oaths given during mystic initiation ceremonies; for instance, oaths in which a neophyte member of the union would swear to obey the union's rules or face death as a penalty for disobedience. Union meetings were accompanied by rites of a religious nature, and union leaders were regarded as a living embodiment of the saints whom they also resembled in their unreasoning obedience. Masked trials were often held, and unions had secret execution squads which carried out their sentences using firearms, vitriol or flaming torches with which they burned down the homes of those who had been sentenced. The campaign of terror waged by the unions on one side and the authorities on the other had a mutually inciting effect, and each provided the other with a justification and rationale for the tactics which they adopted.[1]

The irrational form assumed by the social protest movement and the fragmented and amorphous state of the factory workers helped to promote the spread of religious cults. Whilst union activities were dressed up in the colourful vestments of religious rites, the workers were endeavouring, with the active co-operation of Methodist preachers, to imbue the traditional religious ceremonies with a class content. In the chapels it was quite normal to hold prayers for the success of a strike or to call on God to punish the strike-breakers.[1] The influence of religious practice on the first industrial trade unions did not, however, end there.[2]

Earlier in this chapter I tried to trace the processes by which the new kinds of union activity among the journeymen craftsmen were absorbed in the old forms that had been evolved and bequeathed to them by the guilds. The factory workers were not the inheritors of the guild tradition. Even if they had been, the machinery of the guilds was based on the distinct stratification of a self-organising community, and it was concentrated on the conservative tasks of maintaining that community's social status. Thus it could not be adapted for use in the completely different structure of factory work, or for dealing with altogether different social problems. In consequence, the religious tradition played the same sort of role in the first industrial unions as the guild tradition had played in the first craft unions. The forms of religious organisation which played a particularly strong role here were those of the most democratic and popular of the Nonconformist religious bodies, the Methodists. The pioneers of the union

1 Cf, for instance, Williams, *Magnificent journey*, pp. 35–6.
2 R. L. Galloway, *Annals of coal mining and the coal trade*, II, chapter 14, Colliery Guardian Co., London, 1896.

movement in the factories turned instinctively to Methodist forms of organisation, as the only forms of social activity with which they were familiar and which they used in practice.

This was why such institutions as the open-air meetings introduced by such Methodist founding fathers as John Wesley and George Whitefield found an unexpected renaissance in the open-air gatherings of the first trade unionists. These meetings were closely modelled on the religious ceremonies of the early Methodists, and they retained a religious guise, albeit one which covered concerns that were entirely mundane.

The internal organisation of the Methodist body set up by Wesley in 1747 proved of the greatest service to the youthful labour movement, providing a model for union organisations which were set up half a century later. The division of the Methodist society into territorially based 'class meetings for Christian fellowship', the regular Sunday meetings, the principle of raising funds for the society by voluntary weekly contributions from wages, the meeting of 'class' elders, the quarterly general assemblies and conferences—experience of all these organisational techniques was of considerable value to the infant union movement, which lacked any traditions of its own.[1] The Methodist type of organisation became a prototype for the trade unions organised by the factory workers. Every circumstance favoured this development: the plebeian nature of Methodism, its position as the only organisation in the social lives of the factory workers; its adaptability to the social programme of the labour movement; and, finally, the tendency of the pioneers of the union movement to accept religio-mystical rationalisations which inclined them to turn to religious models.

Nevertheless, the existence of organisational models was not by itself enough to ensure that the workers' societies would be reasonably stable. The factory workers were desperate and highly excitable, and their constant alternation between turbulence and total apathy—both easily induced and quickly spread—made it difficult to set up organisations that were likely to endure. The difficulties were enhanced by an almost complete absence of the habits of organised life, and above all by the total or partial lack of any natural social bonds which could have served as a stable foundation on which a union could be built. In consequence, the first union organisations in the factories were extremely unstable. They were set up on the spur of a desperate impulse; but when a worker who was more far-sighted than his fellows succeeded in organising the protest, the organisation would break and vanish without a trace at the first setback or halt to progress. The same thing could happen if the union's organiser lost

1   R. F. Wearmouth, *Some working class movements of the nineteenth century*, Epworth Press, London, 1948, pp. 31–2, 48, 66, 144.

his social prestige, for reasons which were often completely irrational, or simply because the temporary access of energy had once more given way to depression and collapse. As a result, the successive spates of endeavour towards setting up union organisations failed to produce any lasting organisational structures.

Unions sprang up and vanished so rapidly and left so little material trace of their existence that the majority of them are remembered today only because they are mentioned in the records of the police or the Home Office security branch. Trade unions often collapsed even before the authorities could strike at them. On the other hand, official counter-action was sometimes so rapid that a union disappeared even earlier than it would otherwise have done. For instance, the organisation of farm workers set up in 1833 in the remote Dorset village of Tolpuddle owes its renown entirely to the brutal reprisals that fell on its organisers. In reality it was a feeble organisation which had no chance of lasting more than a few months.[1]

A typical example of this kaleidoscope of ephemeral unions may be found in the history of the union movement among the English miners. This is not an irresponsibly one-sided example, because the miners, while they were fragmented and beyond the pale of society like other categories of industrial workers, had an advantage over the others in being a long-established community with old traditions, which had from its very beginnings succeeded in evolving certain basic elements of an internal structure. In spite of this, not even the miners could escape the fate of other pioneers of the industrial union movement in the period under discussion.

The earliest surviving document of a miners' trade union was published in 1825. It was headed 'Voice from The Mines' and its signators were 'the Miners of the United Society of Durham and Northumberland'. This document is similar in character to the peasant 'lamentations' familiar in Poland. It contains a collection of the miners' complaints, backed up with a shocking account of their working and living conditions. It is the only record of the existence of the United Society. The Society's fate is completely unknown; probably the production of this list of complaints was its only act, and thereafter it ceased to exist. In the years that followed we find scattered and fragmentary information about vaguely identified mining organisations bearing a great variety of names; but all of them were alike in having extensive aspirations which were quite unrelated to their actual fortunes.

The miners' union in the Tyne and Wear valleys was set up to organise a strike. The strike began on 10 March 1832. At a mass meeting the miners passed a resolution to the effect that, just as the common people, who were

1   Selley, *Village trade unions*, p. 11.

oppressed in every era, had succeeded in vanquishing their enemies if they were united, so they, the miners, would follow the example of those who in the past and present had risen and destroyed their oppressors.[1] The strike involved half the mines in the area. Those union members who were working in pits where there was no strike paid a voluntary contribution of sixpence in the £ towards strike pay for their striking comrades. As the strikes continued, however, the inflow from this source decreased. The members began to rebel against the continuing financial burden and finally, in August, they one after another withheld further contributions and simultaneously withdrew from the union. For lack of funds the strike ended in a disastrous failure. The men returned to work, exhausted and even more impoverished than before. The union collapsed at the end of September after finally losing all authority among the miners.

In the next decade a similar fate overtook the Miners' Association of Great Britain and Ireland. Although this union was led by Martin Jude, probably the most talented trade unionist of the period, it failed to recover from the blow dealt it by the failure of the strike of 40,000 miners in the Durham and Northumberland valleys. The final *coup de grâce* was the depression of 1847–48, which caused the demise of this belligerent but shortlived organisation. In the years that followed some attempts were made by Jude to resurrect the union, but without success.[2]

Everything about the miners' unions and the way they functioned is typical of the history of the industrial trade unions in general at this period. Among these characteristics were: a short lease of life; the unmethodical manner of collecting dues; the need for a strike as the principal incentive to induce workers to organise; the ease with which the men's enthusiasm ebbed as soon as setbacks were encountered; the vulnerability of the flimsy union organisations to economic depression; the lack of continuity between successive workers' organisations; the attempts to organise unions not on an occupational but on a broad class basis, at a time when solidarity consisted of a short-lived flare of enthusiasm. To sum up, the unions were highly ephemeral creations—the froth on the surface of the working class. In consequence, they had hardly any influence on the internal situation, the structure or the social position of that class.

An extremely important trait which differentiated the first industrial associations from the craft unions was the fact that they were formed not on an occupational but on a class basis. Occupational stratification among

1   *Newcastle Chronicle*, 1832.
2   Unless particular references are given, the information on the beginnings of the union movement among the miners is drawn from the following: J. L. and B. Hammond, *The skilled labourer*; R. Page-Arnot, *The miners*, Allen & Unwin, London, 1949; Webb, *The story of the Durham miners*.

industrial workers was at that time so germinal and fluid, differences of status between one job and another so slight, and changes of job so easy and habitual, that there seemed to the working groups in different factories and mines to be a clear identity of class affiliation between the different occupational categories. A weaver was not so much a weaver as a worker; the same was true of a spinner or a railwayman. Even a coal miner regarded himself rather as a worker than as a miner; in spite of the long traditions of his occupation and the relative geographical isolation of a mining community the mineworker, or at least his parents, were new-comers from another sphere of production. In the event of his losing his job in mining, the pitman would seek employment in an entirely different type of work. He was, after all, part of a completely skilled labour force. The feeling of solidarity among workers in various occupations was the natural outcome of the free flow of industrial workers between different manufacturing industries, factories and branches of production. The value of a trade was rated low on the factory exchange. Manufacturers bought their labour force in a simple and unspecified form, putting the highest valuation on overall efficiency and physical strength and giving preference to the rawest and thus most flexible labour force over specialised workers, who had been shaped into a rigid mould by the long drawn-out monotony of their unvarying jobs. In consequence, if any social interest competed with class interests within the labour movement of this period, it was on a local and not an occupational basis.

Local distinctions, and sometimes even differences between working groups, worked against the establishment of stable 'general' unions. In discussing the question of labour migration I drew attention to the fact that in England there were no large-scale migrations from one region to another, despite the rapid growth of manufacturing centres. The paucity of transport facilities meant that the majority of the working population could only consider moving as far as the nearest urban centres. The many 'general' workers' unions, which were set up on a class basis, disintegrated rapidly; but they gave way not to unions based on occupation but to local unions drawn from many occupational groups. It was far more difficult to bridge the barriers between geographical centres than those between occupations. It was even more difficult to cross these geographical boundaries because the means of communication at hand were so primitive. Take, for instance, the march to London by the twelve delegates of the mineworkers (the Twelve Apostles, as they were called) during the strike of 1844 to give a guarantee of the solidarity of the working people of the Durham area.[1] It would, however, be an over-simplification to believe that distance and communication problems were the real reason for the

1   Webb, *The story of the Durham miners*, p. 44.

internal weakness of the many 'general' unions that were set up all over the place throughout the whole of the period we are considering, especially during the 1830s.

The proliferation of these unions and the persistent attempts that were made to create them are evidence that they were manifestations not of Utopian notions but of the trends that were gaining momentum within the working population as an expression of its more or less conscious interests. For instance, the existence was reported between 19 August and 7 September 1818 of an organisation called 'The Philanthropic Hercules', whose aim was to recruit all workers regardless of their occupational differences. Home Office reports show that an identical attempt was made in 1826. 1830 saw the brief but heroic epic of the National Association for the Protection of Labour; during the course of a few weeks the membership of this organisation grew to an unprecedented total for that period (several hundred thousand), but after some months it too disintegrated into local groupings. In 1832 a country-wide building workers' union suddenly came into existence. It reached far beyond the boundaries of the traditional occupations connected with the building trade, but was flimsily based and faded away with the same speed as the others. 1834 saw the rise of the most ambitious attempt of all—the Grand National Consolidated Trade Union, set up, with great effort, on a nation-wide basis, its aim being to organise the workers as a class to take over the reins of the economy.

None of the societies just mentioned can be properly described as a 'trade union' so long as we are using the terms 'trade' or 'occupation' in their usual sense. These societies were the organisations of a class, or attempts to set up such organisations; in practice, the connotations of the terms 'trade' and 'working class', as applied to the groups from which their members were recruited, were co-extensive. The mantle of a 'trade' organisation covered a class organisation, representing the interests of all its members and setting itself the task not of defending the interests of a particular trade but of radically uplifting the status of the class as a whole. To maintain, or even to improve, the status of a trade or occupation does not require the transformation of the social structure. On the contrary, it requires the petrification of the social system, which provides the frame of reference for the curve on the graph of occupational mobility. On the other hand, to lift a whole class up from the depths demands the overall transformation of social relations, the overturning of social hierarchies and the revolutionising of prevailing value systems. The trade unions in their proper form were therefore conservatively inclined, whereas the mass organisations which we are now discussing were nonconformist in disposition—like the milieu which gave rise to them.

None the less, these mass organisations had a survival capacity of only a few months, even shorter than the butterfly existence of the industrial trade unions. The disintegration of these organisations was always a disaster for the labour movement; it helped to destroy smaller unions which had been in existence before the mass organisations were set up and for years afterwards deterred workers from the very idea of organising themselves—as, for instance, happened with the building workers after the downfall of their mass union.[1]

The weakness of these mass organisations arose from the fact that they carried the germs of disintegration and death within them from the very beginning.[2] This was because they were built directly on the shifting foundations of an atomised class. In seeking to organise scattered individuals, who were not yet linked together by even more elementary kinds of social bonds—atoms that were not joined together in molecules—these combinations created a bond that was superficial, artificial and incapable of binding a social group with a lasting tie. Their organisational links were brittle and sundered easily at the first check. The mass unions were buildings without foundations, or rather they were the outer walls of a building with no interior framework. A breach in the wall would reveal an empty space inside, unequipped and not divided up into different storeys or smaller, more compact sections. Once the outer wall collapsed all trace of the organisation vanished and the working class reverted to its former state of almost complete fragmentation and amorphousness. The fabric never lasted long enough to leave any enduring traces of its existence in the structure of the class.

The industrial section of the Chartist movement which was known as the 'physical force' section had the same sort of characteristics. The failure of the Chartists' attempts at industrial organisation and their general lack of success were not the result of error or lack of foresight among their leaders. The attempt to set up a broadly based and enduring political organisation amidst what was not yet a class but an aggregate of isolated individuals unconnected by natural ties was doomed to failure. Despite the immense success of the Chartist mass rallies for workers, the massive scale of the

---

1   Postgate, *The builders' history*, pp. 115 *et seq*.

2   To quote a contemporary observer: 'During the first burst of enthusiasm, brought about by what they think emancipation from thraldom, those [local interests] may be forgotten or thrown aside, and all may join heart and hand in the promotion of what they suppose the cause . . . No sooner were the effects of the vast drain upon their money resources felt—no sooner the first excitement passed away —than the natural interests of each separate town or body were again brought into play and want of general cordiality and unanimity of acting soon rendered the great combinations partially inoperative.' (Gaskell, *The manufacturing population*, pp. 305–6.)

occasions, demonstrations and campaigns and the occurrence of violent localised operations like the Newport insurrection, none of these should suggest that any real historical possibilities of creating a mass political organisation existed. A spontaneous mass movement and a political movement are distinct social phenomena, set in different social conditions, and the existence of the first by no means implies the inevitability of the second.

Thus we have to consider two different types of phenomenon: just as in the case of the structure of the working class, so also, in that of the working class movement we are confronted by such opposed phenomena as journeymen's unions and industrial unions; the manifestations of occupational interests and of class interests; conformism and nonconformism; conservatism and radicalism; peaceful protest and violent struggle; occupational segregation and the trend towards mass organisation on a national scale; political indifference and deep political involvement; organisational solidarity and extreme organisational weakness. The two components of the labour movement are opposite extremes in type.

3

The structure of the elite
of the labour movement

The clubs of the journeymen craftsmen were small-scale associations, usually confined to one local centre. Their functions were uncomplicated, their funds meagre and their spending patterns simple. There was thus no need for those who managed club affairs to possess any particular qualifications—or, at any rate, to possess qualifications over and above those common to the majority of members. Such associations were, after all, for craftsmen whose occupational background was likely to equip them with a certain amount of organising ability and with the book-keeping and financial skills needed to run a workshop. The management of these clubs, with their modest resources and functions, required qualifications of the same kind as those needed for managing a workshop.

Moreover, positions of leadership in the journeymen's unions did not assure their holders any additional prestige or authority in comparison with the prestige and authority which were conferred by the craftsman's status *per se*. In reality the union official who was performing certain functions was simultaneously and above all a craftsman. He carried out his union duties after work, as a sort of social obligation; the scope of union functions did not require that officials should be given time off from their work, and in consequence his social position was defined not by his union function but by his occupational status. The regulations about union discipline assured him a certain esteem and obedience from his union brothers during his term of office; but this was a brief one, because the union offices were honorary ones, and in the long run the prestige of the union official came down to the measure of his position in the occupational, and not the union, hierarchy.

In the matter of exerting special influence or authority in decision-making on questions of importance to the union, the democracy which formally prevailed in the journeymen's unions may not have been so complete as contemporary accounts would suggest, and the amount of influence exerted on the decision-making process probably varied, or so it seems to me. Even so, all the evidence points to the fact that the basis for this variation was to be sought not in the union hierarchy but in the occupational hierarchy. The relationships of subordination and superordination evolved by the occupational hierarchy of the guilds were more lasting and extensive than the blurred and flexible stratifications set up by the union hierarchy. These relationships were in any case so deep-rooted that the impermanent union hierarchy could not provide any sort of counterweight. The process of advancement towards emancipation, the ownership of one's own workshop, even the journeyman's training period, all meant more than a position of doubtful social importance in the journeymen's club—work that was half administrative and half disciplinary.

To sum up: the union clubs did not provide the basic conditions for the creation of their own union elite. The fact that union offices were held in rotation by virtually all members without dispute affords proof of this. The history of the first clubs offers no evidence that would enable one to posit the existence of any kind of 'leadership struggle' or attempt to retain authority for longer than the usual period. On the contrary, we have a fair amount of material to show that it was difficult to find members to fill the union offices, and that the holding of such positions was in fact regarded not as an honour but as a duty.[1] The application of a compulsion clause during elections of union office holders is clear evidence that the social consequences of these functions were insignificant.

Although the artisan movement made only infrequent and sporadic political appearances, its large-scale nature afforded certain opportunities for the emergence of an elite. Nevertheless, the period of its activity was short, its achievements were inconsiderable, and the social status it acquired was modest. There was thus little probability that it could act as an effective catapult for the more active section of the artisan community. William Lovett and Thomas Attwood, the leaders of the 'moral force' section of the Chartist movement, admittedly owed their renown and their place in history to their position within that movement and not to any functions performed outside it. Yet Lovett was a prosperous master cabinet-maker with middle class aspirations and Attwood was a banker.[2] They came into the movement from these conspicuous social brackets

---

1 Here are two characteristic instances. 'The officers—President, Stewards (who kept the door and fetched the drinks) and Committee-men—were generally chosen to serve in rotation. To take one's turn of office was compulsory, the penalty for refusal being a fine varying from a shilling to half a guinea. As the societies expanded, and branches or lodges had to be formed in different localities, the same idea of sharing the burden of office by rotation was extended to these lodges. The head-quarters of the Union was regularly moved from place to place, each lodge taking it in turn to act as the "Governing Branch", and its officers and committee thereby becoming the central executive for the time being.' (Lloyd, *Trade unionism*, p. 48). The 1806 articles of the Society of Journeymen Brush-makers laid it down that the president be chosen on each evening the society met; thus in practice the union had no regular administration. In order to persuade union members to take on this function, article VII of the statute provided an honorarium for the president of one shilling "for his trouble", and a fine of sixpence for those who refused to "serve the office". (Kiddier, *The old trade unions*, p. 37.)

2 Dodds, *The age of paradox*, pp. 87 *et seq.*

and returned to them after it had collapsed. The heady vicissitudes of the movement were certainly of importance in their lives, but they were only episodes. Because of their socio-economic positions they were firmly placed on relatively high rungs of the social ladder, rungs higher than those to which the movement could have raised them. Chartism gave them an evanescent popularity, and it could probably satisfy the vanity of individuals in search of fame; it could not, however, ensure the achievement of social positions which could act as foci for a nascent social stratum with a higher status than that of the movement by which this stratum had been created.

The second sector of the labour movement of this period—the movement of factory workers, farm workers and miners—evolved in a totally different way, as we have already pointed out. The stage of evolution achieved by its leadership was similar in many features to that of the journeymen's movement—particularly in the fact that the people who headed it had no possibility of developing into an elite. At the same time, as one might expect, there were a large number of differences.

In contrast to the journeymen's organisations, those of the factory workers were superimposed on milieux that lacked internal cohesion and on loose human agglomerations that were not welded together into lasting social groups. This kind of organisation was not a superstructure built on existing natural ties but a substitute for non-existent ties. Usually it was the only bond connecting a particular milieu. Furthermore, such organisations arose among people who were not used to the kinds of activity that characterise organisational life. The factory workers, in contrast to the journeymen, lacked administrative skills, a knowledge of book-keeping and the management of finances, none of which could be learned at their everyday work. Thus such organisations were something external to their lives, which could be set up only in response to an outside impulse emanating from circles other than the ordinary community of factory workers or miners.

There is the further consideration, already mentioned, that the attitude of the factory workers to the wider society was totally nonconformist and that their occupational differentiation was only rudimentary. In consequence, their earliest organisations were characterised by a tendency to become mass movements and to be based upon general class support, not on an occupational or even a local basis. Clearly, the role of the leadership in the organisational life of such associations had to be much greater than in the journeymen's clubs. The existence of these leaders and their moral influence on the mass membership was after all the chief, if not the only, bond that held together these large, loosely associated groups of people. The durability of such organisations was a function of the characteristics of the leadership. The abilities, virtues and defects of the leadership, its capacity to keep the energies of the mass membership at a high pitch of preparedness, its ability to gain and retain lasting authority and the confidence of its members determined the fate of the organisation. The chronicles of a particular organisation were usually linked with the names of one or two individuals. An organisation died with its leaders, or as soon as they lost their authority. These organisations lacked the continuity that flows from the hereditary character of functions in even a rudimentary kind of administration. In such circumstances the leaders of workers' unions needed to possess special qualities that were somewhat rare in the ordinary working community of the period.

It was a state of affairs which opened up wide horizons for leaders of a charismatic rather than a nomocratic type, leaders who owed their decisive position in the movement not to an ingeniously constructed bureaucratic apparatus but to the aura of an exceptional mission conferred on them personally by the mass membership. The bonds linking the leader with the members as a whole were not institutionalised in a permanent, hierarchical bureaucratic apparatus. They were simple, and functioned without intermediaries. The cult of the leader often had a messianic tinge, and relationships within the organisation were surrounded by a religio-mystical glow. This cult embodied the people's need for continuity and security of existence; it was a reification of the need to set up a rational force in opposition to blind historical necessity, and the need to promote consciousness of individuality in a situation of depersonalising social degradation. The social situation of the class in which this mechanism functioned provided a rationale for myths, linking them with living people instead of legendary figures. But the social images of leaders were the sum of the qualities which those who held them felt were so gravely lacking in their own situation.

The personal characteristics which designated the man who possessed them as a potential leader of a workers' organisation were determined by the social milieu in whose terrain the organisation was to function. Thus there were certain differences between regions, connected with their class structure and the stage of development which had been reached. Nevertheless, there were more important common characteristics which were always apparent in all the charismatic leaders of this period. A leader had to know how to exploit the laws of crowd psychology, and in addition to have a profound understanding of the needs and moods of the working masses. He had to know how to explain in simple language what the workers felt but were themselves incapable of grasping in a rationalised form. The organisations could survive only on the fragile foundation of the workers' enthusiasm. The extent to which that enthusiasm was fuelled and kept in a state of incandescence depended on the leader. Moreover, the mystical aspects of the cult of the leader involved heavy demands on his personal moral character, including sacrifices and even martyrdom in order to satisfy the notion of redemption that was inherent in these social situations. There were even specifications for the external appearance of the leader, his gestures and facial expression, his way of addressing those around him, and so on.

Because of this, certain groups within the population were predestined to take charge of the first trade union organisations. There is plenty of contemporary evidence to confirm the hypothesis that there were many active Methodists among the leaders of the unions mentioned earlier. Obviously, accurate statistics cannot now be reconstructed, but it would seem that the proportion of Methodists was higher in those communities which were more backward and less developed as regards class awareness.[1]

Most leaders of the first workers' unions were drawn from amongst the workers themselves, from the factories and mines, although they consisted of individuals with qualifications and talents beyond the average. In contrast to the colourless and frequently changing sequence of officials in the journeymen's associations, the leaders of the factory groups generally stood out above their fellow workers because of their special and exceptional merits. In some cases—for instance that of John Doherty, the eminent trade union organiser of the 1830s—they acquired maturity and stature during their union activities and moved further up the social ladder as individuals without needing support from the movement which they had not always been able to carry along with them.[2]

There were cases like that of Tommy Hepburn, the formidable leader of the great miners' strike of the same period. The failure of a strike ended the personal cult of such men and lost them the adherents who had so recently venerated them in an almost religious sense. Thereafter they would live on in utter poverty, keeping themselves alive by such means as begging or futilely wandering about for miles and miles in bitterly cold weather trying to sell a packet of tea.[3] In either case, however, such leaders lost their whole position in the workers' movement and the whole moral

---

1 Of the six Tolpuddle martyrs sentenced to transportation on 19 March 1834, five were active members of the Wesleyan Methodist sect and three (George Loveless, James Loveless and Thomas Standfield) were Methodist evangelists. These leaders of a village union were also its religious leaders. Indeed, George Loveless, the union's organiser, was a local celebrity, venerated because of the great gift of oratory displayed in his sermons. (R. Groves, *Sharpen the sickle*, Porcupine Press, London, 1949, pp. 19–20.)

2 J. L. and B. Hammond, *The town labourer* pp. 249–50; Cole and Filson, *British working class movements*, p. 242.

3 Webb, *The story of the Durham miners*, pp. 36–7.

capital gained by their earlier work at the moment when their individual cult vanished, as often happened after the first failure of an organised action or the first move by the police. The leaders attained a higher status in the movement because of their personal qualities; they did not, however, move up in the social scale because of their activities in the movement. Even if they formed the elite of the movement on account of their qualifications, prestige and authority, they did not owe their position to the movement's internal mechanisms. Moreover, the structure of the movement was too weak to permit an elite social stratum to form upon it.

Furthermore, it must be realised that, at a time when factory workers were totally underprivileged in the social, economic and political spheres, and in which the movement was characterised by a clear-cut revolutionary outlook, a position of leadership in the labour movement could in no circumstances serve as a step towards social advancement. In the hierarchy of values prevailing in English society, activity in the labour movement offered no chance of advancing up the status ladder. Thus the labour movement itself did not ensure for its leaders a higher social position nor did it offer a channel through which the most talented workers could pass to higher social strata. The labour movement was to solve the problem of social mobility outside contemporary society and in opposition to it. The fact that the paths of mobility were closed prevented the industrial unions from acclimatising themselves to the capitalist system. It kept them in a nonconformist position, as foreign bodies within a capitalist society. No communicating channels linked the union structure with the social constructions of capitalism.

This does not mean that there was no upward social mobility in England, even during that period of profound degradation for the working population. The path which individuals from the underprivileged strata had to negotiate to reach the social elite was narrow and difficult, but it existed. It was not, however, a beaten track: each individual had to clear a way for himself. In no case did it lead through trade union institutions—indeed, no institutions guaranteed a passage. The story of William Cobbett, the well known reformer and political leader, is characteristic of a small minority of individuals who rose from the depths to the heights of society. The most typical aspect of his career is that every level of his backbreaking climb was achieved outside the compass of the labour movement or of any labour organisation at all. Even at the outset of his career Cobbett's development proceeded independently and by his own efforts.[1]

1 In 1834 Cobbett wrote as follows of his desire to write the story of his life: 'I shall entitle my book "The Progress of a Ploughboy to a seat in Parliament, as exemplified in the History of the Life of William Cobbett, Member for Oldham"; and I intend that the frontispiece to the book shall represent me, first in a smock-frock, driving

No account of the leaders of the labour movement among the factory workers, farm labourers and miners would be complete if it were to overlook the role of the 'refugees' from other social classes. I refer particularly to differing types of dissidents or straightforward rebels from the ruling classes—the aristocracy and the bourgeoisie. The labour movement, being too weak to produce enough leaders from its own ranks, afforded a large-scale and convenient field of activity for those to whom birth and upbringing had given a broader political horizon and who found themselves drawn into the movement by a variety of circumstances.

the rooks from the corn; and, in the lower compartment of the picture, standing in the House of Commons, addressing the Speaker.' (*The autobiography of William Cobbett*, ed. W. Reitzel, Faber, 1947, p. 5.) The turning point in Cobbett's life occurred when he was wandering through various small towns looking for work as a gardener's boy, with only threepence in his pocket. To quote from his own account: 'My eye fell upon a little book, in a bookseller's window: *Tale of a Tub*; price 3*d*. The title was so odd, that my curiosity was excited. I had the 3*d*. but, then, I could have no supper. In I went and got the little book, which I was so impatient to read, that I got over into a field, at the upper corner of Kew Gardens, where there stood a haystack. On the shady side of this I sat down to read. The book was so different from anything I had ever read before; it was something so new to my mind, that, though I could not at all understand some of it, it delighted me beyond description; and it produced what I have always considered a sort of birth of intellect.' (*Ibid.*, p. 18.) The *Tale of a Tub* was the beginning. With the pennies that he could scrape together Cobbett bought books, including an English grammar, which he copied out three times. Then he learned it by heart and repeated it every morning and evening. Later he enlisted in the army, saved up his pay and after demobilisation bought a shop, first in France, then in America. In the latter country he also published a journal entitled *The Porcupine*, which expressed pro-British views during the periods of international tension. The shop brought him a fair sum, while the journal brought him an offer of a government post after his return to England, as a mark of appreciation of his services to his country. From that time onwards the road to a political career was open. In his political activities Cobbett was one of the leaders of the reform party. His programme, however, expressed the interests of the bourgeoisie and its growing political aspirations; it did not stretch beyond the framework of the existing social order and was entirely remote from the demands which were being put forward at the same period by the labour movement. The following statements are typical of Cobbett's views. 'I am [at the end of my life] no republican in principle, any more than I am in land and allegiance. I hold that this, which we have [in England] is the best sort of government in the world. I hold that a government of kings, lords, and commons, the last of which chosen by all men, who are of full age, of sound mind, and untainted by indelible crime, is the best of governments.' (*Ibid.*, p. 76.) 'Our rights in society are numerous; the right of enjoying life and property; the right of exerting our physical and mental powers in an innocent manner; but, the great right of all, and without which there is, in fact, no right, is, the right of taking a part in the making of the laws by which we are governed. This right is founded in that law of nature . . .' (*Advice to young men and women, Advice to a citizen*, 1829, quoted by M. Oakeshott, *The social and political doctrines of contemporary Europe*, Cambridge University Press, 1939, p. 30.)

Within this category of people two separate groups should be distinguished. The first was fairly large, comprising the relatively numerous radical reformers of a bourgeois stamp. Their aim was to shatter the anachronistic political authority of the landed aristocracy: they therefore endeavoured to create as broadly based a supporting organisation as possible among different social strata, including the emerging labour movement. Their social programme did not, however, go beyond the broadly conceived framework of bourgeois reform. Their ideology was akin to Lincoln's formula of a government 'of the people, by the people and for the people' or Thomas Paine's doctrine of natural rights and equality among men; but despite its universalistic mode of expression it had a highly bourgeois content in specific historical circumstances. The 'bourgeoisification' of Parliament was, in the view of these reformers, to be a panacea for social ills. It would somehow radically improve the situation of the ordinary working man, who was supposed to be suffering mainly because of the violation of the whole complex of natural laws. This 'bourgeoisification' was also intended to be linked with extension of the State's legislative function.[1]

With all its professions of individualism, the utilitarian ideology that was predominant among the bourgeois reformers of that period played a great part in impressing certain legislative concepts on Parliament which in the century to come were to lead to an extension (not encountered elsewhere) of the range of Parliamentary intervention.[2] An important part of this process was to be the extension of Parliament's writ to cover the regulation of working conditions, and, in particular, factory legislation. Cobden, one of the leading figures in the group that was pressing for this, in consequence regarded himself as a socialist and his reforms as socialist ones.[3]

Nevertheless the whole of this group maintained an extremely loose connection with the labour movement. Its members regarded the workers as the subjects of legislative activity, or sometimes as welcome allies, but not as an independent and autonomous political force with its own programme, one moreover that went outside the framework of the established order.

The case of the second group was rather different. Its membership did not consist of reformers from the bourgeoisie but of individuals who, although they were of middle class or aristocratic origins, had become rabid enemies of their own class. It is difficult to establish in each separate case whether it was hatred of the ruling class, at the other pole of contem-

1   Sydney Smith, *Works*, Longmans, London, 1839, pp. 670 *et seq.*
2   A. V. Dicey, *Lectures on the relation between law and public opinion in England*, Macmillan, London, 1948, p. 310.
3   J. Morley, *Life of Cobden*, Chapman & Hall, London, 1881, p. 302.

porary society, or, on the contrary, sympathy for the workers that led
them to attack their own class. Probably both factors were at work to a
certain extent. In any case, newcomers from the heights of contemporary
British society were to be found at the head of the mass political labour
organisations of that period. The 'Grand National' was in fact run by Owen,
and the acknowledged leader of the party of physical force among the
Chartists was a large landowner, the Irishman Feargus O'Connor.

The latter was incomparably better suited than Owen to the turbulent
years of the 1830s and 1840s. The best proof of this is that he succeeded in
keeping his movement in a state of ferment for an unusually long time,
considering the period. He was, however, exceptionally endowed with
qualities that encouraged the formation of a charismatic cult. O'Connor
had the eyes of an inspired prophet, looking out from beneath bushy eyebrows; a huge beard, usually tousled; a deep, powerful and sonorous
baritone voice; an incisive wit, a rustic sarcasm and a consummate knowledge of popular psychology. For hours on end he could hold the attention
of thousands of people assembled on hillsides, keeping them in a state of
extraordinary suspense and attentiveness. Understanding that the workers'
true desire and need was not electoral reform but social revolution, he
imbued his Chartist gospel with a message that assured him a unique
authority and leadership among the masses of the Chartist leaders: he was
a prophet, a near-saint, the anointed one who was to lead the people out of
bondage.

A group of people with similar qualities gathered around O'Connor,
either because he sought them out or through a process of natural selection.
This group formed a sort of extension of its leader's qualities. O'Connor's
right-hand man, the Rev. J. R. Stephens, was also famous for his ability
to hold thousands spellbound for hours with his oratory.[1]

Nevertheless, not even this group, although it was closely linked with
the labour movement, conformed to the definition of an elite of this
social movement. It was not created by the movement but came in from
outside; after a period it again left the movement and the class that was
its base. The group's prominent position in the movement lasted only as
long as the spell of its charismatic cult; when the revolutionary tide
receded, a relapse into political apathy ruined its authority and left it
outside the confines of the movement. Moreover, the group was a small
one. To pass from the aristocracy, the upper middle classes or even the
petty bourgeoisie to the labour movement at that period did not offer any
prospect of a political career—on the contrary, it meant immediate and
total loss of social standing even expulsion from the relationships and
communities acknowledged as society. In such circumstances there was no

1   Dodds, *The age of paradox*, p. 88.

possibility of a large-scale exodus from the privileged classes into the labour movement, although individual cases did occur, for individual reasons.

To sum up, in this period of history, in which both the working class and the labour movement were split into two sections, each with its separate fate and lines of evolution, we cannot locate in either section of the labour movement a stratum or group of people which could be regarded as an elite within the movement. The boundary between the mass membership and the groups of leaders was either fluid or blurred. Where it was sharply drawn, the leaders were guests in the movement. The main point is that in the initial phase of its existence the labour movement had not yet created the sort of internal structures, nor achieved the kind of position in the structure of society as a whole, that would provide a nucleus for the emergence of a set of leaders, thrown up by the movement itself and endowed with special resources, qualifications, prestige and authority.

II
The movement comes of age
1850–1890

In the period which was the subject of Part I, I distinguished between two different groups within the working population, groups characterised by very different traits. The first dated back to pre-capitalist times and was tending to die out by degrees; in any case, its social role was decreasing. The second group was the product of capitalism: it was characterised primarily by its amorphous and indeterminate nature, and the trade union movement set up by it was weak and left no lasting traces behind it.

In this respect the period during which the labour movement came of age was very different from the preceding one. The second of the two groups moved out in front, assuming an increasingly defined form; it became stratified from within and gradually set up new social units and lasting structures based on the capitalist system of production. Its position in society ceased to be equivocal as it began increasingly to reflect the differences between its component strata. Amorphousness ceased to be its characteristic trait, and fragmentation, with its consequent alienation, remained characteristic of only one stratum within it. Other strata emerged from the social periphery and found a place for themselves in the social network of the system of that time, in which their structures and programmes were gradually absorbed. This place was not achieved without a great struggle; but once the resistance of the existing social structure to this foreign body was overcome its assimilation proceeded by degrees.

The process which we are discussing was the consequence of certain characteristics of British capitalism and in particular its monopolistic position at this stage of the development of world capitalism. I shall not, however, be concentrating on these problems, which have been adequately discussed elsewhere, but rather on the internal structural changes in the working class which allowed this process to take place. Once again, as in Part I, the analysis will be focused on the interrelations between the structure of the class, the structure of its social movement and the structure of the movement's elite—and on grasping the regular interdependences between them. These are not peculiar to the history of English society—it depends on the external conditions of socio-economic history when these regularities begin to operate—but they do operate where and when these conditions appear. Thus their cognitive value is surely greater than would emerge from the exceptional economic position of British capitalism at this particular period.

I

The structure of
the working class

In the middle of the nineteenth century fundamental transformations occurred in the structure of British industry. The historical reasons for them have been recounted many times. One of the most important was the rapid expansion of the railways, which led to the setting up and speedy development of the iron and steel and engineering industries. Simultaneously there emerged new techniques and a new organisation of labour. Physical compulsion slowly disappeared in the factories; it was displaced by planned organisation, which was more efficient in dealing with a labour force geared to the institutionalised stimuli of capitalism, and by the division of labour. The complicated new machines needed a new type of labour force. The process of production made far greater demands than previously on the workers who were operating the machines, in terms of independent action and initiative; it also required a considerable amount of technical instruction and a certain level of general culture. As a result, the new industry produced a new stratum of skilled workers, men with definite jobs and a permanent place in the new system of production. These men were not identical, easily changed components; instead, precisely because of the difficulty of replacing them, and their important part in the production process, they had a lasting position in the social structure of production.

The rise of a stratum of skilled workers and the stratification of the working class proceeded simultaneously. On the face of it this statement may not seem meaningful, for in the preceding period also the working population was stratified, even divided, into two very different social groups. There was nevertheless an important difference between the two types of stratification.

The new stratification took place within that section of the working population which was created by, and owed its existence to, capitalist industry. This group thus had no history which was unconnected with capitalism, no traditions which went back further than the industrial revolution. The earlier stratification was a division that still existed but was disappearing in the trend towards greater uniformity. The new stratification was the result of a break-away from that state of uniformity. The earlier division could be described as a 'stratification' only in a metaphorical sense, since it really involved the coexistence of two groups of differing origins, social positions, prestige and social consciousness. The new stratification took place within the working masses, whose origins were far from uniform but who had become sufficiently homogeneous with the passing of time to ensure that the origins of their grandparents or great-grandparents were not a factor in the stratificatory process. Thus the new stratum of skilled workers was fundamentally different from that of the craft journeymen discussed earlier. They differed in their origins, in the socio-economic system with which their fortunes were linked, and in their actual social position and perspectives. It would therefore be an error of fact and of methodology to take the automatic view that the social history of the new skilled workers' stratum was a continuation, either chrono-logically or logically of the history of the craft journeymen. There was no such continuity in the history of the two succeeding strata, although a number of similarities in their social attitude and ideology might suggest it. This naturally does not mean that the organisational forms and ways of thinking that were characteristic of the stratum of craftsmen did not exert a powerful influence on the evolution of the new stratum of skilled workers. None the less, this new stratum was not the direct successor of the stratum of craftsmen. Instead, it gradually emerged from the plastic, homogeneous raw material formed by the unskilled factory workers and even the rural workers, who were still being driven into the towns by the need to find a living.

The development of the urban centres continued with even greater intensity. At this period, however, the development was concentrated in those areas where coal mining and heavy industry were being developed, not the manufacture of consumer goods. South Wales was an example of such a 'new' area of development, as table 4 shows.

Table 4

Population increase in south Wales as a measure of industrialisation, 1801–1911

District	1801	1861	1871	1881	1911
Population of Cardiff	1,870	32,954	–	–	196,205
Population of Rhondda	–	3,857	–	–	152,781
Number of coalminers in Glamorgan	–	–	34,000	–	150,000
Population of Merthyr	8,800	49,794	–	48,861	80,990
Population of Monmouth, Glamorgan, Brecon and Carmarthen	666,000	–	–	–	1,736,000

Note In the period 1865–75 there was a temporary depression in the iron and steel industry.

Source P. Massey, *Industrial south Wales*, Gollancz, London, 1940, p. 26.

The extension of the centres of heavy industry—the type of industry in which the occupational stratification of working gangs was proceeding most energetically—meant that this kind of stratification was a decisive factor for the history of the whole working class and labour movement at this particular time. There were other parallel branches of industry in which stratification did not take place or occurred much more slowly, so that there were also very considerable sectors of the working population which preserved the traits characteristic of the foregoing period and required a quite different ranking from the new skilled workers, who were most representative of this period. Yet the majority of the historians of the British labour movement, when analysing the third quarter of the nineteenth century, have concentrated almost exclusively on the stratum of skilled workers, following the example of the Webbs. It must be admitted that even though this methodological approach is not entirely supported by the historical facts, logically it is entirely justified. This new stratum of skilled workers was to be important for the future development of the labour movement in England. It was this stratum that was to create and give final shape to the forms of organisation and stereo-typed modes of thought that were assimilated in later periods, when the character of the working class was changing.

All this remains valid, even though statistics may show that the proportion of skilled workers in the working class as a whole was relatively small. In 1867 Baxter estimated that skilled workers made up 21 per cent of the overall working population of England: the percentage of semi-skilled workers was 38, and that of unskilled workers highest of all, 41 per cent.[1] The roles of the various strata were not, however, determined by their relative numerical strength. Instead, they can be accurately assessed by comparing the situations of the skilled and the unskilled strata in terms of a number of other criteria.

The first difference to strike one is that of comparative wage scales. In the previous period, wages had been almost equally low across the entire working population, the most important disproportion being the difference between the scales for men, women and children. Now sharp differences could be noted between the wage scales for different occupational categories in the newly created branches of industry. Baxter records that in 1867 the wages of qualified mechanics in the locomotive building industry in large industrial centres were as high as 30s a week, whereas unskilled workers in the same factories received only about half that amount (15s–16s).[2] Moreover, other estimates show that during the period we are discussing the wages of skilled workers tended to rise gently but steadily, although the

1   Cole, *Studies in class structure*, pp. 57–8.
2   *Ibid.*

prices of consumer goods (and also meat and rents) were falling steadily.[1] According to H. Wood, the retail price index for essential goods and services was down to 86 in 1887, if we take the index for 1850 as 100.[2] Meanwhile the wages of unskilled workers either remained in a state of stagnation or showed a clear downward trend. Table 5 gives a characteristic example of these trends.

Table 5

Changes in weekly wage scales in the engineering industry in Sheffield, 1866–86

Occupation	1866–68		1871		1874		1880		1883		1886	
	s	d	s	d	s	d	s	d	s	d	s	d
Locksmiths	30		30		32		30	6	32		31	9
Turners	30		30		32		30		33	6	32	5
Foundry workers	34		33				32		37		36	1
Blacksmiths	30		31		30		31	6	31		31	10
Blacksmiths' assistants	19	6	21	6	22		20		20	6	21	5
Unskilled workers	21		18		20	6	19	6	20		19	3

Source   Wood, *A glance at wages and prices*, p. 15.

Whereas the wages of unskilled workers rarely exceeded 20s per week, there were many occupations (Hobsbawm[3] gives the total) in which weekly wages were higher than 40s as early as 1865. The qualitative as well as the quantitative meaning of this difference surely needs no further explanation. The divergences of wage scales meant that those who worked in different occupations had very different standards of living.

While the material situation of the 'privileged' workers was undergoing a steady and marked improvement, the living conditions of the mass of unskilled workers remained at a pitifully low level. Such workers were still easily interchangeable and not linked with any particular industry; this often made their position weak in the economic struggle which had to be waged with the employers if they were to improve their lot. In contrast to their skilled fellow workers, they did not play a key role in the production system. Thus it was easy for employers to replace them with other

1   R. Giffen, *The progress of the working classes in the last half century*, Bell, London, 1884, p. 13.
2   Wood, *A glance at wages and prices*, p. 15.
3   Hobsbawm, 'The labour aristocracy', p. 210.

similar workers, who were always available because of the continued existence of a large pool of unemployed. Such replacement was not only easy but less expensive than securing a more stable labour force by increasing wages. In consequence, while the number of people with savings bank accounts rose tenfold over the fifty years between 1831 and 1881, the numbers of paupers drawing public assistance decreased over roughly the same period by only about a hundred thousand, to a total of 803,000 for England and Wales.[1]

The living conditions of factory workers and farm labourers outlined in Part I underwent virtually no change as far as the unskilled workers of the period now under discussion were concerned. To avoid repetition, I propose to refer only to the contemporary situation of one stratum, which might especially appropriately be termed the 'pariahs of capitalist industry'. These were the farm labourers, whose average weekly wage in England was no more than 12s 4d or 12s 5d in 1870, having risen by only two shillings over the preceding thirty-three years. In some areas the weekly wage was even lower than the average: for instance, it was 11s in the Midlands, and 8s for men, 3s for women, in Dorset.[2]

Set against such conditions for the mass of unskilled workers, the living standards of the new skilled stratum afforded a glaring contrast. Because of its higher wages and potentially higher living standards, this stratum in fact constituted the aristocracy *sui generis* of the working class. The use of this metaphorical term is justified in part by the fact that both objectively and subjectively the relationship of this stratum to the remainder of the working class was in many respects reminiscent of the relations of the real aristocracy to the remainder of the English upper and middle classes.

None the less, the social position of the stratum of skilled workers, and particularly those elements within it that gave the stratum its 'aristocratic' quality, can by no means be characterised in terms of relative earnings and the living conditions associated with them. In this connection an observation by Hobsbawm seems extremely apt. He has suggested that six criteria should be distinguished among the many that determine whether a particular group of workers belongs to the working aristocracy: level and

---

1 Giffen, *The progress of the working classes*, pp. 18–19.
2 As Girdlestone recorded, 'The labourer breakfasts on tea-kettle broth—hot water poured on bread and hard cheese at twopence a pound, with cider very washy and sour, and sups on potatoes or cabbage greased with a tiny bit of fat bacon. He seldom more than sees or smells butcher's meat . . .' In *The Beehive* Lloyd Jones wrote of the farm worker: 'In intellect he is a child, in position a helot, in condition a squalid outcast; he knows nothing of the past; his knowledge of the future is limited to the field he works in . . . The squire is his king, the parson his deity, the taproom his highest conception of earthly bliss.' (Quoted by Groves, *Sharpen the sickle*, pp. 33, 36.)

regularity of wages; prospects of social security; working conditions (including treatment by foremen and masters); relation to the strata 'above' and 'below' them in the social hierarchy; living conditions in general; and prospects of future advancement and those of their children. Yet it is difficult to accept Hobsbawm's statement that of all these criteria the first is undoubtedly the most important, or the order of importance in which he ranks these criteria.[1] In my view, the social attitude of the skilled workers' stratum can be explained, if not altogether, then most completely, by the objective position occupied by this stratum in both the working class itself and the over-all structure of society—or, to put it more precisely, by the manner in which this position was achieved. I shall be discussing these points later.

The changes in the structure of industry which gave birth to a new industrial hierarchy, with the skilled worker in an important key position, potentially prestigious, at its top, took place without the conscious participation of the working population. Some time passed before the possibilities of their new objective position were fully appreciated by the members of the new skilled stratum.[2] While they were moving into a new social position, the newly created skilled workers were still deeply rooted in the stereotypes prevailing within the amorphous and fragmented mass of factory workers. It was only by degrees and with some effort that they began to realise their new situation. The path to this awareness of themselves as a stratum proceeded by stages.

The decisive stage, which constituted a truly qualitative leap, was their acceptance of their social position. The working population from which the new skilled workers had imperceptibly emerged was nonconformist in all spheres. It was in revolt not against its position in society but against society itself and the whole social hierarchy. On the other hand, the new skilled workers at some point of their evolution acquiesced in the existence of the hierarchical ladder and in the stability of the existing social system. What is more, they acquiesced in their own position in the social hierarchy, and by acknowledging that position as an immutable fact they determined

1   Hobsbawm, 'The labour aristocracy', p. 202.
2   In his *Notes on England* Hippolyte Taine characterised the skilled English worker as follows: '... He is twenty-eight; he is rich already and spends his day in the following manner: in the morning he goes to the factory, inspects, supervises, takes a file in his hand to show a clumsy workman how to use it properly, returns home frightfully dirty, washes himself and breakfasts. He does likewise in the afternoon ... In the evening he seats himself in a small neighbouring tavern, drinks six penny-worth of beer, smokes his pipe and returns home at ten ... He has neither an idea, nor any curiosity; he can barely spell; he never reads; his own condition alone interests him.' (Quoted by R. Lewis and A. Maude, *The English middle classes*, Phoenix House, London, 1949, p. 52.)

to do everything in their power to extract the maximum advantage from it. If one were to try to convey briefly the essence of their new social attitude, one would have to stress that their aim was the emancipation of the stratum as a whole within the framework of a scale of values that was firmly linked with the capitalist system. What really inspired members of the skilled stratum and determined their social and political attitudes was not the prospect of breaking out of the ranks of their social group but the social advancement of their group *as* a group, and the lessening of the distance between their group as a whole and the strata regarded as 'higher' within the existing social order. Such an aim had to be based on a prior acceptance of the prevailing scale of social values; the new skilled workers were concerned not with overthrowing or changing the latter but with achieving, from their own viewpoint, a better division of what that scale of values had to offer which was worth competing for.

Here we find a basic difference between the attitudes of the new skilled workers and the earlier craftsmen, although they resembled each other in adopting a conformist stand to the social system in which they lived. The journeymen craftsmen had a relatively high social status and wished to defend it against the down-grading which the future augured for them. On their side, the new skilled workers had no socially recognised status but were intruders in the socially recognised hierarchy. They still bore the stamp of the working masses, unruly, easily worked up into a ferment, sunk in ignorance and misery, lacking all broader ambitions in life. The stereotype of the worker that was current in educated society included the traits of a drunkard, a rowdy, an illiterate, a person lacking all respect for ethical norms and established principles of social intercourse, unable to take advantage of benefits or any kind of spiritual nourishment except for some suitably predigested religious pap. Sometimes the catalogue of stereotypes was qualified by the addition of some good qualities: it might, for instance, include an innate kind-heartedness, a basic honesty, gratitude towards benefactors and natural piety. All this, seen in the worst light, went to make up a picture of a socially dangerous thug; at best, it indicated an overgrown Simple Simon with the muscles of a wrestler and the brain of a child. Neither the employers nor the liberal humanists of the time regarded the workers as having qualities that could help them climb the ladder of values accepted by both groups. The stereotype of the workers was almost the opposite of that which referred to the craftsmen, to whom were traditionally attributed the qualities of industriousness, honesty, thrift and a high moral sense.

The new skilled workers were therefore gravely handicapped, starting out from almost the lowest position in society. The weight of tradition operated to drag them back to the milieu from which they had emerged.

On the other hand, there was nothing to propel them upwards in their climb towards the higher rungs of social status. Thus before they could become conservative, like the craftsmen of the preceding period, they would have to win for themselves a status that would be worth conserving. No part of the social position which they desired would be tacitly ceded to them as something that belonged to them by custom. For the time being, everything had to be fought for, everything was linked with ideals which were still to be realised.

In consequence, the conformism of the new skilled workers differed from that of the craftsmen. It was active and aggressive; the new stratum had to prove that it was worthy of respect in terms of the prevailing criteria if it was in fact to achieve such respect. Moreover, it had to prove its active loyalty to the system if its life ambitions were to be linked to that system. It had to absorb the moral code of society, and try to be rated as highly as possible in terms of the values most highly prized by that society. It had to adapt itself to the stereotype of the contemporary hero, the capitalist—a titan of labour who could successfully multiply his wealth; sober, honest in business, decisive, thrifty. Furthermore, the model had to be that of an English capitalist—which meant someone who also possessed the qualities taken over from that unfading social ideal, the English gentleman born and bred. In all this process the *onus probandi* rested on the new skilled stratum.

Thus the integration of the stratum of skilled workers into the capitalist social system began with their ostentatious acceptance of the value system that dominated it. Only after this acceptance did the stratum begin to achieve by degrees a social status which was to become the premise and justification for its conservative social and political attitudes. For the time being, the stratum's attention was concentrated on itself, on self-improvement, on adapting itself to the style of life required by the rules of the classes which set the standards of social prestige. At this time its members' main objective was to entrench themselves as solidly as possible in the society outside whose pale their grandfathers, if not also their fathers, would certainly still have remained.[1]

1 Baernreither gives the following outline of the very moderate life ambitions of an
   English skilled worker: 'What the English workman of today requires is to be able
   to marry and set up a household to live in health and decency, to give his children
   a suitable education, and to be in a position to provide against old age, sickness or
   accident. He wishes to have access in his spare hours to the means of enlarging his
   knowledge and cultivation, so as to work in his sphere for the welfare of his class.
   Family, education, provision for the future, the self-government of his associations—
   these words contain the sum and substance of his "habits and requirements",
   equally far removed from a socialistic Utopia as from indolent submission to a hard
   lot ... "A fair day's wages for a fair day's work"—so runs the formula in which

The programme for self-improvement had a material and a spiritual aspect. The material aspect was expressed in zealous exhortations to save and put something aside for a rainy day, thrift being presented as one of the fundamental virtues. The number of savings accounts increased at a staggering rate—they were opened in a wide range of different savings banks and mutual aid societies serving the needs of the lower middle class. With the zeal of a convert the skilled worker saved money not only for concrete purchases but for the sake of saving, both as a material safeguard of his living standards and as a symbol of moral refinement. The second, spiritual, aspect of self-improvement was expressed in the ever-increasing drive for education and the extension of the self-initiating campaign against the plague of drunkenness, which made thrift impossible and destroyed the prestige of the upwardly mobile skilled group. The desire for learning ran parallel to the pressures of industry, whose increasingly sophisticated technology needed workers with improved skills and background. Education meant an increase in wages. For the time being the skilled stratum regarded it not as a bridge enabling individuals to move up into other classes but as an important element in the social advancement of the stratum as a whole on the ladder of accepted social values.[1]

The temperance movement acquired a similar momentum. In its most extensive manifestations it was positively fanatical, forbidding the drinking not only of spirits and wine but also of beer, and even coffee and tea, while smoking was also banned.[2] In its more popular form the movement was somewhat milder, but in general it went beyond the limits dictated by economic or even health considerations to include elements symbolic of a moral purge. The members of the new stratum were in a hurry to discard

this standpoint is comprised.' (Baernreither, *English associations of working men*, p. 80.)

1   The drive for education from below was supported by similar trends coming from higher social spheres. The motivation was similar in both cases. Here are a few characteristic views expressed in the report of the Royal Commission on Education, 1861, which was set up to enquire into the results of education among the poor. 'It has unquestionably added to the value of their labour—an intelligent workman, other things being equal, being worth more to himself and his employer than an ignorant one. It has also helped them to accommodate themselves more readily to the great and frequent changes in the methods of labour necessitated by the constant discoveries of science.'—Henry Sheats, replying to the commissioners' circular. 'Several large employers in Hull, as well as in the other parts of my district, concur generally that education gives additional value to labour.'—From the testimony of an assistant commissioner. (Ludlow and Jones, *Progress of the working class*, pp. 152–4.) The pressure of industry's needs must indeed have been great for the views of factory owners on this subject to have been completely reversed over two or three decades.

2   Ludlow and Jones, *Progress of the working class*, pp. 246–8.

the garments of their forbears. The fanatical and self-flagellating nature of their abstinence was fostered, if not created, by a desire to make redemption for their origins, which had during the struggle for emancipation acquired something like the stigmata of original sin.

Here we come to what is perhaps the most important question in the analysis of the new stratum of skilled workers: the question of the relationship of this stratum to others, and particularly to the classes that were its immediate neighbours in society.

This was a problem only for the new skilled stratum. The working masses from which it was emerging took up no position in relation to other social classes; nor did they measure their position in relation to other strata, because they were objectively and subjectively alienated from society and had adopted a position of total opposition to it. To accept that society and its principles it was necessary to visualise and consolidate one's own position in it. This position was expressed in terms of one's relationship with other social strata, of the formation of attitudes of inferiority or superiority in relation to these strata and, finally, of the choice of a social ideal.

The remnants of the stratum of craftsmen were the nearest neighbours in the class hierarchy to the new stratum of skilled workers. The former was being eroded at a growing pace,[1] as more and more branches of production that had once been in the hands of craftsmen went over to capitalist methods of production. As these changes took place the social significance of craftsmanship steadily decreased, and the status of the journeyman craftsmen deteriorated. An increasing number of criteria linked them with the working class—and no traditional craft privileges could in fact prevent them from moving into the ranks of hired labour. Yet the continuity of craft traditions persisted in spite of the growing shift from craft to capitalist methods of production; it enabled the majority of craftsmen to keep up at least an appearance of social distinctiveness. The more shaky their actual position in the class hierarchy became, the more diligently did they strive to keep up appearances, increasingly

---

1   Take, for instance, the printing trade: this was mainly a craft trade in the first half of the nineteenth century, but from 1850 onwards it increasingly changed to capitalist methods of production. In 1885, 288 out of London's 423 printing shops still employed fewer than three workers; but the two largest, Clowes and Bradbury Evans, employed over eighty journeymen. Six other firms employed between fifty and sixty journeymen; thirteen, between thirty and forty; thirteen, twenty to thirty journeymen; and eighteen between ten and twenty. The smaller firms were being increasingly squeezed by competition from the larger ones, and the possibility of emancipation for the printers' journeymen was becoming increasingly illusory. (Howe and Waite, *The London Society of Compositors,* pp. 147–9.)

ludicrous though these might seem.[1]

Whatever the reality, the appearances were sufficiently strong and widespread to make the new skilled stratum covet the class position of the craftsmen. Among the elements that attracted them were the legendary and venerable traditions of their craft (particularly strong in English conditions), the unquestioned prestige of their occupation, their way of life, and the dignified nature of their social relationships. All these appealed to the imagination of the new skilled workers, as an accessible model of the forms in which their new lower middle class social situation could be moulded. This desire to attain the level of the craftsmen was, as we shall see later, an exceedingly important factor in inducing the new skilled stratum to copy the organisational forms and statements of objectives handed down by the post-guild craft unions. The lower middle class status that essentially belonged to the craftsmen's stratum became an indicator of the aims of the skilled workers. This circumstance would have brought the two strata together but for the fact that one of them was still aiming to achieve lower middle class status while the other had in fact already lost it.

Here one should emphasise strongly a point whose importance will emerge in later chapters—that the aspirations of the new skilled workers were relatively modest and showed no tendency to expand. Craft status was the upper limit of their ambition in life. There was no question of opening out a path to the upper and ruling social strata. For the time being the objective was not to pave the way for the advancement of the most energetic section of the stratum, only to promote the advancement of the stratum as a whole. But the aspirations of its leaders, which were narrower in scope, though more ambitious, were to superimpose themselves on this spontaneous upward trend among the new skilled stratum; this development will, however, be discussed later.

The skilled stratum derived a feeling of social advancement from the fact that, while it was admittedly ranked below the producers, somewhere near to those at the lowest level, it was definitely above the undifferentiated mass of unskilled workers. Only a short time before it had been part of the fragmented masses, but now it had broken out of the social depths and discovered itself as a separate entity, because of the existence of a stratum to which it could feel superior. This circumstance was a greater measure of

1 Even during the reign of Queen Victoria the exclusive Phoenix Society of Compositors required its union members to attend meetings wearing evening dress and top hats. Carpenters also went to work every day in such formal garments which they carefully put away in a special cupboard. If the employer did not provide such a cupboard, the carpenters would refuse to do their job. (Postgate, *The builders' history*, pp. 32–3.)

the distance the skilled workers had travelled than their increasing proximity to the heights of craft status.

The new stratum was genealogically linked with only one other stratum, that of the unskilled workers below it; its members' pursuit of social advancement was thus expressed both by their raising themselves to the position of the lower middle class and by a definite dissociation of themselves from the unskilled. Fear of being reminded of their base origins drove these newly created petty bourgeois snobs into demonstrations of open aversion to the mass of unskilled workers. The new skilled stratum soon assembled a whole arsenal of defensive stereotypes to safeguard its social superiority.[1]

From the viewpoint of the new skilled stratum, the achievement of craft status was a real social revolution. The ideological leaders of this stratum never ceased emphasising the social importance of the change which was taking place in its position. For them it was a revolution accomplished within the existing framework of the social order, beneficial for society as a whole and carried out in the common interests of the employers and their employees. Moreover, as far as they were concerned it was a total revolution and one that had been carried through to completion. After the skilled stratum had climbed on to a higher rung of the social ladder, nothing remained to be done except for some minor improvements, the need for which would probably emerge from the normal course of social progress. The aims of the struggle had been achieved and it now remained only to institute a dogged defence of the gains already achieved. The problem was not so much how to advance as how to avoid retreating. The inner flame which had stirred the skilled workers to action died down by degrees. They continued to hold the ground they had won, but otherwise gave up even their previous modest aspirations and passively submitted to the political initiatives of other groups. Because the capitalist system was a network which comprised even the lowest social position within it and guaranteed its stability, the skilled stratum became vitally interested in the defence of that system. It therefore acquired a moderately conservative attitude towards its own position and towards the social order as well. The skilled stratum and the organisations which it had set up moved into a stage of stabilisation. It could be shaken out of its lethargy only as a result of some untapped force from outside, since the stratum's own internal possibilities for change, formerly the source of its dynamism, were now exhausted.

1   An 'artisan' or 'craftsman' could in no circumstances be confused with a labourer. The skilled workers believed that labourers were an inferior class and should be compelled to know their place and keep to it. (T. Wright, *Our new masters*, Strahan, London, 1873, pp. 3, 6.)

During the period under discussion, therefore, two processes were occurring side by side which were transforming the structure of the working class. One was the disappearance of the division which had played a fundamental part in the preceding period, a specific division which belonged to the 'prehistory' of the working class; the other was the emergence of a new stratification within the working class that had been created by the industrial revolution. Both processes together marked the end of the first or embryonic period of the rise of the working class. But that class did not become homogeneous as a result of these processes. Occupational barriers remained high, and differences of occupational interests overshadowed any identity of class interests.

In his novel *Sybil* Disraeli made the much quoted comment that the English were not one but two nations—'the Privileged and the People'. This brief aphorism expressed the essence of class relationships in the England of the time. The barrier of money divided the nation and divided it to such an extent that national unity had become a highly theoretical question.

Despite the turbulence and confusion produced over a number of decades by the industrial revolution, social relations in Britain were distinguished by a stability not encountered elsewhere, and by the almost inexplicable stamp which they impressed on the consciousness of all strata of society from top to bottom. The inequality of classes, the fact that some were privileged and others the reverse, the grading of classes in terms of merit—all these were accepted as an axiom, as part of the natural order, dictated by principles which went beyond the scope of human activities. Certain schools of political thought might revolt against blatant inequality, but the 'rights' of the different classes, as exercised by individual members, were respected without any qualification, and the social hierarchy offered a simple and accepted design for advancement for individuals or groups who were suitably equipped to get on in a capitalist society and planned to do so.[1]

This conviction of the permanence of class divisions was deeply rooted in the consciousness of otherwise very different social strata in Victorian

1 Here is an apt description of the situation prevailing in this period. 'In Victorian days life was simplified for most people by the fact that society was conventionally divided into three main classes, upper, middle and lower. One was born into one or the other, and everyone was supposed to "know their place" and—keep it! ... People of one class might choose to ape the manner of a higher class, but each fully recognised the initial distinctions all the same, the humbler grades quietly accepting that position in life to which it had "pleased" providence to call them, and remaining therein without any irreverent aspiration towards the more exalted social spheres.' (M. E. Perugini, *Victorian days and ways*, Jarrold's, London, 1946, pp. 31–2.)

England. One of its sources is probably to be found in the English variant of the emergence from feudalism. This had allowed the aristocracy to preserve its political and social privileges in their entirety and, moreover, to emerge from its struggle for power with the middle classes with its social authority not only not undermined but even strengthened, and with an undiminished influence on the social imagination, if not the social consciousness, of society.[1] The middle classes felt respect for the hierarchical traditions and shibboleths of the aristocracy, and an almost superstitious fear of storming the castles that were their historical possessions. The English aristocracy remained unbroken in both the political and the economic spheres. In the political sphere it retained its monopoly of the key positions in the State administration long after the country's economy had reached a stage which should have led to a political reshuffling of class forces; economically, the aristocracy had emerged from a difficult period with the foundations of its financial strength virtually intact, so that it remained the wealthiest aristocracy in Europe. In political terms, it had not only not been defeated but had actually gained the victory, by inducing the *nouveau riche* stratum to dream of advancement into the aristocratic world. In accepting the superiority of the aristocratic system of social values, the new class that dominated the economy also accepted its own position, in which it had to look up to the aristocracy.

As a result, in spite of the stormy processes of change that were taking place in the lower sectors of the social structure, relations between the classes in Victorian England underwent only small modifications—at least outwardly—and displayed rather conservative tendencies. The stability of the class hierarchy as a whole prevented the development of the kind of fluid and dynamic state of affairs which is usually created when accepted scales of values and their structural bases come under violent attack and which can promote a revolutionary transformation of inter-class relations. In the final analysis, the divisions between classes and their reflection in the social consciousness were particularly stable and acted as an effective brake on the development of more widespread trends of social mobility—not so much in the sense of individual mobility as that of the mobility of strata in relation to a recognised social hierarchy.

This description of class relations in the Victorian era gives some idea of the obstacle encountered by the new skilled stratum in its aspiration to attain a higher rung of the social ladder. While the setting up of new branches of industry made it easy for more resourceful individuals from the skilled milieu to embark on a successful career as technical or admini-

1   A. Sturmthal, 'Comments on Selig Perlman's theory of the labour movement', *Industrial and Labor Relations Review*, July 1951, p. 487.

strative supervisors,[1] the advance of the stratum as a whole was rendered much more difficult. The advancement of individuals meant jumping from one class to another; on the other hand, the stratum as a whole, in so far as it made its living from manual labour, was pushed down by the prevailing social convention—a convention actually accepted by the stratum itself—into the position of the lower class, despite the relative material well-being it had achieved and its own earnest attempts at self-improvement.

The most important characteristic of the history of the new skilled stratum in the Victorian era was that it confined its ambitions in life not only within the sphere of prevailing capitalist relationships but also within the framework delimited by the social position of the 'lower class'; this was a servile affirmation of the fact that it belonged to the lower strata of society. In its move for social advancement the skilled stratum was still trying to achieve quite elementary objectives: acceptance by society, an end to its state of alienation and acceptance of its existence as a part of the nation. As proof of its citizenship it was prepared to offer an obedient and submissive recognition of its social inferiority and give up any idea of trying to reach the level of the classes above it. Contemporary authors have commented on the significance of the appearance of a 'loyal national feeling' in the working class community.[2] The representatives of the new stratum rarely missed an opportunity of stressing their unqualified loyalty to the institutions of the State, their respect for the historic traditions of the ruling class, and their view of themselves as a harmonious segment of the nation as a whole.[3]

The skilled workers' acceptance of the existing society and its criteria for estimating human values, and their attempt to find a permanent place in that society—even if it be in the servants' hall—involved on the one side the endeavour, already described, to dissociate themselves clearly from the remainder of the working class, which was still in a state of alienation; on the other it required them to acknowledge the customs and values set up by the bourgeoisie as supreme, to imitate those customs, and to adapt themselves to social milieux recognised as superior to their own. Thus we

1 Lord Eustace Percy *et al.*, 'The future of the political parties: a symposium', *Political Quarterly*, January–March 1932, p. 21.

2 Ludlow and Jones, *Progress of the working class*, p. 283.

3 Here is a typical instance taken from the TUC presidential address by William Matkin in 1890: 'It cannot, of course, be disputed that the Anglo-Saxon is pre-eminently endowed with great organising faculties. Our colonial expansion, our system of government, our successful local representative bodies, our ancient guilds, and our host of voluntary successful enterprises, all bear testimony to this. Trade unionism is, in fact, an offspring of this spirit.' (Report of the TUC, 1890, p. 25.)

find among the rank and file of well paid workers a deliberate self-restric-
tion to the position of a helot stratum.[1] Among those whose ambitions
drove them somewhat further beyond a state of servitude which was
accepted as a benefaction, there was widespread snobbery, a *nouveau riche*
contempt for their own community, and simultaneously a sense of shame
combined with a greedy acceptance of the most superficial signs of kinship
with the stratum above.[2]

In this way the historical conditions which determined the aspirations
of the skilled artisans ensured that these aspirations did not in principle
go further than a desire for the stratum to be assimilated by society; not
even the most ambitious individuals aspired higher than to the class status
of the lower middle class.

1   Quelch commented indignantly on this attitude: 'Can there be anything more
    exasperating than to hear a skilled artisan, who ought to know that the whole of
    society is living on the labour of himself and his mates, skilled and unskilled, talking
    of his home as "not bad for a working man", his set of books as "quite creditable to
    a working man", his children as "a good-looking lot of kids for a working man",
    and so on? You never hear this abominable servile cant in any other country. Nor
    before the old Chartist movement died down was it nearly so common here. The
    systematic and degrading respect for their "betters", inculcated into the workers
    from their childhood upwards, tells its tale in after years.' (Quoted by H. M.
    Hyndman, *Further reminiscences*, Macmillan, London 1912, pp. 249–50.)
2   As Hyndman wrote, '... For the life of me I cannot understand the respectful
    attitude which they adopt to all the prejudices of the class immediately above
    them ... With the exception of the thorough-going Socialists, nearly all the working
    class leaders I have known have given me the impression that they were rather
    ashamed of belonging to the producers at all. They have most of them tried hard
    to imitate the clothes, manners and speech of their enemies.' (*Further reminiscences*,
    pp. 248–9.)

2

The structure of the
labour movement

The traits which characterised the skilled workers made this stratum exceptionally fertile soil for the germination of the prevailing middle class belief in free trade. The ideas propagated by the Manchester school of economists, which expressed in a rationalised form the interests of the consolidating capitalist enterprises, found easy access to a stratum that was searching eagerly for ways of establishing itself permanently in the social and political system around it.

The ideological *avant-garde* of the middle classes devoted an increasing amount of attention to the propagation of its social views among the working population. The publicity campaign of the Anti-Corn Law League[1] reached well beyond the boundaries of the 'political classes' of the period; it was consciously intended to mould not only the general viewpoint but also the psychological attitudes of the more politically active strata of the working class. It would be difficult to over-estimate the role of this campaign in providing the ideological subject matter for future conceptions about the organisation of the new skilled workers. Even after the end of the League's activities large groups of the middle class continued to provide considerable sums to shape a climate of ideas in which new generations of workers in capitalist industry were steeped and which they absorbed. In the years between 1833 and 1869 the publishing firm of Charles Knight, well subsidised by private funds, was flooding the rather meagre reading market among the workers with an enormous output of brochures sold at specially reduced rates, with such titles as *The consequences of machines*, *Capital and labour*, *The character and consequences of the trade union movement*, etc. Generous private donations also helped to develop the work of the working men's clubs and institutes movement, which endeavoured to fill the workers' leisure time by converting them to a middle class way of thinking; working men's clubs disseminated the ideals of sobriety, the nobility of hard work and moral self-improvement.[2] Faithful replicas of this kind of programme were later to reappear in the declarations of aims and objects set out by the most representative trade union organisations of the artisan stratum.

It was in this philosophical and political climate, under continual pressure from middle class ways of looking at the world, that the skilled

1   S. and B. Webb, *The history of trade unionism*, p. 174.
2   Postgate, *The builders' history*, pp. 196 et seq.

stratum developed, from the time when it first began to take an interest in the society around it and to possess the means of satisfying that interest.

This ideological pressure was not, of course, the reason for the particular form ultimately adopted by the artisans' trade unions. The sources of that must be sought in the internal structure of the class and the position of the class in the overall structure of society—that is to say, in completely objective factors. Nevertheless, the ideological climate played an important role, and one that is difficult to over-estimate, in that it provided ready-made forms for the social aims which were maturing inside the stratum.

A new type of trade union organisation—sharply contrasting with the primitive structures familiar to us in the first half of the nineteenth century, which were ephemeral, disintegrated easily and were aimed at a mass membership—appeared and spread rapidly in the 1850s. This type of union was adapted to the structure and position of the new artisan stratum. Its form was the product both of the stratum's new social position and its new social aspirations, and of the skills and organising experience which its members had recently acquired at work.

The social base for the formation of the new trade organisations was provided by occupation, just as it had been in the former craftsmen's unions, and in contrast to the class base of the unions set up by the unskilled factory workers. Occupation was the natural basis for organisation, since it was occupational qualifications which had raised the new artisans from the uniformly underprivileged mass of unskilled factory workers and had conferred privileges on them. Thus the activities of these unions were aimed at strengthening and defending these privileges. The artisan unions were from the very beginning an institutionalisation not of class but of occupational interests. These interests did not connect but divided the new artisan stratum from the remaining sections of the working class; they even divided particular sections of the artisan stratum from one another. Occupational differentiation became the first premise for the internal stratification and articulation of the working class; the social significance of these unions was based on emphasising and stressing this stratification on behalf of those sections of the working class to whom the stratification brought direct benefit.[1]

The artisans could note the coincidence of the frontier between relative prosperity and poverty with that between skilled and unskilled labour.

1   A leading thinker of this union movement, George Howell, stated, 'The mainten-
    ance of trade privilege doubtless was, and is, the primary object of every Trade
    Union. For that purpose they were originally instituted. This is indeed the essence
    of the Old Trade Unionism' [i.e. of the artisan unions]. ('Trade unionism', p. 118;
    cf also L. Ulman, *The rise of the national trade union*, Harvard University Press,
    Cambridge, Mass., 1955, p. 308; and J. Cunnison, *Labour organisation*, Pitman,
    London, 1930, p. 56.)

They were justified in regarding their skilled qualifications as the bases for both the privileges already won and those that might still be won, and also for their place in the social hierarchy to which they accorded recognition. Practical experience of this, combined with the bourgeois liberal conception of the interplay of supply and demand as the source of all prosperity, made the artisans increasingly conscious of the need for organisations based on occupational criteria aimed at keeping out intruders bent on infiltrating the sphere reserved for the chosen ones, organisations administered on a purely commercial basis, with interest payments guaranteed to those who invested their contributions in them.[1]

The discovery of a suitable organisational model for this social need was made easier in Britain because the craftsmen's unions, which had survived the stormy period of the first half of the nineteenth century, could hand down the traditions of the guild structure; the latter had, after all, been set up in order, *inter alia*, to defend occupational interests. The journeymen's unions and their whole range of organisational concepts and programmes were ready for use as models for the unions now being set up by the skilled workers, whose energies were directed into a channel that had already been defined.

In the 1860s and 1870s we find existing side by side unions of workers in crafts that dated back to before the industrial revolution (building, printing, cabinet-making, tailoring, glass bottle making, bookbinding, coach-building, etc) and in trades created by capitalist industry, chiefly in the iron and steel and engineering industries.[2] The first category of unions was relatively old, the second only lately established, and the first category clearly served as models for the second. During the Victorian era, however, the two components of the skilled trade union movement, with their different antecedents, consistently grew closer to each other. The differences of earlier years faded away as the similarities of their social position and the organisational structure dictated by that position became more obvious.

1 Comparative data show that the need for organisations of this type is associated with this precise stage of development of a working population and not merely with the specifically British version of it. The American example is particularly significant because, as we have already indicated, the prehistory of the working class there followed quite a different course. Yet, there as well, the crystallisation of the stratum of skilled workers led to the setting up of unions based on occupational skills. The first was a printers' union, set up in 1852; five more were started in the 1850s, twenty-one in the 1860s and eighteen more shortly after that. All of them were organised like the British trade unions and had similar aims. (This information comes from an unpublished paper by S. H. Slichter, 'Historical data on trade unions, 1850–1946'. See also R. R. R. Brooks, *When labor organizes*, Yale University Press, New Haven, Conn., 1937, p. 29.)

2 Hobsbawm, 'The labour aristocracy', p. 209.

Since the time of the Webbs, and as a result of their influence, historians of the British labour movement have usually associated the emergence of the 'new model' trade unions with the setting up by William Allan and William Newton of the Amalgamated Society of Engineers. This was in fact the organisation which was to assemble the fragmented accumulation of past union experience into an integrated, complete and universal philosophy of trade unionism. In the history of the ASE this philosophy proved successful and the Engineers' version of it therefore became the most attractive one. But all the elements which, as we shall see later, distinguished the 'new model' union from the unions of the preceding half-century could be found in the journeymen's organisations that existed before the ASE was set up.

For instance, in 1845 the London Society of Compositors was already a wealthy organisation, with high membership fees and a paid executive, whose membership was becoming increasingly professionalised. That year the organisation's annual income was £1,795; one year later it had risen to £2,487. Despite this, it was decided to double the cost of membership in 1847, probably not only for financial reasons but also as a deterrent to the growing numbers of people who wished to become compositors.[1] The activities of the union, never particularly militant, became even more pacific, cautious and motivated by concern for the security of its funds and the prestige of the skilled trade which it represented.[2]

Other printers' unions showed similar characteristics. For instance, the Typographical Association never 'flung open its gates to all and sundry'; 'quality was never sacrificed to quantity'; much of the 'old craft gild exclusiveness' still clung to it. Its membership consisted of skilled tradesmen, who were opposed to the influx of unskilled workers into the printing shops and supported the seven-year apprenticeship.[3]

The organisers of the Scottish Typographical Association had the same ideas,[4] and in general these ideas were to be found everywhere where there still existed craft unions, derived more or less directly from the guild tradition and set up to defend occupational privileges that were being undermined

---

1   Symptomatic of this is the comment made by the historians of the printing trade unions, Ellic Howe and Harold Waite, at the beginning of their account of the history of the second half of the nineteenth century: 'We now enter upon a lengthy period of steady progress and consolidation, and the task of the Society's historians becomes more difficult . . . Comparative lack of spectacular events is rather to the credit of the Society's leaders than otherwise, for the present strength, wealth and influence of the L.S.C. is founded on a century-old tradition of caution and sense of statemanship in the conduct of the Society's affairs.' (*Ibid.*, p. 161.)

2   Howe and Waite, *The London Society of Compositors*, p. 119.

3   Musson, *The Typographical Association*, p. 116.

4   Gillespie, *A hundred years of progress*, pp. 52–3.

by capitalism. We find them among the building trades, as for instance in the painters' society of St Martin or the Phoenix Association, which put up an unsuccessful resistance against the massive and ceaseless influx of un-skilled workers. There were also the stonemasons, who set up a compact and defensive trade organisation long before the engineers.[1]

So far as trade organisation was concerned, the milieu of the 'new' skilled workers was not itself virgin territory at the beginning of the Vic-torian era. Newton and Allan did not set up their union in a void. Skilled engineers held themselves aloof from the revolutionary mass movements of the unskilled rank and file. They kept at a distance from the mainstream of the Chartist campaign and the experiments of Doherty and Owen. Instead they set up the first nuclei of the trade organisations, few in number and very small in membership at first, but based on the principles that were later accepted by Allan: high membership fees in exchange for mutual insurance arranged by the union. These tiny but lively organisa-tions included the Journeymen Steam Engine and Machine Makers' Friendly Society (more popularly known as 'The Old Mechanics'), the Steam Engine Makers' Society, and the United Machine Workers' Associa-tion.[2] Although these organisations were set up in a completely different milieu from that of the journeymen's unions of the period before the in-dustrial revolution, they came increasingly to resemble the latter, both in forms of organisation and in social objectives. As the 'new' skilled workers' social status improved and the guarantees of their trade privileges moved from the realm of aspiration to that of a reality to be defended, there ceased to be a fundamental difference between the conservatism of the journeymen's unions and the increasingly constructive attitude of the new artisan unions.

In consequence, one can observe during the period under discussion a consistent and growing unity between the journeymen's movement and that of the new artisans. It proceeded on a parallel course with the struc-tural changes that were taking place within the working class. On the other hand, the real division within the union movement lay not between the branches that dated from before or after the industrial revolution but between the unions based on occupational interests and the 'general' unions. These were emerging in industries that did not have so definite an occupational stratification as did, for instance, iron and steel. The 'general' unions were organised on a class rather than an occupational basis and therefore operated along class, not guild, lines.

The role of this second type of labour organisation was relatively un-important at the period under discussion. Although such organisations

1 Postgate, *The builders' history*, pp. 144, 145, 235–6.
2 Williams, *Magnificent journey*, p. 89.

were sometimes of considerable size, they did not influence the style of the labour movement nor determine the lines of its development. They were foreign bodies within the ranks of the respectable and prosperous trade union movement of the time. Furthermore, they lacked solidarity and respectability—on which the power of the 'new model' unions was based. In his controversy with the Webbs E. E. Gillespie disputes the thesis that the 'new model' unions automatically achieved a dominant position in the labour movement immediately after 1850. There is a good deal of truth in this standpoint; nevertheless, the Webbs' generalisation has, leaving aside possible corrections of factual detail, grasped the basic trend of the movement's evolution and is thus of heuristic value.

For the sake of historical accuracy, however, one should not overlook the miners' union, or rather unions. These were very different from the 'new model' unions because they were coming into being in an environment in which occupational differentiation was less developed, and which also totally lacked any environmental guild tradition. Nor should one forget that strange and complex creation, the National Agricultural Labourers' Union, founded by Joseph Arch. This 'mass' union,[1] ephemeral in all its traits, artificially inflated, an organisation of the amorphous mass of agricultural workers based on a charismatic link, nonetheless adopted the liberal and pacifistic ideology of the free-trade bourgeoisie and busied itself enthusiastically with organising emigration to the colonies to ease the excessive pressure of work-seekers on the labour market. At the same time, the ritualistic character of proceedings at union meetings and the charismatic cult of Joseph Arch[2] revealed the real social significance of the union. The farm workers' union was a sociological paradox—one of those which frequently crop up on the periphery of an era as complex as the Victorian age. Another indication that the character of the union and the category to which it belonged were defined, not by political or ideological considerations, but by the social structure on which the organisation was based, is to be found in its history. After its stormy debut in the years 1882–84 the initial wave of enthusiasm soon began to ebb; the rural population, only superficially inspired by the brief spell of a charismatic cult, reverted to its fragmented state. In 1879 the union's membership was down to 24,000, in 1879 to 20,000, and by 1889 its remnants apparently contained only 4,000 members.[3] The collapse came suddenly in July 1874, after the first unsuccessful strike.

1 George Dixon reported at a conference in Leamington that the union had twenty-three sections, 982 branches and 71,835 members in 1873; a year later there were 1,480 branches and 86,214 members. (Selley, *Village trade unions*, p. 65.)
2 *Ibid.*; also Groves, *Sharpen the sickle*, p. 45.
3 Selley, *Village trade unions*, p. 72.

In any case, it was the 'new model' branch of the Victorian labour movement, which arose out of the continuation of the journeymen's unions and those of the 'new artisans', that had a decisive significance for the later history of the labour movement in England. It became a forge for the forms of organisation and organisational philosophy which determined the final shape of the labour organisations, and became part of their assets. For this reason we shall focus our attention on this particular branch for the primary purposes of this study, which is aimed not so much at reproducing every detail of the historical mosaic as at eliciting the key regularities which have determined its evolutionary dynamic.

Table 6

Membership and financial strength of the 'new model' unions, 1869–89

	1869	1879	1889
Membership	105,216	155,184	200,666
Annual income	£192,787	£395,319	£531,486
Cash balance	126,422	309,373	623,064

Source G. Howell, 'Trade unionism—new and old' in *Social questions of today*, ed. H. de B. Gibbins, Methuen, London, 1891, pp. 210–20.

The 'new model' unions never experienced short-lived concentrated tempestuous expansion of the kind that characterised the 'Grand National' or Joseph Arch's organisation. Instead, their development was characterised by a systematic stable trend and by resistance to misfortunes—whether it was the sometimes catastrophic consequences of unsuccessful union action or a general economic breakdown. These unions never grew as large as those of the non-skilled workers but their membership figures remained steady; moreover, while the influx of new members was not large, their union funds showed a steady upward trend. In the first year of its existence the Amalgamated Society of Engineers had 121 branches and a membership of 11,829. Its annual income was £22,807 8s 8d and the balance at the end of the year was £21,705 5s. By 1866 the Society had 30,984 members. In the same year other organisations had an even smaller membership. The Friendly Society of Operative Masons had 17,762 members, the Operative House Carpenters' and Joiners' Society 10,000, and the Amalgamated Society of Carpenters and Joiners and the National Association of Plasterers about 8,000 each; the Friendly Society of Ironfounders 10,669 members and the Boilermakers and Iron Shipbuilders 9,000. In all, only sixteen of the 'new model' unions had a membership of over 5,000 in that year.[1] All of them were characterised by a slow but steady increase in numbers and income. The nature of this increase is shown in Howell's table (see table 6), based on the annual balance sheets of the fourteen largest model unions.

Selectivity in the recruitment of new members and concern to build up the union's funds by means of membership fees that were extremely high by contemporary standards were basic principles for the organisation of the 'new model' unions. These two principles emphasised the connection of the new organisations with a select sector of the working class, one which was sufficiently prosperous to accept considerable financial burdens and to contribute the sort of fees on which an interest yield could be paid. They were also excellently suited to the programme of the new-style unions.

Table 7

Some outgoings of the fourteen 'new model' unions in the period 1869–89 (£)

	1869	1879	1889
Funeral allowance	17,141	28,515	29,668
Sick benefit	38,017	74,637	93,159
Superannuation allowance	13,764	33,617	76,154
Accident benefit	6,346	5,996	8,184
Out-of-work allowance	114,987	329,804	75,682

Source   Howell, 'Trade unionism', pp. 90–200; also E. Howe and H. E. Waite, *The London Society of Compositors*, Cassell, London, 1948, pp. 184 *et seq.*

The principle task of the new model unions, whether they were aware of it or not, was to consolidate and safeguard the social status of their occupation. To be successful in this it was necessary to provide material guarantees that the status was a secure one. Thus the unions, following guild traditions, also became as much, if not more, friendly societies. Their major expenditure went on funeral allowances (between £6 and £15), sick benefits (£9–£15), superannuation allowances (2s 6d–10s a week), accident benefits (£50–£100), out-of-work allowances (8s–12s a week), and various other kinds of financial aid, such as emigration grants, reimbursement for tools destroyed in some natural calamity and other kinds of accident. The amounts and trends of such outgoings are shown in table 7, based on returns from the same fourteen unions as table 6.

1   G. Howell, *Labour legislation—labour movements—labour leaders*, Unwin, London, 1902, p. 99; also Ludlow and Jones, *Progress of the working class*, pp. 200–203.

As the dimensions and scope of the insurance functions of the unions increased, it began to exert an increasingly powerful effect on their activities. Insurance of various kinds had a real and steadily increasing significance in the lives of the members. The insurance function was, moreover, linked with the difficult procedure of manipulating large sums of money, which required constant attention; it tended therefore to relegate all other aspects of union activity to a less important position. It came to the point where many unions developed into something like commercial undertakings, geared to pay the best possible dividends and assessing their operations strictly in terms of capital gain. Union finance took on a life of its own; the increase of union funds became an end in itself, and the amount of the dividend received by shareholders came to be the main concern of the organisations. For instance, in February 1880 the founders of the Associated Society of Locomotive and Steam Enginemen and Firemen sent out a prospectus stating the aims and objectives of their organisation which was entirely modelled on the prospectus of an insurance company. The leaflet consisted simply of a detailed account of the registration fee and the membership dues, on the one hand, and of the insurance benefits and premiums on the other. It ended by saying that the association would not cost more than £200 to run in the first year for an active and energetic secretary.[1] It is almost impossible to over-estimate the extent to which unions' policy as a whole was influenced by their operations in the insurance field.

The 'new model' unions were by their very nature opposed to violent forms of struggle which could undermine the reputation of their stratum, which was making a bid for acceptance as part of the social order. The unions therefore regarded strike action as primitive, and disapproved of it as a weapon for achieving their objectives. But these natural tendencies were strengthened by their activities in the insurance field. High insurance premiums and strikes were mutually self-exclusive. The thinking of the 'new model' unions was holistic, and its components were linked. Support for strike action would destroy this philosophy by threatening the security of union funds which were earmarked for the payment of numerous benefits, and thus fulfilled the role of a deposit guaranteeing a secure existence for the individual trade unionist. As the unions' funds increased, the clouds looming over the workers' future were dispelled and an easier and more comfortable life became possible; plans for the future could be entertained and one could acquire a justified sense of one's own dignity and right to social esteem. All these privileges would be demolished at one

---

1 N. McKillop, *The lighted flame*, Nelson, London, 1950, pp. 25–6.

blow if the union's assets were worn down by a lengthy strike. The unions' insurance operations therefore became the basic stabilising factor.[1]

This concentration on insurance activities was one of the elements that made the 'new model' unions different from others and furthered the consolidation and defence of the social status of the privileged stratum of workers. A second element, also deriving from the occupational basis on which the unions were organised, was to be found in the measures they undertook with the aim of regulating the labour market.

In the opening phase of activity of the 'new model' unions both these elements were present in every union, but in different proportions. For understandable reasons the new artisan unions put greater emphasis on mutual aid activities, while other journeymen's unions tended, under the influence of their traditions, to pay most attention to various aspects of the regulation of production. For example, among the building workers the central union's principal function was for a long time seen as the establishment of 'working rules', rules which would regulate all the terms of employment in agreement with the employers. 'Working rules' took precedent even over such vital union concerns as wages and hours of work. The arranging of these was left to local branches while the main union retained the power to establish the 'working rules'. In consequence, the wages of members of the Amalgamated Society of Carpenters and Joiners in 1897 ranged from 5d to 10d an hour according to the locality; and the hours worked per week ranged from 41½ hours in Middleton to 60 in Yarmouth.[2]

The new artisans' unions were just beginning to seize the opportunities afforded by their new situation, but they had no legal or customary guarantees of their emancipation from the mass of workers; initially, therefore, it was natural for them to pay more attention to questions of wages and working hours. Yet the example set by the older and more

1 In *The spirit of association* (pp. 289–90) M. Fothergill Robinson makes an interesting comment on this point: 'It will be readily understood that the offer of tangible benefits in case of accident, sickness, superannuation, or burial is a powerful magnet whereby to induce men to join the unions; and also secures the continuance of their membership when they have once joined. The disciplinary powers which these benefits afford are also considerable and may, indeed, be open to abuse. A man is unlikely to oppose the will of his society, when such opposition would reap expulsion and the loss of prospective out-of-work and sick pay, for which he may have contributed for years.'

Robinson also quotes a characteristic comment by a union leader in 1872: '"As soon as we got means and members, the men struck, drew out all the funds, and we then had to start again." The subsequent introduction of friendly society-type benefits was found to have "the effect of greatly reducing strikes, and of introducing into Labour disputes a spirit of conciliation . . ."'

2 Postgate, *The builders' history*, p. 26.

experienced journeymen's organisations, in conjunction with middle class economic theory, influenced them away from wage considerations towards questions concerned with the regulation of the labour market, i.e. matters which had long been the concern of the journeymen's unions. Eventually, therefore, a relative uniformity emerged in the strategic and tactical emphasis laid on various problems by the 'new model' unions.

Along with their acceptance of liberal economic theory, the 'new model' unions regarded it as axiomatic that wage levels were always determined by the fluctuating relation between supply and demand, and that the wage fund as a whole was a constant amount in all circumstances, so that an improvement in wage rates could be achieved only by means of competition within working groups, and especially by limiting the labour supply in particular occupations. This concept was accepted all the more willingly by the stratum of skilled workers because it provided a con-venient rationalisation for their aversion to the labourers, from whom it was necessary to dissociate themselves in order to stress the social position they had achieved. Thus the unions of the new artisans became organs of the struggle against competitors within the ranks of the workers, par-ticularly against competition from unskilled labour.[1]

The main form of resistance to competition adopted by the unions was to restrict the intake of apprentices. The unions sought to secure for their trades the exclusiveness which had traditionally belonged to the craft guilds. The conflict between workers and employers which shaped the wage structure was almost invariably to a dispute over the number of young workers to be accepted as apprentices. This was regarded as the kernel of the problem and also as the best cure for downwards trends in wage rates.[2]

---

1 That this feature was not fortuitous is also confirmed by the American experience. In the United States a whole series of skilled workers' unions (for instance the boot-makers) were set up to oppose the influx of unskilled labour into their trades. (Taft, 'Theories of the labor movement', p. 57.)

2 Some characteristic formulations of this concept are found in an article in *The Operative* of 12 April 1851, probably written by William Newton: '"Supply and demand regulate the wages of labour"—that is an aphorism unfortunately too true: but as it is a truth and one that could be subverted it is necessary to use it to the best advantage. Now we do not pretend to set up a standard of wages—we do not propose to insist upon a fixed sum, neither more nor less. We are willing, for the time, to submit to the competition principle of having wages regulated by the supply and demand of labour, therefore we are not desirous of dealing with wages at all, in a direct manner. We propose rather to interfere with those principles that regulate wages, preferring to deal with the cause of this effect, rather than with the effect itself. If wages are to be maintained, it is not only by insisting upon a certain amount, without reference to the circumstances by which the trade is surrounded, but by surrounding the trade with fresh circumstances, as will of necessity have a

These endeavours to restrict the supply of labour accentuated the parochial character of the 'new model' unions, and impelled them into incessant conflict with one another. In consequence their declarations were
(often unintentionally) imbued with what sounded like a cynical egoism.
The interests of other sections of their class were set aside without hesitation to serve the interests of a particular trade. The idea of solidarity
among workers, widely accepted in earlier days in the milieu of the unorganised factory workers, was shipwrecked on the rocks of occupational
interests, which entirely dominated the trade unions.[1]

beneficial effect upon its condition. The wages of labour are influenced by the number of men out of employment, by the amount of competition that exists among the
workmen themselves—and unless the number of unemployed is reduced and competition thereby destroyed, wages can never be increased nor privileges enhanced.
To destroy, then, a redundancy in the labour market ought to be the first object of
a Trades Society.'

In 1869 J. Doody, the representative of the United Flint Glass Cutters' Society,
said in a speech delivered at the second Trades Union Congress in Birmingham, 'It
has been affirmed by almost all political economists that trades unions have no right
to interfere with or restrict the number of apprentices employed. This we deny,
as the introduction of an unlimited number of apprentices into any trade would
overstock the labour market, and thereby cause men who are ready and willing
to work to be thrown idle, and moreover cause a reduction of wages to those who
may be retained. It is not called for by the requirements of, or state of, trade, but
often arises from the greed and caprice of unprincipled employers who force into a
trade an unnecessarily large number of youths, who, as they attain manhood,
must either themselves be thrown out of employ or be the means of throwing out
others.'

Third, there is the evidence of Joseph Arch of the Agricultural Workers'
Union before Her Majesty's Commissioners of Agriculture, 1881–82—thirty-six
minutes of evidence, III: 'How do you set about ensuring the labourers' getting
higher wages?'—'We have reduced the number of labourers in the market very
considerably.'

'How have you reduced the number of labourers in the market?'—'We have
emigrated about 700,000 souls, men, women and children, within the last eight or
nine years.'

'How have these 700,000 souls been emigrated; out of which funds?'—'I went
over to Canada, and I made arrangements with the Canadian Government to give
them so much and we found so much from the funds of our trade.'

'That is out of the funds of the association?'—'Yes.' (From J. B. Jeffreys, *Labour's
formative years*, II, Lawrence & Wishart, London, 1948.)

1   The following passage from William MacDonald's *The true story of trades' unions*
exemplifies a characteristic argument used to justify claims. 'What does the assumed
monopoly of Trades Unions cost the nation? Professor Jevons himself says they
cannot raise wages at all in the long run; "they may seem now and then to gain an
advantage of five or ten per cent." We shall take the highest rate, and suppose
that the skilled labour of England costs the country ten per cent more than it
should do. I should say that there has never at any time been more than a quarter
of a million of members in all associations of the United Kingdom; but allow half a

The idea of restricting the labour market gradually became an obsession with the 'new model' unions. It was the prism through which union leaders viewed all problems concerned with the workers, and it provided them with guidelines for settling every sort of problem and argument. Unskilled and unorganised workers existed for them only in so far as they constituted an element that could interfere with the market privileges of their particular trade.[1]

A third element that was typical of the 'new model' unions and closely associated with the two already mentioned was their extremely conciliatory and deferential attitude towards the employers. It was justified by means of the same objective premises and the philosophy deriving from them. The starting point of this philosophy was the conviction that the capitalist system would last for ever. The prospect of a thousand years of capitalism was accepted as axiomatic and was implicit in every theoretical concept of the political thinkers of the union movement. It assumed an

million, and say four millions of workmen; that is, one in eight is a monopolist, and the other seven free labourers. Do you think if only one landlord in seven had been a monopolist that ever we should have agitated, for twenty years, to repeal those starvation laws? They would have repealed themselves . . . And I think, sir, if our half million of educated workmen have been able to receive ten per cent more than the market price, the three and a half millions who have had no unions have got ten per cent less than they should have done, and consequently the loss to the nation or the capital of the country has been restored sevenfold.' (*The true story of trades' unions: a reply to Dr John Watts, Prof. Jevons*, Manchester, 1867, p. 19.)

1 This viewpoint came up incessantly at Trade Union Congresses. In 1883 a Mr Toyne from Saltburn said that at the present time there was 'a tendency in the rural districts to monopolise the land; to convert small farms into large ones. The small farmsteads were being knocked down, and the land absorbed into large estates. The present land system was driving men from off the land into the mines and factories to compete against the artisan in the labour market. The working men of the country wanted relief for this immediately.' (Report of the TUC, 1883, p. 39.) In the following year the president of the TUC, J. C. Thompson, said in his presidential address, 'Through these conditions being allowed to exist, we know for a fact that many of our farm workers are but poorly fed and even more deplorably housed. Their circumstances are such as lead them to exclaim, "Any life than this life!' and so they are driven into the towns and cities to destroy what would otherwise be a normal labour market. We have employers of labour who are continually grasping for this kind of cheap labour.' (Report of the TUC, 1884, p. 16.) In 1889 the presidential address of the then president of the TUC, R. D. B. Ritchie, contained the following passage: 'In the ordinary course of things the unskilled or inferior workman is the first to suffer by a lessened demand for labour, and the last to benefit by increased demand; thus a margin of unemployed labour is created, which is brought into competition with the more skilful class of workers, thereby tending to lower wages, and acting as a drag upon the efforts of our workers to maintain a condition of comparative comfort in their respective trades.' (Report of the TUC, 1889, p. 15.)

opting out of war against the system and the acceptance of a place in that system. In such a situation the inevitable complement of the initial assumptions was the axiom that the interests of employers and workers—at least, skilled workers—were basically in harmony. Thus disputes were seen to arise chiefly because of misunderstandings and to be aggravated because of mistakes made either by one side or by both at the same time. It was considered possible to prevent them altogether then and in the future by the simple process of explaining mutual interests, demands and desired spheres of influence, and then keeping to the arrangements on which agreement had been reached.

According to this way of thinking, harmonious co-operation and friendly relations were a normal state, while disputes were ordinarily a temporary disturbance of the usual equilibrium. Thus the vocation of the unions was to see that the regrettable periods when normal harmony was disturbed were reduced and to stress the community of interests between the two conflicting sides within the capitalist unit of production.[1]

This way of thinking was the natural outcome of the predominant aspiration among the new unionists to escape from a position of social estrangement and to occupy a legally sanctioned place in capitalist society, a place of honour according to the prevailing notions of honour.

The conviction that there was a community of interests between employers and employees was rationalised by appeals to the national interest —something of great importance[2]—and also by references to the economic theory already mentioned; apart from other aspects this made the workers into co-partners of their 'own' capitalist employer, with their wages dependent on the successes achieved by the manufacturer who employed them in his struggle against his competitors in the market. A manifestation of this way of conceptualising the relations between the two groups

---

1   T. J. Dunning, the leader of the London bookbinders, wrote, '... After all, the true function of employer and employed is that of amity. They are each, notwithstanding these occasional disagreements, the truest friends of the other and neither can inflict an injury on the other without its recoiling on himself. Capital and labour should go hand in hand ... Neither class can injure the other without at the same time injuring itself. Both are so essential to each other, and so intimately connected, that one cannot be injured without the other feeling it, and consequently no triumph can be gained at the expense of justice by either class over the other with impunity.' (*Trade unions and strikes*, London Consolidated Society of Bookbinders, 1873, pp. 31, 61.)

2   In his address to the electors of Stafford in 1874 Alexander MacDonald said that 'all questions affecting the interests of capital and labour would have my constant and individual attention, believing, as I do that it is only by a more peaceful relation of these interests that the greatness and strength of our country can be maintained'. (From A. W. Humphrey, *A history of labour representation*, Constable, London, 1912, p. 52.)

was the idea, put forward by several unions, of the 'sliding scale'—a scale which made the wage rates of workers dependent on the current selling price of the product made by a particular factory. Another instance was the frequently recurring idea that the trade unions had nothing against honest employers and would therefore maintain a united front with 'honest' capitalists against the 'dishonest' ones who, motivated by an excessive lust for profits, used below-the-belt practices to sell their goods.[1]

For obvious reasons the unions adopted a decidedly uncompromising and negative attitude to strikes. Strikes were undesirable in all respects. They were a charge on union funds, and they damaged relations with the employers, making it more difficult for the unions to consolidate themselves in a position of accepted and respected partnership. An aphorism coined by Odger, one of the members of the Junta, gives the essence of the 'new model' unions' attitude to strikes:[2] 'Strikes are to the social world what wars are to politics ... they become crimes unless prompted by absolute necessity.[3]

In the same way as all other aspects of trade union activity, strikes lost all semblance of class warfare; they were regarded as commercial moves, calculated to obtain direct and immediate financial advantage. Quite apart from condemning the whole idea of a strike as an enterprise likely to damage the respectability of the trade unions, every strike that actually

1 Cf the following passage from the presidential address at the 1877 Trades Union Congress: 'There are a large number of honourable and respectable employers who do their utmost to give their workpeople good wages, and make every necessary arrangement for them whilst at work. This class of employers never find fault with trade unions; they know the workers are right, and that their own establishments derive advantage from them. There is a class of employers who are never easy without having their goods produced at a cheaper rate than their neighbours; they go into the market and undersell the more honourable portion of employers. The result of this is clear enough: either the trade unions must deal with the evil by getting the men out on strike, or else the honourable employers must reduce their work-people to the same level.' (Report of the TUC, 1877, p. 11.) In consequence, when attempts at reconciliation failed and industrial conflict ended in strike action, trade unionists were ready to admit that the fault was on both sides and that the authors of the trouble should be sought on their side as well as on that of the employers. Cf, for instance, the presidential address of T. J. Wilkinson to the TUC, 1869 (W. J. Davis, *The British Trades Union Congress*, I, Labour Year Book, Co-operative Printing Society, London, 1910, p. 8).

2 Cited by W. H. G. Armytage, *A. J. Mundella*, Ernest Benn, London, 1951, p. 53.

3 The same motif is repeated again and again. 'I venture to say that we are fools—almost criminals—if we resort to a strike.'—from the presidential address of Thomas Burt to the TUC in 1891. (Report of the TUC, 1891, p. 53.) 'I believe it to be an act of criminal folly to hint of or recommend a strike until all the resources of civilisation have been exhausted in the endeavour to avoid such a forlorn hope; ...' —Samuel Monro, TUC president in 1893. (Report of the TUC, 1893, p. 32.)

took place was, irrespective of its cause, rated in terms of the relations between the extent to which union funds were depleted and the size of the wage increase achieved. In his account of the colliers' strike in 1858 George Howell expressed disapproval on the grounds that during the strike the colliers had lost £45,720 in wages, plus a further £8,005 4s 1d which had been raised by subscription for the benefit of the strikers.[1] Henry Broadhurst also condemned the London gas workers for calling a strike, against his advice, without considering the union's funds.[2] The prevailing view was that unions could flourish only in conditions of industrial peace, and that the strength of the unions was the supreme good, something that was good in itself.[3]

The logical consequence of such an attitude to strikes was that many 'new model' unions instituted far-reaching measures to prevent their being called. Among other steps, the central committees of some unions gradually and permanently deprived their local branches of the right to call a strike, by inserting clauses to that effect in their constitutions.[4] Of all the payments made out of union funds, outlays on strike pay were regarded as the least profitable—virtually a loss, as the budgetary allocations indicate very clearly. Even the most militant 'new model' union, in the most intensive period of strike action in its history, paid out only £108,404 18s for strike action out of a total expenditure of £554,267 10s 6d.[5]

In the fourteen 'new model' unions already referred to, the overall expenditure on strike pay came to £10,140 in 1869, £60,222 in 1879 and £10,906 in 1889. One has only to compare these amounts with the other

1   Howell, *Labour legislation*, p. 116.
2   H. Broadhurst, *Henry Broadhurst, MP: the story of his life*, Hutchinson, London, 1901, p. 60.
3   'A strike is as much a calamity to a Trade Society as it is to anyone else. It is in time of peace, when work is plentiful and wages high, that the society flourishes; the immediate effect of a strike is necessarily to deplete its coffers and circumscribe its resources.' (Ludlow and Jones, *Progress of the working class*, p. 217.)
4   Such rules were inserted in the constitution of the Stonemasons and Ironmoulders (Lloyd, *Trade unionism*, p. 20), the Operative Masons, the Coachmakers and the Amalgamated Society of Carpenters and Joiners. Ludlow and Jones commented on these provisions: 'Surely it is impossible to surround a declaration of war with more precautions and formalities. Would to God it were as difficult for an English Minister to involve the Empire in hostilities as it generally is for a Trade Society to enter upon a strike!' (*Progress of the working class*, p. 29.) The constitution of the Operative Potters put the prevention of strikes in first place. In the event of a local dispute the local branch was to attempt to reach a settlement within its own sphere; if this were unsuccessful, the dispute was to be referred to the regional office, and thence to union headquarters. Only the latter could decide, if all efforts to reach a settlement failed, whether strike action was necessary. (Cole and Filson, *British working class movements*, p. 475.)
5   Howell, 'Trade unionism', p. 217.

types of expenditure given in table 6, to understand the part which strike action played in union activity as a whole.[1] It would be hard to find a more classic expression of the philosophy on which this approach to union activity was based than Broadhurst's comment on the annual report of trade union activities: 'We congratulate the trades on the comparative industrial peace experienced since our last meeting. No great national labour contest has occurred to strain the resources of our unions or to disturb the relations between capital and labour.[2]

Table 8

Increase in the membership of some friendly societies in the second half of the nineteenth century

Name of society	Period covered	Amount of increase
Foresters	1854–84	527,535
Grand United Oddfellows	1874–84	34,654
Shepherds	1874–84	6,697
Rechabites	1879–84	18,000
United Ancient Druids	1877–84	4,692
National United Free Gardeners	1874–84	7,000
Nottingham Imperial Oddfellows	1874–84	10,068
National Oddfellows	1874–84	9,000
United Mechanics	1876–84	4,131
Sons of Temperance	1874–84	8,000

Source J. F. Wilkinson, *The friendly society movement*, Longmans, London, 1891, p. 221.

The same kind of thinking inspired the friendly societies, which reached their stormy heyday in the years between 1850 and 1890. The commission set up to conduct an enquiry into the activities of such societies reported that towards the end of this period there were 32,000 friendly societies in England and Wales, with a total membership of four million, and £11 million in their current accounts.[3] The speed at which the societies developed is shown in table 8, which gives figures for some of the better known friendly societies.

The large number and variety of friendly societies derived in large measure from the residual guild tradition, and the period of their efflor-

1 *Ibid.*, pp. 121–3.
2 Report of the TUC, 1888, p. 13.
3 Baernreither, *English associations of working men*, pp. 162–3.

escence was drawing to an end. A number of small friendly societies were still winning new members and enlarging their funds, but there was also an increasing trend towards concentration in accordance with the general laws of capitalism. One indication of this was that the proportional increase in membership and funds of the largest societies was faster than that of the smaller ones. Table 9 gives some figures illustrating the growth of the two largest friendly societies.

Table 9

The growth of the two largest friendly societies over the period 1872–89

		1872	1882	1884	1889
1	The Grand United Oddfellows (Manchester Unity)				
	(*a*) No. of members	436,918	550,352	593,850	651,890
	(*b*) No. of lodges	3,551	3,565	–	–
	(*c*) Capital assets	–	–	£6,034,587	£7,301,186
2	The Ancient Order of Foresters				
	(*a*) No. of members	400,217	531,987	633,288	675,918
	(*b*) No. of lodges	3,738	3,957	–	–
	(*c*) Capital assets	–	–	£3,584,165	£4,392,662

Source Wilkinson, *The friendly society movement*, pp. 112–13.

The friendly societies were even more deeply rooted in the guild tradition than the 'new model' trade unions. As a rule they preserved the whole set of magic oaths, formulae, passwords, rites and bizarre mythological explanations of a particular organisation's name and offices, all of which had been discarded by the unions and were in ludicrous contrast to the societies' hard-headed commercial operations. Certainly, the strongly emphasised antiquity of the friendly societies succeeded in attracting the new artisans. The latter, like most converts, were particularly sensitive about the traditions of the community which had only just become theirs.

The friendly societies also provided a social arena in which the new artisans came into contact with independent tradesmen, shopkeepers, shop assistants and other members of the town middle class—for this was the social cross-section from which most of those who made use of the friendly societies' services were drawn.[1] These contacts helped to shape their ambitions, their views on their own interests and their *mores*, with a single, shared lower middle class mentality; in particular, they furthered the assimilation by the new artisans of lower middle class culture in its ready-made form.

In many respects the friendly societies fulfilled the role of guarantors of the social security of their members more thoroughly than did the unions. When he paid his contributions to a friendly society the skilled worker got in return the certainty that in his old age he would not have to face the workhouse or almshouse which awaited the infirm labourer. This consciousness of social security served to link the stratum of skilled workers even more closely with capitalist society; it also inclined them to the defence of peace and order within that society, since there must be order if they were to achieve the reward of their lifelong exertions.

A similar kind of social influence was exerted by the co-operative movement, also expanding at a tremendous rate during this period. This simultaneous development of three kinds of labour organisation, all equally subordinated to commercial principles and the laws of the capitalist market, probably gives the best idea of the position of the skilled workers in the social structure of the time. It is worth stressing that the ideas of the consumers' co-operative movement had been propagated in England for some while, but they had fallen on unprepared ground and had therefore had no lasting results. In the second half of the nineteenth century, however, the situation changed completely. The change was initiated by the setting up of the Rochdale Equitable Pioneers, an organisation founded on sound commercial principles (which included, *inter alia*, an absolute prohibition of credit sales). This meant the exclusion from membership of the mass of unskilled workers, as was the case with the trade unions and friendly societies. The Rochdale Pioneers also adopted the principle of paying a dividend based on the value of goods purchased by each member. This not only put the better-off workers in a privileged position but was equitable from the viewpoint of commercial good sense. In the auxiliary enterprises which it set up, the co-operative movement applied prevailing capitalist norms for the hiring of labour to its workers and officials. As G. D. H. Cole tells us, 'the Co-operative Manufacturing Society was converted into an ordinary profit-making concern'.[2]

In consequence the co-operative movement flourished, with a total in

1   Baernreither, *English associations of working men*, pp. 221–5.
2   G. D. H. Cole, *A century of co-operation*, Allen & Unwin, London, for the Co-operative Union, Manchester, 1947, p. 90.

1881 in England alone of 971 branches, 547,000 members and an annual turnover of nearly £15½ million.[1] Moreover, it made a major contribution to the establishment of living conditions for skilled workers of a kind which linked them more and more closely with capitalist society.

In the literature concerned with the history of labour organisations in Britain one not infrequently encounters an over-simplified view which maintains that the main objective of their activities during the period under discussion was to improve the material living conditions of the contemporary aristocracy of workers. Such an interpretation can be based only on a simplification of the processes which produced the conformist and even conservative attitude of particular sections of the working class. The struggle to improve its material lot and to achieve a certain degree of social security was only one element in the process by which the stratum of skilled workers was integrated into society—the process by which the stratum moved upwards along the value scales prevailing in that society and deriving from its socio-economic system.

The documents which relate to this period leave no doubt that this was the case. All the workers' organisations were concentrating on efforts aimed at gaining for the new artisan stratum greater social prestige (also within the scope of the concepts accepted in capitalist conditions) to the point of achieving its total assimilation in the system of capitalist relationships.[2]

The new-style trade unionists regarded the elimination of any kind of special legislation concerned with workers as an essential part of their emancipation. They were particularly concerned to ensure that any privilege they gained should have no tinge of charity, but should derive from the laws operative in society as a whole. In accepting the low position of their class and giving up any excessive aspirations to upward social mobility they demanded in return that capitalist society should recognise

---

1 *Ibid.*, p. 179.

2 At the 1875 TUC an essay competition on the trade unions was set by Alexander MacDonald. The entry which gained first prize contained the following views: 'The raising of the rate of wages is undoubtedly the principal means to that end [the bettering of conditions for members], but to say it is the "sole aim" is to mistake the one for the other . . . Unlike most kinds of individual effort, the object is not to assist men to lift themselves out of their class, as if they were ashamed of it, or as if manual labour were a disgrace, but to raise the class itself in physical well-being and self-estimation.' (Quoted by Jeffreys, *Labour's formative years*, pp. 41–2.) A leaflet published in 1865 by the National Council of Practical Miners, the 'new model' miners' union, contained the following appeal: 'Join yourselves at once into Lodges . . . Do this and you will not only emancipate yourselves but secure respect and esteem.' (Quoted by Cole and Filson, *British working class movements*, p. 249.)

their stratum as an integral component of that society, subject to the prevailing civic codes and norms.[1]

The goal of the unions was to ensure that the skilled worker achieved a legally protected occupational status similar to that possessed by the members of the liberal professions. This was the extent of their occupational aspirations, and the criterion of success for union activity. The struggle to restrict the recruitment of apprentices was based on something more than economic considerations. It was equally, if not primarily, concerned to accentuate the distinction between those who belonged to the skilled occupations and the undifferentiated masses of factory workers, and to secure social recognition for the prestige due to the skilled trades. The object was to increase the social distance between the artisan stratum and the remainder of the working class.[2]

It has already been pointed out that the great bulk of the new artisans displayed no ambition to clear a path for their elite into the higher spheres of national life, particularly into the ranks of the country's political elite. Their position in society restricted them to much more modest aims. Moreover, it was characteristic of them that when individual union leaders were appointed by liberal administrations to government office (not, incidentally, to the highest posts) this was regarded as a matter for pride, as yet another manifestation of recognition of the stratum's social worth. This pride contained no element of aspiration to attain political control,

---

1   In an electoral address in 1852 William Newton said, 'Bare [subsistence] is not all that is required. The labourers of the country do not require charity, but the independence of honest labour . . .' (*Reynolds' Newspaper*, 25 April 1852.) George Potter, president of the TUC, said in 1871 that if there was one thing they had to demand more than another it was that the working men who belonged to trade organisations should be free from exceptional legislation. (Davis, *The British Trades Union Congress*, p. 15.)

2   Cf the following extract from the rules of the Journeymen Steam-Engine Machine Makers, and Millwrights' Friendly Society: '"The youth who has the good fortune and inclination for preparing himself as a useful member of society by the study of physics, and who studies that profession with success so as to obtain his diploma from the Surgeons' Hall or College of Surgeons, naturally expects, in some measure, that he is entitled to privileges to which the pretending quack can lay no claim;" . . . He [the skilled worker] is therefore urged to join the society, which aims at securing the same protection of his trade against interlopers as is enjoyed by the learned professions.' (Quoted by S. and B. Webb, *The history of trade unionism*, p. 218.) The artisan printers usually called their occupation not a 'trade' but a profession, and often stressed that it was worthy to be ranked within the aristocracy of the working classes. (*Typographical Gazette*, June 1846.) The compositors maintained that the object of their union was . . . 'to advance the claims of their profession to that rank among the working classes of England, to which it is predestined by virtue of its intellectual character and higher utility.' (*Compositors' Chronicle*, September 1840.)

or even a greater influence on government, which remained in the hands of other classes.[1]

In its endeavours to achieve a recognised position in society the stratum of skilled workers had no aggressive designs on the privileges of the classes above them in the social hierarchy. On the contrary, they protested strongly against any insinuations about their rebellious tendencies arising out of memories of their Chartist past.[2] Their leaders missed no opportunity of emphasising that the avoidance of all manifestations of hostility towards the employers was a natural trait of union activity—a trait that was regarded as a virtue.[3]

The objective of the skilled workers' organisations, pursued with all their strength, was to make the capitalist class acknowledge them as suitable bodies with which to co-operate and as solid partners who merited respect. Step by step they achieved this recognition in wider and wider circles.[4]

The political activities of the unions were exceptionally meagre by comparison with the scale of those undertaken in later periods, and they should

1 Broadhurst commented on his appointment as under-secretary at the Home Office in 1884: 'I think we are making great and rapid progress. The days are fast coming when mere rank and pedigree will no longer take the premier position in the country, for brains and moral worth, capacity and patriotism are fast assuming the superiority over the ancient privileges of birth and family.' (Report of the TUC, 1884, p. 28.) In his presidential address F. Maddison made the following comment on the appointments of Broadhurst and Burt: '... in a very signal manner the unionists of this country were honoured by the elevation of our late secretary (Mr Broadhurst) to a responsible place in the Ministry ... These are significant signs of the times and reflect great credit upon the Ministers who brought them about.' (Report of the TUC, 1886, p. 25.)

2 A resolution referring to the Criminal Law Amendment Act which was proposed by Potter and carried unanimously by the 1873 TUC contained the following passage: 'This Congress, consisting of representatives from lawful associations, repudiates all intention of conspiracy with a view to the injury of an individual or any class of individuals, and indignantly protests against the law, under whatever form or name, which renders workmen liable to such an odious charge ...' (Report of the TUC, 1873, p. 3.)

3 Cf the commendation of the Congress proceedings by the president in his summing up in 1887: 'The tenth annual trade congress was, on the whole, moderate in tone and altogether free from anything like bitterness towards employers or invective against society.' (Report of the TUC, 1877, p. 32.)

4 As an ironmaster wrote (in a letter quoted by W. Trant), 'I look upon Trade Unions as admirable training schools for the workmen, where they will soon outgrow their theories on the subject of capital and labour ... The uneducated workmen are, as a rule, a rather violent set of fellows, it will be admitted; but I can see that, under the training and leadership of the foremost men in the Unions, they are fast becoming a very small minority, as they are very plainly and forcibly told that the old way of settling disputes with their employers is about the very worst that could be adopted.' (Quoted from W. Trant, *Trade unions*, Kegan Paul, London, 1884, p. 163.)

be assessed as an element in the skilled workers' aspiration to achieve general social acceptance for the social prestige of their situation. Such activities were in no way the consequence of any desire to take over political power.

In essence, the entire political activity of the 'new model' unions was marginal, playing no decisive part in union life. The tasks which the trade union movement was built up to perform did not require the intervention of Parliament or of the executive for their success. On the contrary, the unions, being subject to the overall laws of a bourgeois economy, were set up in some sense on commercial lines; they thus required a field of activity that was free from State intervention, a 'free market' for the play of economic factors. In consequence, they took extremely little interest in Parliament. Time and again short-lived campaigns were started up to secure representation for the workers in the House of Commons, but they always took place on the fringes of the trade union movement. As institutions representing occupational and not class interests, the unions naturally had no need to bid for influence in Parliament. Moreover, their activities were dispersed, with only sporadic collaboration, usually for a single operation, whereas an assault on the portals of the House of Commons could ultimately be carried out only by the united forces of the union movement as a whole.

In the first half of the nineteenth century, therefore, there were only a few attempts to co-ordinate union activity. One such attempt was the National Association of United Trades for the Protection of Industry and the Employment of Labour in Agriculture and Manufacture—an organisation with an impressive name but little influence. It arose about 1848 and quietly expired a few years later.[1]

Of much greater consequence was the London Working Men's Association, founded in the 1860s by George Potter; this set itself the ambitious task of correlating the fragmented operations of the whole existing union movement towards goals that were not only union-oriented but also political and social.[2] The Association gained a certain influence among London unions, but the most important unions, which were also those most representative of the 'new model' unions, stayed outside. Moreover, there was no discernible tendency among trade unions to unite. What was significant was the differences between occupations, which at that time had no common characteristics or interests in terms of which their actions could be measured and compared.

For extraneous reasons this situation suddenly changed at the beginning of 1867, when the Boilermakers' Society sued the treasurer of its

---

1 Jeffreys, *Labour's formative years*, p. 87.
2 Cole and Filson, *British working class movements*, p. 561.

Bradford branch in order to recover £24 which he owed the society. The
union referred the case to the local court, which unexpectedly ruled that
trade unions, as organisations with a tendency to act 'in restraint of trade',
were still illegal (although not criminal) organisations; their funds were
therefore also illegal and thus outside the scope of the Friendly Societies
Act of 1855. Appalled by this decision, the union took the case (which had
by then acquired some renown as that of Hornby v. Close) on appeal to
the High Court, which confirmed the original ruling. This set up a legal
precedent, with the unions suddenly finding themselves in the situation
of illegal associations, deprived of State protection. It is easy to imagine the
gloom of union officials faced with the prospect that henceforward looting
the union's till would be an act that would go unprosecuted by the courts
and could thus be done with impunity. The court ruling struck with equal
force at the social position of the unions, particularly because it cast doubt
on their civic rights and their overall soundness as institutions.

As a consequence of these two immediate threats, the sporadic attempts
at co-ordination, which had brought no results for so long, at last fell on
more fruitful ground in the trade union world. Two months after the
court ruling, not one but two union conferences were called in London
to debate measures aimed at achieving two goals: to obtain for the unions
the same rights as those possessed by other incorporated bodies and to
ensure that representatives of the trade unions should sit on the Royal
Commission appointed in 1867 to investigate the whole subject of trade
unionism, following the Sheffield outrages of 1866. One of the two conferences was known as the St Martin's Hall Conference, the other as the
Conference of Amalgamated Trades. They were called simultaneously
and in competition. The first, which was led by Potter, adopted a more
radical attitude. The second was led by the so-called 'Junta', a group of
the leaders of the most powerful 'new model' unions, whose chief care it
was to ensure that no irresponsible persons should appear before the commission in the role of representatives of the trade union movement.[1]

The first two years of link-ups between unions were filled with bitter
strife between the two rival nuclei. The Junta's victory was, however,
inevitable, being determined by the essential character of the union
movement at that period. The danger threatening the very foundations of
the 'new model' unions was so great that a lower priority was given to
secondary differences dividing the two rival groups. Under Junta pressure
Potter dropped the more radical points in his programme; and a notice
summoning union representatives to meet on 14 October at the Bell Inn,
for the first Trade Union Congress was signed by all the most important

1   Armytage, *Mundella*, pp. 50–100; A. E. Musson, *The Congress of 1868*, TUC, London,
    1955, pp. 21–40.

leaders of the trade union movement, from the radicals to the extreme conservatives.[1]

Thereafter Congress met every year, its proceedings being almost entirely devoted to the two objectives which had led its member societies to join forces. At this stage of its existence Congress constituted some kind of pressure group, called annually to promulgate a definite campaign. The unions' spokesman in the Commons was the radical MP A. J. Mundella, a Nottingham hosiery manufacturer, who had introduced a system of industrial conciliation in his own works by agreement with the union—a concept that was taken up with alacrity by the union as a whole. Persistent pressure on public opinion by Congress and on the House of Commons by Mundella resulted in the passing in 1871 of a Bill giving legal recognition to the unions, and enabling them to protect their funds by registering under the Friendly Societies Act. The passing of this legislation contained indications of the fact that middle class opinion took an increasingly sober and realistic view of the 'revolutionary' character of the new generation of trade unionists and the extent to which they constituted a 'threat' to the existing capitalistic order. The unions' lengthy struggle to achieve the rights of citizenship in a capitalist society was producing results.

The second part of the desired legislation, exempting trade unionists from responsibility under the Criminal Law Amendment Act for their organisational activities, was passed by Parliament only in 1874. Thus in the sixth year of its life the objectives which Congress had been set up to achieve were attained. The extent to which Congress's activities were concentrated on securing the desired legislation during this period is shown by the fact that a considerable number of trade unionists considered that the 1875 Congress should be the last, and that the TUC had no further work to do.[2]

The TUC nevertheless survived this critical period. It is difficult to say definitely to what extent its survival was dependent on the growing habit

1   The proclamation was signed by Allan, Applegarth, Guile, Odger, Coulson, Potter, Dunning, Howell, Shipton and Leicester. Potter's militant organ, *The Beehive*, which was later taken over by the Junta, commented that these names had not appeared together for a very long time, a fact which indicated the serious nature of the crisis which had led to the reconciliation. *The Beehive*, 26 September and 3 October 1868.

2   This view was expressed in a speech by the chairman of the TUC's Parliamentary Commission, Mr J. D. Prior, at the 1875 congress: 'The Criminal Law Amendment Act has been repealed; instead of the old Masters and Servants Act, there is a better one in existence now; . . . we do not want so much legislation now that these penal laws have been amended . . . It has been prophesied that the Newcastle Congress would not be a success. It has been said by some people that the questions which led to their establishment have passed away, and that we do not want any more congresses in the future.' (Report of the TUC, 1875, p. 5.)

among union leaders of getting together to discuss certain problems—or on the desire to conserve the potential influence gained during the period of Parliamentary lobbying. There was also an element of inertia arising out of the organisation which had grown up over this period, equipped with an embryonic administrative and bureaucratic apparatus. The Congresses, therefore, continued to meet annually, although over the next fifteen years the proceedings were rendered increasingly colourless by the limited aspirations and growing conservatism of the 'new model' unions; these features also deprived the unions' superstructures of expansionist tendencies and practical influence on the development of either the labour movement or the course of national politics. It was only in the next phase, when the mass of skilled workers became socially aware, that the organisation which had been created for other ends and was virtually in a state of vegetation suddenly took on new life.

The endeavours to secure Parliamentary representation for the workers were renewed sporadically; they constituted the second element in the political activities of the 'new model' unions. During the period under discussion the unions never, not even in their most radical publications, made any claims that workers' representatives should gain control of Parliament with the aim of changing national policy and carrying out some specifically working class programme. In principle their aspirations were confined to the notion of finding a place in Parliament, side by side with the representatives of various land-owning and industrial interest groups, for representatives of the interests of different working occupations. Comments on the class-bound nature of Parliament were rarely heard, and this, indeed, was true of class warfare in general. Parliament was seen as an assembly of experts from different spheres of social life, whose purpose it was to order the affairs of the country in as professional a way as possible. The representatives of the trade unions would be experts on labour questions, experts whose absence from Parliament was felt acutely. Their presence would mean that factory legislation would be worked out with greater expertise, and this would be an advantage to a government that was managing national affairs on behalf of all interest groups.

This argument was repeated without variation during each successive election campaign. It would appear, however, that it was a faithful reflection of the motives behind the trade union movement's interest in Parliament during the early period. Later it was to persist through force of habit, since union activity in this sphere had come to be motivated by entirely different factors, which will be discussed later.

The first period of union interest in Parliamentary affairs was in the years which preceded the setting up of the TUC. Surviving documentary evidence indicates that in different years over this period at least four organisations were concerned with the question of workers' representation in the House of Commons.[1] These organisations not only propagated the idea of extending the suffrage but also attempted to put up working class candidates for Parliament. Nevertheless, none of them managed to reach the masses. In this early period emphasis was only occasionally placed on the working class origin of candidates;[2] instead the stress was usually laid only on the fact that they should represent the interests of the workers irrespective of the milieu from which they sprang.

In the second period—following immediately on the setting up of the TUC—the motif of working class origins became predominant. In the manifesto *Our platform*, published by the London Working Men's Association in 1867, there was a clear demand that 'men who had actually experienced working class disabilities'[3] should be got into Parliament; considerations relating to the political programme were relegated to second place. The manifesto did not envisage that MPs of working class origins would carry out any separate working class policy. What was important was the actual fact of their presence in Parliament.[4]

The Labour Representation League, formed in 1869 and working with the TUC, set itself the goal of introducing working men to Parliament 'without reference to opinion or party bias'.[5] From that time onwards this approach was to become increasingly important. In Parliamentary campaigns the primary objective was to open up the gates of Parliament—the 'best club in London'—to carefully selected representatives of the working class community.[6]

1 They were the Northern Reform Union, the Manhood Suffrage and Vote by Ballot Association, the National Reform Union, and the National Reform League. (Cole and Filson, *British working class movements*, pp. 518 *et seq.*)
2 Cf for example, Gillespie, *A hundred years of progress*, pp. 97–102.
3 G. D. H. Cole, *British working class politics*, Routledge, London, 1941, pp. 43–4.
4 The same text contains the following sentiments: 'Providing a careful selection of working class candidates be made, there is no reason why they should stand isolated as a class in Parliament any more than the special representatives of other interests now sitting there . . . We believe that after the first novelty of their appearance in the House has worn off, they will, insensibly and imperceptibly, blend with the other members in the performance of the usual duties expected from members of the Legislature . . . We presume that the working class candidate, in addressing a constituency, would do as all other candidates do—appeal to the electors generally, and not to those of a particular interest.' (*Ibid.*)
5 Humphrey, *History of labour representation*, p. 33.
6 Cf the following references to this aspect of the matter at annual Trades Union Congresses. From a resolution proposed by Broadhurst in 1873 (and adopted): 'This meeting calls upon all trade societies to put forward and suggest at the coming general election candidates of their own class.' (Report of the TUC, 1873, p. 6.) In 1874 as many as five separate and independent resolutions were put forward relating to this matter. (Report of the TUC, 1874, p. 28.) In 1876 John Batkin, of

Leaving aside all other marginal considerations, therefore, the union movement's Parliamentary interests went through three basic phases. The first was concerned with representation for occupational interests in the political arena of Parliament; the second with opening up a road into Parliament for MPs of working class origins. The third was concentrated clearly and explicitly on making seats in Parliament available for leading trade unionists. These three phases are like three concentric circles, each smaller than the last, and they point to an important social phenomenon— the birth and consolidation of the new social elite of the labour movement. This elite nursed growing aspirations; it was geared towards the higher strata of the social hierarchy, unlike its own stratum as a whole, which barely aspired to lower middle class levels. Its Parliamentary interests were the sum of the interaction of two forces: pressure from the skilled workers' stratum as a whole to achieve mobility for that stratum as a whole up one more rung of the ladder of the capitalist social order, and pressure from the elite of that stratum, seeking to advance higher on the ladder than the rung which would ultimately be attained by the stratum as a whole. The second force was reinforced by the first: it owed its vitality to the dynamism of the first force and became weaker when the dynamism decreased. The social energy of the stratum of skilled workers in its striving for social emancipation was sufficiently strong to secure the entry of some five to eight leading trade unionists into Parliament; more than this number, however, it could not manage.

Moreover, from the moment when the basic demands of the skilled workers were met—in other words, when the social prestige and socio-economic status of the stratum had reached a level which accorded with the possibilities arising out of the new position it had assumed in the social structure—its social dynamism, organisational flexibility and capacity

Birkenhead, said, in a speech dealing with working class representation in Parlia-ment, that 'such classes and interests should be represented by men identified with the class and interests they represented, and who by association, general experience, culture and abilities were most likely to know the requirements of their constituents, and were most competent to take an intelligent and disinterested part in the councils of the nation . . .' (Report of the TUC, 1876, p. 21.) Seven years later Mr Garrie, from Barrow in Furness, proposed as an amendment to the resolution that 'none but duly qualified trade unionists be recognised labour candidates'. Replying, Mr J. Battersby (Glasgow) pointed out, with reference to the proposed amendment, that 'a hundred different definitions of who was a *bona fide* working man might be made. Some might be inclined to say that Mr Broadhurst, who had ably represented the cause of labour in Parliament, was a *bona fide* working man.' Mr Bailey (Rotherham) thought they had had 'quite enough of gentlemen from London to undertake these duties' and that they wanted 'men like Mr Burt and Mr Broadhurst'. (Report of the TUC, 1883, pp. 43-4.) With each year that passed the debate focused increasingly on the demand that the trade union elite should be elected to Parliament.

to exert effective pressures suddenly began to decrease. In consequence. the pressure exerted by the elite lost its main driving force. In point of fact the leaders of the working class elite remained within the political elite into which they had been catapulted by the labour movement at the time of its expansion. On the other hand, they no longer relied on the support of the movement, which henceforward dwindled and grew weaker in the atmosphere of conservative complacency that increasingly overwhelmed it. The labour movement went on to achieve stability in the positions of lower middle class prosperity which it had already won—while those branches which had shot up too exuberantly and precociously during the movement's dynamic phase gradually wilted for lack of a supply of life-giving sap. About 1880 the Labour Representation League ceased to exist even on paper.[1] Social security for the stratum had been won and legally guaranteed; there was therefore no reason for further expansion, a process which, like every risky enterprise, would threaten the social standards and position already attained.[2]

Attention should, however, be drawn once again to the fact that, even in the period of their greatest intensity, the Parliamentary interests of the labour movement did not involve the promotion of any independent political conceptions. For example, as William Newton pointed out, his union—the Amalgamated Society of Engineers, which was representative of the 'new model' unions—did not permit the discussion of any political matter.[3] This subordination to occupational, not class, interests led the unions to accept a liberal ideology, and in consequence liberal political policies. In the political arena the unionists as a rule supported the Liberal Party. The support was, however, passive; the unions did not introduce

---

1 Cole, *British working class politics*, pp. 75–6.
2 Here one should draw attention to an identical lack of interest in the legislature shown by Samuel Gompers, the leader and major intellect of the American equivalent of the 'new model' unions. His view was that the workers had no further claim on the legislature once their rights in the labour market were guaranteed. (G. G. Higgins, 'Union attitudes towards economic and social roles of the modern state' Industrial Relations Research Association, *Interpreting the labour movement*, p. 151.) Nevertheless, the later history of relations between the labour movement and the legislature developed along different lines in the United States and Britain. The contemporary situation of the trade unions in the USA may afford a picture of the way in which the British trade unions could have developed if the lines of development set by the 'new model' unions had been preserved, instead of being shattered by the rise of the masses of unskilled workers as they came to life politically. The political institutions would not have become, *inter alia*, a platform for incorporating the working class elite into the political elite of the capitalist State; this process would simply have taken place in the economic sphere, as was the case in the United States. (I shall be discussing this question in more detail in later chapters.)
3 W. Newton, *Masters and workmen*, London, 1856, p. 30.

into the body of Liberal doctrine any element of their own working class programme which had not been there already. This renunciation of an active political role meant in practice an unconditional surrender to the policies of bourgeois liberalism, and also a docile acceptance of the upper classes' monopoly of government.[1]

The second Reform Act of 1867 extended the right to vote, particularly in the boroughs, where it went to all occupiers of houses who had been in residence for at least one year and to lodgers paying £10 or more per annum; this gave the franchise to almost all skilled workers. It did not, however, introduce any new political forces beyond those already engaged in the Parliamentary confrontation. As voters, the skilled workers exerted no perceptible influence on the country's political life. Both electors and candidates from the working class regarded themselves as an inherent component of the Liberal Party and wished to be ranked among its most loyal supporters—possibly in the hope that they would thereby appropriate to themselves a particle of the respectability and glory of that venerable bourgeois party, with its Whig antecedents.[2]

The trade unionists were just as zealous in their defence of the alliance between Liberals and workers as were the Liberal leaders themselves, whose vital interest it was to keep their hold on working class votes. As late as 1895 the leaders of the 'new model' unions sharply attacked the young Independent Labour Party for opposing the Liberal Party, on whose behalf leading trade unionists were standing for Parliament. The ILPs behaviour was, in the view of John Jenkins, chairman of the TUC at that time, anti-labour and anti-trade unionist.[3] The 1895 Congress even went to the length of excluding ILP leaders from taking part in the annual Congresses, by means of a casuistically framed amendment altering the system of representation and voting at Congress.

In consequence, the radical trends that were emerging in British politics during this period—trends that produced the ideological climate in which

---

1   Lloyd Jones, who was the first secretary of the Labour Representation League, commented that the workers had apparently only enlarged the number of electoral districts, without contributing a single plank to the Liberal platform. (*Industrial Review*, 27 July 1878.)

2   Broadhurst, who was the successful Liberal candidate in Stoke on Trent in 1880, regarded his victory simply as a victory for the Liberal Party from the political angle: 'We have won a glorious and honourable victory—a victory which is already flashing its news throughout the length and breadth of the land to stimulate our fellow Liberals to still greater exertions in the contest to come.' (Quoted from H. Hopkinson, 'The life of Henry Broadhurst', MS, British Library of Political and Economic Science, London, p. 31.) The reference to 'our fellow Liberals' must have given Broadhurst great satisfaction, for it was a victory in itself.

3   Report of the TUC, 1895, p. 28.

'British socialism[1] was to be born a little later—developed outside the framework of the labour movement of the time. They developed without its co-operation and even in the face of its unequivocal hostility. Men like Joseph Chamberlain and Charles Dilke, who put forward a wide-ranging programme of social legislation that was the ideological grandparent of the welfare State concept, were members of the middle class and represented the views of the more far-sighted groups within that class. The stratum of skilled workers, at that time the only socially active stratum in the working class, was still deeply involved in classic liberal conceptions of the 'welfare factory' and regarded the liberal radicals as disturbers of the social order in which it was vitally interested.

The reason for the peculiar position adopted by the trade union movement towards politics and Parliamentary government has already been discussed. It was due to the fact that the struggle in Parliament for working class representation was based on a wish to ensure for those in the growing vanguard of the movement far-reaching possibilities of upward social mobility. A good if unintended instance of this kind of motivation is to be found in Broadhurst's comment after the 1878 elections in Stoke on Trent: 'I observed that the work people of these towns is the most intelligent and broad-minded of any industrial communities I had hitherto met. Their one desire was that I should succeed and to ensure my success they wisely recognised the necessity of obtaining the support of all classes.'[2] In Broadhurst's eyes, a desire that he should win was a criterion of the intelligence and other intellectual qualities of the working population. It was also his justification for diluting working class demands in a solution of middle class liberalism.

To sum up the findings in this chapter: the labour movement of the period served to institutionalise the parochial interests of particular trades. At the same time it was the sum of two pressures towards social mobility: that of the stratum which was seeking to free itself from the amorphous mass of factory workers; and that of the elite of this stratum, seeking to clear a road along which individual members could advance further up the social ladder. In practice, both pressures were an expression of the labour movement's increasing integration in middle class society, its structure and hierarchy of values, a process disclosed by the exceptional intensification of conformist trends.

---

1   *British socialism* is the subject of my own earlier study of that title, published in Polish in Warsaw in 1959.
2   Broadhurst's autobiography, p. 95.

3
The structure of the elite
of the labour movement

The changes that were taking place in the structure of the working class shaped the model of the labour movement. In its turn the structure of the labour movement determined the most essential characteristics of the stratum which led the movement.

This particular period in the history of the labour movement was distinguished by, *inter alia*, the rise of a working class elite created by the movement itself. The two elements essential to this process, hitherto lacking had now made their appearance: First, the new structure and function of the labour movement permitted its leadership to be recruited from the ranks of the working class itself. Second, as the movement achieved stability the leadership also was transferred into a relatively stable structure, whose key position within the movement was based on comparatively dependent foundations.

The above statement refers exclusively to the 'new model' union movement. While the labour movement of the Victorian era was not confined to the 'new model' movement, the latter was nevertheless its most important branch, exerting a decisive influence on the profile of the whole. For this reason I propose to concentrate on the processes by which elites were formed in the 'new model' unions.

These processes were based on a series of changes that were taking place in both the structure of the working class and that of the labour movement.

In the first half of the nineteenth century the trade clubs of the journeymen craftsmen had not accorded their officers any additional prestige deriving from the union functions they performed; nor had any special qualifications been required from them which the average member of the club did not possess. In the 'new model' unions, on the other hand, the situation underwent a fundamental change. The unions were gradually evolving into organisations which in size and functions were not far removed from friendly societies, or indeed commercial undertakings: they administered considerable funds, were burdened with many administrative tasks and carried out extensive and varied operations. The administration of such organisations required people of wide horizons, exceptional abilities, a developed administrative sense and the capacity to think in categories beyond the experience of their own backgrounds. In short, it required qualifications that were not an indispensable characteristic of the social stratum within which the movement was arising. The occupational proficiency of the skilled worker did not accustom him to the techniques of large-scale leadership or of carrying out large financial transactions. In this he differed from the journeyman craftsman, who had to be familiar not only with the secrets of his trade but also with the management of an independent workshop. In consequence, the running of a 'new model' union demanded additional qualifications beyond the capacity of the rank-and-file members. This led to the emergence of objective grounds for the formation of a qualified elite, owing its position as an elite to the mechanism of the labour movement and dependent on the latter for its own existence.

This differentiation of qualifications made it possible to differentiate objectively in terms of social prestige. The performance of functions that required a particular skill conferred a particular aura on members of the nascent elite by qualification—an aura deriving not from the special qualities which they possessed, independently of the movement, in the outside world, but from the fact that they were in charge of union affairs. Whereas the chairman of a journeymen's club enjoyed only such prestige as was conferred on him by his craft qualifications and occupational success, the leader of a 'new model' union enjoyed prestige deriving from the fact that he was the union's leader. Moreover, his qualifications as a one-time worker or craftsman ceased to play any part in his union career. The qualities that created his prestige lay in his organisational and administrative qualifications, as measured by the successes achieved by the union, not in qualifications which were measured by the success of a private workshop. The conditions thus arose for the formation of an elite of prestige as well, an elite which, like the elite by qualification, was strongly based in the union movement itself, and not in formations external to it.

Because of their increasing size and bulging coffers, the labour organisations required both administrative continuity and regular attention from those charged with their administration. It was no longer sufficient for union officials to perform their functions on a part-time basis in their leisure time. The rotation of different teams of officials was also highly damaging to the activities of the organisation and the extension of its social influence. Moreover, the rotatory system was hampered by the fact that the number of individuals who possessed the fairly high qualifications required by the new union structure was comparatively small. In consequence, the running of a union gradually became a paid occupation. This enabled the new teams of leaders to devote themselves entirely to union work, instead of dividing their time between that and their jobs. At the same time the system of rotation was gradually being replaced by stability of tenure among office holders. All in all, these two processes were encouraging the rise of the full-time union official. A union leader was no

longer a workman or a tradesman, occupationally linked to the same group
of people from which membership of his organisation was recruited. He
was a union official by profession. As a result of this occupational separation, the elite by qualification and prestige within the labour movement
could gradually separate itself off into a more or less isolated stratum; it
could create its own internal variants of the social bond, shape its autonomous interests to a certain extent, and so on. In short, it could transform
itself into a comparatively permanent stratum with its own heritage of
social characteristics.

The increased size and changed functions of the union organisation also
made it less easy for rank-and-file members to influence the direction
of union affairs as these grew in complexity and changed in character.
Financial problems in particular were coming to the fore, and these had, by
their very nature, to be handled consistently and efficiently. This meant
that the number of officials in direct charge of affairs had to be limited.
Quite apart from any difficulties of communication, the transition from
journeymen's clubs to unions with their thousands of members was a
transition from small assemblies to large agglomerations receptive to
stimuli of an irrational type. This made it all the more necessary to limit
the size of the group that was actually in charge of union affairs; it also
necessitated the emergence of a power elite, a set of people who would have
a greater share in the taking of vital decisions in the life of the union.

Associated with the phenomena already described, we can picture the
formation of an elite of the labour movement as a stratum differentiated,
on the basis of occupations, in terms of all three criteria—expertise,
prestige and power. I have tried in the previous chapter to show the inter-
dependence of the three criteria of the process by which these elites were
formed.[1]

1 Different elements in this process, generally in abstraction from one another, have
   been discerned and described by various authors. Here are some examples from
   the works of the Webbs and Baernreither. 'The attempt to secure the participation
   of every member in the management of his society was found to lead to instability
   in legislation, dangerous unsoundness of finance, and general weakness of administration. The result was the early abandonment of the initiative, either by express
   rule or through the persistent influence of the executive.' (S. and B. Webb, *Industrial
   democracy*, Longmans, London, 1897, p. 26.) 'Self-government in the workers has
   developed a level of official class. The hierarchical composition of these unions, the
   necessity of carrying out large schemes of organisation and actuarial business, conducting the publications of the order, and arranging the general meetings, have led
   to the appointment of permanent secretaries. These are standing, salaried officials . . .
   Practically, however, they are far more than mere executive organs of the central
   committee, since they represent the permanent element of administration as
   opposed to the changing composition of the committees.' (Baernreither, *English
   associations of working men*, p. 224.) The only new element which Michels added to

The formation of the stratum of union officials was not an automatic or straightforward process. The potential candidates for this new-born stratum stressed the increasingly urgent objective need for it. Against this need, however, was ranged the passive but persistent resistance of the mass of members, who were attached to the built-in democratic traditions of trade unionism. It was fairly characteristic of the stratum of new skilled workers that resistance to the setting up of a permanent officialdom would take the form of financial or economic objections, and that it should be overcome by means of arguments of the same nature.[1]

The first full-time union secretaries were closely watched, and every opportunity was taken to cut down the pay which had been allocated to them. Particular care was taken to ensure that their pay should not exceed the earnings of the average skilled worker. Indeed, in many cases it was lower, a circumstance which at times even led to the misappropriation of funds.[2] When the London Trades Council was set up in 1861 its first

his observations was to put together a number of disparate statements in the form of a fundamental law, and to assess the process he was describing from the viewpoint of the assumptions of direct democracy. Seen from this angle, the rise of a permanent executive was synonymous with the alienation of the elite and the destruction of democracy. We cannot accept such a view. The existence of an elite *per se* is not only not a negation of democracy; on the contrary, it is a condition of its functioning. The question of the extent to which democracy exists can be answered only after ascertaining to what extent the activities of the executive elite reflect or oppose the trends that are current in the social circles, class or stratum that constitute the social base of the organisation under discussion. This is why I wish to separate the problems of the elite and the processes that create such an elite from the context with which it has traditionally been entangled, one which has been taken over from Michels by contemporary sociologists. These problems are not concerned with the growth or diminution of democracy, nor in general with making any sort of value judgment. I should like to concentrate exclusively on the following matters: first, on an analysis of the mechanism of the actual process of creating an elite; second, on an analysis of the traits of the elite; and, third, on a comparison of the characteristic traits and trends found in the elite and in the movement which gave birth to it, with the object of discovering what correlations exist between them. On the other hand, I reject the whole 'demoniac' part of Michels' theory, which is weighed down with a pronounced ideological ballast.

1 Mr Baker, the first National Organiser of the National Amalgamated Society of Enginemen, Cranemen, Boilermen, Firemen and Electrical Workers, wrote in his first half-yearly report, 'All kinds of blank ruin were prophesied for the society should an organiser be appointed, some going so far as to say that we would be compelled to withdraw money from the bank to pay him with. Yet the fact remains that we are £440 richer than we were six months ago, having banked this amount during that period.' (Quoted by Sir A. Pugh, *Men of steel*, Iron and Steel Trades Confederation, London, 1951, p. 23.)

2 Such cases were not very frequent. One was that of Thomas Short, general secretary of the stonemasons' union. In 1843 the union cut his weekly pay from 38s to 30s. Short had a wife and children to support and also lived in Birmingham, whereas

secretary, George Odger, was from time to time paid half a crown—which was supposed to represent a weekly salary. It was only the third holder of the secretary's office George Shipton, who succeeded in extracting the arrears of pay owed to his predecessor and in establishing a regularly paid though modest salary for himself at £150 per annum. Here one should recall that at that time this was the most important union office in the whole of England.[1]

In return for these rather modest sums, which kept them within the socio-economic status of the stratum of skilled workers, the full-time managers of the first 'new model' unions, who at the outset were left to their own resources, without any clerical or administrative assistance, were obliged to undertake a vast and wide-ranging set of tasks; these tasks, which demanded immense effort and self-sacrifice, were in later years carried out by a whole staff of officials. The leader of the union, usually the secretary, conducted negotiations; he was simultaneously spokesman and legal expert; he travelled up and down the country to establish new branches, settle disputes with employers and so on.[2] The work of a union leader in the opening phase of union activity required considerable courage and self-sacrifice. It was a good thing if a union leader could, by persuading his union to pay him a regular salary, become independent of the employers' whims. In the reverse case, when he had to earn his living by factory work, he was usually a target for deliberate harassment; if he was not simply dismissed, as happened in earlier times, he was likely to be sent to the worst and most unrewarding jobs, and to be deliberately subjected to unpleasant working conditions.[3]

The annals of the emerging trade union elite are thus full of examples of self-sacrifice, idealism, even heroism. The traits that were to characterise the average trade union official of medium calibre—rigidity, a 'red tape' mentality and insensitivity—made their appearance considerably later; so did the conservatism and self-satisfaction which made stability an organisational ideal. These traits emerged as a result of the operation of the evolving union machinery, and not—as some crude versions would have it—because of the particular qualities of a certain group of individuals

the union's offices were in London. Finding himself unable to get by on so low a sum and being permanently exposed to temptation because he was handling considerable sums of money for the union, Short took a few shillings for himself every now and then. When this was discovered there was a public outcry. Intensified financial checks were introduced for Short's successors in the post, while Short himself was immediately dismissed (Postgate, *The builders' history*, pp. 122–32.)

1   Howell, *Labour legislation*, p. 135.
2   Pugh, *Men of steel*, pp. 58 *et seq.*
3   Cf, for example, N. Edwards, *History of the South Wales Miners' Federation*, Lawrence & Wishart, London, 1938, p. 17.

who had by machiavellian means succeeded in usurping power in the trade union movement.

The traits which characterised the people who formed the first generation of the elite of the British labour movement were a product of the organisation's situation, and the similarity of people who held analogous positions in different unions indicates clearly that cause-and-effect factors of a more comprehensive nature were at work, not simply coincidence. Irrespective of occupational and local differences, the 'new model' unions, as they became stronger, required men with specific qualifications and psychological traits for their management. Such men appeared simultaneously in fairly considerable numbers at the head of the trade union movement.

Unlike the situation which prevailed in the workers' unions of the first half of the century, these people were not outsiders from the ruling classes, rebellious *emigrés* from the middle classes and the aristocracy. They came from the ranks of the workers and were themselves skilled workers who possessed greater abilities, breadth of vision and ambitions than their fellow workers. In common with the rest of their stratum they had extricated themselves from a situation of extreme poverty and humiliation. And in common with their stratum, but more urgently and clearly, they felt the need to strengthen a social position that was a little higher than before, the need to be integrated into a society until recently had been alien and unintelligible to them. They were thus far from any thought of attacking the social order and were appalled by the idea of an intractable mob of workers, prone to facile outbursts. Instead they desired order, harmony, peace and a rational gauging of aims in relation to strength. They saw it as their goal to avoid all disputes with the employer class, which for them personified the solidity and durability of the existing order. They did not wish to destroy the capitalist fortress, but merely knocked humbly at its gates in the hope that they would be let in.[1]

The social programme and organisational conceptions of the new generation of trade union leaders were based on the assumption that even if capitalism were not everlasting, union operations should be organised as if it was. The existence of capitalist social relations was so absolutely recognised as the starting point for all discussions about the tasks of the unions that this recognition was equivalent to an acceptance of them. From the

1 This viewpoint found its fullest theoretical expression in the writings of Howell. 'Mr Frederic Harrison has long been teaching that "order is the law of progress". Pope years ago declared that "order is Heaven's first law". Trade Unions have been more or less inculcating the lesson for at least a generation. The discipline taught by the unions has done much in the propagation of the doctrine and in imposing its authority . . . Threats are dangerous, and they are unnecessary. Violence is indefensible. Intimidation is an irritant, and is valueless as a remedy for labour's wrongs.' (Howell, *Labour legislation*, p. 488.)

moment they became more established, the unions had been built up on this assumption needed to defend the existing order if they were to operate effectively.

As long as the maintenance of capitalism was an axiom, the unions' task was to squeeze every possible benefit out of it. The union leaders, who had a sober and rational assessment of the capabilities of the stratum which had accepted its position at the lower levels of the social hierarchy, realised that their objective would not be achieved without the setting up of a flexible and cohesive organisation to protect occupational privileges. Historical circumstance made the organiser, the administrator, the financial expert and the negotiator the heroes of the day.

Allan, Applegarth, Odger, Coulson and other figures who were representative of the union leadership at this period were first and foremost men who combined a strong and determined character with exceptional administrative ability. While they in no way conformed to the model of the popular charismatic leader so often encountered in earlier decades, they were none the less strong and outstanding men in their own way; men of iron who, in an exceptionally unfavourable climate of opinion, forced through the new conception of legal and loyal trade unions which were essential if capitalist society was to function normally. They were the first men of working class origin in Britain to succeed in the difficult task of constructing trade union organisations that were not only complex and extensive but also lasting and stable. The setting up of organisations that were efficiently administered and financially well endowed was their main task, and the measure of their personal qualities and skills was the increase in the number of members and the size of their unions' bank balances.[1]

1   After the death of John Kane, the founder of the Amalgamated Malleable Iron-
    workers' Association (1862–67) and then of the National Amalgamated Association
    of Ironworkers (1868–74), his wife wrote the following comment in a letter to the
    union: 'The Society was in a very low state when we took over the books in 1868;
    there were but twelve lodges, which numbered not more than five or six hundred
    members, and they were all in the North of England, excepting one in Sheffield. How
    we worked to raise the workmen once more and to give them an interest in them-
    selves will be seen by the increased number of lodges and members we had at the
    Birmingham Conference in 1872 . . . We had then above two hundred branches
    with over 20,000 members not only in the North of England but in North and South
    Staffordshire, Wales and Scotland.' (Quoted by Pugh, *Men of steel*, p. 57.) In the
    mining district of Northumberland, Burt broke decisively with the traditions of
    Chartism and anti-capitalist ideology. This was in contrast to the policy of William
    Crawford in the Durham mines, where he endeavoured to set up the traditional
    forms of union activity. An argument for the superiority of Burt's conception of
    trade unionism was based on the fact that during his tenure of office his union's
    membership rose from 4,250 in 1865 to 17,561 in 1875. This example was also ad-

In the next generation, after the unions had been consolidated and occupied a legalised and permanent place in the social structure, their leaders were colourless men, administrators lacking any individuality, working their way towards the top of the union hierarchy by virtue of an amenable disposition and an ability to adopt the sort of moderate position that would not arouse opposition in any milieu. During the period when the unions were being set up, however, their leadership required a strong will, nerves of steel, unscrupulousness in putting over one's own policy, and a determination to break down every kind of obstruction. For such men a show of polish borrowed from the City was no more than a fig leaf.[1]

The chief strength of the union leaders, however, was their capacity—one typical of businessmen—for concentration on detail, prudence, and assessment of all the pros and cons before taking a decision. The planning of union operations was for them, as for the directors of City companies, a matter of balancing estimated profits and losses. A modest but assured profit was always preferable to a larger one involving risk. The golden rule was that the union's membership or funds should not fall below the level already attained. The characters of the union leaders bore witness to the fact that they had been shaped by contemporary capitalist society to conform to and resemble the positive heroes of the society—the businessmen.[2]

vanced as the reason for Crawford's 'conversion' to Liberalism. (Page-Arnot, *The miners*, p. 53.)

1 Cf the following description of Applegarth: 'Applegarth gained none of his successes by Christian mildness and patience: he had much more of the devil than the angel in him. When younger, he was a restless, dark-faced man, autocratic and brooked no opposition, within or without the union. He could work well and harmoniously with men who, like Coulson, were in close agreement with him. But if a man or an executive defied him, he broke them. He used fair means if he could, foul if he needed. No suspicion of personal motive ever seriously touched him and for that reason he felt the more justified in using the most questionable methods. The Junta, in fighting George Potter, used crooked methods and slander, and the main inspiration of the Junta was Applegarth.' (Postgate, *The builders' history*, p. 184.) It is worth recording that Applegarth's personality, which was ideal for the first years of the 'new model' era, showed itself to be too powerful and individualistic only a few years later, once the unions moved into a new situation of conservative stabilisation, which required a more balanced, legalistic and down-to-earth leadership. Applegarth soon found himself outside the trade union movement, pushed out by the machine which he had helped to create.

2 Broadhurst made personal notes about some trade union leaders who were his contemporaries. These are of sociological importance not only because of the individuals described but also because of the light which they throw on the writer himself. About Allan, Broadhurst wrote, 'His great strength was his marvellous power for detail and administration. He was the sort of man from whom are made the heads of great departments of State. Mr Allen was a man of the highest char-

Given a strong character, combined with far-reaching cautiousness and avoidance of all drastic action, union leaders could establish themselves firmly in office, and these traits furthered their transformation into professional, lifetime officers. In this period, for the first time in the history of the British trade union movement, we find a considerable number of trade union leaders who performed their functions on a life tenure and could not in practice be removed from office.[1]

If the unions were to be drawn into the machinery of capitalistic society, and win recognition from the employers and the State, it was necessary for them to show that they possessed the traits that combined to make up the bourgeois concept of decency or respectability. The quest for this respectability represented the most essential and at the same time the most dramatic chapter in the annals of the leadership of the 'new model' unions. The union leaders showed the utmost zeal in donning the constricting garments of the worthy bourgeoisie. This zeal sprang from their own initiative and their deepest convictions. They spared no effort to cleanse themselves and the organisations they led of the shameful stigma left by the stormy years of the 1830s and 1840s, which they regarded as the mark of their exclusion from society. This was the reason why they condemned the more violent methods of union activity with as much feeling and indignation as did the employers themselves. Frequently they outstripped the ruling classes in their denunciation of the traditional forms of working class self-defence, reckoning that their zeal would gain them the respect of middle class public opinion.[2]

acter and respectability . . . In appearance he gave one the impression of a well-to-do City man.' Of Odger, Broadhurst had this to say: 'George Odger was a man of singularly broad mind and benevolent views. His nature was that of a high-bred gentleman of the olden times, and meanness in any form was an affront to him. He was a most wise counsellor in committee. His caution and care in coming to important decisions were remarkable. This characteristic saved many mistakes and toned down many declamatory resolutions . . . In Congress he always poured oil on the troubled waters . . . Anyone hearing him for the first time would credit him with having a good middle-class education; but such was not the case. All his attainments were the result of self-effort.' (Quoted by Hopkinson, 'Life of Henry Broadhurst', pp. 17, 18.)

1   For instance, in all the trade unions among building workers only one instance is known of a union leader being dismissed (Short). Three more (McGregor, Rennie and Carter) retired at their own request. Others, like Richard Harnott, George Cherry, William Matkin, Edwin Coulson and James Charles Lockett, were officials in perpetuity. (Postgate, *The builders' history*, p. 143.)

2   Howell emphasised this aspect strongly. 'I was personally acquainted with almost every man of prominence in the labour world during these anxious years [the 1860s] and was associated with them in all labour movements; and this I can honestly say, that I never heard one of them excuse or palliate the outrages complained of, much less sanction or condone them. They were as honest in their denunciations

The union leaders gradually worked out a broad range of measures which were intended to lead to the attainment of the desired 'respectability', in line with prevailing and accepted middle class categories and values. To this end the unions' annual budgets were released to the press, and their bank balances were published. Newspaper offices were flooded with monthly reports of the activities of union executives. Public lectures about union matters were held, and endeavours were made to secure the participation of union speakers at academic conferences concerned with social problems. Everything possible was done to ensure that the employers should regard the union organisations as sufficiently respectable for their representatives to be invited to the same conference table without derogating from the dignity of the middle class participants. Starched collars, ties, neat clothes conforming to the prevailing middle class mode, good manners and a solid financial background—all these elements were combined in the most unexpected proportions in the struggle to achieve middle class respectability.

The leaders' concern over the state of union funds was to a large extent derived from the role which those funds were supposed to play as one of the elements essential for carrying the campaign to a successful conclusion. Rayner observed with wit and accuracy that the Junta regarded its funds in the same light as the former king of Prussia his army—rather as a source of prestige than as something to be used in battle.[1] The idea that the people whose power was derived from wealth would treat only wealthy institutions seriously was deeply embedded in the consciousness of the union officials, while the actual process of accumulating union funds obscured the aims for which the process had been initiated.

The conception of a trade union which held sway among the union leaders included the view that it was a function of the union to promote self-improvement among the skilled workers who were its members. 'Self-improvement' was interpreted as 'raising' them to the level of the generally accepted norms of behaviour which bourgeois society recognised

as employers and others, and were far more insistent in their demands for a thorough investigation into all the allegations made than most of their critics.' (Howell, p. 161.) Applegarth gave the following reply to workmen who were refusing to return to work until the employers posted a formal notice of withdrawal of abnoxious conditions which they had in fact abandoned: 'I tell you honestly that if I had been in Birmingham I should have been at my bench side on Monday morning last. Whenever the employers have tried to humiliate you and bring you to your knees I have been in the front to defend you; now you are trying to humiliate the employers I will be no party to it.' (Quoted by M. Cole, *Makers of the labour movement*, Longmans, London, 1948, p. 34.)

1   R. M. Rayner, *The story of trade unionism*, Longmans, London, 1929, p. 34.

as worthy of esteem.[1] Abstinence, self-education, restraint in sexual relations, self-control, thrift, hard and honest work at one's trade—these were the chief elements in the moral campaign undertaken by the unions among the stratum of skilled workers. The proposition that a change of personality must precede social reform was constantly repeated by the union leaders and the need for a strict moral code was the most frequent subject of their public declarations.[2] Simultaneously, the great majority of the leading trade unionists of the period under discussion were actively engaged in the operations of the mushrooming temperance societies, which were stubbornly combating the growing plague of drink in the working class communities. They were also involved in organisations that advocated thrift—a habit as yet unfamiliar to the skilled worker, who had only recently started to earn more money than was sufficient to meet his basic needs; in societies promoting various forms of self-education and popular enlightment;[3] in campaigns against prostitution and sexual licence; and in movements advocating birth control—particularly in application to working class families, which were usually prolific.

    While it is true that the union leaders were recruited from the working class, they came from a particular sector of that class. In fact they were drawn from the small minority of those who had made exceptional efforts and renounced much to reach a certain level of knowledge and education, had found some white-collar occupation and accumulated some savings. The most extreme example of a man drawn from such circles was Alexander Macdonald, the Liberal leader of the mineworkers, who later became an MP. After his day's work in the mines he would study Latin and Greek, and make the journey to a small town several miles away to attend evening classes. After he had graduated he obtained a place at Glasgow University, where he studied on a near-starvation diet; during the summer vacations he worked down the mine to earn money for his studies during the winter. Macdonald's story may be an extreme case, but the urge for some form of self-education and emancipation in one direction or another,

1   Cf, for instance, a statement by Applegarth reported in *The Beehive*, 13 February 1869.
2   Cf a characteristic extract from the rules of the Amalgamated Society of Carpenters and Joiners, passed in 1860: 'We shall be faithless to our fellow working men . . . if we omit to record our honest conviction that this much-to-be-desired condition must be preceded by the equally universal spread of the principles of economy and sobriety, which would be accelerated by our meeting for business in public halls or private rooms, where, by the establishment of libraries and listening to the voice of the lecturer on all subjects connected with our interests, we and our sons should become respectful and respectable, and make rapid progress in the onward march of reform.' (Quoted by Postgate, *The builders' history*, pp. 192–3.)
3   H. L. Beales, 'Has Labour come to stay?' *Political Quarterly*, January–March 1947.

along with the final achievement of comparative material independence, emerge to some extent in every biography of the union leaders of the period, including those of other miners' leaders such as John Weir and Andrew Sharp. One possible exception was William Pickard, who at the time of his marriage still could not read or write.[1]

The bulk of this group of emancipated workers were denied the possibility of scaling class barriers in Victorian times; they saw their place as being at the head of the stratum which was claiming a higher place in the social hierarchy. The social pressure exerted by the stratum of skilled workers, aspiring towards the social advancement of the group as a whole, reinforced the aspirations among this group to achieve individual advancement; indeed, such pressure was essential if individual aspirations were to be fulfilled. On the other hand, the better-educated working class elite, with its relatively broader outlook, was more fully aware of the aspirations of the stratum; the latter was only vaguely conscious of its social needs, and could neither formulate them rationally nor set about fulfilling them in an organised manner.

The interests of both groups required that persons of working class origin be assured a monopoly of leadership of the labour movement. Positions in the unions had to become their exclusive preserve, and for this objective it was necessary to get rid of competitors from other classes. In theory, such people would, if they wished to undermine the labour movement, have at their disposal greater talent for organisation and be more familiar with administrative methods than the less qualified workers, even if the latter were potentially as capable. The question was probably an academic one in essence, since the low prestige of the trade unions at that time would have meant degradation for any middle class person who wished to devote himself to union work. There were thus no grounds for fearing a massive influx of intruders from other classes into the labour movement. For this reason little emotion was wasted on stressing working class self-dependence in the matter of running their own organisation; this could only have been stirred up by a real threat of competition. Yet here and there, particularly during the beginnings of the 'new model' unions, one can find declarations attesting to the fact that the working class elite had not relaxed its vigilance in this respect.[2]

---

1 Williams, *Magnificent journey*, p. 116; W. Hallan, *Miners' leaders*, Bemrose, London, 1894.
2 Here is a characteristic statement by G. J. Holyoake, who himself belonged to the 'self-made' category, and was one of the first advocates of self-dependence and self-sufficiency for the labour movement of the 'phase of respectability': 'Mr Owen, in his *Instructions to the Missionaries*, in 1839, speaks to the purpose on this point—his words are: "the middle class is the *only* efficient *directing* class in society—the working class never did *direct* any permanent successful operations". In his Egyptian

Apart from countering potential middle class competition, the other side of this process of digging in on the workers' home ground was the campaign to get their position recognised by the employers. The union leaders' objective was to induce society to accept their status as the only legal representatives of the workers—as one of the two equally important sides participating in the industrial process. The object was to bring about a fundamental change in the middle class image of the unions—from that of tiresome, importunate intruders in industrial relations to that of allies whose help was needed and desired in the task of assuring that work in the capitalist factories proceeded peacefully and without disturbance.

The pioneer of industrial arbitration, the middle class radical Mundella, was expressing the very essence of the aspirations of the labour elite when he told a Royal Commission in the 1860s that 'we [the employers] could have done nothing without the organisation of the unions'. This radically changed the view of the unions that had hitherto prevailed in the employer class. Mundella was continually putting forward the view that discussion between the employers and labour should not only be allowed a legal status but should also be deliberately promoted.

From the workers' side, such discussions should not, he believed, 'consist of a deputation of workers meeting the masters at the end of the table' but should be 'carried on round a table, with every person treating his neighbour as an equal, and agreements being reached without the necessity of the chairman having to give a casting vote'.[1] At first Mundella's views were regarded by middle class public opinion as the ravings of a madman, but they gradually made headway in the employer class as a result of the real benefits that followed their application.

It was clearly to the advantage of the employers to build up the social authority of the working class elite if by so doing its physical and spiritual authority within the labour movement could be consolidated. The employers began to look favourably on the union organisers whom they had formerly anathematised and expelled from the shop floor, seeing them as a quite useful cog in the industrial machine. After the death of Kane the owners of the various ironworks in which his union operated collected among themselves the sum of £500 to buy an annuity for the dead man's widow.[2] Furthermore, Odger's funeral, as Broadhurst recalls, drew the

Hall lectures in 1841, he declares that "the working classes are too inexperienced even to know their real position, and that they will pass from one error to another".'
(*The Movement*, 20 April, 1844.) Holyoake criticised these views sharply, maintaining that the workers were capable of directing their own fortunes and of producing their own leaders from their midst.

1 Armytage, *Mundella*, pp. 320–21.
2 Report of the TUC, 1875, p. 17.

largest assemblage of persons from different classes that had ever been present to pay their last respects to a working man.[1]

The working class elite as a whole gradually achieved a status that was recognised by the employers. Particular individuals from this milieu went even further, penetrating the capitalist class and by one method or another reaching affluence on a middle class scale. This they sometimes did by taking advantage of the possibilities which their position in the union afforded them (though never, so far as I have been able to ascertain, by misappropriation of union funds). John Hodge, the general secretary of the British Steel Smelters, Mill, Iron, Turnplate and Kindred Trades Association (1886–1918), and his brother owned a group of prosperous grocery stores, trading as Hodge Brothers.[2] More characteristic than such individual instances, however, was the acquiescent view that prevailed among the working class elite about the integration into capitalist society, not so much of the whole stratum, as of individual union leaders. At the Trades Union Congress in 1889 the young Keir Hardie, whose attitude towards the old elite was a militant one, condemned Broadhurst for holding shares in the firm of Brunner Mond & Co., whose workpeople were poorly paid and overworked. The subsequent debate was concerned, not with the general ethics of a trade unionist's owning shares in a capitalist firm, but with the question as to whether the workers at Brunner Mond were well or badly paid. The information that Broadhurst owned industrial shares was not a revelation in itself.[3]

Personal meetings between the working class elite and the middle class also occurred in another milieu—the Parliamentary one, within the Liberal Party. I have already described the social significance of the unions' campaign to secure representation for the workers in the House of Commons. In this campaign two dominant motifs recurred: the idea that only union officials could perform the role of experts on labour affairs in Parliament and the idea that union members would not restrict themselves to representing the occupational interests of the workers but that they would in practice, like other MPs represent all classes which made up their constituency. Both these ideas, propagated from two different sides, expressed chiefly the aspirations of the workers' leaders for social advancement rather than the advancement achieved by their stratum as a whole.

The Parliamentary campaign reached its greatest intensity during the

1 Hopkinson, 'Life of Henry Broadhurst', p. 17.
2 Pugh, *Men of steel*, pp. 86 *et seq.*
3 This is how Chisholm Robertson described the incident: 'Mr Keir Hardie charged Mr Broadhurst with what was a heinous crime, that of investing money in a concern without making full inquiry as to how the concern worked.' (Report of the TUC, 1889, p. 23.)

period when the 'new model' unions were at their most dynamic, but bore fruit only when the unions were moving into the phase of conservative stabilisation. For this reason the trade union MPs found themselves entirely dependent on the goodwill of the Liberal Party. The Liberals made them members, by offering them safe Parliamentary seats; in return they demanded absolute subservience in Parliament to the political decisions of the Liberal faction. Here it must be added that the union MPs usually found it extremely easy to carry out this demand.

The trade union MPs who were dependent on Liberal goodwill earned no renown in any sphere of Parliamentary history. With the exception of two or three individuals they were all colourless, unobtrusive figures. Their qualifications had brought them to the top of the union movement, which was itself congealing at the level of the socio-economic status of the lower middle class. They proved completely inadequate to the performance of any role in the House, which was brimming over with old Parliamentary hands reared in rich and highly sophisticated political traditions which sometimes spanned many generations. Furthermore, the labour movement had begun to grow an increasingly tough shell even before the union MPs entered Parliament; this process eliminated all possibility of expansive activity in the Commons and gave the union MPs the feeling that they were only on the fringes of Parliament.

At this period the working class MPs regarded their presence in the House of Commons as an end in itself, as the last and highest stage of the social revolution which had been accomplished in the life span of their generation. They were men of extremely practical views, who regarded with repugnance the diffusion, towards the end of their period, of what they regarded as Utopian fantasies about the rebuilding of society from its foundations on socialist principles. These leaders occupied the highest positions which their own potentialities and those of their movement allowed, and they adopted a decidedly hostile attitude to the young movement which was challenging the Liberal Party. The charge brought by this new movement against the Liberal Party was that it was capable neither of meeting the workers' needs nor of guaranteeing genuine representation for the workers in Parliament. Such a charge was literally beyond the comprehension of the working class MPs who had for many years been accustomed to receive the highest honours from Gladstone and his party.[1] The elite of the 'new model' trade unions was heart and soul

---

1   The following list of trade union MPs elected to Parliament with the support of the
    Liberal Party illustrates the evolution of the tendency for the party to absorb the
    labour elite:

    1874   T. Burt, A. Macdonald.
    1880   T. Burt, A. Macdonald, H. Broadhurst.

with the Liberals for having opened up a road for them to distinctions which, as they saw it, could not have been achieved without Liberal help.[1]

If one put together the manifold characteristics of the leaders of the 'new model' union period, one gets a picture that is in polar contrast to the silhouette of the leaders of the factory workers in the first half of the century. The 'new model' leaders were the complete opposite of the charismatic type of leader. They felt much more at ease in an office or seated at a table than at mass meetings. They could trust in their own powers of reasoning at conferences but were powerless to cope with mass gatherings. They based their authority on an efficient administrative apparatus, not on personal charm—a quality in which they were not accustomed to put much confidence. They were concerned with minutiae, lacked a wider vision, and were over-rational in discussing everyday matters. Professions of principle got a derisive reception while annual balance sheets and financial reports were treated as holy writ. They were responsive to flattery from above and armoured against complaints emanating from below; quick to drop anything that would make them seem different from the average middle class standard, and to emphasise everything that differentiated them from the average factory worker. At first even this too-sober attitude to life became a cause of self-sacrifice and gave rise to considerable pioneer romanticism. But it rapidly reverted to its natural form, shaking itself free of all remnants of poetry and accepting prose as the most appropriate form for conveying its message. In short, we have to do here with a type of labour leader different from anything that had gone before; different both from the charismatic leaders of the weak mass movements of the 1830s and 1840s, and also from the leaders of the journeymen's clubs, men of modest abilities who had left practically no mark on the history of the labour movement.

One must, however, stress that the type of Victorian labour leader so far

1886 W. Abraham, J. Arch, H. Broadhurst, T. Burt, W. R. Cremer, W. Crawford, C. Fenwick, G. Howell, R. B. Cunninghame Graham, B. Pickard, J. Rowlands.

1892 W. Abraham, J. Arch, M. Austin, J. Burns, T. Burt, W. R. Cremer, E. Crane, G. Fenwick, J. Keir Hardie, G. Howell, B. Pickard, J. Rowlands, J. Wilson, J. H. Wilson, S. Woods.

(Humphrey, *History of labour representation*, pp. 192–3.)

1 Lord Snell wrote ironically in his memoirs, 'The Gladstonian hold over the trade union leaders was increased by the method of control by favour and by appointment. In this Gladstone merely continued what others had begun, but the effect of the appointment of Henry Broadhurst in 1886, and of Thomas Burt in 1892, to ministerial positions was to harness to the Liberal machine the whole of the trade union movement. A certain number of working-class leaders were to be assisted to enter Parliament as supporters of the Liberal Party, and nearly every trade union leader of the time promptly held out his hand and said: "Here am I, send me!"'. (Lord Snell, *Men, movements and myself*, Dent, London, 1936, p. 139.)

described was found only in association with the particular type of labour organisation which has been defined as the 'new model' type. As I have said, these 'new model' unions were based on those sections of the working class which underwent the process of occupational crystallisation; they thus extricated themselves from the state of amorphism and, by securing an improvement in their material conditions, ceased to be estranged from society. The type of labour leader we have been describing so far emerged from, and was the logical product of, this type of movement and this particular stratum.

None the less, alongside the stratum of the new skilled workers, which was undergoing far-reaching changes, there still continued to exist an even larger section of the working class which in many respects remained in exactly the same situation as the factory workers of the first half of the century. This consisted of an unorganised mass of unskilled factory workers, still undifferentiated occupationally, together with a similar mass of workers in the rural areas, the majority of them miners. In these sections of the working class there were no grounds for the crystallisation of occupational interests or the emergence of unions of the 'new model' type and the sort of labour elite which has been described earlier.

It would, however, be a simplification to assume that such a glaring dichotomy within the working class, between two groups with fundamentally different social characteristics, would give rise in the period under discussion to two completely different types of labour elite, appearing and evolving in complete isolation from each other. Such total isolation clearly could not exist. Each section of the labour movement influenced the other, the overriding influence obviously being exerted by the more powerful section, not the weaker one. In the outcome, the evolution of the labour movement among the amorphous factory population was bound to be influenced by the presence or absence of strong, cohesive factory unions of skilled workers. In contrast to the preceding period, no purely charismatic figures like O'Connor are to be found in the Victorian era. From the moment they achieved influence the charismatic leaders were rapidly subjugated by the ruling machinery of the 'new model' unions, and even more by the all-powerful set of rules created by that machinery. This led to the emergence of figures with blurred outlines, who constituted a strange melange of two different sociological types.

The most characteristic example of such a mixture of types was the agricultural workers' leader, Joseph Arch. By origin he was a farm labourer, who had mastered what was then the remunerative trade of hedge cutter, and thus attained a relatively independent material position. Because of his trade he was constantly on the move through the rural areas of England and this gave him a comparatively broad outlook and a considerable store of experience. He had exceptional authority among farm workers: he was one of them but at the same time he had succeeded in escaping from the poverty and humiliation in which they lived. He was far more eloquent than they and was enveloped in the aura of the great world which they knew only from tales. Arch was a Methodist preacher as well, and his sermons quickly became famous over a wide area for the tense emotional reactions which they aroused in those who heard them. It was not surprising that one evening a delegation of waggon drivers, half-dead with overwork, knocked at Arch's door to beg him to take their part and organise them for industrial action.

This was the beginning of an epic campaign, entirely reminiscent of the old Chartist days. Thousands gathered on hillsides, held spellbound by Arch's thundering orations. Organisations were born out of the feeling engendered at the mass meetings and fell apart after the departure of the leader, who was venerated in an almost religious manner. Stories circulated from village to village about the coming of a Messiah who had been called to deliver the farm workers from afflictions which were an affront to human dignity. Social energy, often revolutionary in its mode of expression, was intensified by the Messianic legend, but it died away at the first counter-blow, being sustained only by the spell of the half-mystical leader.

Arch was not so far from regarding himself as a Messiah. He wrote of himself: 'I know that it was the hand of the Lord of Hosts that led me that day; that the Almighty Maker of Heaven and earth raised me up to do this particular thing; that in the counsel of His wisdom He singled me out, and set me on my feet in His sight and breathed of the breath of His spirit into me and sent me forth as a messenger of the Lord God of Battles. So I girded up my loins and went forth.'[1]

Arch's conviction of his divine calling made his behaviour highly arbitrary and led him to be intolerant and contemptuous towards those about him. He was a magnificent orator but no organiser. After the first overwhelming successes the union which he had founded disintegrated rapidly. Arch himself became the captive of the Liberal Party—his union's expansion thrust him up and he suddenly found himself in Parliament as a Liberal MP. Not surprisingly, his mystical qualities did not shine as brightly in the atmosphere of the Commons as they had done at mass meetings, where they were enhanced by the spell of woodland nights. Compared with the sophisticated Parliamentary orators, Arch appeared surprisingly colourless, and was lost to view among his Lib–Lab colleagues. After his term had expired, Liberal members bought him an annuity on which he lived many years, but outside the labour movement.

1 Quoted by Selley, *Village trade unions*, pp. 93–101.

Arch's closest collaborator, George Mitchell, was the son of a mason, who had with his own resources built up a prosperous wholesale business in marble. Like Arch he was an excellent speaker at mass meetings, with a tongue that could be both sharp and laden with pathos. He was full of hatred for the class of which he himself had become a member. This hatred added an especial violence and fervour to his speeches and leaflets, and led to clashes with the other leaders of the union, among whom there very soon emerged a group modelling itself on the 'new model' type of leadership. After Arch and Mitchell the leadership of the farm workers' union was held by such colourless administrators as George Edwards, Holmes and Tom Higdon. The union was gradually absorbed and assimilated by the existing labour movement, built on 'new model' lines.[1]

The story of George Potter affords an example of an even more rapid assimilation of leaders of the militant type by the 'respectable' union movement. Potter was an infallible expert in techniques of agitation, an excellent speaker at mass meetings, an advocate of radical measures, who kept up the Chartist traditions. He was a figure from another age, who lived either too late or too early, in times which were least propitious for his programme and his temperament. The labour elite of the day abused him roundly as an irresponsible adventurer who threatened the existence of the movement. The Junta smashed him without scruples and he succumbed after only a few years' resistance, yielding to its programme and practices.[2]

Arch and Potter were, however, exceptions. The victory went to another type of labour leader, more firmly rooted in the contemporary era and better fitted to the structure of the most socially active section of the working class and also to the structure of the labour movement created by it.

It would now seem timely to list the basic characteristics of this dominant type of union leader. Instead, one may try to give an outline of Henry Broadhurst, for many years the secretary and in actuality the leader of the Trades Union Congress, who had immense influence on the British labour movement of the period under discussion as well as being its product. The career of this man included and exemplified all the most general and most typical features of the careers of the whole stratum of labour leaders.

Broadhurst was the son of a quarryman in Gloucestershire, and learned the trade under his father's supervision. He and his father moved from the quarries into stonemasonry and he worked as his father's assistant in small teams doing repair work or extensions to churches and university colleges.

---

1   The information about the farm workers' union is taken from Selley, *Village trade unions*, pp. 93–101, and Groves, *Sharpen the sickle*, pp. 39–110.
2   Musson, *The Congress of 1868*, pp. 14–15.

This work needed training, was artisan in character and was carried out using almost artisan methods.

Broadhurst made himself independent and went to work in the prosperous stonemasons' firm of a certain Mr Lloyd, a master craftsman with a very patriarchal attitude to his journeymen. The master and his journeymen often travelled the country in search of work together, eating together in wayside inns and talking over their pipes. This warm relationship with his master had a profound influence on Broadhurst's mind.

Broadhurst had a natural shrewdness which offset his lack of formal education, a ready wit and keen powers of observation; he quickly and unobtrusively gained an uncommon authority among his fellow stonemasons, and in the natural course of things proceeded to union work. Being a highly ambitious man, he involved himself deeply in union activity, in which he rightly discerned the possibility of an outlet for his energy and the most promising arena for displaying his abilities. As he was later to recall, the beginning of his political career was the year 1872, when he finally ceased to work as a stonemason and became a full-time trade union official.

A clever and able administrator, he advanced rapidly up the rungs of the trade union ladder. In 1873 he was appointed secretary of the Labour Representation League, and a year later to the leading post in the union movement of the day that of Parliamentary secretary to the TUC. From that time onwards for a dozen or more years Broadhurst was the real leader of the whole union movement in Britain. Throughout this period he was the chief advocate of industrial peace, of union loyalty to capitalist society, and of harmony between employers and their labour force.

Broadhurst's new social position, which grew in importance along with that of the unions, brought him into direct contact with the leading figures of the economic and political world. Once a stonemason, now a leader of the unions which had until recently been scorned by the rulers of that world, Broadhurst was respected and flattered by the celebrities among whom he moved. He dreamed of such recognition and strove to achieve it along with his trade union colleagues. He was stunned by the brilliance of the world that suddenly opened up before him. In such a situation a man needs a very obdurate nature if he is to avoid the temptation to become snobbish and to accept the honours that are proffered. Broadhurst did not have such a nature—moreover, this headlong advancement was the objective sought, consciously or subconsciously, by him and by those like him. There was no reason why he should draw back before reaching the goal of his endeavours—particularly at a time when that goal was at last beginning to seem a real one. Thus Broadhurst was to write quite frankly in his memoirs, 'It is exciting and pleasing to be able to engage the attention of 5,000 persons, to amuse them, to use their plaudits, to be observed and to be talked about.' He also complained that 'when I first won for myself a seat in Parliament many courted and flattered me, sought and obtained my help. Since I have ceased to be in Parliament they don't know me'. (This was after 1892, when he ceased to be an MP for four years.) In a chapter about his acquaintances, he described with gusto his relationships with such men as the aristocratic lawyer Sir James Stephen and Professor Toynbee (who, according to Broadhurst, personally asked him if he would take part in the Trades Union Congress). Broadhurst went into raptures in writing about the social gatherings at which he rubbed shoulders with 'society'.

> There was one fashionable function which I attended for years in succession. This was the garden party at Marlborough House. As a spectacle it is always worth seeing, for in addition to all the leaders of the political, literary, artistic, and ecclesiastical worlds in this country, many foreign notabilities attend . . . The brilliance of the dresses, the beauty of the garden, and the pleasing strains of the band, made this function a most acceptable diversion in the commonplace round of a workaday world.

In his memoirs Broadhurst could not resist quoting *in extenso* a letter from the Prince of Wales inviting him to spend a weekend at one of the royal seats. Afterwards he described the visit in detail, stressing how, on his arrival, 'His Royal Highness personally conducted me to my rooms, made a careful inspection to see that all was right, stoked the fires, and then after satisfying himself that all my wants were provided for, withdrew and left me for the night'.

For Gladstone, 'our beloved leader', Broadhurst reserved his highest praise, almost to the point of idolatry. In every sentence of his memoirs which refers to Gladstone, he used the most rapturous terms about the Liberal leader to show his gratitude for the State honours bestowed on him. He described Gladstone's greetings and congratulations after Broadhurst had delivered his maiden speech in Parliament, commenting that nobody had shaken his hand or greeted him in a more friendly manner, nor given him so much encouragement as had the great man himself.

Broadhurst's thoughts also returned to Gladstone when he was summing up the course of his life. His memoirs end with an account of the death and funeral of the Liberal leader:

> My place in the procession was a little in advance of the coffin . . . My eye involuntarily sought the clock tower, on whose tall flanks I had worked, chilled to the bone, nearly thirty years before . . . The contrast was almost

overwhelming: then unknown and penniless; today in a place of honour, the sorrowing colleague of the greatest Englishman of the century.[1]

Broadhurst's career marks the ultimate landmark on the road taken by the labour elite of the 'new model' period: some achieved this in actual fact while for others it was only a psychological incentive, which defined the mentality of that elite. His view of his own story is an expression of this mentality, which made the labour elite of his time the most submissive towards the ruling class and the most conservative in relation to the aspirations of its own stratum in the history of the British labour movement.

1   All these quotations are taken either from Hopkinson, 'Life of Henry Broadhurst', or from Broadhurst's own autobiography.

III

The evolution of a mass labour movement 1890–1924

We have seen how in the preceding period the structural forms of the labour movement came to maturity, passing in the last phase into a process of stabilisation, consolidation and ossification of the developed structure. The movement lost its initial dynamism and elasticity when it had achieved its initial aims, imposed by the social position and evolutionary tendencies of its social base. This stable labour movement became the scaffolding for an equally stable elite of qualification, prestige and authority. The stabilisation of the movement, as of its elite, was conditional upon the attainment of vertical mobility by the stratum and its individual members, to the degree that was permitted by the socio-historical situation of their social base and the overall structure of society.

The process of stabilisation to which we have referred could not, however, be long-drawn-out, still less final. The increasingly rigid structure of the movement was based on a relatively small stratum of the working class, separated off from the rest as a result of occupational differentiation. The movement was an institutionalisation of occupational interests and as such was bound to collide with class interests.

In these circumstances the stabilisation of the movement could endure for as long as the stratum of skilled workers, on which it was based, were its exclusive spokesmen. The mass of unskilled workers, who had so far stayed on the sidelines, either not organising themselves at all or creating organisations with only a butterfly's life span, were still there as a powerful reserve; their engagement in the political struggle must inevitably shake the very foundations of the conservative edifice of the skilled unions and provide an injection of new energy of hitherto unknown dimensions, energy which would be capable of smashing a too feeble structure to bits.

The process of its engagement is the subject of Part III. The mass of unskilled workers, awakened to political life by factors that will be discussed later, came up against a system of organisation that was geared to defend the interests of a narrow stratum with comparatively low aspirations, a system that was quite inadequate to secure the advancement of a powerful class. The result of this clash of interests was a sharp increase in the structural elasticity of the movement. This in turn led to the abolition of old forms and the creation of new ones adapted to the new social content of the movement.

I

The structure of
the working class

As a result of the metamorphosis that took place in the preceding period, the stratum of skilled workers at the beginning of the new era was linked in terms of culture, ideology and political attitudes with the lower middle class. The skilled worker copied the models set up by the lower levels of the middle class in such matters as the furnishings of his home, his style of life and his preferred recreations. He sent his children to the same schools and instilled into his offspring ideals of advancement in life which were borrowed from the lower middle class. He voted for the same political party as the lower middle class. Like the main body of that class, he was moderately conservative in his attitude to life, feared novelty and valued social peace and order above all else as the surest guarantee of his modest but quite important privileges. He was more zealous than the aristocracy or the upper middle class in expressing his patriotism and devotion to the Crown, because he retained a subconscious fear that his status as a citizen in a capitalist society was still uncertain. In fact the skilled workers had even in outlook thrust their roots into the capitalist system, to merge with the stratum that occupied an intermediate place between the two polar classes of the capitalist structure. In consequence, a deep gulf divided them from the mass of unskilled labourers in the factories, on the land and in the mines, who still remained semi-alienated outcasts from a society ruled by the bourgeoisie and its system of values.

We may recall that the social emancipation of the stratum of skilled workers was based on occupational differentiation. This differentiation began with the development of heavy industry, and was also in some degree a consequence of the durability of artisan traditions in those branches of production which underwent technical change by a course of fairly straightforward evolution. In the process of emancipation of the skilled stratum the characteristic trait that is easiest to test, because it can be measured, is the level of wages. Contemporary calculations show that the most financially privileged group of workers at the end of the nineteenth century was concentrated chiefly in the engineering industry and the other branches of production just mentioned. According to Hobsbawm's analysis of the 1906 census,[1] the largest concentration of highly paid workers (i.e. earning 45s a week and over) was in the foundries, in machine production and

---

1 Hobsbawm, 'The labour aristocracy,' pp. 216–20.

boiler-making and shipbuilding—and, on the other hand, in building, cabinet-making, printing and hosiery. The best paid trades were those of engine driver, welder, tool-maker, turner and so on. In accordance with a custom already hallowed by tradition, the 'privileged' occupations were considered as belonging to the category of 'artisans'—probably as a result of the aspirations of the skilled workers of capitalist industry, in their quest for emancipation, to insinuate themselves into the only social stratum endowed with an accepted social status since guild times. In place of the generalised concept 'worker', which was rarely used, it was general practice to apply the divisive and narrower concepts of 'artisan' and 'labourer'.

The artisans made up a considerable portion of the labouring population in the great cities (above all, London[1]), which had large numbers of establishments producing consumer goods and luxury articles; these establishments were geared to supplying the aristocracy and bourgeoisie, and those who worked in them had to possess craft qualifications and individual artistic skill. On the other hand, in the ordinary provincial industrial towns the artisans constituted a relatively thin layer on the surface of the great mass of labourers. This numerical disproportion is particularly striking if one considers not only the factory workers and artisan strata, in which the skilled stratum was fairly well established, but also the mass of all types of navvying, farm work, mining and so on, in which the percentage of skilled workers was minimal. One can therefore assume that over the country as a whole the labourers considerably outnumbered the artisans.

In consequence, the stratum of skilled workers, which had mobilised the labour movement of the preceding period, was actually only a small part of the working class; the great majority of the latter still, towards the end of the nineteenth century, lived in poverty, often in destitution, on the periphery or even beyond the borders of society. The fact that only the skilled stratum was able, by virtue of its articulateness, to speak in the

---

1   Charles Booth (*Labour and life of the people*, II, Williams & Norgate, London, 1891, p. 383) gives the following statistics for the working class districts of London, showing percentages of labourers and artisans as part of the whole population in 1891:

District	Labourers	Artisans
Central London	16·8	20·7
Shoreditch	16·0	44·9
Bethnal Green	18·7	41·7
Whitechapel, Stepney	30·4	28·0
Mile End	22·7	29·4
Poplar	32·1	29·9
Hackney	11·2	24·7
Battersea	20·9	27·8

name of the working class meant that an outside observer could easily get a wrong idea of the true situation of the workers in Britain and of the degree to which social conflicts had developed.[1] And yet the gap between the artisans and the rest of the working class assumed dimensions that were found hardly anywhere else. The skilled workers were reaping the benefits of a strong trade union organisation while the mass of unskilled workers hardly knew how to set about improving their living conditions. As a result, a gulf yawned between the two sections of the working class, growing deeper until the 1890s. The division was not merely one of resources but also existed in the sphere of social prestige, possibilities of social advancement for the group and the individual, relations with other classes in society, and so on.

The skilled workers enjoyed greater opportunities for education, and their chosen trades were fenced around with protective barriers. In consequence they gradually became a hereditary stratum, like the master craftsmen at the time of the disintegration of the guild system. The son of an artisan was generally trained to the same trade as his father, unless he went on to become a clerical worker or even a member of the technical or administrative supervisory grades. There were very few instances of an artisan's son dropping to the level of unskilled work; if this happened it was usually the result of exceptional circumstances.[2] The privileged position of artisans' children, as compared with that of labourers' families, made itself felt even in the primary and secondary schools. Booth showed that in the secondary schools of the East End of London there were, out of every hundred pupils, an average of only two labourers' sons, compared with as many as twenty-six sons of artisans.[3] On the other hand, the stratum of unskilled labourers was no less self-perpetuating than that of the artisans. The labourer usually handed down to his children his own social position along with a complete lack of opportunities for individual advancement. Interchange of members between these two strata became so minimal that the stratification of the working class acquired certain characteristics of an estate system.

For such reasons the terms 'skilled' and 'artisan' achieved an acknow-

1 Cf the following observation by Eduard Bernstein: 'The difference between the artisan and the uneducated working man in the matter of wages and cultivation was, for the most part, until lately, very much greater in England than with us; which explains, among other things, why the German, on coming to England, having read that the English worker is better paid, and works shorter hours than the German worker, at first receives the contrary impression.' (*My years of exile*, Parsons, London, 1921, p. 207).

2 B. Seebohm Rowntree, *Poverty: a study of town life*, Macmillan, London, 1901; revised edn., Longmans, London, 1922, pp. 102–3.

3 Booth, *Labour and life of the people*, II, p. 557.

ledged social position combined with considerable prestige at the lower
middle class level. On the other hand, the terms 'unskilled' and 'labourer'
had a pejorative flavour, and even an unfavourable moral connotation.
The word 'unskilled' was used within the artisan group with an undertone
of scorn; when addressing unskilled labourers it was used with embarrassment, as if the word itself were abusive. Unskilled workers themselves
rejected the name, which they regarded as offensive; they replaced it with
a term of their own coinage—that of 'general worker'.[1]

There are numerous estimates relating trends in the movement of real
wages during the latter part of the nineteenth and the earlier part of the
twentieth centuries. They are fundamentally in accord in showing that
average real wages for the whole of the working class rose slowly over the
period 1860–90 because of wage increases, and in the period 1890–1900
because of a fall in prices; on the other hand, in the remaining years up to
the first world war wages drifted slightly downward.[2] Yet even if this over-
general average wage was accurate, it conceals two very significant processes. In the first place, during the period of wage increases various strata
of the working class did not benefit from them evenly, so that the only
authoritative figures would be those calculated for each stratum separately. Secondly, even an increase in wages did not eradicate poverty within a
large part of the working class.

The statistics collected by Charles Booth for London and by Seebohm
Rowntree for York can convey some idea of the misery that prevailed in
urban areas at the end of the nineteenth century. Table 10 is compiled
from statistics taken from the findings of both these broadly planned and
carefully conducted surveys. A conflation is made possible by the fact that

---

1   Ben Tillett, the first organiser of the great union of unskilled workers, frequently
     condemned the use of the term 'unskilled'. He also wrote as follows about one of
     the largest sections of unskilled workers, the dockers: 'So real was the stigma
     attaching to dock labour that those of us who earned a living by it concealed the
     nature of our occupation from our family as well as our friends. A contractor would
     speak of the dock labourer as the "dock oaf".' 'No public man in that period would
     condescend to take part in a Sunday meeting of casual workers and disdained to
     lower his pride in competing with the gutter oratory of the Salvation Army.'
     (*Memories and reflections*, Long, London, 1931, pp. 89, 92.) In his presidental address
     to the TUC in 1891, attended for the first time by a considerable number of repre-
     sentatives of unskilled unions, Thomas Burt made the following embarrassed
     excuse: 'We have the unskilled labourers represented as they never were before. I
     would say less skilled, because all labour, even the rudest, requires a considerable
     amount of skill' (Report of the TUC, 1891, p. 53.)
2   Cf, for instance, A. L. Bowley, *Wages and incomes in the United Kingdom since 1860*,
     Cambridge University Press, 1937, p. 30; M. L. Yates, *Wages and labour conditions in
     British engineering*, Macdonald & Evans, London, 1937, p. 104.

both works use basically similar systems of classification; one must, however, in using the table, take account of some differences in the system of
classifying particular groups, natural enough in two surveys conducted
separately and according to somewhat different criteria.

Table 10

Classification of the working class population of London and York according to their
material condition at the end of the nineteenth century*

Material condition	Percentage of the working class population		Percentage of the whole population	
	London	York	London	York
Lowest	1·1	4·2	0·9	2·6
Very poor	9·2	9·6	7·5	5·9
Poor	28·0	33·6	22·3	20·7
Total poor	38·3	47·4	30·7	29·2
Relatively well-to-do	61·7	52·6	51·5	32·4

*According to Seebohm Rowntree (*Poverty*, p. 101), this included (*a*) the
families of skilled workers and artisans, and (*b*) families of unskilled workers
containing several wage earners (children of working age).

Source C. Booth, *Labour and life of the people*, II, Williams & Norgate,
London, 1891, p. 21; B. Seebohm Rowntree, *Poverty: a study of town life*,
Longmans, London, 1922 edn., pp. 102–3.

Even when one takes into account all the reservations that can be advanced on methodological grounds in relation to such a comparison, there
is a striking correspondence between the results of the two surveys, undertaken independently in two different areas. We can, therefore, without
risk of serious error take it that at the end of the nineteenth century, in
urban areas dominated by the engineering industry, about 30 per cent of
the total population and about forty per cent of the labouring population
lived in poverty, that is to say, lacked the means to provide for their most
basic needs. Of this number, Rowntree estimated that, on the basis of an
analysis of the most extreme instances of poverty, more than half the
labourers who did not earn the minimum required for the barest physical
needs were in this position because the wages of the main breadwinner

were insufficient even to maintain a family with two children.[1] Rowntree concluded that 'the wages paid for unskilled labour in York are insufficient to provide food, shelter, and clothing adequate to maintain a family of moderate size in a state of bare physical sufficiency'.[2] The areas in which unskilled workers were concentrated (for a considerable section of the artisan group gradually settled in districts of a lower middle class character) were nuclei of appalling poverty of the kind observed and described by Booth in the hundreds of shocking instances reported in his study of London.[3]

The sustenance of the average unqualified labourer was described by Ben Turner, the well known trade union leader.

> We had porridge to breakfast, porridge to dinner and porridge to tea, until my father got another warp in and could earn some more food. I can remember later on turning up my nose at porridge. Mother thought it was stupidity; probably it was, and nausea. In those days it wasn't porridge followed by something else. It was porridge warm, porridge cold, porridge with milk and with treacle, and sometimes porridge and point, that is you had a hole in the centre of the basin of porridge and you pointed to where the milk or treacle should be.[4]

When the English towns emerged from the Victorian epoch which had brought prosperity to the stratum of skilled workers, they contained large areas inhabited by people who were sunk in the utmost poverty. For the time being this section of the population was not a source of direct political problems. Those in it were worn down by chronic hunger, inhuman living conditions, disease, and growing drunkenness and gambling. They were not as yet capable of making conscious and organised effort to attain

1   Seebohm Rowntree, *Poverty*, p. 136.
2   *Ibid.*, p. 133.
3   In this connection one should not forget that in addition to those living in 'average poverty' there were also 'relatively well-to-do' areas, and others in which extreme poverty was widespread. For instance, Booth notes that the area between Blackfriars and London Bridge had a total population of 33,000, of whom as many as 68 per cent were in the grip of poverty. Other districts of London in which over half the population was living in extreme poverty were: Southwark, 67·9 per cent, Greenwich 65·2 per cent, Goswell Road 60·9 per cent, Bethnal Green 58·7 per cent, Bermondsey 57 per cent, Kings Cross 55·2 per cent, Horselydown 55 per cent, Bromley (West) 51·5 per cent. (Booth, *Labour and the life of the people*, II, pp. 27–31.) It was precisely this concentration of poverty in certain closed residential communities, to which in principle the unskilled worker's horizon of knowledge was confined, and not the country-wide average that was one of the great realities which shaped the social and psychological make-up of the mass of workers who lacked qualifications.
4   B. Turner, *About myself*, Cayme Press, London, 1930, p. 21.

their rights as human beings. In most cases they were not even fully aware of those rights and accepted as inescapable the conditions of life to which they were condemned. Nevertheless, they remained potentially a powerful force which, once set in motion, could bring about a total upheaval in the balance of forces that had been established in Victorian days.

Such was the position within the working class at the outset of the period which will be analysed in this chapter. But it was this period which saw the beginnings of profound changes in the structure of the working class, changes which led to no less profound changes in the model and the social content of the British labour movement.

At the back of these changes, both at this time and earlier, lay the continuing evolution of the structure of capitalist industry. The rise of the iron and steel and engineering industries had brought differentiation to a working class that had once been uniform in its amorphousness. The continued improvement of machines, the widespread diffusion of techniques, semi-automation, the mechanisation of a considerable number of processes of production, the advent of the internal combustion engine, the rise of industrial chemistry, and a general reorganisation of the technology of production combined with the new techniques—all these led to a renewed and gradual unification of the working class, though, obviously, on a different level of evolution and in a different manner than in the earlier period of economic primitivism. This was the basic social significance of the metamorphosis which capitalist industry underwent at the turn of the century.

The social gulf that divided the skilled stratum from the unskilled masses was to a greater or lesser degree a function of the occupational gulf—that between highly qualified workers and the unskilled labour force. This occupational gulf was now diminishing rapidly, followed considerably later by a diminution of the social gulf that was its superstructure *sui generis*.

The occupation gulf began to narrow from both sides. In the first place, the need for unskilled manual labour began to decrease as modern, progressive techniques came into general use. Machines combined with competent organisation of work proved more economical and brought greater profit than ordinary unskilled labour, even when the latter cost very little. In the docks, quarries and so on the use of cheap manual labour was to hold the spread of mechanisation for a long time to come. But even these industries saw the beginning of a technical revolution of sorts, under the influence of the structural transformation in other branches of production—principally in manufacturing industry—and the related increase in the cost of unskilled manpower. In the basic branches of production the elimination of the unskilled labour force continued at a relatively fast tempo, with a consequent decrease in the numbers of the 'lowest' stratum of the working class.

What happened to that section of the workers which moved out of this stratum ? As industry developed and machines began to be used more and more widely in the different phases of production, the entire work-force, not simply the artisan cream, was required to be generally knowledgeable and familiar with technical processes, and to have some elementary technical training which would enable it to operate uncomplicated machinery at least. The machine was the 'skilled worker', but there had to be a man to set it going or stop it in accordance with the requirements of the technological process. Even general labourers, who might seem to be the lowest category of unskilled worker, were gradually faced with technical problems as machines appeared in spheres which had traditionally been the domain of manual labour.

The shrinkage in the numbers of 'totally unqualified' workers led to the growth of a new stratum of semi-skilled workers—a stratum that had been far smaller in the preceding period. The significance of this stratum also changed fundamentally. It was not just that the semi-skilled stratum was increasing in numbers. This stratum had formerly included those workers in clearly defined trades who, being less accomplished in their craft than the stratum of skilled workers, were charged with performing the less complex auxiliary functions in a given craft. Now, however, the term 'semi-skilled' came increasingly to refer, not to a trainee in a particular trade, but to a worker with a general though limited technical training. It meant a worker who was in principle able, after a short period of training, to operate any machine with simplified controls; a worker without any precise trade, who could be transferred with ease from one factory department or stage of production to another, but who was capable everywhere, and in every situation, of meeting the demands of modern manufacturing techniques.

The far-reaching division of functions in the production process, which was the significant element in technical progress, finally led to its own contradiction. From the viewpoint of the men who set the machine in motion, all mechanised operations were increasingly coming to resemble one another; the diversity of goods produced became less important, because the operation itself—the most essential thing from the operative's angle—was becoming more and more uniform, regardless of the type of work performed by the machine. Thus technical progress gradually blurred the dividing lines between occupations. While it brought about a steady rise in the level of demand for technical qualifications from the average worker, it removed the need for any specific skills. The unskilled worker advanced to the status of a semi-skilled operative without at the same time experiencing the process of internal differentiation which had exerted such an influence on the fortunes of the stratum that had freed itself from the uniform masses of factory workers in the middle of the nineteenth century.

As I pointed out earlier, the process of levelling out the occupational gap between the two sections of the working class was also getting under way simultaneously from the other side. With the exception of a few branches of production, chiefly involving luxury goods and certain precision instruments, the role of fine craftsmanship in the production process was gradually decreasing in the great majority of industrial and transport undertakings. The value of manual expertise fell as mechanisation was extended to even the most complicated operations, bringing automation to functions that had formerly required a trained eye and a skilful hand. This mechanisation was accompanied by extensive simplifications in the operation of machines and semi-automated instruments. In consequence, there was a contraction in the area of employment dominated by monopolistic trade, mysteries at one time learned during a long and arduous apprenticeship served with masters who zealously guarded such secrets. Moreover, the barriers between particular trades slowly grew fewer even within this diminished artisan sphere of employment. They did not disappear altogether, but lessened to the point where it was in practice no longer out of the question for a worker to move from one trade to another, but simply required a relatively short period of adaptation and training. Thus the skilled workers not only lost their key role in production to the semi-skilled workers with technical training but could also be interchanged with one another. The importance of occupational interests within the skilled stratum diminished; at the same time the interests that were common to different occupations, i.e. the interests of various strata and, gradually, the most general interests, those of the class as a whole, increased in importance.

In this way, over a period spanning several successive decades, a profound stratificatory process took place step by step within the working class. The strata at either extreme contracted in proportion to the whole, while the middle stratum, that of the semi-skilled, was the only one to go on growing and to display tendencies towards further development. This process took place so imperceptibly that the semi-skilled stratum was not distinguished at all in contemporary statistics; its existence was recognised only *post factum*, when it had led to far-reaching changes in the social structure of the working class. Moreover, the upper and lower boundaries of this new, numerically dominant stratum were both fluid and difficult to fix, in contrast to earlier boundaries between strata. In the third quarter of the nineteenth century there was no difficulty at all in differentiating 'skilled' from 'unskilled' workers. By the beginning of the twentieth it was in many cases becoming much more difficult to establish where the unskilled stratum ended and the semi-skilled stratum began, or where the latter ended and the skilled began. The various strata of the working class shaded into one another fairly smoothly, their differences having been levelled off by technical progress.

The working class, which had been relatively homogeneous in the embryonic period of its evolution, i.e. in the first half of the nineteenth century, was then bisected by the sharp line of stratal boundaries. Now, however, it again began to move towards homogeneity, becoming a fairly cohesive whole. But the new homogeneity was not just a repetition of the former one: it was at the same time its antithesis; it was *sui generis* the negation of a negation, since it still included, though in an altered form, the characteristics which had emerged during the period when the strata were split.

The earlier homogeneity of the working class—or, strictly speaking, of the human material out of which the working class was to be fashioned— had been the homogeneity of a heterogeneous mass, torn from different social milieux, bereft of ties with former environments and groups, amorphous, fragmented and socially estranged. In the new epoch all these characteristics were replaced by their antitheses. The move towards homogeneity was accomplished inside a class with established communal traditions many centuries old. This class was based on occupational differentiation, with a distinctive internal structure, and at least one section of it was strongly rooted in the existing social structure. Thus the appearance of similarity should not lead us into error. The social content of the formally identical processes is different. It is, however, precisely that social content in a specific historical class and context, and not the formal characteristics, which can explain the rationale of the processes which were taking place within the labour movement. We must therefore pay particular attention to that aspect.

Unfortunately there are no criteria which would make it possible to present in statistical form the whole of the process described above, and by which it could be assessed. The semi-skilled stratum was in a state of flux which makes it impossible to expect too much accuracy from the various attempts to collect direct statistics. So one has to have recourse to fragmentary accounts of the process, which set out the whole of the problem from one side only; it is, however, the side which is most easily expressed in statistics. This kind of fragmentary description can consist of a comparison between the wages of unskilled and skilled workers, taking into account the occupational changes that were taking place within the stratum whose members were traditionally described as 'labourers'. A considerable number of calculations have been made independently of one another and for different branches of production. They show clearly that, from the 1890s onwards, there was a tendency almost everywhere for the disproportion between the wage levels of the skilled and unskilled workers to decrease. The extremes came closer to each other as a result of the rise in the lowest wage levels. At the same time there was an increase in the number of intermediate wage categories which lay between the two extremes.[1]

However one-sided the picture given by wage rates alone, it does offer some reflection of the overall process of social levelling out which was taking place between the different strata of the working class. This levelling out was the result of a kind of 'invasion from below' by the mass of formerly unskilled workers into the positions in which the vanguard of the working class, the artisan stratum, had entrenched itself earlier. At first the skilled workers reacted to this process in the traditional manner of the guilds and the guild-like artisans' unions. At union conferences and in union publications increasingly frequent protests were made by the representatives of skilled workers against the employment of men who had not served a period of apprenticeship in the trades traditionally reserved for the chosen few. Yet it was only the blinkered habit of thinking in guild-like categories that prevented them from seeing the obvious fact that the 'dilution' issue was not a matter of ill-will on the employers' side. Several decades earlier no employers, however malevolent, could have found a way to replace the arduous and lengthy apprenticeship that was essential for those who were to do skilled jobs in industry. Now the influx of unskilled labour into the factories was simply the result of the technical changes which had blurred the differences between the semi-trained worker who had not learned the 'secrets' of a trade by undergoing an apprenticeship lasting several years and the

1 Here are two examples of such calculations. G. D. H. Cole states that about 1914 typical weekly wage rates for skilled and unskilled workers were respectively 37s and 24s–25s—a difference of 50 per cent. Half a century earlier the respective figures were 30s and 15s–16s—a difference of 100 per cent. (Cole, *Studies in class structure*, pp. 57–8.) The movement of wage rates in the building industry is given in the accompanying table (from Postgate, *The builders' history*, p. 455).

The movement of day rates in the building trade, 1850–1920

Years	Carpenters, masons, bricklayers		Plumbers		Plasterers		Labourers	
	s	d	s	d	s	d	s	d
1853–61	5		5		5		3	
1872–73	7	1	7	1	7	1	4	4½
1914	8	7½	9		8	7½	6	
1920	18	8	19		18	8	16	8

high-class artisan who had until now stood on the peak of the old occupational hierarchy and solicitously guarded the mysteries of his craft.

This mass invasion of the technical occupations struck at the very *raison d'être* of the social privileges won and consolidated by the artisan stratum. That system of privileges was built on the foundation of trade monopoly, a monopoly which, because of its exclusive character, gave access to only a few. The channels of social advancement, which were an indisputable element of the privileged position, were scaled to the needs of a stratum of modest numbers; they were, therefore, incapable of letting through a much larger stream of candidates for advancement. The whole carefully constructed system of stratal superiority could only crumble into ruins under the pressure of the mass of workers who were trained in the new capitalist techniques. The system was not suitable for adaptation, but had to be completely rebuilt. The new social movement could not *en route* avoid smashing the constructions put up by its predecessor, which were too narrow for its requirements, but as it smashed them it simultaneously assimilated the well tested assumptions on which they had been based.

We have indicated that the process by which the working class became uniform was not a one-way movement but came from both sides simultaneously. The unskilled masses acquired bases from which to climb out of the slough of despond in which they were sunk; meanwhile the foundations of the privileges of skilled workers were giving way. The latter process was reinforced by the fact that the old channels which had linked the artisans with the classes above them in the hierarchy were beginning to be blocked. In the nineteenth century many workers had trodden a straight path of advancement up which an artisan could move into the technical supervisory staff. Now this path was becoming choked with obstacles. The new techniques which made higher technical demands on workers also required that those who supervised production should have higher qualifications, which could be acquired only through a formal technical education. Thus a new social frontier was appearing from above, and this emphasised even more strongly the blurring of social frontiers below. Moreover, a new and rapidly growing stratum was emerging between the strata which had formerly been immediate neighbours, i.e. the skilled workers and the factory management; this new stratum consisted of employees who were half manual, half white-collar, employed in the fast-expanding supervisory grades. Whereas the actual process of production was becoming relatively simpler, in the sense described above, and the manual trades were becoming less differentiated, the process of supervising production was, on the contrary, becoming more complex. Moreover, it was rapidly creating new and specialised jobs which were from the very start classified on a higher level than the manual trades.

A new stratum of white-collar workers was also emerging. Formerly it had been numerically small and socially unimportant, but now it was assuming an increasingly important role in the process of production, and increasing in size at a hitherto unheard-of rate. There was no passage from topmost rungs of the labour hierarchy to even the lowest rungs of the clerical ladder, which demanded a different type of education. Thus yet another barricade was set up on the earlier routes of upward social mobility for individuals in the stratum of skilled workers. This circumstance, like the separation of the technical supervisory staff, pushed the skilled stratum towards the mass of semi-skilled workers moving up from the bottom, and promoted the process by which occupational interests became subordinated to the interests of the class as a whole.

As a result of all these processes operating on the working class, unifying it internally and separating it from other classes externally, it became more and more a class in the true sense of the word—a social whole with a developed and integrative internal structure and with common unifying interests. Yet that unity existed for the time being in the sphere of a *Klasse an sich*, and not yet in the sphere of a *Klasse für sich*. Objectively, there were increasing structural reasons for the levelling out of internal barriers within the class, but this fact, in its rational form, did not penetrate the consciousness of any of the existing strata. The objective differences between strata which derived from their place in the process of production were already much smaller than the differences in their social position, standard of living and prospects of advancement. The old hierarchies of privilege and deprivation still survived, even though they had lost their objective grounds for existence. Moreover, new relationships could not take their place until the new interests attained a formal institutionalisation which would cement together the *Klasse an sich* and the *Klasse für sich* and give articulate expression to objective trends. The old relationships did not of their own accord give way to the new ones; this required a conscious struggle between social forces.

This conflict between the altered reality of relationships in the production process and their outdated social superstructures is, in my view, the key to the interpretation of the processes which were taking place within the labour movement of this period. In using this key, however, one must remember that in the programmes and operations of various sections of the movement this conflict appeared in a distorted form, deriving from the fact that the requirements of the new situation were perceived by these sections in terms of the life experiences and habitual ways of thinking of the old-established strata. Members of the upwardly mobile stratum of workers which was trained for the new phase of mechanisation regarded themselves as 'unskilled', although the term 'general worker' indicated that their position was above that stratum. The downwardly mobile stratum of skilled workers still continued to look at itself through the prism of guild privilege, guaranteed to those who were masters of the most important individual crafts in a particular industry. It is therefore extremely important, from a methodological viewpoint, to detect, in the views expressed by representatives of different strata about their own and other strata, the decisive objective trends which derive from the social structure, although it is not always possible to find such trends reflected in a rational programme.

This is why there was a long period of inter-stratal conflict within the working class before the unity to which I have referred was attained in practice. During the preceding decades these strata had been living in quite different social conditions and had undergone different experiences, which were consolidated in the form of stratal traditions.

On the one side there was the great mass of workers, unskilled until recently but at this time possessing some technical skills; despite this, they were still living in lamentable conditions and aiming, consciously or unconsciously, at raising their social position in accordance with the possibilities offered by the new organisation of industry. These workers lacked the tradition of occupational protection; even at this date they had no objective grounds for paying special attention to occupational differences, and therefore from the very beginning they saw their interests as those of the workers as a whole, not those of particular occupational groups. Their interests could not be met by changes of income within the working class, because they themselves constituted the whole of the class. In consequence, this mass of workers had a natural inclination to set itself up as a whole in opposition to contemporary society as a whole. The shallow stratum of artisans could carve itself out a place in society without harming the latter's internal structure by adapting for its own needs the hierarchies already created by society. Such a development was unthinkable in the case of the unskilled and semi-skilled workers. All the existing hierarchies were too fragile to take the weight of their numbers, so the satisfaction of their social aspirations required the rebuilding of established social institutions. These working masses were therefore inherently anti-conservative by disposition.

On the other side, there was a relatively well-to-do stratum whose members, by contrast with other workers, possessed certain additional financial advantages derived from their role in the process of production—though, naturally, within the limits of the criteria of the capitalist system—and were thus not likely to adopt an attitude of social protest. This stratum had for many decades been accustomed to regard its occupational exclusiveness as the most enduring foundations of its well-being and had reduced its social problems to occupational questions, even conceiving of its stratum as a federation of trades. The privileged position of this stratum was a function of the social structure; the members of the stratum therefore adopted an affirmative, conformist and conservative attitude towards it. This stratum felt itself to be a fully enfranchised section of the existing social set-up, and was not conscious of any need for changes in the system in order to achieve the gradual satisfaction of its own requirements.

Thus the process of integrating the working class involved a conflict between two social groups with very different characteristics. As we shall see later, this fact gave the labour movement of this period an exceptional internal dynamism and flexibility of forms.

While it was becoming internally consolidated, the working class was rooted in a society in which the class hierachy was exceptionally powerful; moreover this hierarchy was fixed in the social consciousness of almost all strata as a result of the specific character of its historical genesis, and particularly the peaceful integration of the landed aristocracy into capitalism, and of the capitalist class into the aristocracy. In the period under discussion the English aristocracy was still one of the wealthiest in the world. It was strongly placed to retain its economic power in the new conditions, and, in consequence, to retain many key political positions as well.

Of a total of several hundred members of the aristocracy, however, only thirty-seven had pedigrees dating back before the seventeenth century. The paint was scarcely dry on the armorial bearings of the ever-growing number of peers entitled to a seat in the House of Lords. At the turn of the century the accumulation of a sizeable fortune was regarded as a service to the nation, something which entitled a man to try for a title. The influx of middle class intruders was an expression of the capitulation of the new ruling class to the old one and its recognition of the superiority or aristocratic values in the hierarchy of social values. On the other hand, however, it was bound to lower the social worth of a title and to blur the frontiers between the aristocracy and the middle class to some extent. In the social hierarchy the higher grades of this class were almost coterminous with the aristocracy. On the other hand, an increasing number of people of aristocratic background were entering the middle classes by practising one of the professions—something which had been extremely rare in earlier times.

The frontiers of the middle class were probably less defined than those of any other class. We have already mentioned the fact that its upper boundary was blurred, but the class as a whole was an unbroken chain of strata which were interconnected and afforded easy passage from one to another.

These strata included such categories as owners of industrial, distributive and transport undertakings of widely varying sizes, representatives of the professions, administrative staff of different types, and an extremely diversified and undefined petty bourgeois stratum; at the lower extreme this passed into the stratum of privileged workers and craftsmen. The rise and rapid growth of the white-collar stratum added still more to the complexity of the concept of the middle class. This extensive social diversity made the class division of English society incomparably less clear-cut than in the Victorian era. In the period we are concerned with here, although the definitions of the basic classes in society retained their value, it was much more difficult to apply those definitions correctly in determining the increasing number of borderline cases. This development is the more important for our particular enquiry in view of the perceptive observation made by Lewis and Maude that the English middle classes are more open from inside than from outside[1]—that is to say, that an impoverished member of the middle class retains the mentality and political attitudes appropriate to the middle class for a long time, while a well-to-do worker rapidly adopts the consciousness of the class to which he does not in fact belong.

For this reason we must not overlook the fact that, despite the existence of objective class divisions, class movements were not always confined to specified classes. For instance, as it entered a working class that was becoming increasingly uniform, the stratum of skilled workers brought with it the established and lasting ties which linked it in many respects with the middle class or bourgeoisie.

In the new situation of increasing uniformity the social contacts with classes higher in the hierarchy, which had in an earlier period separated the skilled workers from the rest of the working class, now assumed a new role. Within the increasingly integrated working class these contacts began to function as an ideological guide to the *mores*, the ideals of life and the value systems peculiar to the bourgeoisie—a guide for that part of the working class whose general situation had until this time immunised it against the invasion of elements of the bourgeois view of the world. This proposition about the new function of the old social conflicts retains its force, even though the new characteristics of the system of production were destroying the channels along which individuals had in a single generation advanced from skilled status to higher grades of the middle class. For one should not confuse such advancement with social contacts between classes: these two indicators can coincide but need not do so. The drying-up of the channel of intragenerational advancement did not lead to an immediate revolution in the cultural traits that characterised the skilled workers.

1   Lewis and Maude, *The English middle classes*, p. 18.

2

The structure of the labour movement

As the nineteenth century drew to a close the majority of the British working class were living in conditions which differed little from those obtaining in the first half of the century. Only those working in a strictly limited number of trades had succeeded in extricating themselves from a degradation that shamed human dignity. Not only were the mass of unskilled workers condemned to exist in a state of chronic poverty, but they also had to suffer the humiliating attitude of all other strata in society; in particular, they were treated as less than human in the work-places where they earned the means of subsistence. This situation was nothing new. It had lasted for many decades without provoking reactions of self-defence, owing to the unorganised and fragmented state of the unskilled stratum. In the conditions which had evolved towards the end of the nineteenth century, however, the same situation began to produce social consequences of a different kind from those which had been seen until then.

The situation was influenced to a certain extent by the pressure of socialist propaganda, and also by the visible success of the skilled trade union movement. Neither of these would, however, have had any effect but for the structural transformations that were, as has already been described, taking place within the unskilled sector itself. The gradual transition from simple manual labour to work that was in some degree complex put the masses of hitherto unskilled workers in a new situation, assuring them a new position in the production process. Nevertheless, the rise in social status and prestige that corresponded to this situation were not accorded automatically; indeed, this could hardly have come about without a conscious endeavour and struggle. Our purpose here is to pinpoint not only the social premises for this struggle, but also its eventual course and the forms which it assumed. The mass of labourers was galvanised with protest, and both historical circumstances and the operation of external forces defined the direction in which that protest exploded and the intensity of the explosion.

The labourers' revolt was directed more against their humiliating social status than against their miserable living conditions. In this respect the rejection of the very name 'unskilled' as a symbol of social disapproval[1] is

---

1 The leader of the first labourers' union, Ben Tillett, wrote in his memoirs, 'Unskilled labour—a phrase I detest, not merely because it is untrue but also because it is patronising.' Similarly, Philip Snowden commented in his introduction to those

symptomatic. The term was linked in the consciousness of the labouring masses with their treatment by the ruling classes as the dregs of society, and by the skilled factory workers as a passive agglomeration unfitted for organisation. Even the protest against poverty arising from low wages took the form of a revolt against conditions which offended human dignity. The fight for better pay was regarded by the unskilled as a small part of the overall campaign for decent living conditions; it was linked in a single unbreakable whole both with demands that their factory overseers should accord them some respect and with calls for self-indulgence that were now multiplying and becoming widespread. In this sphere the unskilled workers were carrying on the same fight as that waged by their skilled colleagues four decades earlier;[1] the scale was, however, incomparably greater.

None the less, the first barrier which the unskilled workers came up against at the very beginning of their struggle was the skilled unions

memoirs, '. . . the so-called "unskilled" labourers (a term which, like Ben Tillett, I despise as being not only derogatory but untrue).' B. Tillett, *Memories and reflections*, pp. 20, 8.) From a social psychological viewpoint, it is instructive to note how a term which was entirely technical in origin evolved into a stereotype which was a focal point for sharp clashes of an ideological nature.

1 In his memoirs Robert Smillie gives the following description of the conditions that drove him and his colleagues to rebel, and of the forms which this fight assumed: 'Vividly there rises before me at this moment the form of an old miner, his voice hoarse with many freezings, as he came up from the perspiring pit with the thermometer above ground at zero, or thereabout, so that his clothes became like icy mail before he reached the hovel he called home . . . And with the eagerness of youth, and with the high hopefulness of inexperience, I vowed to give my life to the betterment of the conditions under which, even then, the miner still dragged out a life which was no life for a man made in God's image.' Smillie goes on to recount his conversation with a forge superintendent which ultimately led to the organisation of the workers. 'Now, Gallacher, we have been working our hardest and doing our best for you, and up to now we have had nothing but abuse; I'm here to tell you that we're all tired of it, and we are determined not to strike another blow until you have promised to stop swearing at us, and to treat us as free men and not as slaves.' (R. Smillie, *My life for labour*, Mills & Boon, London, 1924, pp. 11–12, 18.) At a mass meeting of cab drivers in Hyde Park, John Burns, the leading figure in the unskilled labour movement, shouted, 'Now do make a reasonable use of the higher wages which you have fought for . . . Don't drink, but give the money to the missus.' As this evoked various interruptions, he continued, 'Oh, I know you; you can't take me in. Your wives are worth more than you are. And this is certain, if I find out that the extra pay is being drunk, the next time you will have me against you, not for you.' (Bernstein, *My years of exile*, p. 260.) In summing up the results of several years' operations by the dockers' union, Ben Tillett gave priority to the following contributions: 'We have seen the men of our own country become lighter and better with a brighter environment; a better race of men, better husbands, fathers and citizens have come along to understand the finer meanings of life.' (B. Tillett, *A brief history of the dockers' union*, Dock, Wharf, Riverside and General Workers' Union, London, 1910, p. 46.)

themselves. The latter were going through a period of conservative stabilisation; they were satisfied with their achievements, tightly closed against
intruders and already suspicious and on their guard against attempts by the
unskilled masses to encroach on their monopolistic positions. These unions
were strongly entrenched in the field as the official and legal representatives of the entire working class and labour movement in dealing with
government and the employers, although in fact they had substituted
their own narrow occupational interests for the interests of the class movement as a whole.[1]

The conflict between the aspirations of the unskilled and the monopolistic position of the skilled workers within the labour movement was
sufficiently obvious to be quickly realised by both sides. It was bound to
lead to a sharp conflict between the 'new' and the 'old' trade union
movement. (The 'new model' unions suddenly found that they had become the 'old' unions—although the majority of them were only twenty
to thirty years of age—and I shall refer to them thus hence-forward.) The
type of social position which the artisan stratum had won for itself precluded the possibility of assimilation *en masse* of the upwardly mobile
unskilled stratum; in the same way the type of organisation created by the
artisan stratum made it impossible for the old unions to assimilate the
unskilled masses. The whole meaning and conception behind the old
unions required that they should be exclusive and their membership
open only to relatively well-off workers who could pay the high membership fees in return for equally high insurance benefits. Moreover, in the
1890s the structure of the old unions was adapted to the defence of existing
gains, whereas the unskilled masses were only starting to fight for positions
which would be worth defending. Lastly, the interests of the skilled stratum could still be satisfied on an occupational basis, a fact which was reflected in the structure of their unions. On the other hand, the interests of
the working class as a whole required a much broader organisational
plane and a more universal target for their demands than the local employer.

All this in conjunction precluded the possibility of organisational assimilation and made it necessary for the unskilled to organise themselves
outside the skilled unions, alongside them and independently of them.
Then, however, there arose all along the line the problem of mutual
relations between the two types of labour union, and in particular the
problem of the monopoly of representing the working class which had
been usurped by the skilled unions. Before long this monopoly was bound
to become the object of attacks by the new trade union movement. And
this is what happened. The struggle began, and the position taken up by

1   See Cole, *Organised labour*, p. 24.

either side throws considerable light on the social characteristics of the two sections of the labour movement.

The main charge levelled by the unskilled section against the old unions was that of occupational egoism, aimed against the interests of that part of the working class which had no occupational protection. In statements made by the representatives of the new movement one finds many comments on the incompatibility of interests between the two sections of the movement. Such statements maintained that an important task facing the new unions was to defend the economic interests of unskilled workers against the selfishness of the skilled union.[1]

With this object in view it was necessary to organise the unskilled workers as rapidly as possible, and to even out the disproportion in the degrees to which skilled and unskilled were organised. For instance, as late as 1899 among trade union members in York the ratio of skilled to unskilled workers was as low as 446 to 2,093.[2] Furthermore, it was necessary to

1   For instance, one of the leaders of the new movement, J. R. Clynes, told an audience, 'So far as I can speak for the general labourer, I should say that he has in the realm of trade union organisation up till now been the sufferer to a greater extent from causes over which he had no control than any other class of workmen or artisans in the field of labour. The labourer has been, as it were, between two stools—(hear, hear)—he has been ground often between two forces—the employer of labour has often inflicted loss and punishment upon the labourer without having an immediate quarrel with the general labourer. The blow that the employer has intended to inflict upon the skilled workman has very often missed that workman and fallen with very great force indeed upon the innocent, and upon the non-competitive general labourer. (Hear, hear.) Not only has the labourer had to suffer in that way because of the attacks and the aggression of the employers but the labourer has had to suffer even because of the battles which the skilled workman naturally wages in his own interest, so that, between the two, the labourer in turn was made the victim of industrial warfare over which he had little or no control.' (General Labourers' National Council and National Transport Workers' Federation, *Report of special conference on amalgamation*, Caxton Hall, Westminster, 8 July 1914, pp. 8–9.) Tom Mann and Ben Tillett also sharply attacked the old unions for neglecting the interests of unskilled workers: 'Mr Shipton, [the General Secretary of the TUC] is one of the "old" school, happily a diminishing one, who considered it impossible to organise the unskilled labourer, thus practically avowing his own incapacity to rouse this class of workman . . . The old societies [were] so utterly callous to this poverty as not to make any special exertion to alter matters for the better. Thus, the Amalgamated Engineers, in 1879, had 13 per cent of their numbers out of employment, and another 4 per cent on sick and superannuation benefits, while outside the society were three times the number in the same trade, eligible for membership in the Amalgamated Engineers, beside 300,000 handy men and labourers employed in that trade, all waiting to be organised and helped; but no encouraging word was held out, no elaboration of policy, no real concern was manifested by the unionists —everything was dead.' (T. Mann and B. Tillett, *The 'new' trade unionism*, Green & McAllan, London, 1890, pp. 3–4.)

2   Seebohm Rowntree, *Poverty*, p. 408.)

organise the labourers in separate unions, not subordinated to the self-interest of the skilled unions and based on entirely new conceptual assumptions and methods of operation.

It may be recalled that the awakening of the unskilled worker occurred in the period when the artisans' unions had entered a phase of ossification and had lost almost all their original dynamism, which had been characterised by a flexibility of structural forms and a capacity for absorption. The rigidity and conservatism of the old unions were in glaring contrast to the dynamic energy of the class that was now making its appearance in the social arena, and provided a target for better attacks and denunciations from the leaders of the new movement.[1]

Closely connected with these charges was the attack on the very concept of organisation on which the old unions were based. The system of social insurance which was increasingly gaining a key position in the activities of the old unions led to two consequences which were equally opposed to the interests of the unskilled. For this system dissociated the less prosperous workers from the union movement; at the same time it effectively exerted a restraining influence on union policy and helped to spread conformist attitudes towards the existing social order.[2]

1   To quote Tom Mann's angry words, 'To Trade Unionists I desire to make a special appeal. How long, *how long*, will you be content with the present half-hearted policy of your Unions? I readily grant that good work has been done in the past by the Unions, but, in Heaven's name, what good purpose are they serving now? All of them have large numbers out of employment even when their particular trade is busy. None of the important societies have any policy other than that of endeavouring to keep wages from falling. The true Unionist policy of *aggression* seems entirely lost sight of; in fact, the average Unionist of today is a man with a fossilised intellect, either hopelessly apathetic, or supporting a policy that plays directly into the hands of the capitalist exploiter.' (T. Mann, *What a compulsory eight-hour working day means to the workers*, Modern Press, London, 1886, p. 11.)

   Again, the same Tom Mann wrote, together with Ben Tillett: 'We could, if need be, call together hundreds among the most valued members of the Amalgamated Engineers ... who would readily testify to the most frightful apathy prevailing in their union even five years ago ... We attribute the apathy of many of the wealthy unions to the lack of new vitality, many of them up till within recent years not being in advance of the stage where they have been left by the men who suffered imprisonment and starvation for their convictions.' (Mann and Tillett, *The 'new' trade unionism*, pp. 4, 14.)

2   In 1887, on the eve of the birth of the new trade union movement, its ideological spokesman, John Burns, made the following comment on 'old' trade unionism in *Justice*. 'Constituted as it is, Unionism carries within itself the source of its own dissolution ... Their reckless assumption of the duties and responsibilities that only the State or the whole country can discharge, in the nature of sick and superannuation benefits, at the instance of the middle class, is crushing out the larger Unions by taxing their members to an unbearable extent. This so cripples them that the fear of being unable to discharge their friendly society liabilities often makes them sub-

Another target for attack, and one consistent with the nature of the new movement, was the occupational basis on which the old unions were organised. It has already been pointed out that occupational differences played little part in the social structure of that section of the working class which was now moving towards emancipation. The clannishness of the guild tradition was something fundamentally alien to this sector. Class, not occupation, was regarded as the right basis for the setting up of an organisation. Because of the rapid turnover of unskilled and semi-skilled labour and its easy exchangeability between different branches of industry and different types of work, a broad-based organisation which would unite workers from the most varied occupations and industries was required if this sector's interests were to be defended effectively. On the other hand, such fluidity and interchangeability precluded any attempt to institutionalise any particular non-artisan occupation. 'Clannishness in trade matters must be superseded by a cosmopolitan spirit; brotherhood must not only be talked of but practised'—this was the cry of the new trade union movement.[1]

The concept of the 'general union', based not on occupation nor even on a particular industry but on class, was evolved as the practical counterpart to this slogan. A union of this kind was by its very nature supposed to attempt to cover all workers, regardless of their occupational training or connection with any particular industry. This assumption was the exact opposite of the principles which actuated the skilled unions. It is worth noting that the idea of the 'industrial union', i.e. one union for all the employees in a given branch of industry, never struck deep roots in Britain.[2] Only with the National Union of Railwaymen and the National Union of Mineworkers were attempts made to set up this kind of union, and even they were not completely successful. In principle, the British trade union movement consists of two types of union—the craft union, institutionalising the interests of one or more trades of a particular character, and the general union, which endeavours to institutionalise the interests shared by the mobile semi-skilled work groups in different industries and transport services and in different production teams.[3]

mit to encroachments by the masters without protest. The result of this is that all of them have ceased to be Unions for maintaining the rights of labour, and have degenerated into mere middle and upper class rate-reducing institutions.' (Quoted by G. D. H. Cole, *John Burns*, Fabian Biographical Series, No. 14, Gollancz, London, 1943, p. 21.)

1   Mann and Tillett, *The 'new' trade unionism*, p. 15.
2   See, for instance, J. D. M. Bell, *Industrial unionism*, University of Glasgow (Department of Social and Economic Research) occasional papers, No. 2, McNaughton & Gowanlock, Glasgow, 1949, p. 9.
3   This dual organisational structure found in Britain's trade unions is not, apparently,

an isolated one. Different union structures have evolved in different countries depending on varying historical circumstances; nevertheless, the history of the trade union movement shows similar trends in the majority of countries. Yet this occurs only on one condition, i.e. if a working class political movement either has not evolved at all in a given country or appeared only after the trade union movement had struck deep roots. In brief, it occurs when the union movement is not a creation of the political party, stamped with the social concepts of its creator, but has evolved spontaneously without an organisational centre. This reservation will be more easily understood if we contrast two cases which are totally dissimilar from each other—the trade union movements in Britain and pre-Nazi Germany, about which Bernstein commented in an apt simile: 'The relation of the English labour movement to the German may be compared with that of a primeval forest to an orderly plantation laid out upon virgin soil.' (*My years of exile*, p. 276.) The Allgemeiner Deutscher Gewerkschaftsbund was essentially the creation of the SPD. The system of 'one industry—one union' was the realisation in material form of the socialist ideals of a party which was set up before the unions came into being. In addition, the German labour movement dispensed with the stage of craft unions and also that of general unions. In the latter case this was probably because there was a strong central bond, though not a federal one, between the unions; this bond was adequate to meet the need for institutionalisation of those general interests whose requirements in the British situation had to be satisfied by the general unions. In consequence, the structure of the German unions was much simpler and more clearly defined. In 1912 there were only fifty-two trade unions in Germany (Rayner, *The story of trade unionism*, p. 123), compared with a total of over 1,000 in Britain. A similar observation can be made about the Confédération Générale de Travail, originally set up in 1895, in France, in spite of the fact that a few weak unions were actually in existence in that country before the French socialists began to organise the union movement, and also that the exceptional popularity of syndicalist principles gave the *bourses de travail* an importance such as was never possessed by their British equivalents, the trades councils. On the other hand, in countries where the unions sprang up spontaneously and occupational interests became ossified ahead of class interests, one is struck by the similarity of the organisational structures set up to the two basic types in Britain. An example of this may be found in Denmark. There, one large general union with aspirations to recruit all workers, but in fact covering unskilled and semi-skilled workers, has grown up alongside trade unions still tracing their origins back to the guild tradition. In 1949 the membership of the large general union comprised 38 per cent of all Danish Federation members, while the rest were divided among the other sixty-nine craft unions. (Galenson, *Comparative labor movements*, p. 122.) In the history of the American labour movement the Knights of Labor were a phenomenon somewhat outside the compass of the trade union movement (like the trades unions of Britain in the 1830s). In the brief period between their lightning upsurge and downfall the Knights of Labor made themselves known as supporters of a mass organisation on Owenite and syndicalist lines. On the other hand, the IWW was emerging as early as 1905 as the opponent of the conservatism and stagnation prevalent in the skilled unions organised in the AFL; it countered the guild-like clannishness of those unions with the model of a general union that would unite under its aegis workers with all kinds of qualifications and from all possible branches of industry, so that the whole fighting force of the working class might be concentrated together. (B. Stephansky, 'The structure of the American labor movement', in Industrial Relations Research Association, *Interpereting the labour movement*, p. 49.)

The trend towards a broad type of general union was expressed in a long-drawn-out series of amalgamations between unions. These continued at a steady pace throughout the period under discussion and into the early years of the period between the two world wars. Fusions took place between the most varied and specialised unions from all branches of the economy; the only trait which they shared in common was that their membership consisted of unskilled and semi-skilled workers.[1]

1   Listed below are the names of unions which met in 1914 to discuss the question of amalgamation. I am giving it in full to illustrate the variety of unions from which the 'general unions' were set up and the popularity of the idea of a 'general union'. Indeed, the names of many of the unions which amalgamated already expressed their aspirations in this direction:

The British Labour Amalgamation
Navvies', Builders, Labourer' and General Labourers' Union
The Workers' Union
National Amalgamated Union of Labour
Amalgamated Society of Gasworkers, Brickmakers and General Labourers
Amalgamated Union of Machine and General Labourers
Amalgamated General and Warehouse Worker's Union
Amalgamated Society of Watermen, Lightermen and Bargemen
Amalgamated Stevedores' Labour Protection League
Dock, Wharf, Riverside and General Workers' Union
Labour Protection League
National Union of Gasworkers and General Labourers
Hull Seamen's Union
Mersey Quay and Railway Carters' Union
National Amalgamated Labourers' Union
National Union of Dock Labourers
National Union of Ships' Clerks
National Union of Vehicle Workers
Scottish Union of Dock Labourers
North of Scotland Horse and Motormen's Association
United Carters' Association of England
United Order of General Labourers
Upper Mersey Watermen's and Porters' Association
Weaver Watermen's Association
Cardiff, Barry and Penarth Coal Trimmers' Union
Scottish Horse and Motormen's Association
North of England Trimmers' and Teemers' Association
National Amalgamated Coal Porters' Association
Irish Transport Workers' Union
London and Provincial Union of Licensed Vehicle Workers
Glasgow Ship Riggers
United Society of Boiler Sealers
Mersey River and Canals Watermen
Amalgamated Protective Union of Engine and Crane Drivers.

(*Report of special conference on amalgamation*, pp. 2–6, 27). The number of unions

The labourers' unions, which had from the start been dissociated from the old unions and had adopted a hostile attitude to them, had groped their way forward without the possibility of falling back on any ready-made organisational models. If one looks at their external forms, the continuing birth of new unions was an illusory reminder of the history of the sudden creation of new unions in the upsurge of protest during the first half of the nineteenth century.[1] The new movement was spontaneous and to a large extent dependent on transient emotional tension; it lacked the sober calculation of profit and loss which was the basis of the skilled unions. In the first phase of their existence the general unions were frequently held together only by a charismatic bond, and were just as impermanent as their predecessors of the first half of the century. However, a successful strike in direct conflict with the employers would immediately increase the members' confidence in their own forces and enhance the feeling of strength which is conferred by an organised and united campaign. The victorious union would gain massive support in no time at all; if it succeeded, before the first setback, in setting up internal links that were more lasting than those based on charisma, then it would continue to exist, no longer dependent for continuity and reinforcement on a frequent recurrence of *ad hoc* successes. Before the great dock strike of 1889—the first great strike victory of the labourers—the Tea Operatives and General Labourers' Union led by Tillett had 300 members. Immediately after the successful strike, and as a result of it, this union developed into the Dock, Wharf, Riverside and General Labourers' Union, with a membership of 30,000.[2] The increase was enormous for that period, and only the Amalgamated Society of Engineers had more members.

The case of the dockers was far from being an exception: its wide fame came from the shock effect among the ruling classes of a major dock strike involving the threat of future explosion by no means confined to the economic sphere. Nevertheless the course of events in many other branches

whose names contained the term 'general' or otherwise indicated universalistic aspirations is significant. It is not a mere matter of coincidence but expresses the trends of that particular era.

1 This is how Ben Tillet described the setting up in the 'Royal Oak' public house in 1887 of the powerful dockers' union, a direct lineal ancestor of Britain's largest general union of today, the Transport and General Workers': 'It was talk, talk, shout and jeer and cheer; the air was electric; the tune of life was playing on our heartstrings, but it lacked direction . . . I was driven along the cataract of passion and feeling until I found my frightened voice; but I knew we wanted direction; we wanted the machinery; we wanted a base, a starting point; we wanted authority . . . It was agreed, agreed before I could estimate that my sense of the obvious was what we had all been trying hitherto to express.' (Tillett, *Brief history of the dockers' union*, p. 3.)

2 Williams, *Magnificent journey*, p. 179.

of industry was similar. For instance, immediately after the dockers' strike (and probably in emulation of its example) a strike of semi-skilled employees in London printing houses took place. In protest against their low rates of pay—three times less than those of qualified printers—the printers' assistants at the firm of Spottiswoode & Co. led a march from one printing house to another, calling on all workers to join their strike. This unusual strike led to the swift capitulation of the majority of printing house owners. Its outcome was the setting up of the first union of semi-skilled printing workers—the National Society of Operative Printers and Assistants. A certain George Evans, compositor, is said to have advised the printing workers to preserve the sense of community which had sprung up spontaneously during the strike.[1]

In consequence of this and similar developments, a considerable number of unskilled and semi-skilled worker's unions sprang up like mushrooms after rain. Their representatives began to appear in ever-increasing numbers at the annual Trades Union Congresses, which had until then been the feudal bailiwick of the group of the wealthiest 'old' unions. These representatives of the 'new' unionism began to press ever more insistently for changes in the role and administration of the T.U.C. and to utter accusations against the old unions at their own union conferences.

The old unions were thus brought face to face with the fact that a new and more powerful force had been born, one which did not fit into the traditional forms of the union movement. Everthing in the new unions—their belligerence and aggressiveness, their lack of financial reserves, their administrative weakness and propensity to strike, the dubious social stability of the stratum from which their members were recruited—all ran counter to the inclinations and habits of the stable unions of the old, established trades. The old unions responded by counter-attacking. The new unions' enthusiasm for strike action compelled the old ones to compete in the sphere least convenient for themselves. Strikes were a negation of their general philosophy and also constituted an intolerable threat to the rich funds which were the old unions' greatest achievement. Furthermore, they cast doubt upon the respectability which the old union movement had fostered with such care, and also created an atmosphere in which the old union leaders, who dressed in middle class style and were used to the conference table and desk work, simply felt ill at ease. The hot-headed, fiery-tongued leaders of the younger generation of unionists found the atmosphere of a strike congenial. Whether a particular strike ended with victory or defeat for the workers, it could easily mean personal defeat for the existing chairman or secretary of a union, and his replacement by

1   G. G. Eastwood, *George Isaacs*, Odhams Press, London, 1952, pp. 37–41.

another individual who felt more at home in the fray.[1] The skilled unions regarded the whole 'new' union movement as an attack on the privileges they had won; and their leaders considered the new activists as adventurers who were making claims on the well merited honour of their own organisations. When Keir Hardie delivered the new movement's visiting card at the 1887 Congress with his bitter attack on the established leadership, Broadhurst's answer, part astonished, part indignant, was to ask how long his attacker had sacrificed his life to trade unionism and politics and what part he had played 'in the great struggle which had lifted labour up from the position it was in fifty years back, when Odger, Howell and all the other champions of labour were fighting their battles?' This attempt to justify contemporary inactivity by recalling the heroic past was understandable enough to those who used it but entirely failed to convince the younger generation, whose heroic phase was still to come.

In their defence against the would-be usurpers the old unions made herculean endeavours to adapt themselves to the new conditions. Such adaptation demanded above all that they should give up their claims to occupational monopoly—something that was not easy for the old union movement to swallow. In any case, if some unions made efforts to accede to such demands, this attests to the strength of the pressure exerted by the working masses once they were aroused. The doyen of the old unions, the Amalgamated Society of Engineers, was forced to open its doors to groups of less skilled workers in the iron and steel trade, groups which had hitherto not been allowed to join—and by 1900 its membership had risen to 87,672.[2] The Operative Society of Bricklayers, whose membership had for decades not exceeded 7,000, rose to 17,000 in the 1890s, and the Boot and Shoe Operatives' Union trebled the number of its members over the same period.[3] Somewhat later even the exclusive Scottish Typographical Association began to admit not only compositors, stone-hands and machine minders but also less skilled printing workers, although to the very end it remained essentially an organisation for the higher grades of the printing trade.[4]

In spite of these endeavours, no genuine adaptation of the old unions to the needs of the mass movement of workers was possible. More precisely, it was possible, but at the price of destroying in the old unions those special elements which made them what they were and which enabled them to satisfy and fulfil the needs of the skilled stratum in the years 1850–90. In admitting unskilled workers to their ranks the old unions would have

1 Hyndman, *Further Reminiscences*, pp. 460–1.
2 V. L. Allen, *Power in trade unions*, Longmans, London, 1954, p. 108.
3 Rayner, *The story of trade unionism*, p. 62.
4 Gillespie, *A hundred years of progress*, pp. 147, 231.

ceased to be 'old style' unions; they would have lost their ability to serve the interests of the skilled stratum efficiently. Quite apart from this, expansion was made difficult, if not impossible, by the fact that the machinery of the old unions was creaky and its structure ossified. This was why despite intensive efforts, they failed to keep up with the flexible and dynamic 'new' unions in organising the great mass of workers not yet caught up in the union movement.

For this reason, relations between the old and the new union movement were characterised more by infighting than by straightforward competition. The old unions deployed against the new ones a heavy artillery barrage of charges which were highly disparaging in terms of the old union ethic. They accused the new unions of wanting to 'do less work, and get more pay'; of believing in 'loose forms of association'; of 'relying upon demonstrations, bands and banners'; of being 'led by the academic middle class' and being 'manipulated by men outside . . . the special trade in which they are moving spirits'.[1] Without going into the accuracy of these charges, it is worth pointing out that in any event they reflect the views of the leaders of the old unions on the new unionism, and the fears which the latter's emergence had aroused in their minds. The leaders of the old unions indicted those who were active in the new unions with far greater energy than they did the capitalist employers,[2] and were liberal with their abuse and accusations.[3]

The sources of the bitterness which characterised both sides in the first phase of the struggle should be sought on two levels simultaneously. On the one hand, there was a genuine opposition of interests between the elite stratum of skilled workers, entrenched in their lower middle class comfort and rooted in the capitalist political system, and most of the rest of the working class, which still remained in a state of poverty or near-poverty and was excluded from general society. On the other hand, there was a

1   Mann and Tillett, *The 'new' trade unionism.*
2   Cf, for example, the Association of Locomotive Enginemen and Firemen and the Amalgamated Society of Railway Servants. (McKillop, *The lighted flame*, p. 78.)
3   The report of the Parliamentary Committee to the TUC in September 1889 contained the following passage. 'Those who support dissension in the Unions . . . and seek to destroy Unionism, by vehemently attacking its prominent representatives, we unhesitatingly declare to be people unworthy of confidence and who should be shunned accordingly. Their [the socialists'] emissaries enter our camp in the guise of friends in order that they may the better sow the seeds of disruption. Let the worker beware of them . . . We point out the danger and unmask their policy; it is for you to decide whether your enemies shall triumph or you yourselves will continue to hold the field of unionism . . . No progress can be made while dissensions are in our camp. Those who create discord are not worthy of the association of earnest men.' (Quoted by Page-Arnot, *The miners*, p. 129.)

source of friction, to some extent derivative but nevertheless automatic, in the conflict of interests between the two labour movements, which had been built on the bases of stratal interests and class interests. The skilled union movement was protecting its monopoly of the right to represent workers' interests, a monopoly which gave the movement a political role greater than its particular social base would otherwise have afforded. The unskilled and semi-skilled union movement, on the other hand, was struggling to gain a social position for itself, with that monopoly constituting one of the main obstacles in the struggle.

The duration and intensity of the struggle depended in the final analysis on the extent to which the two above-mentioned conflicts were resolved and on the speed with which this was done. On the one hand, it depended on the degree and rapidity with which the socio-economic positions of the various strata of the working class were evened out in accordance with the increasing proximity of their roles in the production process. On the other it depended on the extent to which the new alignment of the labour movement, and particularly its newly extended range—opening up, as it did, completely new horizons for social action—were making the monopoly of the old unions obsolete. That monopoly had been exercised only within a labour movement of relatively small proportions, playing an insignificant political role; it now faced the powerful onsurge which was gradually being generated by the newly awakened class movement. The fortress of the old unions, assiduously though it had been guarded, was soon left far behind in the movement's first attack on a wide front.

Thereafter, probably as a consequence of the completion of these two processes, a gradual tapering off of the struggle between the new and old unions is discernible. After the full-scale clashes of the 1890s, the first signs of a truce appeared at the beginning of the twentieth century. In the years immediately preceding the first world war this truce was succeeded by a thoroughgoing standardisation of programmes and political organisational patterns between both branches of the movement.

The trade union movement that took shape as a result of this move towards uniformity was an alloy of the old and the new. It was linked with the old unionism by its final acceptance of the existing social structure and of its own place within that structure, while the indelible influence of the new movement resulted in an immeasurable increase in union aspirations. In the final analysis, the social content of the union movement that ultimately emerged was found to differ from that of the old unions in only one respect. It wished to exploit the opportunities for upward mobility which now existed for individuals and groups, opportunities that were much more far-reaching than any the old unions had created. For this purpose it wished to exploit the possibilities of the existing capitalist order.

It therefore aligned its programme with the system of capitalist relationships, accepting these relations and rejecting the idea of reversing the scale of social values which prevailed under that system.[1] When one of the most militant and restless leaders of the new unionism, Ben Turner, who in the 1890s had inveighed thunderously against the capitalist system of nepotism, later took stock of his life's struggle, he found it justified only in that he had 'had a good deal to do' with getting the wages of male workers in textile factories up from about 21*s* a week in 1890 to 54*s* 10*d* in 1929. He ended with a comment of which no ideological associate of Broadhurst or Howell would have been ashamed: '. . . and certainly it has helped, and not hindered, the employers, for it is always the same; the best wages get the best work and even the best profit.'[2]

In 1910, moreover, Ben Tillet, the man who was almost the symbol of the new unionism, defined the relationship of the new unions to the old as follows (it should be noted that he was no longer using the pejorative term 'old union'): 'We have achieved results transcending the benefits obtained by the skilled unions. The uplift was greater, because the depths were so low from which to rise.'[3] Instead the balance sheets of the hundred largest unions, both old and new, showed a steady rise in the proportion of expenditure, while there was no increase in outgoings for strike action, in spite of the unions' increasing potential in this sphere. These trends are illustrated by Table 11. The increase in the amounts paid out on strikes in 1908 and in the three-year period which began in 1910 was an exceptional phenomenon, a sudden 'bulge' in the fairly straightforward basic trend due to several unusually long strikes which occurred in these years.

From the sociological viewpoint the most interesting question is why these once aggressively militant unions became 'domesticated'. For it must not be forgotten that the labour movement of the factory workers of the first half of the nineteenth century, whose determined methods had resembled those of the new unions, had led not to conformist organisations rooted in the capitalist system, but to the revolutionary Chartist movement—and thus to consequences entirely different from those which ensued for the new unions in the early part of the twentieth century.

One reason why these superficially similar movements developed so differently was the difference in the historical situation. It has already been shown how the unions of the early nineteenth century arose in a social

1 S. Perlman, *A theory of the labor movement*, Macmillan, New York, 1928; reprinted Kelley, New York, 1949, pp. 131–2. Perlman attributes his attitude to the 'new unionism', not to the movement which evolved as a consequence of the 'synthesis' of the old and new unions. This view is contradicted by the facts.
2 Turner, *About myself*, p. 135.
3 Tillett, *Brief history of the dockers' union*, p. 3.

Table 11

Variations in the local expenditure of the 100 principal trade unions, 1901–10 (£'000)

Year	Unemployed	Sick and accident; superannuation; funeral	
	A	B	B:A
1901	2·0	5·9	2·95
1902	2·3	6·5	2·85
1903	1·5	7·0	4·7
1904	1·2	7·4	6·1
1905	2·2	7·8	3·5
1906	1·6	8·4	5·25
1907	1·2	8·9	7·4
1908	6·1	9·4	1·5
1909	1·6	9·3	5·6
1910	3·5	9·2	2·6

Source C. M. Lloyd, *Trade unionism*, Black, London, 1921. p. 127; cf also H. B. Lees Smith, *Trade unionism*, Christian Social Union pamphlet No. 9, p. 12.

milieu that was completely undifferentiated, fluid, and unused to organising itself in any way. The journeymen's clubs kept aloof, because the stratum of craftsmen had no tradition of community with the working population in the factories and mines, or on the estates. The new unions were born in a situation in which a considerable part of the working class that had been created by capitalist industry already possessed a definite occupational structure, a stability of social status and a cohesive organisation that was proof against changing circumstances. The structural network of the old unions was the framework on which the new unionism was built.

After the first dizzying successes, achieved through the violent release of the hitherto dormant energies of the working masses, the new unions faced the complicated problem of consolidating the organisations which had been born amid such turbulence.

Once again the sociological dictum was confirmed that it is incomparably easier to transform the energy of the workers into an explosive outburst than into regular, monotonous, everyday effort; it is easier to rally the workers to the standards of a militant organisation than it is to keep them there. If the unions were to maintain their existence, without losing the power so suddenly acquired, and to consolidate what had been achieved by their rapid onslaught, it was essential to replace the unstable charismatic link with the only type of social bond capable of guaranteeing long life to an association—the bond of a nomocratic organisation. This is the most difficult stage to reach in the development of a new social structure from its birth to its establishment. In the case of the new unions the crucial step was greatly eased by the existence of the old union movement. In the preceding century the protectionist craft unions had supplied the unions of the new skilled workers with a convenient model of organisation; the old unions now performed a similar role for the new unionism. In a sense, the movement of skilled workers went through the period of maturing both on its own account and on behalf of the unskilled and semi-skilled unions simultaneously. When the new unions emerged from the state of confusion which followed the stormy struggles that accompanied their birth, they found themselves confronted by a ready-made structure which made it possible for them in practice to omit the period of maturation and to adopt the most enduring and well tried forms of organisation without a preliminary period of trial and error. This was all the easier for them because the leaders of the new unionism naturally attended the Trades Union Congresses as the principal workers' organisations of this period. Despite the aggressive attitudes which they at first displayed there, they gradually succumbed to the moderating influence of a solid, established union structure. Nor was it without significance that the leaders of the unskilled workers were as a general rule skilled workers, trained in the old unions and reared in their atmosphere.

Another element which helped to assuage the initial militancy of the new unions was the social position which had been achieved by the old union movement for at least some manual occupations, for the union movement and for the occupation of union official.

The labourers' unions of the first half of the nineteenth century were conducting their struggle in a vacuum, in conditions where there was no tradition of organising factory workers and no social position for a workers' leader. The stereotype which prevailed at that period classed workers' organisations among the enemies of a sacrosanct social order, outside society and its legal system. The new unions, on the other hand, were subsumed almost automatically and without effort under the stereotypes which had been evolved by the associations of skilled workers in the eyes of society at large. These public stereotypes were entirely different from those referred to above: they involved not only the acceptance of the unions' right to exist but even the recognition of their social utility for the consolidation of the prevailing social order. The unions' status was established, and the role of union organiser was also accepted as that of a reliable person, worthy of respect and needed by society. In this situation the transition from the stage of a union's birth to that of its establishment could be an especially rapid one. It could occur all the more easily because the new unions, in order to take advantage of the convenient positions in the social hierarchy prepared by their predecessors, had also to take over all the related organisational forms evolved by the old unions, including their tactical methods and their organisational symbols. The new social content of the unions, which was an institutionalisation of class, not occupational, interests, had to be clothed in the livery of organisational forms already designed on an occupational basis. One consequence of this was that, *inter alia*, class interests in the British labour movement were somehow superimposed on occupational interests. This was an institutionalisation of the interests of a class which had already been crystallised into occupations and had learned its brand of social action in the course of its struggle for occupational interests. In short, the existence of the old unions shortened the process of maturation for the new ones, and facilitated their assimilation by the capitalist social system.

A factor which furthered the assimilation of the new unions into the existing set-up was the need to adapt their structure to everyday requirements.[1] In consequence, the new organisations developed a bureaucratic type of administrative apparatus—a network of permanent agents and organisers, personifying the social bond which held them together. From the moment of its emergence the administrative machinery itself became a factor which helped to hold the new organisations together from within. Apart from the dull routine of its everyday functions—such as negotiations with employers and efforts to build up union funds—this machinery was the most effective antidote to the romantic ups and downs of strike action. The clerical machinery of the new movement, like the unions which belonged to it, slipped easily into the grooves hollowed out by the old union movement. From the very outset the union officials achieved a socially recognised status which was a considerable social advance; this encouraged them to make efforts to ensure that elected office should be held for as long a term as possible and that their administrative posts should be permanent.

Table 12 illustrates the dimensions achieved by the bureaucratic administration of the new unions. The table indicates that the establishment of their administrative machinery was proceeding considerably faster than had been the case within the old unions. In fact they reached roughly the same level of development in a much shorter period—precisely because they were developing on terrain already prepared by the skilled unions. The figures for expenditure on administration per union member shown

1 For theoretical discussion of this problem see Max Weber's *Theory of social and economic organisation*, Hodges, London, 1947; V. O. Keys, Jr., *Politics, parties and pressure groups*, Cromwell, New York, 1948.

Table 12

Pre-war* expenditure of certain trade unions analysed

Name of union	Proportion of total spent on management, 1913 (per cent)	Expenditure on management per head, 1913
1. Unions of skilled workers		s d
Amalgamated Society of Carpenters and Joiners	17·6	9 6½
Friendly Society of Ironfounders	9·8	9 4½
London Society of Compositors	9·2	8 3½
Amalgamated Society of Engineers	16·5	8 2
Steam Engine Makers	18·6	7 8½
Amalgamated Association of Operative Cotton Spinners, etc	17·6	13 4
2. Unions consisting largely of less skilled workers		
Workers' Union	40·9	3 2½
National Union of General Workers	61·3	4 6½
Dock, Wharf, Riverside and General Workers' Union	74·3	7 7
National Union of Railwaymen	62·4	5 5

*1914–18.

Source   G. D. H. Cole, Organised labour, Allen & Unwin, London, 1924, p. 166.

in the table are much lower for the new unions than for the old, but only because the new ones had a much larger membership. On the other hand, the proportion of administrative expenses in relation to total expenditure was far higher in the new unions; overheads definitely outweighed expenditure on insurance of various kinds.

The average pay of union officials at the end of the nineteenth century was about £2 4s a week.[1] Such wages were nothing out of the ordinary; but as a rule they exceeded the weekly wage of even the most highly skilled worker, and put the professional union official in privileged

1   Tillett, Memories and reflections, pp. 107–108.

material circumstances. For instance, the annual pay of the secretary of the Typographical Association rose from £100 to £225 over the period 1868–1908 (the change from weekly to annual pay implied, *inter alia*, acceptance of the 'professional' character of the occupation of union official). This rise occurred notwithstanding the fall in prices that took place over the same time. In terms of both the total increase and the speed with which it was attained, the union secretary did far better than the average skilled compositor—the most highly privileged worker in the printing trade.[1]

The basic salaries of union officials were often augmented by various increments. Very characteristic of this type of union was the commission of ten per cent on all union dues paid by newly enlisted members; this was granted to John Hodge, secretary of the British Steel Smelters, Mill, Iron, Tinplate and Kindred Trades' Association in January 1888.[2] In this particular instance the basic salary was relatively low—£2 a week—to give its recipient adequate economic incentive for energetic recruiting. All this still did not make a union job a glittering prize. As we shall see, the union administrators never achieved the astronomic salaries paid to their American counterparts, for reasons which I shall try to explain later. A union post was nevertheless sufficiently appealing to even a skilled worker, and such an appointment was an undoubted step up the social ladder. Obviously, this provided an additonal incentive to officials to strengthen the union structure. At the 1920 Trades Union Congress, Robert Smillie, the miners' leader, gave a depressing picture of the intrigues which accompanied appointments to union posts as a matter of course; they included cheating voters by unscrupulous methods and even straightforward buying and selling of votes. These practices, said Smillie, brought shame upon the trade union movement.[3]

The privileges attached to the position of a professional union official were not confined to higher pay or even to the higher status that derived from the while-collar nature of the work. The fact that the ruling class accepted the unions as an integral part of the 'establishment' meant that there were many additional posts, as lucrative as they were prestigious, awaiting the more able union officials as hand-outs of the capitalist State. This was an additional and exceptionally tempting incentive—and the officials of the new unions encountered its effects from the moment they appeared on the social arena, whereas it had been necessary for men like Applegarth or Shipton to initiate such incentives.[4]

1 Musson, *The Typographical Association*, p. 131.
2 Pugh, *Men of steel*, p. 88.
3 Report of the TUC, 1920, pp. 247–8.
4 On 9 September 1915 Beatrice Webb made the following comment in her diary on

All the factors so far mentioned undoubtedly played a large part in domesticating the new union movement. Yet the integration of the movement into the 'establishment' was not merely a carbon copy of the 'old union' model on an appropriately extended scale. The difference in size was so great that it established a basic qualitative difference. The movement which had emerged from the integration of the old and the new unions, after finding its place in the structure of capitalist society, established itself on a quite different and considerably higher level, as a power not only in economic but also in political terms. This was the basically new characteristic of the stage now under discussion. It is, however, impossible to explain its meaning without an attempt to analyse in sociological terms this new phenomenon in the history of the British labour movement—the political labour parties. For in contrast to earlier periods, and particularly that which immediately preceded this one, it was not the trade unions but the political parties in which were concentrated the principal qualities which characterised this particular phase of the labour movement's evolution.

The political party, not the trade union, was the appropriate form for a movement which from its beginnings and in its very essence was the institutionalisation of class and not of occupational interests. The interests of selected occupations could be satisfied by means of an economic struggle such as could be waged by the unions; and the social prestige which the trade union movement conferred was all that could be afforded by a movement based on a single narrow stratum. An entirely different situation arose when the subject of social action became the class. If its demands, even in the economic sphere, were to be met, laws had to be forced through Parliament to guarantee and protect the elementary rights of the

the TUC meeting at Bristol. 'My net impression was that the Trade Unionists were more sophisticated but no abler than thirty years ago at Dundee. The trade union official of today has too many different jobs to be efficient at any one of them. And he is apt to be "retained" by the Government, not only by the hope of getting a highly paid job in the civil service on committees, etc . . . There is very little that is sinister or actually corrupt in the British Trade Union movement, but there is appalling slackness, moral, intellectual and practical.' (*Beatrice Webb's diaries*, 1912–24, ed. M. Cole, Longmans, London, 1952, p. 45.) George Lansbury made this comment on the same situation: 'We all talk, write and preach about the dignity and glory attaching to a ploughman or a domestic servant, but few of us desire these occupations either for ourselves or those we love. We Labour members of Parliament, drawn, as most of us are, from the ranks of the workers, find ourselves thrown into the midst of a society which is artificial and quite out of harmony with the conditions which formerly dominated our lives. From the sheltered libraries, reading and dining rooms of the House of Commons it is a little difficult to realise the class war and all these two words mean in moral, mental and material degradation to those who remain in the mental and material abyss from which we have, at least for a time, escaped.' (*My life*, Constable, London, 1928, p. 276.)

unions. Moreover, there had to be continued pressure for constructive legislation, in consequence of the completely altered view of the sphere of interests pertaining to the State, which hitherto had kept away from the domain of the rights of capital. If the demands of the new working class were to be satisfied, therefore, a genuine and lasting political organisation was needed which would exert the necessary pressure on the legislative and executive organs of the State. This was one of the reasons why the men of the old trade union movement were stubborn supporters of Liberal doctrines in their classical form. On the other hand, those active in the new unionism were generally socialists or, more precisely, collectivists. If we are to be even more precise, they were in favour of a considerable extension of the activities of the legislature. Political scientists regard the nomination of Parliamentary candidates as an essential criterion distinguishing a political party. But from a sociological viewpoint—from the viewpoint of the relations which arise between social structures and the interests which they institutionalise—every general union (and there were very many of them at the turn of the century) was basically more a political party in embryo than a trade union, in view of the types of interests which it represented and the possible ways of satisfying those interests. The need for an organisation on a class basis was visible behind the spontaneous organising of 'general' unions, yet the only method of meeting that need was to set up a political party which would serve all the formal requirements of its definition.

The need to solve the problem of social mobility, with a mass movement involved, was an additional element calling for the creation of a political party. The trade unions had secured vertical mobility for their elite, to the extent that their stratum was capable of exerting pressure to promote this mobility. The social movement of the numerically largest class in the nation was a far stronger driving force, and the union movement's outlets proved too narrow for the new objectives. Moreover, even the modest number of high-level places which the Liberal Party had made available for leading trade unionists proved quite inadequate. The elite of the working class movement was far more numerous, had higher aspirations, and stronger social backing; it was thus bolder than the elite of the union movement. What was needed, therefore was not just a political party but a labour party, separate from those which already existed; a party to serve the purpose of advancing the labour leaders and securing the election to Parliament of upwardly mobile individuals of working class origin in numbers such as would be unthinkable in the existing middle class parties.

The emergence of class interests ahead of occupational interests was the factor which caused the old unions to align themselves with the new ones in support of a party of labour. This did not happen immediately, nor without bitter resistance. The leadership of the skilled unions was strongly involved in the machinery of the middle class political parties, through whose good offices its aspirations to social advancement were met. Attitudes changed only when the old unions realised the new range of possibilities which would be opened up to a party of labour, and—most important of all—when changes took place in the situation of the skilled stratum itself.[1]

Classic free-trade liberalism had created a climate of ideas that was suited to the trade union phase in the evolution of the labour movement. Similarly, at this time socialism was the ideology which created a suitable emotional climate for the transition from trade union to party political methods of operation. It was, however, a special type of socialism, linked with collectivist concepts and at the opposite extreme from theories of revolutionary socialism.

Elsewhere I have attempted to justify my view that British socialism has been the principal antagonist of Marxist socialism: all the remaining shades of the conflicting ideologies within the labour movement are blends which contain elements of these two variants in differing proportions. British socialism is thus the purest form of collectivist ideology, springing not from a total rejection of the existing structure but from a willingness to adapt that structure. This attitude is characteristic of a class of which whole sections have, as a consequence of its evolution into a vocal and articulated entity, become rooted in the existing structure before the question of satisfying its overall interests as a class is raised. The need for a socialist type of ideology emerged in the history of the British labour movement only after the process of assimilating the class into the structure of capitalist society was well under way. This is why British socialism is diametrically opposed to the revolutionary and totally nonconformist concepts of Marxism. It is far less radical; it is oriented towards the institutions of the existing society and concerned to effect their transformation as quietly and peacefully as possible, in conformity with the general liking for social order which is characteristic of the petty-bourgeois strata of the British working class.[2]

1 As J. Grady, then president of the TUC, said in 1898, 'Specialisation, making what was skilled work unskilled, is the order of the day. The effect of this is that the apprenticeship system has become obsolete . . . The drift, although unconscious so far as its own world of capital is concerned, is distinctly towards collectivism.
     Having agreed, then, that the objective of trade unions is collectivism, as the only possible outcome of a long series of its own actions, as the only logical expression of the trend of modern industry . . . as practical men we must use every agency at hand, industrial and political, to work consciously towards this goal.' (Report of the TUC, 1898, pp. 43 *et seq*.)
2 Cf this typical statement by Tom Mann, who was, after all, one of the most radical and restless spirits in the socialist movement in Britain: 'The effect of the better

In Britain socialist ideas were not disseminated by middle class intellectual circles. The philosophy of the Fabians and the Social Democratic Federation was the most articulate of the many kinds of collectivist ideology being proclaimed in Britain at this period—but, as we shall see later, it evolved on the sidelines, away from the mainstream of the development of working class socialism. The men who did most to create an ideological climate for a separate labour party were the supporters of an ILP-style socialism in its most spontaneous variant, one which in consequence most completely reflected the spontaneous mood of the working masses who had not yet been subjected to ideological influences. The situation of the British working class at the end of the nineteenth century, a situation that was internally contradictory and full of conflicts, found its fullest reflection in this kind of socialism. In it we find the intense protest of the labouring masses, as against the sober practicality of the stratum of skilled workers; the call for a crusade for justice as against admonitions about the need to preserve respectability, a need which derived from a respect for the social order; a critical attitude to various social institutions, combined with a simultaneous acceptance of the values expressed by those institutions and a decisive rejection of all methods of bringing about their violent transformation.

The ideology of ILP socialism, which was the least sophisticated and intellectualised of the social ideologies, was the closest to the feelings and most urgent desires of the working masses. This does not, however, mean that it was accepted by the working class without difficulty. The stratum of skilled workers was protected against ILP ideas by an armour of Liberal concepts. As for the labouring masses, they were hauling themselves out of their state of material and intellectual deprivation and only gradually became capable of apprehending any kind of political ideology. Initially, therefore, the ILP leaders lacked any mass support. Instead they formed a group in relative isolation from the mass movement, and evolving outside the machinery of the existing institutions of the labour movement. Moreover, this group was attacked simultaneously from many sides; for instance, such attacks came from the prevailing majority opinion of the ruling classes; from the conservative trade union movement; and even from

education of late years has been to impart a desire for culture and refinement, and, as might have been expected, it has carried with it a determined revolt against those conditions that prevent proper expansion intellectually and materially. We have truly a "revolt of labour" in this country, but it is not the revolt of despair, it is not a wild desire to demonstrate strength, nor a reckless willingness to be a nuisance. It is the direct outcome of careful thought given to the great industrial problems by men who have the best interests of the country at heart. It is the necessary accompaniment of progress.' (T. Mann, *The regulation of working hours*, London, 1891, p. 8.)

slum dwellers, who detected insults to their dignity as human beings in the exposures of the ILP. Socialist campaigners sometimes ran into trouble at street meetings if they called the labourers' dwellings 'dens' or 'warrens' and their way of life a wretched one, unworthy of men and women.

The initial isolation and the need for continuous resistance to attacks which were often unscrupulous imbued the activities of the working class socialists with an aura of heroic martyrdom and produced the social type of an ascetic evangelist, devoting himself utterly to the propagation of an almost gospel-like ideology. Lansbury's biographer describes the ILP-er of the years before the first world war as easy to recognise, not only because of the red enamel button with the gold S (for Socialism) in his lapel but because of his white face, bearing the marks of asceticism and the stamp of under-nourishment and over-work which was still typical of working men's faces.[1] At this time the pioneers of working class socialism rose to heights of heroism and self-sacrifice which were never to be reached later, when their work had borne fruit.[2]

---

1   R. Postgate, *The life of George Lansbury*, Longmans, London, 1951, p. 95.
2   The biographies of these pioneers make fascinating and edifying reading. As Lord Snell wrote, 'The young Socialist advocates were not political adventurers, they were preachers filled with the Holy Ghost. The fervour of their appeal was immediately arresting and highly infectious; its hopefulness passed from soul to soul, awakening, energising and transforming. Its zealots quarrelled among themselves concerning methods, they laughed merrily at their own follies, and stood united before the enemy. Without money, social prestige or political experience, and opposed by the united power of the politicians and publicists of the land, they created by their enthusiasm and their faith an organised social force ... The almost fanatical fervour with which our attack was made ... was scorching and cleansing, a spiritual ecstasy the like of which I shall never again see.' (*Men, movements and myself*, pp. 99, 100.) Some men who in their later years achieved high position in the capitalist political hierachy were to recall the entirely different atmosphere of their ILP youth. Take, for instance, the following passage from Ben Turner's autobiography: 'I never regretted those days. They were the days of soap-box and street-corner oratory. There was no pay for the job. Many of us have travelled many miles, spoken at a Sunday morning meeting, had a snack meal in a coffee house, gone to an afternoon meeting elsewhere, had tea with a comrade, done another meeting at night and gone home poorer and prouder for our task.' (*About myself*, pp. 163–4.) Philip Snowden, one of the few leading trade unionists who followed Ramsay Macdonald into the Conservative Party, was also a socialist campaigner in his youth. This was particularly difficult for him because he was lame. One leg had been crushed in an accident and gave him life-long pain: 'When I look back on those years and recall the hardships I endured I marvel how I stood it. I walked with difficulty, with the aid of a stick, every step a deliberate effort, carrying my bag in the other hand. I made all the journeys alone. I spoke in practically every large town in Great Britain, in most of them very often, and in hundreds of smaller towns and villages. I often had to travel long distances between meetings, and frequently was

The pioneers of British socialism did not expect any reward for their endeavours. The work of a socialist campaigner was no sinecure at this time: the work of an ILP supporter was pure self-sacrifice devoid of any kind of material motives or reasoning calculations. To be a party official in the ILP was not a career in terms of the values which prevailed in society.[1] It carried practically no income, but the scanty pay, quite unrelated to the efforts expended on the work, was not the only reason why it was not seen as a career. Another was that the social position of a socialist campaigner was that of an outcast, depreciated in unison not only by the ruling classes but by all the vocal strata which had a corporate voice and thus an influence on public opinion. In the public view the occupational role of socialist campaigner was something disgraceful: it lowered the person who performed it in the scale of social dignity and respect. A man who became active in labour politics had to be aware that he was declaring war, if not on society as a whole, at least on the views which prevailed in that society; and that he could expect no support, at least in the short term, from any existing institution.[2] Working class socialism was excluded from the category of social respectability. Its advance along the scale of social prestige came about not only as a consequence of the endeavours of the ILP and the type of socialist leader of working class origins just described but also on account of increasing changes in the consciousness of the ruling classes from the turn of the century onward.

unable to get food between breakfast time and evening, except sometimes a railway refreshment room cup of tea and a sandwich. Cabs were a luxury we seldom could afford, and I usually had to walk considerable distances to and from the meetings.' (P. Snowden, *An autobiography*, 1, Nicholson & Watson, London, 1934, p. 82.)

1   In his memoirs Will Thorne mentioned an entry made in the 1892 balance sheet: 'Expenditure—Mr Clynes—away from home—allowed 2s.' (*Souvenir history of the National Union of General and Municipal Workers*, London, 1929, p. 5.) Later J. R. Clynes was the leader of the Parliamentary Labour Party, Lord Privy Seal and deputy Leader of the House of Commons. Clynes himself wrote of the early days: 'My agent asked one of them [active campaign supporters] what had been his expenses. He answered that the fare to Manchester was only a small amount— 1s 4d. "I'm not going to let you go away like that!" said the agent, and thrust a two-shilling piece into his palm. Think of a general election speaker getting two shillings nowadays!' (*Memoirs*, 1, *1869–1924*; 11, *1924–37*, Hutchinson, London, 1937, p. 107.)

2   The attitude of the old trade union movement has already been described. Its aversion to working class socialists and to projects for setting up an 'independent labour party' was far stronger than its dislike of the new unionism. When the number of 'Lib–Lab' MPs dropped a little after the 1895 general election, the Labour Electoral Association commented bitterly, 'Disaster has fallen on us, not from *without* but from *within*. The Labour barque has been treacherously piloted upon rocks by frothy, ecstatic dreamers and administrative failures, who seek to ruin and destroy, by spite and spleen, all homogeneity and unity in the ranks of Labour.

The awakening of the stratum of skilled workers in the middle of the nineteenth century had for the first time drawn the attention of the ruling classes to the problem of autonomous labour organisations and their place among the institutions of a capitalist society. After a long struggle this later development led to the acceptance and legalisation of the status of the unions and of union officials characteristic of the 'new model' type. The *de facto* and *de jure* recognition of the union movement as a compenent part of the machinery of the existing social structure was not, however, extended to socialist doctrines. These posed the problem of the emancipation of the working class on a completely different plane, a political one, even if the socialism actually in currency repudiated all forms of social revolution. The old union movement neither desired nor was in a position to achieve such an expansion of the position it had won for itself. It was only when the labouring masses became politically conscious, and the workers entered the political arena as a class, that an effective campaign could begin to change the attitudes of the ruling classes, not only in the matter of the socio-economic emancipation of a relatively small group of skilled workers but also in that of political autonomy for the working class as a whole.

It was the labourers themselves who reminded the ruling classes of their existence and forced them to pay attention to them. Suddenly, simultaneously and independently, many politicians, scholars, writers and rich middle class philanthropists made the 'discovery' that poverty was rampant in the heart of the capital of the world's greatest empire, in every industrial centre and on every flourishing farm. This was no coincidence, but the

Save our representatives, our old men, our wages, our unemployed, our hearts and houses from their cruel, crossheaded and blighting influences.' (Quoted by Page-Arnot, *The miners*, p. 295.) The attitude of the ruling classes to socialism and its spokesmen was even more uncompromisingly hostile. In 1909 C. F. G. Masterman gave an apt account of the feelings of the aristocracy, which still retained its position in the political elite: 'Its fear today is Socialism, Socialism which it does not understand, but which presents itself as an uprising of the uneducated, suddenly breaking into its houses; their clumsy feet on the mantelpiece, their clumsy hands seizing and destroying all beautiful and pleasant things. So it lies awake at night, listening fearfully to the tramp of the rising host, the revolt of the slave against his master.' (*The condition of England*, Methuen, London, 1909, p. 64.) The ruling classes spared no effort or expense to set up as extensive a counter-propaganda machine as possible in opposition to socialist propaganda. They had access to far greater financial resources than did the socialists, and lavishly subsidised organisations like the Anti-Socialist Union of Great Britain, whose 'only aim' was to attack and defeat the forces and organisations working in Britain on behalf of socialism. This organisation published for mass circulation books and pamphlets with titles like *The socialist conspiracy to win control of the trade union movement; The socialist tyranny; Socialism, the enemy of Christianity; What you lose through socialism; Successes without socialism*, etc.

result of an awareness of danger brought on by events in Britain and abroad, an awareness that the poverty which afflicted millions of human beings over vast urban and rural areas had a highly explosive potential. The fast-rising tide of humanitarian and philanthropic sentiments did not amount to a feeling of fear that the existing order was unstable, as a result of the existence of an immensely powerful and extensive social protest. The upsurge of this tide was probably determined by a partly conscious, partly instinctive aspiration to defuse these tensions without damaging the surrounding structure or letting the controls out of the hands of those against whom such feeling would be directed in the event of an explosion. The aim was to keep the working class, or the poor (for the social significance of a class was perceived in terms of wealth and poverty) as a stratum in receipt of assistance. The working class was to be the passive object of social measures but not their active subject.

This aspiration was common to all the many and varied social movements focused on the problems of poverty seen as a social phenomenon, which emerged simultaneously in different sections of the aristocracy, middle classes, and middle class intellectual circles. It was common to social movements in the universities, among artists, within the Anglican Church and numerous Christian sects, and also among politicians belonging to the middle class parties. These movements assumed different forms, and adopted different approaches, ranging from those of the Kyrle Society, whose members devoted their leisure time to painting works of art on the walls of East End slum dwellings,[1] to the dissemination of far-reaching programmes of social reform and an organised system of legally regulated social assistance. To express concern with the problems of the newly discovered world of poverty, no separate political movement was formed among the ruling classes which would have a complete programme and tend to become institutionalised as a political party. The concern with poverty was common to those who adhered to all the varieties of political opinion then prevailing among the political elite. It was an addendum to these concepts, not an alternative—which again supports the assumption that the penitential pilgrimage made by wealthy employers and rentiers to the slums, the scene of their crimes, did not mean that a section of the middle class elite was moving into the ranks of the labour movement, as was to happen in the next period of its history. For the time being this movement was only an extension of the fear, shared by the whole capitalist class, of the consequences of an uncontrolled explosion of social protest. Those who were most active in urging that something must be done about

---

1   R. A. Woods, 'The social awakening in London' in R. A. Woods, W. T. Elsing and
J. A. Riis, *The poor in great cities*, Kegan Paul, London, 1896, pp. 27–8.

the problems of poverty included representatives of all possible shades of
political opinion in the nation at that time—Tories, Liberals, radicals,
nonconformists, supporters of free trade, of home rule (Optionists),
republicans, Catholics, the Salvation Army, and members of every possible
Church and religious sect. In its most general form, concern with the problem of poverty was a movement above politics; it was a reaction by the
bourgeoisie as a class to the new phase in the conflict between capital and
the proletariat.[1]

1   The memoirs of men who were active in the emergent socialist movement give a
    colourful picture of the state of confusion to which the ruling classes were reduced
    by the 'discovery' of working class poverty. Hyndman writes: 'Suddenly the West
    End of London, the fashionable dwellers in Belgravia and Bayswater, Mayfair and
    South Kensington, awakened to the fact that there were some 2,000,000 or 3,000,000
    people in the brick and mortar wilderness beyond the Bank of England, many of
    them in very woeful distress. It became quite the proper thing to go down East.
    Guardsmen and girls of the period, rich philanthropists and prophets of Piccadilly,
    students of human nature and cynics on the make, betook themselves with hearts
    and pockets bursting with charity to the choicest rookeries to be found along the
    riverside.' (*The record of an adventurous life*, Macmillan, London, 1911, p. 50.) Robert
    Blatchford, the author of *Merry England*, describes a characteristic incident: 'I took
    him [the manufacturer, Mr (later Sir) Edward Hulton] into a slum hovel where the
    husband, who had just died of consumption, was laid out dead on the deal table.
    There was no fire and no bed. Three young children cowered together on the floor
    with a couple of sacks over them and the widow sat on an empty box crying herself
    blind. Young Hulton looked round, emptied all the money out of his pocket and
    walked out without a word. When I spoke to him he could only shake his head. He
    was unable to control his voice. And he would not go into another house.' (*My
    eighty years*, Cassell, London, 1931, p. 189.) While some reacted to the discovery of
    poverty by creating a new variant of social snobbery or patronage, and some by
    philosophic endeavours, others endeavoured to get to the source of this appalling
    phenomenon. Beatrice Webb, *née* Potter, writes about the reaction of her own family
    circle, which belonged to the intellectual elite. In her childhood and youth the out-
    look of the family circle, though unusually extended and diversified, did not include
    the world of labour: 'The very term labour was an abstraction which seemed to
    denote an arithmetically calculable mass of human beings, each individual a
    repetition of the others'. (*My apprenticeship*, Longmans, London, 1926; Penguin
    Books edn., Harmondsworth, 1938, pp. 36–7.) With the emergence of an organised
    labour movement the situation changed. The term 'labour' ceased to be interpreted
    as an abstraction, and the phenomena which it denoted began to be regarded as
    worthy of investigation. The enquiry led to the discovery of poverty, and the
    investigators reacted with a consciousness of the sin that had been committed against
    the masses of workers. Beatrice Webb wrote in the same book: 'When I say the
    consciousness of sin, I do not mean the consciousness of personal sin: the agricultural
    labourers on Lord Shaftesbury's estate were no better off than others in Dorset-
    shire: Ruskin and William Morris were surrounded in their homes with things
    which were costly as well as beautiful; John Stuart Mill did not alter his modest but
    comfortable way of life when he became a socialist; and H. M. Hyndman gloried in
    the garments habitual to the members of exclusive West End clubs. The conscious-

This about-turn in the position of the middle classes was, however, an intellectual movement above all. The middle class parties began to think seriously about a broad programme of reforms only after they faced the direct threat of a labour party in Parliament, but the ideological ferment among a section of the middle class intelligentsia started much earlier. Great attention was paid to the message of the later works of Mill and Ruskin; Carlyle and Dickens were re-read.[1] It was chiefly from them, and also from Henry George, the advocate of the single tax, that this group learned about the significance of social problems and drew the inspiration for its collectivist or interventionist ideas.

This intellectual ferment was part of the more general phenomenon of the focusing of middle class concern on the problem of the working class; within it we find only a few relatively small movements of a socialistic tinge. These movements were probably the product of the above-mentioned reaction of the middle classes to the new phase of social relations. They were distinctive in that for one reason or another their programmes for countering the evil of poverty went further than the average consensus of opinion among the ruling classes: further in the direction of a radical rejection of the policy of free trade and in the direction of extending social control to take over areas previously left entirely to private initiative.

The most significant, and also the most enduring, of the movements which showed socialist tendencies proved to be the Fabian Society. It began in the 1880s with a division of opinion within the 'Fellowship of the New Life', an intellectual society founded by Thomas Davidson. This

---

ness of sin was a collective or class consciousness: a growing uneasiness, amounting to conviction, that the industrial organisation, which had yielded rent, interest and profits on a stupendous scale, had failed to provide a decent livelihood and tolerable conditions for a majority of the inhabitants of Great Britain.' (*Ibid.*, p. 155.) Arnold Toynbee's reasoning was similar, but heavily imbued with the theme of penance and redemption; behind these can be clearly perceived the desire that the ruling class should be persuaded to agree to repair the faultily constructed machinery of society itself. In his lecture 'Mr George in England', delivered on 18 January 1883 in St Andrew's Hall, London, he said, 'We—the middle classes, I mean, not merely the very rich—we have neglected you; instead of justice we have offered you charity, and instead of sympathy we have offered you hard and unreal advice; but I think we are changing. If you would only believe it and trust us, I think that many of us would spend our lives in your service. You have, I say—and clearly and advisedly—you have to forgive us, for we have wronged you; we have sinned against you grievously—not knowingly always, but still we have sinned, and let us confess it, but if you will forgive us—nay, whether you will forgive us or not—we will serve you, we will devote our lives to your service, and we cannot do more.' (*Lectures on the industrial revolution*, London, 1896, p. 318.)

1 E. R. Pease, *The history of the Fabian Society*, Fifield, London, 1916, pp. 22–3; *ibid.*, typescript version with personal remarks of Sydney Webb and Bernard Shaw, British Library of Political and Economic Science, p. 19.

group had set itself the objective of 'cultivating a perfect moral character' , and its chief principle was 'to subordinate material things to spiritual'.[1] The division was made and the new society formed by a group of young intellectuals from aristocratic or middle class backgrounds, whose studies and discussions had led them to the conclusion that the way to improve social morality was to improve social relations. This group was closely connected with the liberal bourgeoisie by family ties, traditions, inherited ways of thinking and the interests of the particular social class to which its members belonged. The group's members nevertheless came to the conclusion that the position of the middle class intelligentsia could be maintained only if they operated not as part of the ruling class but as a team of individuals attempting to influence the government, adapting themselves to the changing situation within Great Britain.[2] Their origins and the class ties which they retained separated the Fabians from the groups of working class socialists, who were distrustful of these rich, sophisticated highbrows from the ruling class. On the other hand, the aspiration to secure a mutal adaptation of collectivist ideas and of the existing social structure, an aspiration which dominated the Fabians' thoughts, isolated them from the groups of revolutionary socialists, from whom in any case they firmly dissociated themselves. The Fabian society was born and developed quite independently of the Marxist ideas which at that time were filtering through to the British intelligentsia. The majority of Fabians had an extremely hazy idea[3] of Marx's theory and most of those who had read his works rejected his teaching as being at variance with their conception of social evolution.

Elsewhere I have discussed the philosophical, social and political views of the Fabians at greater length. Here I should like to concentrate on the problem which is most essential from the sociological viewpoint—that of the position adopted by the Fabian Society in relation to the contemporary political and social structure, and particularly the different sections of the labour movement.

The Society did not aspire to perform the role of a political party. Its wish was to exert an indirect influence on political life through the existing

1   Lord Snell, *Men, movements and myself*, p. 100.
2   G. K. Lewis, 'The present condition of British political parties', *Western Political Quarterly*, June 1952, p. 235; K. Martin, *Socialism and the welfare State*, Fabian Tracts, Fabian Society, London, 1951, p. 17.
3   In the original version of the history of the Fabian Society its leading figure and long-term secretary, E. R. Pease, wrote of 'theoretical socialists who held, with Marx, that the exploiter's profits arose, exclusively, from the final hours of the day's work.' (*History of the Fabian Society*, typescript of chapter iv, p. 28.) It was left for Shaw to remind him that the theory to which he was referring originated with Nassau Senior and was fiercely contested by Marx.

political parties, principally the Liberal Party; the Fabians regarded themselves as an organisation for educating professional politicians and influential people in general.[1] The majority of Fabians belonged to the Liberal Party, and some were persons of considerable influence within the party, a fact which made this mode of operation possible.[2] It would seem that the choice of the Liberal Party as the main subject for activity was dictated by these connections, which were in any case the product of the particular class ties of that party as a whole. According to Shaw,[3] however, the Liberal Party was chosen not because it was a liberal party but because it was the party that was in opposition at the time and therefore more likely to take up seemingly revolutionary demands.

Bernstein draws a brilliant comparison between the Fabian movement and the Saint-Simonian movement of 1830 in France and with the scientists, officials, scholars, men of letters and artists who constituted a majority of the public at socialist lectures and open debates and were present at the meetings in the Rue Monsigny, the Rue Taranue or the Rue Taitbout. At the same time, however, he does point to one essential difference: that in Britain the movement which corresponded formally to the Saint-Simonian movement was developing alongside a labour movement that was already powerful and self-aware.[4] This feature is a most important one for a sociological analysis of the role of the Fabian movement.

It was probably Shaw who most fully grasped the essence of the Fabians' relationship to the labour movement. He wrote: 'We knew that we could collaborate at full speed solely with our own class and not with casual artisans and labourers with a different mental background and rooted class prejudice against us.'[5] Many years earlier, in his novitiate, this same author, who was himself representative of the Fabians, had asserted that the reason for the Fabian movement's isolation from the workers' organisations was that 'the workers could not go our pace or stand our social habits'.[6] These assertions are frank. From many sources it is clear that the Fabians regarded the working class organisations with a considerable measure of contempt and irony. Even when, following publication of the memorable pamphlet *To your tents, O Israel*, the Fabians changed their tactics and began to support the idea of an independent labour party, attendance at the conference of this party was regarded as the 'hobby-

1 B. Webb, *Our partnership*, Longmans, London, 1948, pp. 122–3.
2 Pease, *History of the Fabian Society*, p. 111.
3 *Ibid.*, typescript of chapter VI, p. 20.
4 *My years of exile*, p. 223.
5 G. B. Shaw, *Early days: the Webbs and their work*, ed. M. Cole, Muller, London, 1949, p. 7.
6 Pease, *History of the Fabian Society*, typescript of chapter IV, pp. 2–3.

horse' of Edward Pease, the Society's secretary,[1] and the decision of the trade unions to give financial support to the Society was received with considerable distrust and reluctance.[2] The attitude of the Fabians to the party with which they were formally co-operating was radically different from that adopted several decades later by the large number of middle class intellectuals who joined the Labour Party. The social content of the two phenomena was, however, also entirely different.

In any case, the leaders of the labour movement also behaved towards the Fabians in the same sort of way as the Fabians did to them. They did everything possible to restrict the participation of the Fabians in the running of the new-born Labour Party,[3] and they regarded with suspicion the projects for legislation submitted by the Fabians to its Parliamentary wing. The Fabian intellectuals never played a role in the British labour movement similar to that played by intellectuals in the German or French labour movements. Continental European writers of all political views are, in my opinion, inclined to overrate the role of the Fabians in the history of the British labour movement. This tendency is probably due to the fact that everyone who studies the British labour movement owes his knowledge of the basic facts about its history to the Fabians. I think that the tendency to over-estimation is even more attributable to a methodological bias, deriving from a familiarity with Continental models.

In reality the Fabians, like other intellectuals of non-working class origins, exerted only a minimal influence on the structure, organisation, attitudes and even the general programme of the party of labour. The Fabians were active on the fringes of the movement throughout; and they had a far greater influence on the thinking of the enlightened circles than on the views, let alone the actions, of those groups which played a decisive part

1 Postgate, *Life of George Lansbury*, p. 94.
2 Shaw, *Early days*, p. 9.
3 In his writings Shaw frequently reverts, as to a very painful matter, to the time when, during the foundation conference of the Labour Party, an adroit manoeuvre by Keir Hardie eliminated him from the central executive of the party. (E. Hughes, *Keir Hardie*, Allen & Unwin, London, 1956, p. 102; Lord Elton, *The life of James Ramsay MacDonald*, Collins, London, 1939, p. 97.) The official report shows how this was done. A certain T. Burgess gave notice of an amendment to the party constitution, to the effect that the size of the executive should be reduced from eighteen to twelve members. Hardie supported the amendment on the grounds that it would save money (maintaining that a session attended by all eighteen members would cost £30). As a result of the amendment's acceptance (Report of the Labour Representation Committee, 1900, pp. 13–14) the number of Fabian representatives on the executive was cut from two to one, and Pease alone remained. It is, however, interesting to note that much later Ben Turner recalled that he had voted against the acceptance of Shaw on the executive (*About myself*, p. 163)—a statement which would seem to confirm Shaw's own interpretation.

in the British labour movement. The socialism on which the Labour Party was founded was not Fabian socialism but the socialism of Keir Hardie, Burns, Blatchford and others like them. This was a misty kind of socialism, more a way of thinking than a theory. It was not a conception based on studies of social structure and of a rational consideration of the conclusions resulting from these studies; instead, it was a set of ideas which were emerging spontaneously in working class areas, and which reflected the possibilities and aspirations of the working class during the process of its gradual merging into the system of capitalist relations.

There was another wing of intellectuals which remained almost without influence on the labour movement in Britain. These were grouped in the Social Democratic Federation, and also, for a certain period, in the Socialist League. This group, in contradistinction to the Fabians, was sectarian, revolutionary and extremist. It propagated Marxian theory in the most dogmatic form and with no concern for the complexities of contemporary problems. The SDF was never a large group, nor did it take roots in any major working class concentration. It had a small group of workers as members—mostly skilled men of above-average education and abilities— but intellectuals, rarely of working class origins, formed its mainstay. Their motives for becoming socialists varied. Most were, however, influenced by their reading or by ethical reactions of the kind experienced by the whole ruling class of this period. In their case, however, the reaction was felt more profoundly and more seriously.[1]

The SDF ideology was decidedly nonconformist, and was usually expressed in angry speeches filled with hatred for existing social order. It gained a hearing only from a small group of workers of considerable broadmindedness and sensibility. It was the SDF which produced John Burns, the most able of the working class leaders of the late nineteenth and early twentieth centuries.[2] It was in the SDF that George Lansbury and Tom Mann took the first steps in their political careers. Thereafter their careers developed

---

1   *Beatrice Webb's diaries*, p. 10. H. H. Hyndman, the leading light of the SDF, was a wealthy scion of an Ulster family whose grandfather had made a fortune in the West Indies. Asked how he had come to be a socialist, he mentioned a conversation with Mazzini, the experience of the Paris commune, which he had observed as a correspondent of the *Pall Mall Gazette*, and Marx's *Das Kapital*. He also spoke of his aversion to ugliness and his great desire to avoid anything unpleasant, including sights which could evoke moral or aesthetic disgust. Another eminent leader of the SDF, Ernest Belfort Bax, gave as reasons his meetings with Herman Jung and Paschal Grousset, and his reading of the works of Marx and Hegel. Others, too, like Morris, Crane, Scheu and Lee, also referred to works they had read or experiences of an ethical or aesthetic nature. (In *How I became a socialist*, Social Democratic Federation, London, 1896.)

2   J. Burns, *The man with the red flag*, London, 1886.

along different lines, but all of them sooner or later escaped from the cage of dogmatism and entered the ranks of a movement more adapted to the resources of the typically English structure of the working class. Charles Bradlaugh's opinion of the socialist movement as consisting of 'poets and cranks' reflected a view of the SDF which was not confined to middle class intellectuals.

The SDF displayed a total lack of understanding of its own situation and of the balance of political forces in society. It forecast approaching victory in the 1885 general election, in which its candidates got only a handful of votes. The SDF regarded the unemployed demonstrators of 1886–87 as the beginning of the socialist revolution, and Hyndman always carried a list of members of the first socialist government in case a violent revolution should unexpectedly bring him to power.[1] When revolution failed to break out he was convinced that it was the fault of William Morris, who had broken away from the SDF with a group of friends to found the even more ephemeral and unrealistic Socialist League.[2] Furthermore, the SDF's dislike of the trade unions was shown much more clearly and openly than the Fabians'. The Federation spent most of its political life fighting the 'reactionaries of the TUC', thus cutting itself off even more from the organised labour movement.

The kind of ideology which found support under the name of socialism in working class circles, and particularly among the new unionists, differed fundamentally both from the cohesive revolutionary theory of the SDF and from the over-sophisticated programmes of the Fabian intellectuals. It was more primitive but at the same time more hazy. Among the workers who found this type of ideology congenial the term 'socialism' was associated with an undefined solution of all their troubles and cares.[3] Among the more experienced working class leaders of the ILP, 'socialism' was understood very dimly as meaning the ascendancy of collective over individual action, and the need to replace *laisser-faire* by State-directed economic policies.[4] As the assimilation of the new union movement proceeded, this kind of socialism became more and more moderate, as did the ILP too, ridding itself of even the few elements of nonconformism which it had possessed.[5]

1   Lord Snell, *Men, movements and myself*, p. 110.
2   Hyndman, *Further reminiscences*, p. 360.
3   *Public opinion on socialism*, preface by W. Bull, Cuspley, London, 1909 (a collection of essays which were received following a public enquiry).
4   Dicey, *Lectures on the relation between law and public opinion*, p. 259.
5   'Organised socialism . . . has, as a result of this success through peaceful methods, become steadily more moderate. One hears, even in Hyde Park, where on Sunday afternoons advocates of every cause hold noisy rivalry, less of fiery harangue, and more about uniting for the sake of keeping up wages and of getting representatives

With the passing of time this type of socialism was compressed into a single issue: one which had at the outset been regarded as a means leading to a socialist end but which gradually became an end in itself, dominating all the remaining truths, even the most fundamental, which were basic to the ideology in its original version. This single issue consisted of the achievement of large-scale representation for the labour movement in Parliament. It became the platform on which agreement was attained between socialists from the ILP and former Liberals from the TUC. The arguments of Keir Hardie and his comrades induced the union movement to agree to the setting up of something in the nature of an independent labour party. This was, however, the only issue out of the extensive ILP arsenal which the unions took seriously; ideological discussions about the programme of the future independent labour group in Parliament were left to those who got particular satisfaction out of them.

One must remember that, in the period when the Labour Party was being formed, the structure of the party system was subordinated to electoral goals. The two great parties were essentially two teams competing for political power within the political elite, whereas the mass organisations which supported each party had grown up as auxiliary institutions, with the object of winning votes for members of the elite.[1] This characteristic of the parties became even more marked as a result of the increasing standardisation of their social composition and the interests which they represented, a process which was steadily accomplished in the second half of the nineteenth century. In the 1868 Parliament the Liberal side had contained many representatives of the commercial world, while the Tories were overwhelmingly drawn from the landowners and gentry. By 1900, however, the process of standardisation had moved a long way. Of the Liberal members 14 per cent were drawn from the landowners, com-

---

into the County Council and into Parliament. William Morris's Social League, which still represents the poet's impatience of all mechanical methods, and clings to his fantastic revolutionary hopes, has been growing weaker and weaker, until it has now almost dwindled down to the single group which has a meeting in a hall at the back of Morris's house, in Hammersmith, on Sunday evenings, and sups in common afterwards.' (Woods, 'The social awakening in London', p. 35.) 'The character of the Labour propaganda has been changed by the advent of the Labour members to the House of Commons. It has now become wholly political, dealing with current questions. The old Socialist propaganda has been abandoned, and with its disappearamce a good deal of the idealism had been lost . . . Socialism has grown by its moral and idealistic appeal. I do not think the Socialist movement has ever recovered the enthusiasm and moral fervour which inspired it in those early days.' (Snowden, *An autobiography*, p. 151.)

1 J. A. Hawgood, 'The evolution of parties and the party system in the nineteenth century' in *The British party system*, ed. S. D. Bailey, Hansard Society, London, 1953, pp. 34 *et seq.*

pared with 30 per cent of Tories. On the other hand, 84 per cent of Liberals
and as many as 70 per cent of Tories came from the world of industry,
commerce and the professions.[1] This process was to continue in the future,
with the result that both parties lost the distinctive class character which
had been so important in the nineteenth century and came more and more
to express the interests of the same uniform economic elite, interests
divided by party programmes and electoral rivalries. Thus the conception
of a political party as an apparatus geared to support a Parliamentary
group was deep-rooted in the British political system. To put it more
precisely, it was the Parliamentary group that was regarded as the party
proper, while its supporting branches were seen, not as an organisation of
adherents of a particular political conception which shaped the policy
of the party, but as a tool intended to maintain discipline among the
voters and to organise electoral campaigns. Following British political
tradition, a political party outside Parliament came to life only for the
purpose of organising electoral campaigns and faded away in the years between elections. The conferences of party representatives were intended
rather as confrontations between the views of the Parliamentary party and
the feelings of the voters than as occasions on which the policy of the
Parliamentary group should be determined by its supporters throughout
the country. This conception of a political party was accepted by the
labour movement, together with the political tradition into which the
labour movement had been merged gradually and unawares. The labour
politicians got their Parliamentary experience in the ranks of the Liberal
Party, and it was there that they formed their ideas about political life.
Furthermore, this kind of conception of a political party was best suited to
the aims which the new labour party had set itself. Because of these
factors, the party of labour in Britain, so far as the sociological machinery
for functioning was concerned, adopted from the outset a model which was
to be constructed by the social democratic parties of the Continent only
as a result of many years of evolution. Not for a moment was the labour
party a foreign body within the British political system, unlike the first
Continental social democratic parties in their respective political systems. In
the early years of their existence these Continental parties sought to put
into effect the completely different conception of a political party as the
organisation of a class, not an auxiliary apparatus for election campaigns.

   The conception of a party of labour as an electoral apparatus was victorious at the actual foundation conference of the Independent Labour
Party. The conflict of the two different conceptions of the party assumed
the form of a conflict over its name. George Carson and Robert Smillie

1 J. A. Thomas, *The House of Commons*, University of Wales Press Board, Cardiff, 1939,
   pp. 14–20.

proposed that the party should be called the Socialist Labour Party. Ben Tillett and other delegates attacked this proposal sharply, arguing that the party's object was to capture the trade unionists, 'a body of men well organised, who paid their money',[1] and that over-emphasis on socialist aims could frighten them away. Ultimately the name that was accepted laid stress exclusively on the 'independent' aspect of the party: this indicated the party's intention to build up its own Parliamentary party, not as a licensee of the existing parties, but set up by the labour organisations. Emphasis was continually placed on the need to gain the support of the trade unions, at the price of giving up the socialist aims which the union movement was unwilling to accept. This meant that the opening up of a way into Parliament for the vanguard of the workers was being given priority over the aims of setting up a labour party, although the assumption was not stated in so many words. Keir Hardie, Bruce Glasier and other ILP leaders like them were probably inspired by socialist ideas, in however hazy a form. But in this particular situation these ideas, analysed in sociological terms, became an ideological screen for the growing expansion of the elite of the labour movement, which was itself being firmly welded into the capitalist system.

The ILP focused its attention not so much on propagating socialism as on detaching the labour movement from the Liberal Party, which had set unduly restrictive bounds for its labour representatives. The ILP remained in opposition to the two great parties, but more opposed to the Liberals than the Conservatives, because the Liberals were their chief rival in the contest to gain the support of the trade union movement. As early as the 1893 Trades Union Congress, Keir Hardie proposed that 'the labour members in the House of Commons should be unconnected with either the Liberal or Tory Party, and should sit in opposition to any government until such time as they are strong enough to form a Labour Cabinet.'[2] This proposal was rejected by a majority vote. The union movement had not yet acquired ambitions to match its size. None the less, the expansion of the movement, especially by the influx of a considerable number of representatives of the 'general' unions, combined with the decreasing importance of craft interests and privileges, reinforced the conception propagated by the ILP. Year by year the number of supporters of Keir Hardie's conception grew within the TUC. The vanguard of the labour movement felt more and more uncomfortable within the confining framework of the Liberal Party, and was therefore increasingly willing to listen to proposals for setting up an independent ladder of upward mobility.

1 Cole, *British working class politics*, p. 141.
2 Report of the TUC, 1893, p. 48.

In the set of proposals that was ultimately accepted by the trade unions, this matter of the ladder of advancement was the only one which remained of the comprehensive programme of the ILP. The movers renounced all their other proposals in turn, leaving only the task of establishing a group to represent trade union interests in Parliament, without any restrictions on the political programme of these representatives, or even on their Parliamentary tactics.[1] The Labour Representation Committee was set up in 1900. At first it was regarded merely as an auxiliary branch of the TUC, intended for the organising of election campaigns in collaboration with the existing labour organisations or those connected with the labour movement. Of all the functions included in the definition of a political party, the Labour Representation Committee carried out only those which were involved with elections. Moreover, it had neither its own declaration of ideological goals, nor its own political programme, nor even a precise outline of tactics to be adopted in relation to most questions which were likely to be raised in Parliament. A letter which the committee circulated to labour organisations on 23 March 1900 defined its tasks as the organising of wage earners to 'support trade union principles and ideals by political methods'.[2] It was not felt necessary to formulate distinctive political tasks for the political branch of the trade union movement; the cramped framework of the protectionist legislation in which the union movement had traditionally been interested was regarded as adequate.[3]

1   At the foundation conference of the Labour Representation Committee (which in 1906 renamed itself the Labour Party), the following resolution put forward by MacDonald was decisively rejected. It called for the creation of 'a distinct party, with a party organisation separate from the capitalist parties based upon a recognition of the class war, and having for its ultimate object the socialisation of the means of production, distribution and exchange.' Instead, conference passed an amendment by Keir Hardie to establish '. . . a distinct Labour group in Parliament, who shall have their own whips and agree upon their policy, which must embrace a readiness to cooperate with any party which for the time being may be engaged in promoting legislation in the direct interest of labour . . .' (Report of the LRC, 1900, pp. 11–12.)
2   Report of the LRC, 1900, pp. 11–12.
3   The apolitical character of the committee was even more blatantly expressed in its constitution, approved at the 1903 Congress. The second clause under the heading 'Object', reads: 'To secure, by united action, the election to Parliament of candidates promoted by affiliated societies, who undertake to form or join a distinct group in Parliament, with its own whips and its own policy on Labour questions, and not to oppose any other candidates recognised by this Committee.' (Report of the LRC, 1903, p. 25.) This independence of policy was confined to labour questions, and even in this narrow context it was not defined in 1901. Bruce Glasier moved a resolution stating that the 'final object of all democratic effort must be the transfer of all such private monopolies to public control as steps toward the creation of an Industrial Commonwealth founded upon the common ownership and control of land and capital . . .' The text of this resolution was sufficiently ambiguous and the

If any kind of concrete political programme was accepted, this could reduce the number of labour representatives in Parliament, and the latter was the chief, if not the only, concern of the LRC and later of the Labour Party. This was because there was a great variety of views within the political movement, so that, if a candidate's political attitude was too sharply defined, the support he received from various groups could decrease. There was also the consideration that meek assent by the labour representatives to the policy of the Liberal Party and willingness to hold back their own programme assured labour candidates of direct Liberal support through the withdrawal of Liberal candidates in areas where LRC or Liberal men were standing for Parliament. In Clitheroe in 1900 the ILP put Philip Snowden forward as a candidate. MacDonald, then secretary of the LRC, intervened personally to have him replaced by Shackleton. At that time Snowden was a socialist and Shackleton was a Liberal; thus the latter was a guaranteed winner, which was not the case with Snowden. In the following years the LRC supported Will Crooks and Arthur Henderson in by-elections at Woolwich and Barnard Castle, which they won. Both were Liberals by conviction.[1] This electoral policy was followed consistently up to the outbreak of the first world war. As late as 1913 Snowden wrote that the labour representation in Parliament at that time was there chiefly by courtesy of the Liberals, and would vanish if active resistance took the place of their goodwill.[2] In the first stage of its existence the Labour Party was an organisational adjunct to the union movement and a political adjunct to the Liberal Party. But it was also the embryo of an organisation with objectives of a new kind. Supported by the structure set up by the early Labour Party, the labour elite was later to rise into the

possibility of supervising its execution in practice sufficiently doubtful; nevertheless, the proposer thought it necessary to add that it was 'not intended to be a test resolution in respect to candidates'. (Report of the Labour Party, 1901, p. 20.) In 1907 Atkinson moved a resolution which would have made 'public ownership and control of all the means of life' the ultimate goal of the party. This was rejected by 635,000 votes to 98,000. (Report of the Labour Party, 1907, pp. 51, 56.) This aversion to formulating any kind of political programme was based on the acceptance of the structure of capitalist society. The object was advancement within the framework of that structure, and not its reconstruction. Thus there were no bases for conflicts over programmes with the Liberal Party—at most there was room for striking bargains to increase the volume of labour questions to be dealt with by legislation. For, as Will Crooks declared, the Labour Party was for 'creating decent, honest citizens of an empire, trusting in their own strength—citizens of that empire which begins in the working man's home'. 'Does the Labour Party intend to blow up the Empire?' he asked, [and answered,] 'It intends to blow up a few slums.' (Report of the Labour Party, 1906, p. 71.)

1 Lord Elton, *Life of Ramsay Macdonald*, p. 177.
2 *Labour Leader*, June 1913.

political elite of capitalist Britain. The first signs of this new role indicated both the end of the evolutionary phase of the mass labour movement and the beginning of the phase of stabilisation.

During the first two decades of its existence the Labour Party grew at tremendous speed, as table 13 indicates. The growing power of the Labour Party was itself a factor making for its emancipation from the tutelage of the union movement. But the expansion of the labour group in Parliament was a factor which operated even more strongly in the same direction.

Table 13

Labour Party conferences, 1901–18

	1901	1910	1918
Number of delegates at conference	82	448	879
Number of members	45,638	1,486,308	2,465,131
Income of General Fund	£243	£3,053	£11,130

Source   Report of the Labour Party, 1918, p. 150.

Intricate issues of Parliamentary procedure were beyond the scope of the matters which fell within the everyday duties of union officials. They demanded special qualifications, new areas of competence, separate institutions to make plans and decisions. Thus authority over the Parliamentary group slipped out of the hands of the union executives, and the Labour Party slowly secured its own separate sources of power, in the shape of a strongly established Parliamentary group. This slow but consistent trend was soon reflected in the relations between these two structures.

At the 1900 foundation conference it was decided that the LRC executive should make regular reports on its operations to the annual Trades Union Congress. This was equivalent to an official confirmation that the Parliamentary machinery was a branch of the union movement. But as the issues reported on by the political branch became more complex, and following the great electoral success of 1906, the practice of reporting to Congress was slowly replaced by an expression of 'fraternal greetings'. This did not come about without union attempts to resist it. S. Lazenby at the 1905 conference and Ben Tillett in 1907 moved motions demanding that the right of affiliation to the Labour Party should be granted exclusively to the trade unions, and that non-union delegates should be forbidden to participate in debates.[1] Whatever kinds of argument were used, it is

1   Report of the LRC, 1905, p. 45.

difficult to regard either of these resolutions as anything other than attempts to restore the absolute dependence of the Labour Party on the union movement and to preserve for the union elite all the fruits of the Labour representatives' electoral successes. On the other hand, it must be said that as soon as the organisational skeleton of the political wing of the movement began to show signs of life following the election successes of 1906, this wing tried to attack the union machine in order to gain greater independence for itself. The Labour Party executive moved a resolution demanding acceptance of the decisions of annual Congresses and conferences merely as expressions of their views and not as binding rules; it also demanded that the labour political group should retain the right to decide the time and manner of putting these views into practice.[1] The resolution was without any shadow of doubt aimed at the trade unions which, because of their numbers and wealth, dominated the annual conferences and dictated their will there.

A second, even more important step was taken towards the emancipation of the political elite from the union machinery with the introduction of individual membership of the Labour Party. The party executive first brought this proposal up in 1912.[2] At the time, it was rejected but when brought up again in 1918 it was passed after bitter debate.[3] The proposers left little doubt that their object was to secure independent support for the party—i.e. support that did not depend on the machinery of the federated organisations.[4] Once this change in the constitution was approved, local party organisations sprang up all over the country; these came directly under the party executive, and constituted its exclusive domain and counterbalance in wrangles with the union executives and also in tangles with the Parliamentary group. At the same period the Labour Party inserted in its programme a demand for nationalisation of the means of production.[5] This change of party programme signified not so much the 'socialisation' of the party as the final breakaway from the Liberals and the conscious imitation of a policy calculated to transform the Labour Party into one of the two teams competing for power within the capitalist political system. The change was the grand finale in the expansion of the British labour movement to the masses—a phase which culminated in the growth of a mass political organisation based on the institutionalisation of

1 Report of the Labour Party, 1907, pp. 54–6.
2 Report of the Labour Party, 1912, pp. 54–5.
3 Report of the Labour Party, 1918, p. 99.
4 Arthur Henderson, who was the party's secretary at that time, gave this justification of the proposal, asking, 'Are we to stop being a federation and begin to build from a new foundation a political organisation based only on individual membership? . . . If we were to start afresh this would be just the ideal to which we should aspire.'
5 Report of the Labour Party, 1918, p. 140.

class, not occupational, interests and on the structural emancipation of that organisation from both the trade union movement and the machinery of middle class political structures. The organisational development of the labour movement was over so far as its basic outlines were concerned. After a period of dynamism and flexibility, the movement resumed the process of integration into the structure of capitalist society, but this time at a higher level, and on the political, not the economic, plane.

To sum up: by the end of this period, the labour movement in Britain had, from a sociological viewpoint, achieved its completed form: all the strata of the working class had been absorbed by the movement, although the number of those who were its formal members was far less than the total membership of the working class. No section of the working class any longer remained outside the compass of the movement, as had been the case at the outset of this period. Thus no section remained whose entrance to the stage of social activity might set up a need for organisational adaptation, which would stir the movement into a new state of flexibility and give it a new internal dynamism.

In spite of all this, the labour movement was strongly embedded in the structure of capitalist society, for the reasons already given. It was imbued with conformist attitudes towards that structure, and the upward advancement of the class and its leadership, as shaped by the movement, was to take place within the framework of the structure and in accordance with the scale of values linked with it.

3

The structure of the elite
of the labour movement

The analysis both of the movement's elite and of the labour movement itself in the preceding historical period was made easier by the fact that the movement was evolving in one direction only, and that its structure was relatively simple and uniform. An analysis of the labour elite of the period now under discussion is far more complicated, because the movement lost its former simplicity, while a number of comparatively independent structures were formed within it, the majority of which were, moreover, in a dynamic and flexible state.

On the threshold of the period we are now considering we found only the elite set up by the 'new' union movement; this elite was still in the same state as obtained after the movement had lost its initial dynamism and entered into a phase of conservative consolidation. This fact gave the elite a stability of sociological characteristics which was appropriate for mature social formations and made it easy to draw a complete sociological profile of it. As the new period began, however, we noted the appearance of a new union movement, violently expansionist in character, and with it a new elite, which was, like the labour movement, in a state of permanent metamorphosis. The old and the new elites contributed to the elite of the movement traits that were dissimilar, and sometimes even diametrically opposed. In consequence, the executive group of the movement formed a highly heterogeneous structure, and its social balance was upset. Gradually, however, as the fusion of the two union movements proceeded, the process of uniting the two sections of the labour elite took place. The process ended with a new union elite which was the product of the integration of two formerly separate formations.

This was not, however, the only elite-forming process to be observed during the period under consideration. In addition to the union movement there also arose a political movement, a structure of a political party type. In view of its place in the political structure of society and the functions it fulfilled there, this structure demanded from its elite a completely new set of qualifications, unknown in any of the sectors of the union movement. It therefore created a new category of elite, differently recruited and endowed with new characteristics. The new qualifications entailed new sources of prestige. The aura pertaining to the elite of the political movement was, however, greater than the social prestige which would derive from the type of qualifications possessed by a political elite. This was a new phenomenon, unknown in the union movement. The prestige of the elite of the union movement was a simple function of the prestige of the movement itself. A union leader had as much prestige as was guaranteed to him by the organisation he led. In the case of the political structure, the situation was different. An institution such as a political party serves to guide a given group of individuals into the ranks of the society's political elite—an elite which no longer rests on the structure of its own organisation but on that of the political institutions of the society as a whole. If a social organisation is sufficiently powerful to lift its elite up to the level of the overall political elite, this is followed by a qualitative upsurge in the prestige of that elite and also in the authority which it possesses. This prospect in turn faces the organisation's elite with a demand for higher levels of the requisite qualifications than would result from the internal needs of the organisation itself. To sum up, a trade union-type organisation does itself in some measure determine the extent of the qualifications, prestige and authority appropriate for its own elite; on the other hand, an enquiry into the characteristics of the elite in a political organisation cannot be restricted only to the study of the organisation's internal structure. Instead it must be extended, more particularly to the dynamic relationship of a given organisation with the structure of the national political institutions.

All of these considerations make the problems of the period of mass expansion a much more complicated study than those of the preceding period.

At the end of that period, except for a diminishing group of veterans, the contemporary trade union elite had already constituted an elite created by the union organisations. It no longer consisted of men who had built up the organisations out of nothing, but of those whose advancement and place in the elite had been mapped out by a organisation older than themselves and superior to them. These men took the organisation for granted, not as a matter of discussion. Their personal careers depended on climbing up the rungs of a ready-made organisational ladder. The organisational machinery selected the candidates for advancement and determined their opportunities in this sphere.

The initial situation of the men who were later to form the elite of the new union movement was different. They had only just set up the organisations which they were to head. They found only untilled ground in the masses of unskilled and semi-skilled workers who were unused to any kind of organisation. In addition there was an absence of any kind of prepared structures. These men had to possess qualifications of a charismatic type, in the same way as the union leaders of the first half of the century. They did not need administrative abilities, but an essential quality was the capacity to arouse enthusiasm, which took the place of the nomocratic link that was missing as yet. At the outset such qualities determined the prestige which the later members of the elite succeeded in winning among the workers whom they had organised. This prestige, generally speaking, was not a function of the position they occupied in the movement but was derived from certain other attributes unconnected with the movement; it was based on scales of social values external to the organisation.

The mass of unskilled and semi-skilled workers were still in a state of alienation from society and thus imbued with a nonconformist attitude towards that society. It was only natural that they should feel distrustful of people from the ruling classes. On the other hand, they lacked confidence in their own powers, felt conscious of their underprivileged state and helpless to deal with the dangerous and unintelligible social forces that confronted them. Thus they eagerly sought the leadership of men who were better educated, experienced in social action, and familiar with the machinery of social behaviour. This natural predisposition created a convenient situation for a group of people who, while they were part of the working class, were also endowed with special capacities and an education and general culture higher than the average. Hence most of the first leaders of the labourers' unions were highly qualified artisans. The leaders of the first unskilled workers' unions were as a general rule recruited from other occupations than were the members of those unions, and from occupations or trades which required skilled qualifications. The most outstanding lecturers of the unskilled workers included skilled mechanics, textile workers and printers. Clynes, Burns, Mann, Tillet and Thorne were all skilled tradesmen from the most exclusive trades.[1] The skilled workers had acquired the traditions of organisational skills and practices characteristic of their particular stratum, but they were of course also members of the working class. They thus possessed all the qualities

1   In 1892 Clynes, who was a skilled textile worker, was appointed secretary of the Oldham branch of the National Union of Gasworkers and General Labourers, although by trade he had nothing in common with the workers organised in this union. He wrote, 'The Oldham men who wanted to form a local branch of this union were all of them older than I. But they needed a secretary who "had eddication", and my peculiar fondness for books was well known. Also my "Piecer" letters [articles in the local paper] and my platform talks had gained me a certain local fame.' (*Memoirs*, I, p. 62.) I have already referred to the manner of Tillett's becoming leader of the dockers (see p. 159). The appointment of Burns came about in a very similar manner. Burns was also conscious of his responsibility as a skilled artisan to educate the unskilled: 'I have done my best as an artisan to educate my unskilled fellow workmen'. (*The man with the red flag*, p. 5.) In addition, he was aware of his superior class status. As he said, 'We are not going to tell them how much power they have until they become sufficiently educated to be worthy of it.' (Quoted by R. A. Wood, *English social movements*, Swan Sonnenschein, London, 1892, p. 21.)

which were needed in order to win obedience and prestige among the unskilled working masses. The elite of the unskilled workers' movement was recruited from skilled workers because, during a lengthy period of industrialisation, the union movement among skilled workers had taken shape and achieved lasting successes long before the awakening of the labouring masses.[1]

Clearly, it was the most outstanding representatives of the skilled stratum who became the leaders of the new union movement. They were the most outstanding not because of their occupational skills—as had been the case in the earlier journeymen's clubs—but because of their education, breadth of vision and wide interests. The case of Joseph Arch, described in Part II, was to be repeated on a massive scale. All these leaders possessed certain attributes in common: the stubbornness of the self-taught, a great love of books, a lasting hunger for knowledge. All of them had travelled a good deal, judged by the average worker's experience, and their life stories were more varied than those of the average worker. All had been favoured by nature with exceptional intellectual faculties, much above the usual level in working class communities. John Burns was a genius in his own way. Engels went so far as to compare him to Cromwell, whom he considered the military equal of Napoleon and a better statesman than the great Frenchman.[2] Burns was a voracious reader and a confirmed collector of books; he possessed a wide knowledge of a large variety of subjects, great oratorical talent, a sharp wit and penetrating mind. Compared with contemporary leaders of the old type, he was a colossus among dwarfs. Ben Tillett commented, '"I never learned upon what meat our Caesar fed, to make him grow so great".'[3] The leader of the miners, Robert Smillie, wrote of himself: 'Like Adam and Eve, I knew that I was naked, and I made haste to clothe myself.'[4] He would save pennies from the money

---

[1] The existence of such a cause-and-effect relationship is also confirmed by comparative data. In Denmark, during a stage of development of the labour movement similar to the one we are now discussing, the leading positions in the mass movement which institutionalised working class interests were Peter Knudsen, a glover; Emil Wiindblad, a skilled painter; Thorwald Stanning, a cigar maker; and Hans Hedtoft, a lithographer. The stratum to which these people belonged had formed its own organisations, in Denmark as in Britain, long before the rise of an organised movement among unskilled workers. In Norway, on the other hand, the process of industrialisation was violent and relatively late by contrast with Denmark, with the result that, when the mass movement began, no lasting traditions of a skilled labour movement had yet grown up. The mass movement was therefore headed almost exclusively by intellectuals of middle class origins. This contrast, in conjunction with other factors, had some influence on the political attitude of each movement. (Cf, for example, Galenson, *Comparative labor movements*, pp. 149 *et seq*.)

[2] Bernstein, *My years of exile*, p. 208.

[3] *Memories and reflections*, p. 116.

[4] *My life for Labour*, p. 15.

intended for his food to buy the novels of Scott and Dickens. By the time he was fourteen years old he knew the poetry of Burns and the plays of Shakespeare. He subscribed to the *Popular Educator* and succeeded in ferreting out from the used book stalls some volumes of *The world of wit and humour* and also of an old edition of the *Encyclopaedia Britannica*; all these he read from beginning to end.[1] As for Ben Tillett, he spent his youth in a travelling circus, and then served in the Royal Navy and the merchant navy in succession. When fortune sent him to work in a tea warehouse the experiences of his youth kept him yearning for wide horizons and open spaces. He went hungry in order to buy books. He studied Latin and tried to learn Greek. His dream was to become a barrister.[2] Ben Turner began his working career as a pedlar, an experience which he never regretted, 'for it taught me a lot about human nature'.[3] After that he was an insurance agent for a year, and then he became a journalist, first with the *Yorkshire Factory Times*, later with the *Workman's Times*.[4] J. R. Clynes was twelve years old when he bought an old dictionary for sixpence—two weeks' pocket money: 'I became like a character from an old romance, my body walking and talking by day, but my soul coming to life only at nights under the potency of the magic words I culled from my sixpenny dictionary.'[5] Clynes learned the dictionary's contents off by heart, and the resulting tendency to linguistic purism remained with him to the end of his life. He was famous as the labour leader with the most elegant speaking style, and he frequently startled employers whom he met at the conference table with his matchless knowledge of literature.[6] Harry Quelch was a blacksmith's son who began to work in a factory when he was ten years old. He was a passionate student of social problems, and taught himself French so that he could read the French version of *Das Kapital*. He astonished those who knew him by the profundity of his knowledge in the sphere of the humanities and the universality of his erudition.[7] Such attributes were not only characteristic of the most outstanding leaders, whose names have become part of the history of the British labour movement. They set the standard for the average official of the new union movement, at both higher and lower levels. Men whose names are today forgotten were cut according to the same pattern: they included some of the many first-class officials who rose out of the ranks of labour, some of those who abounded

1   *Ibid.*, pp. 49–53.
2   *Memories and reflections*, p. 94.
3   *About myself*, pp. 76 et seq.
4   *Ibid.*
5   *Memoirs*, I, pp. 34 et seq.
6   *Ibid.*
7   F. J. Gould, *Hyndman—prophet of socialism*, Allen & Unwin, London, 1928, pp. 77–8; Tillett, *Memories and reflections*, p. 189.

in the period when the working class woke to active life. Examples of such men were Harry Orbell, one of the pioneers of what was later to become the Transport and General Workers' Union; and A. A. Watts, a compositor active in the labourers' movement, who knew *Das Kapital* by heart and could explain the theory of value with such clarity that a child could have understood it.[1]

There was an element of mystical devotion in all these men. They gave themselves totally to the work, without consideration of their own comfort. They dressed carelessly, whether because they wished to stress their contempt for social conventions or simply because they attached no importance to the matter.[2] At the time when the activities of the old unionists had generally come to be confined within the four walls of their well organised and respectable offices, the new generation of leaders were spending their lives at public meetings and in working class slums; they were also functioning as couriers, distributors of publications, street agitators, turning their hands to any sort of work that helped the cause, regardless of their 'dignity'.[3] These men expected no reward for their activities; they even rejected all proposals which would have ensured them a more tolerable existence and a trouble-free life as a slur on the purity of their intentions—as when George Lansbury refused to accept Lord Swathling's lucrative invitation to become his secretary.[4] They found fulfilment when they found themselves in a situation of great danger which required self-sacrifice. Ben Tillett rightly ended his memoirs with a line by Walter Savage Landor, 'I warmed both hands before the fire of life.'

In their almost monastic fanaticism the leaders of the new movement were merciless in their condemnations of people and phenomena they regarded as meriting condemnation. They paid no heed to social conventions or considerations of good taste, and used pungent language to flay their targets. When Ben Tillett attacked Henderson, Shackleton and other Lib–Labs he called them 'sheer hypocrites', 'liars at five and ten guineas a

1   G. Lansbury, *Looking backwards—and forward*, Blackie, London, 1935, pp. 191–8.

2   In his report on the 1890 Trades Union Congress Burns commented, 'The "old" unionists differed from the "new" not only physically but in dress. A great number of them looked like respectable City gentlemen, wore very good coats, large watch-chains and high hats—and in many cases were of such splendid build and proportions that they presented an aldermanic, not to say a magisterial form and dignity. Amongst the "new" delegates not a single one wore a tall hat. They looked workmen. They were workmen . . .' (Quoted by Postgate, *The builders' history*, p. 343.)

3   Clynes wrote, 'I had no office or staff, and did all the work myself. I addressed meetings which I had previously organised, distributed handbills at street corners, went all over the country speaking to the builders, gas-workers, umbrella stick makers and others.' (*Memoirs*, I, p. 67.)

4   Lansbury, *My life*, pp. 75–6.

time', 'betrayers of their class', 'press flunkeys to Asquith'.[1] During a dispute with Blatchford, Burns called him 'a yellow-press scribe lying like a gas meter'.[2] This was, however, mild compared with the language which Burns was apparently capable of using.[3]

The leaders of the new unions felt most at ease at mass meetings. They all possessed some degree of oratorical talent, and knew how to capture a crowd with the power of their eloquence and the force of their arguments.[4] They were thoroughly capable of controlling unruly gatherings of revolutionary-minded workers, and understood the psychology of the labourers and the psychology of crowds. At a major rally of the unemployed in Trafalgar Square the police, helpless and alarmed, asked Burns to get the crowd under control for them.[5] And he did so. Carried on the shoulders of workers, with the red flag in his hands, he led the excited crowd past the elegant West End clubs to Hyde Park, where, having skilfully damped down their revolutionary fervour, he allowed the meeting to break up.

Here again, as in other cases, the attributes of the stratum of leaders of the new movement appeared in their most striking form in the most extreme individuals. Such a one was Jim Larkin, leader of the Irish Transport Workers' Union. The exceptional conditions of poverty in which unskilled workers lived in Ireland, their complete impotence in organi-

1 Lord Elton, *Life of Ramsay MacDonald*, p. 147.
2 L. Thompson, *Robert Blatchford*, London, 1951, p. 69.
3 *Ibid.*
4 John Burns's gifts as a popular speaker were described as follows. 'He had a voice of unusual range, a big chest capacity; and he possessed great physical and nervous vitality. His method of attracting a crowd was, immediately he rose to speak, and for one or two moments only, to open all the stops of his organ-like voice, roar like a bull of Basham, when the crowd, always fickle and ready to desert for any diverting novelty anyone to whom they were listening, would immediately leave other meetings and crowd round his platform with an eagerness which could not have been more marked had he been giving away something that they greatly desired. The crowd once secured, his vocal energy was modified, but his vitality and masterful diction held his audience against all competitors.' (Lord Snell, *Men, movements and myself*, p. 6.) Of Ben Tillett, Snowden wrote (in his foreword to *Memories and reflections*, pp. 8–9), 'He has, to a greater extent, I think, than any man I have known, the gift and the power to move vast bodies of men by his eloquence and sincerity . . . It is recorded of him that, addressing a great mass meeting of dockers on Tower Hill at the time of the historic Dock Strike, he so roused his audience to a state of religious fervour that in response to his call for three cheers for the greatest labour agitator, the Carpenter of Nazareth, these thousands of rough, non-Church-going men took off their caps and shouted themselves hoarse in response.' Bernard Shaw records how, at the 1896 conference of the second International in London, Burns energetically applauded Jaurès for his oratorical style, although he understood not a word of the speech just delivered in French, and had known little about Jaurès himself until then. (Pease, *History of the Fabian Society*, typescript version.)
5 Gould, *Hyndman*, p. 104.

sational matters, the extraordinary ugliness of their residential districts and the ignorance which made their lives quite without sense—all this constituted a completely out-of-the-way terrain of action for a leader with highly developed charismatic tendencies. Larkin became such a leader. His actions had a considerable element of the myth of penance and redemption, and he gladly submitted to ill-treatment to ease the lot of the workers who trusted him. He identified himself with the class he served, regarding the blows aimed at him as successive links in the chain of sufferings laid on his class. These people had been deprived of any sort of human dignity throughout their whole lives; they were despised by every other stratum in society; they died on the same musty pallets on which they had been born. But Larkin told them they were the salt of the earth, that they were a force, that they were capable of anything, provided only that they would unite their efforts, which until then had been unco-ordinated. When he stood in the dock he called on the magistrates to bow down before him, a labourer's son. His history had an element of the legend of Samson. Moreover, his own legend, well salted with mysticism, grew up during his lifetime and travelled like the tidings of a Messiah through the towns and villages of Ireland.[1] Larkin was as much an extreme personality as the extreme milieu in which he was active. For this reason the characteristics which are discernible only in an embryonic form in less 'extreme' individuals emerge in full in his case.

To recapitulate, it can be said that in the elite of the new union movement and the elite of labour socialism (the two were in fact an entity, both typologically and in terms of the actual people involved) a group of leaders had arisen that was new in the annals of the British labour movement. In certain respects they were a remainder of the charismatic leaders of the first half of the century, but they differed from them considerably in the degree of emancipation which they had achieved for themselves. They had emerged from the stratum of skilled workers, a stratum which at this time had climbed a considerable way towards a higher socio-economic position. So far as energy and devotion were concerned they had something in common with the leaders of the 'new model' unions in the brief early period of that movement; but they differed from them fundamentally in their relation to society, their political outlook and their nonconformist attitude to the prevailing hierarchies of social values.

The elite stratum of the new union movement, had, moreover, proved to be short-lived. Its great days were the period when the existing structure of the labour movement was breaking up; when the movement, set hard in its conservatism, established and no longer expansionist, was suddenly

---

1   R. M. Fox, *Jim Larkin*, Lawrence & Wishart, London, 1957.

thrown off balance and galvanised into dynamic motion by the arrival on the scene of a new and socially active element, the hitherto fragmented labouring masses. As the two branches of the movement united, and the movement returned to a state of equilibrium, and as the mutant energy of the reunited movement became exhausted, the period of the new elite passed. A stable movement with a rigid structure, embodied in the structure of the surrounding society, required the same type of elite as before. This meant a return to the conditions which had favoured the dominance of the type of elite described in Part II, although clearly allowing for all the changes connected with the new plane on which the labour movement, socially uniform once again, was merging into the structure of capitalist society.

The agitator and the administrator are two distinct types of leader, marked not only by different traits of character and different skills, but also by an entirely different psychological make-up, way of thinking and temperament. Sociology can produce few examples of a combination of these two very different sociological types. Even if such a combination occurs, it is an exception; their separation is the rule. For the agitator and the administrator differ from each other not only in overall personality but also in the fact that they are called into being and shaped by different historical eras. Times of upheaval and great changes in social bonds, times when old structures are demolished and new ones set up, times when social divisions are extremely malleable—these are the eras of the agitators. The latter can, because of their charismatic qualities, integrate the scattered masses and give an articulate voice to the fragmented strata. In consequence, however, they prepare the ground for a renewed consolidation of society, to calm the masses which were set in motion, and to allow the newly created social structures to harden. The newly formed social bonds are strengthened by an organisation of a bureaucratic type—the only organisation capable of assuring them a real stability.

But this is the moment when the administrators become the exponents and defenders of the unity and cohesion of the social groups. Agitators are of no use in a bureaucratic organisation. Their qualities have no application in its work; on the contrary, they can only disturb the smooth working of the well oiled machinery. Looking at it from the agitators' viewpoint, they generally do not see in the machinery the realisation of the ideas for which they fought. They feel alien and unnecessary to the machinery and are incapable of using it. They do not know how to manipulate it, nor do they understand how it is constructed. They do not realise what this machinery requires from those who control it. Thus they feel somehow betrayed. Not a few succumb to the illusion of social triumph which the power of the new organisation confers, and enjoy the pinchbeck glitter of that victory.

Others withdraw to one side, embittered and appalled, to seek consolation in the belief that they alone are the ultimate support of the ideas for which the masses once fought and which have been jeered at and sold out to the administrative Molochs. But neither group of agitators, irrespective of the nature of their individual reactions, is capable of taking over organisations which grew up casually and imperceptibly as a seeming by-product of their activities as agitators. Those who have not quit of their own choice are dislodged from the key positions by the new generation of leaders and administrators, and at best the administration gives them some sort of annuity such as befits veterans who seemingly served the cause well once but have now become cranky and old hat.

For the agitators the organisation is something which has grown up before their eyes, something that is from the outset secondary and subordinated to the cause; it is only a means to an end. The administrators come into an established organisation, or, to be more precise, they are the product of the organisation, and owe their being to it. To them it is an existing reality, superordinate, a starting point for discussions and actions. Behind it there is a cause, but the cause is served through the medium of the organisation; the latter is the supreme good and its reinforcement the principal task, to which one should devote all one's zeal, enthusiasm and talents. Ben Tillett, James Sexton, John Burns, Tom Mann and dozens of men like them were present without realising it at the cradles of what were to be strong labour organisations. But those organisations grew up of their own accord, without the leaders playing a conscious part, and in any case they were not an embodiment of the ideal model which had existed in the leaders' minds and to which they had planned to give material form.[1] *Their* supreme goal was the activation of the masses, and an intimate, day-to-day contact with them. On the other hand, the administrative leader Pickard, head of the powerful Miners' Federation, said a few months before his death, certainly with deep conviction, 'I have to confess to you I love this Federation of Miners more than any one man I know.'[2] Those who were present at the birth of the great labour unions lacked the qualifications which a union leaders should have, according to Clynes—the combination of an orator, a statesman, lawyer, financier, negotiator and supervisor. The mercurial Tillett, with his quicksilver gift of oratory, was the father of the most powerful trade union in the country, the Transport and General Workers'. But he was astonished to learn that the gift of words, which had carried him in his time to the heights of the mass movement, was a highly fallible weapon when confronted with the genius for organisation which Ernest Bevin, then rapidly scaling the administrative

1 Allen, *Power in trade unions*, pp. 187–8.
2 Quoted by Page-Arnot, *The miners*, i, p. 322.

ladder erected by his predecessors, brought into the already creaking organisation. Bevin was 'an organiser in the sense that some men are writers or artists. He found in organisation his mode of self-expression: it was a primary tool of his personality'.[1]

The charismatic leader of an emergent movement had to stand head and shoulders above the rank-and-file members of his movement. The secret of his authority derived from the fact that he embodied qualities which the fragmented masses lacked, and for which they had undertaken their struggle. He was an embodiment of power, by contrast with the impotence of the underprivileged masses. Once the period of fragmentation and alienation had passed, to be followed by an era when the gains which the masses had won were being consolidated, a leader of this kind would arouse distrust and a contemptuous shrug. The new hero of the day, the administrator, was not really a hero at all. He was supposed to be exactly like the members of his organisation and to express their newly acquired feeling of their own dignity, self-respect and social solidarity. He was supposed to be hard-headed, level-tempered and rational, and his personality to comprise, though in a greater degree, all the qualities possessed by the members of his organisation. The credentials needed by the agitator, the charismatic leader, were, on the contrary, to possess all those attributes which his supporters did *not* possess.

Thus the heroes of the new era afforded a contrast to the elite of the new unionism—they were colourless, dry and dull. They did not relish the spotlight, but were in their element in an office; they preferred the dry but hard-headed language of statistics to fiery speeches. Nor did they understand high-flown deliberations about ideals; their intellectual energies were entirely devoted to settling the problems of day-to-day administrative practice.[2]

---

1 F. Williams, *Ernest Bevin*, Hutchinson, London, 1952, p. 100.
2 Cf the following description of Arthur Henderson, the second secretary of the Labour Party and an outstanding member of the generation of administrators. 'He had started political life as a Liberal agent, and in a sense he was never anything else. He was the consummate Party organiser. He had not yet assumed the Socialist label, and when circumstances had transformed him from solid Liberal agent into solid Labour candidate, so far from undergoing a startling conversion there is no evidence that he was ruffled by the slightest spiritual or institutional change. And though he had shared and felt for the hardships of his class, it is difficult to resist the conclusion that spiritually he belonged always to the bourgeoisie.' (Lord Elton, *Life of Ramsay MacDonald*, pp. 134–5.) Another example was William Adamson a typical trade union leader, who in 1917–19 found himself heading the Parliamentary Labour Party and thus leader of the Opposition. Beatrice Webb gave this brilliant sketch of him following a visit to the Webbs: 'He is a middle-aged Scottish miner, typical British proletarian in body and mind, with an instinctive suspicion of

All this made the life span of the elite of the new union movement a brief one. The harsh demands of the new stage in the evolution of the labour movement—a stage which was the direct consequence of their activity—made this elite obsolete even before its members died off from natural causes. Thus almost all the heroes of the romantic years of the 1890s moved to the periphery of the movement, which outgrew them. Only a few of their number succeeded in adapting themselves to the new demands.

While the fortunes of the elite of the labourers' movement were identical in terms of sociological process, they followed two patterns in so far as different individuals were concerned.

The leaders of the factory workers' unions of the first half of the nineteenth century had in some measure remained outside the law of the society in which they lived right up to the end of their days. Not only was the function of a union official not accepted by society, it actually put the man who was performing it outside society. To choose to perform such a function amounted to declaring war on the established social order, on prevailing public opinion and on the prevailing hierarchies of values. It meant something in the nature of social suicide, acceptance of an outcast's position, a life full of ill-treatment and the loss of any hope of achieving a respected position in the social hierarchy.

The elite of the new union movement belonged to the same sociological category of leaders as did those who headed the unions of the first half of the nineteenth century. Their situation was, however, entirely different. By contrast with their predecessors the founders of the new unions transformed themselves into an elite—a fairly stable stratum supported by the

all intellectuals or enthusiasts . . . He is a total abstainer and is, I am told, domesticated and pious. He has neither wit, fervour, nor intellect; he is most decidedly not a leader, not even, like Henderson a manager of men. He has pushed his way up from hewer to checkweighman, from checkweighman to district agent, from district agent to miners' agent, to miners' M.P., by industry and trustworthiness and the habit of keeping himself to himself, making no enemies and never giving himself away . . . He had brought with him a typewritten paper and read from it the requirements which he and his pals among the Labour members had decided were necessary to enable the fifty-eight to tackle Lloyd George and his immense following. "Two clerks, three typists—we cannot do with less," he deprecatingly insisted. But what exercised his mind most were the messengers. The Liberals in the last Parliament, he said, had had three messengers; he *thought*—and it was clear from his wrinkled forehead and slowly emphatic tone that he thought strenuously on this question—he *thought* that the Parliamentary Labour Party might take over one of these messengers to fetch members to important divisions. He waited anxiously for Sidney's reply . . . Sidney cheerfully agreed but gently implied that the Parliamentary Labour Party would require more than three clerks, two typists and one messenger . . . "Ye-es—" (this dubiously) "concise rules, statistics, facts, that is what we want."' (*Beatrice Webb's diaries, 1912–24*, pp. 14–23.)

increasingly solid structure of the union movement. This transformation into an elite was accomplished during a period when the function of the union official had long ceased to be outside the law. Moreover, the occupation of union official existed, was socially recognised and had a fair amount of prestige attached to it. Its respectability was firmly consolidated in the scheme of lower middle class esteem. It had a good rating on the scale of capitalist value hierarchies, and could even be a springboard for an honours-laden career as MP, with a safe seat on the back benches of the House of Commons, and for lifelong membership of one of the many lesser governmental committees. Irrespective of their nonconformist and hostile attitudes towards a social order which they did not accept, the leaders of the new unionism suddenly found themselves, because of their occupations, in a position which was socially recognised and esteemed and also legitimated by bourgeois norms and bourgeois law. They found themselves in this position from the outset, without any intentional effort on their own part. They took over the widely respected executive functions in the Trades Union Congress and were elected to local government councils. They were among the candidates for Parliamentary seats and finally landed up in 'the best club in London' a few benches behind men whose names personified the power and wealth of the Empire. Selected individuals even got as far as the front bench and rubbed shoulders with men who had been set on a pedestal even during their lifetime. The confrontation between their avowed ideals and the political reality had an even more shattering effect on the leaders of the new movement than had been the case with the pioneers of the 'new model' unionism, for they immediately encountered conditions which were glaringly at odds with the moral code which they preached with the deepest conviction. The 'new model' leaders had at least known clearly what their goals were; their achievements thus came as no surprise to them but as the realisation of their avowed ideals.

It was as a result of this rebellion against society that John Burns—'Honest John', the 'Man with the Red Flag', the 'working man's Cromwell'—found himself, quite contrary to his own expectations, in such a respectable institution of that society as the London County Council, of which he was a member, together with Will Crooks, George Dew, Harry Gosling, Will Steadman and Ben Tillett, in the Progressive group led by Lord Rosebery. This group was lavishly financed from the plentiful funds of the Liberal Party, which was also the source of generous maintenance for Burns and Crooks.[1] After several years of association with Lord Rosebery and his Liberal colleagues, and several years of the respectful attention which the worthy citizens of London accorded to the words of

1 Lansbury, *My life*, p. 77.

this 'red rebel', Burns was moved to say at the 1900 Trades Union Congress that he was 'getting tired of working class boots, working class trains, working class houses and working class margarine'. He went on to express his belief that the labour movement had reached a stage at which its members should no longer be 'prisoners to class prejudice, but should consider parties and policies apart from class organisation'.[1] When Burns finally got a seat in Parliament this once confirmed socialist, now representing the Liberal Party, accepted the office of President of the Local Government Board from Asquith with gratitude and enthusiasm.[2] Once upon a time Burns used to say that no man was worth more than £500 a year. Asked how he reconciled this view with his current salary, which was several times larger, he replied nonchalantly, 'Oh, I just took the rate for the job.'[3]

Two years after the violence-filled dockers' strike led by Ben Tillett, the latter became an alderman on the London County Council. There he inadvertently addressed the Duke of Norfolk as 'Mr Norfolk', a *faux pas* which he later recalled with embarrassment in his memoirs. Fortunately the Duke accepted 'Alderman Tillett's' apology with affability, and the leader of the militant dockers commented with relief and surprise that the Duke was a gentleman.[4] Clynes, who had organised the most socially debased strata of labourers, became MP for Oldham because he was at the head of a powerful and recognised union. There, as delegate for the trades council to the Oldham chamber of commerce, he 'sat at the same table with employers and learned to understand their points of view' (though he does admit that he seldom agreed with them).[5] In his memoirs Will Thorne devoted as much attention to his visit to Lord Birkenhead to borrow a fur coat for his visit to Russia after the revolution as he did to the visit itself.[6] Another example was that of Ben Turner, who began a chapter on 'People I have known' by mentioning Sir Charles and Lady Dilke.[7] The working class public was inundated with a spate of autobiographical works bearing steretyped titles of the genre of *From the coal mines to Westminster*. Snobbery, that chronic disease of the *nouveau riche*, was corrupting the ranks of the new elite of the politically youthful working class labour movement, an elite which was exposed to innumerable temptations.

1   Quoted by Cole, *British working class politics*, p. 156.
2   Cole, *John Burns*, p. 3.
3   L. MacNeill Weir, *The tragedy of Ramsay MacDonald*, Secker & Warburg, London, p. 166.
4   Tillett, *Memories and reflections*, pp. 167–8.
5   Clynes, *Memoirs*, I, p. 85.
6   Allen, *Power in trade unions*, p. 194.
7   Turner, *About myself*, p. 317.

Some leaders were infected by the disease of snobbery; others, whose idealism made them proof against it, resisted its poisonous action. But sooner or later the members of both groups found themselves far to the rear of the labour movement as it continued on its headlong course of expansion. They were more astonished than alarmed at the dimensions assumed by the elemental force which they had let loose, but lost all authority over it and imperceptibly came to the end of their union careers. They knew nothing of administration, and had no desire to learn. In 1914 John Burns, who still retained a rebellious spirit, resigned from government office as a protest against the war. It was the end of his political career. He did not become an active pacifist but simply disappeared from the political scene, fading like a flower deprived of water. In fact he lived on for thirty more years, into an entirely new historical period which was incomprehensible to him, moving among his old acquaintances like a ghost of the past. He collected books and spent hours in his club boring listeners with incessant reminiscences of time long gone by. In 1918, *à propos* of Arthur Henderson's plan to introduce the principle of individual membership to the Labour Party, the restless spirit of the innate anti-bureaucrat came to life in him again. G. D. H. Cole records him as commenting brusquely that it was all on the wrong lines and that what was needed was a 'straight' socialist party, with no nonsense about it, and no attempt to compromise.[1] Writing of Tom Mann, Tillett quoted Byron's lines in *Childe Harold*: 'Quiet to quick souls is hell . . . his breath is sedition.'[2] Following his tremendous success in creating a movement 'out of nothing', Tom Mann was made general secretary of the Amalgamated Engineering Union, a position which was an honorary and trouble-free berth for life. But he was as much of a failure at the administrative work which it involved as he had been successful in his earlier operations. Bureaucratic walls irked Mann unbearably and every proposal for compromise drove him to indescribable rage.[3] As for Tillett, he died in 1943, a quarter of a century after the death of the movement which he had helped to create. For the greater part of those twenty-five years, in recognition of his former services, he was retained as chairman of the Transport and General Workers' Union—a sinecure carrying no authority at all—in the shadow of that titan among administrators, Ernest Bevin.[4] The union was expanding

1 Cole, *John Burns*, pp. 4–5.
2 *Memories and reflections*, p. 193.
3 Clynes, *Memoirs*, I, p. 264.
4 'To the younger generation he became no more than a scarcely considered legend, a voice out of the remote past as, small, wizened and loquacious, with bright bird-like eyes, he sat in a corner of the Trades Union Club telling of triumphs long gone and of the way in which Bevin, the man he had 'found and made', had pushed him to one side. He had become by then a pathetic yet infinitely attractive figure, a

on account of the flexibility of its administration, in which Tillett never felt at home. Instead he spent hours lunching at West End hotels; when criticised for this he would answer 'Only the best is good enough for the working man.'[1]

There were few exceptions to this rule. Only a small number managed, like Clynes, to adapt themselves to the new conditions and requirements—and even then they did not usually rise to such heights in the new conditions as they had done formerly.

An even smaller number succeeded in preserving their revolutionary fervour despite all temptations. One of these was Keir Hardie, whom I shall be discussing later, and another was George Lansbury. When the question of gaoling three suffragette leaders was raised in 1912 the latter pushed his way to the Treasury bench and shook his fist in the Premier's face, saying, 'You are beneath contempt . . . You drive women mad and then tell them to walk out! You, to talk of principle! And you, too,' he said, turning to the Conservative benches, which were yelling at him by now. 'You ought to be driven out of public life.'[2] Such men were, however, exceptional and few and far between.

The drowsy atmosphere of Parliamentary life changed the elite of the new movement. They were stunned by the Parliamentary tradition of centuries of rule by the aristocracy, a tradition hallowed in its customs and rules of procedures. They were seduced by the good manners and dignity which were traditionally attached to the social position of a member of Parliament; and the combustible energies of impatient hot-heads were exhausted in beating against the hard walls of immutable Parliamentary procedure and suffocating in the soporific atmosphere of endless ineffectual debates.[3]

relic of a more heroic more tragic, gayer and more bohemian past; driven now to brooding on the battles and comrades of his youth and on his own eclipse as he slowly lived out his life, a pensioner of the great Union he had helped to make possible'. (Williams, *Ernest Bevin*, pp. 108–9.)

1   Quoted by Williams, *Ernest Bevin*, p. 67.
2   Lansbury, *My life*, p. 123.
3   Here are four different but not altogether inconsistent impressions given by four leaders who entered Parliament. 'During our first days in the House nearly all the new Labour Members of the 1906 Parliament were inclined to resent the cumbrous formalities imposed by the ceremonies of the place. We were burning with impatience to set the world to rights, and had not yet discovered that this gigantic task could not be completed as the result of a few sincere and somewhat hasty speeches . . . Since that distant day we have learned a lesson that has to be acquired by each succeeding generation of Members. Behind the cumbrous formalities of Parliament lies the wisdom of long experience.' (Clynes, *Memoirs*, I, p. 116.) 'I have elsewhere endeavoured to describe the emotions of a thoughtful man on the day when, for the first time, he becomes a member of the British Parliament, and the

This raw material was moulded into shape by Parliament; swiftly grew into a labour group, modelled on the middle class groups, and ceaselessly wasting the energies unexpended on reformist action in imitating the manners, way of life, and political and social attitudes of older Parliamentary colleagues from the middle class political elite. A group developed of which J. J. Stephenson, chairman of the 1907 TUC, could say with pride, 'In terms of its good sense, capacity for adaptation and dignity, it has taken first place in the British House of Commons, leaving rivalry for the second place to others.'[1] The majority of union MPs quickly began wearing top hats; this led a well known Liberal leader who always appeared in a top hat to change his headgear to a soft hat, in order that, as he declared, he should not be mistaken for a Labour member.[2] With typical sarcasm, Hyndman described his attitude to the Labour Party in the language of an Irish peasant, saying, 'That pig doesn't weigh as much as I thought it would, but then I never thought it would.'[3] No less sarcastic opinions were, however, heard from other sources which were not emotionally engaged.[4]

> thrill that he feels when he makes his first appearance at its doors . . . If the new member is a normally healthy human being, possessing some knowledge of the history of his country and the place of Parliament in its wonderful story, he will probably regard this as the greatest day of his life . . . If our new member is not moved to emotion as he enters upon his great heritage, or if he remains unaware of his partnership in the great fellowship of service which the House of Commons represents his life there may be useful but it can scarcely be happy . . . These words were a description of my own emotions on becoming a Member of Parliament, and they represent my present feelings'. (Lord Snell, *Life of Ramsay MacDonald*, pp. 206–7.) 'Members when they first enter the House are inclined to think that much of the ceremony is old-fashioned nonsense. It is not long before they come to realise that it serves the real purposes of contributing to the proper authority of the Chair and to orderly debate, and of emphasizing the dignity and corporate spirit of the House . . . I am sure that it helps in identifying King and People and Government, in breaking down the antithesis between the "we" who are governed and the "they" who do the governing, which must be removed if a democracy is to be truly popular . . . Much of the pomp and ceremony is valuable because it helps Parliament and the parliamentary system to keep their hold on the imagination of the people.' (H. Morrison, 'British Parliamentary democracy,' *Parliamentary Affairs*, autumn 1949, p. 349.) 'Old members smiled at the impatience of the new members. They reminded us of the time when they first came to Paliament full of an earnest enthusiasm to achieve some good purpose; but despair had entered into their hearts, and before the advent of the Labour men, they had resigned all hope of ever being able to move that cumbersome machine at any reasonable rate along the path of reform.' (Snowden, *An autobiography*, p. 127.)

1 Report of the Labour Party, 1907, p. 44.
2 Snowden, *An autobiography*, pp. 124–5.
3 Hyndman, *Further remininiscences*, p. 259.
4 'They look less like a set of revolutionary malcontents than an excursion of Nonconformist lay preachers. Nor was the group over-burdened with Parliamentary

The failure of the group of Labour MPs was no accident. The political elite of the labour movement was in only a very embryonic state of evolution. During the period under discussion, up to 1918, the Labour Party was in organisational terms a superstructure on top of the union machinery, while its elite had no support of its own in any structure independent of, or even separate from the structure of the trade unions. It thus had only as much capacity for expansion as the unions allowed it, and such frontiers of social mobility as the union structure could afford. Even after the introduction of individual membership the Labour Party Parliamentary group remained a branch of the union structure for several more years. The fundamental breakthrough really came in the years 1922–24, when the Labour group became first of all a team which was competing for a mandate to govern the country, and later one of the two elite political teams which governed the nation by turns.

Until this happened, however, the union officials who made up the bulk of the Labour group in Parliament regarded a Parliamentary seat as an end in itself, the highest and most coveted promotion on the scale of social honours. Dreams about governing the country spoiled their delight in the heights which they had already attained. The trade unions did not let their fancy stray so far. The Labour Party's constitution contained no reference to the task of winning a majority in Parliament; it was confined simply to the maintenance of a Parliamentary group.

At the outset of the period under consideration no section of the labour movement had risen to the level of the political elite. In the years 1870–92 *The Times*, whose pages reflect, if not the political history of Britain, at least the history of the prevailing political viewpoint, did not include a single biography of a labour leader among the dozens of biographies of eminent politicians which it published over that period.[1] The fact speaks for itself. In the consciousness of the labour leaders, too, these heights were regarded as beyond their reach, and were not taken into account. Clynes recalls how, after he told his family of his success at a large meeting organised by himself, he was told: 'Well done, lad. We shall see our Jack on the town council some day, at this rate!' Clynes goes on to comment ironically that if the scene had been set not in Oldham, but in Greek legend, this would have been the time for Mercury to appear, accompanied by a clap of thunder, and to say dramatically: 'He shall be, not town councillor,

---

ability . . . In the House, where, for the most part, they spoke little and spent much time in the smoking room, they seemed to many to represent little more than what Hyndman bitterly described as "a dull and deferential respectability."' (Lord Elton, *Life of Ramsay MacDonald*, p. 133.)

1   *Eminent persons: biographies reprinted from 'The Times'*, Times Publishing Co., London, 1896.

but His Majesty's Secretary of State for Home Affairs!'[1] Of the ILP found-ing conference in 1892, he comments: 'None of us, I think, realised that the conference would make history, or that we were assisting at the birth of a new Parliamentary party whose leaders should one day, and in our day, accept seals of office from the King.'[2] When the Labour group at last made its appearance in Parliament a considerable majority of its members still did not realise the significance of the event. On the contrary, they did everything to play down their presence in the House of Commons, to avoid attracting attention or standing out in any way, and to lose them-selves in the uniform mass of MPs from the bourgeois parties. This Labour group had no political ambitions for the future. All their aspirations had already been realised once for all, in their view, and the end of their struggle had been reached. When Burns became a Minister the group simply acknowledged him as a lost leader, not as a pioneer of the migration of labour members to the peaks of the political hierarchy. The Labour group's aspirations did not extend sufficiently far for Burns's advancement to stir their imagination: instead, he was simply regarded as no longer one of them.

In 1918 Henderson's proposal to introduce individual membership, a move which finally enabled the Labour Party to grow into a formal political party, encountered decided opposition from a considerable section of trade unionists. This resistance was the result not only of apprehension about the emancipation of the political party but also of aversion to the idea of any more far-reaching political ambitions linked with the func-tioning of the party. The opposition, led by the textile worker Tom Shaw, wished the Labour Party to remain an auxiliary branch for trade union officials to operate in the House of Commons as a group conducting regular negotiations with the 'real' political parties, and thereby assuring Ministerial or lesser offices for the leadership of the trade union move-ment.[3] This conception did not have majority backing but the support for

1 *Memoirs*, 1, p. 48.
2 *Ibid.*, pp. 69–70.
3 Tom Shaw's idea, in its purest, most extreme form, appeared in the United States, where, starting from the stage of new model unionism, the labour movement had developed in a different direction from the British one: i.e. towards the full develop-ment of the trends comprised in the 'new model' type of union. The pundit of this movement, Samuel Gompers, argued—and this argument was adopted as a strategic guide for the movement—that 'a few thousand voters, easily mobilised and shifted from one candidate to another, were more powerful in politics than a million or two separatists formed in a minority party of their own'. (H. Seidman, *Labor czars*, Liveright, New York, 1938, p. 217.) It must be stressed that the elite of the Amer-ican labour movement made its way into the overall elite by climbing the eco-nomic, not the political, ladder. This was probably the principal factor behind most of the differences between its evolution and the history of the elite of the British labour movement, which it so resembled in class terms.

it was unusually large. The decision to introduce individual membership was taken after bitter debate and was approved by a very low majority. This clearly shows how far, even a few years before the first Labour government, the British labour elite was from thinking about accomplishing the last and highest leap of its career. Indeed, even in 1922 Clynes accepted the fact that he was the official leader of the Opposition and the first choice as Britain's next Prime Minister with astonishment and a certain tinge of disbelief.[1]

The fact that the structure of the labour political movement afforded such modest opportunities for advancement and was subordinated to the trade union organisation meant that the social elite of the movement was drawn almost entirely from the working class. The labour movement could provide its leaders with Parliamentary places, although activity in the movement was still socially degrading for the stratum of bourgeois intellectuals. Even if it was no longer degrading, it certainly did not offer any impressive prospects for a political career. The movement was not yet large enough for any spreading of its wings. Moreover, within the movement the union elite, which dominated it absolutely, eyed the intellectuals suspiciously. Their help was not essential to the trade unionists to perform the kind of Parliamentary functions which the latter deemed adequate. In such conditions the influx of intellectuals could in their view mean only the threat of unwanted competition, without any compensating advantages. For both reasons, therefore, circumstances did not favour a massive influx of intellectuals into the ranks of the labour movement. This is not to say, however, that certain sections of the intelligentsia did not gather round the movement.

The members of the Fabian Society and the executive of the Social Democratic Federation consisted mainly of intellectuals drawn from the aristocracy and middle classes. In no circumstances, however, could either of these two groups be reckoned among the contemporary elite of the labour movement, whether political or trade unionist. The position of the two groups was not determined by the structure of the movement. Furthermore, because of their social connections and socio-political attitudes, both of them remained outside the basic structure of the labour movement.

I have already pointed out that students of the labour movement frequently exaggerate the influence of Fabian socialism on the genesis of the political wing of the labour movement in Britain. The role played by various Fabian activists in the creation of the Labour Party and its organisational framework has also—in my view—been similarly exaggerated. In neither an ideological nor an organisational sense were the intellectuals present at the cradle of the British labour movement, whether in its

1   Clynes, *Memoirs*, I, pp. 323, 329.

trade union or political version. This was the outcome not of chance but of the internal structural requirements of the evolution of the labour movement in Britain. The Fabians did not fit in with the unambitious elite of the old union movement, nor with the fiercely nonconformist and rebellious elite of the new movement. They were later to join the elite of the mature political movement, not as its creators or its basic nucleus, but as a group carrying out definite tasks set by the organisational structure which had been shaped independently of them.

As a social group the Fabians were far from homogeneous. They comprised writers, higher civil servants, businessmen and landowners: such people owed their social status not to their organisational functions but to their extra-organisational ties. They differed greatly in status, and the organisation did not contribute to uniformity. The association of high functions in the State or the business world with social ideas could at times produce ludicrous consequences—as in the case of Sidney (later Lord) Oliver, who was Financial Secretary in the Jamaican administration and later became the colony's Governor. While in London on leave in 1897 he protested sharply against the proposal that the Fabian Society should contribute 10s towards the decoration of the Strand for the diamond jubilee of Queen Victoria, one of whose representatives he was in the government of the colony.[1]

Except for Annie Besant, the Fabians did not mix with the mass movement. They felt ill at ease at large gatherings and, being neither orators nor agitators, preferred discussions in small groups and on a high intellectual plane. Sidney Webb, the most influential figure among the Fabians, had a profound, analytical mind and was an extremely hard worker. He produced works of great enduring theoretical value, and was at the same time admirably suited to be at the head of an upper division of the civil service. At night he read as fast as he could turn the pages, and from his reading remembered everything that was worth recalling. He was a polyglot who could speak a number of European languages fluently; during his years of education he had won every scholarship that was available. Yet with all this he had none of the skills that could have enabled him to lead a minority movement [2] Not all the Fabians had the same good qualities as Webb, but almost all of them had the same defects.[3] The Fabians were more a part of the intellectual elite of the Liberal Party than of the Labour Party elite. The Liberal milieu was their proper milieu in terms of class and occupational structure and ideological attitudes. The Labour Party was to inherit the Fabians at a later period in the same way

1   Bernstein, *My years of exile*, pp. 239–40.
2   Shaw, *Early days*, p. 4.
3   Pease, *History of the Fabian Society*, p. 55.

as it inherited the Liberal milieu, Liberal politics and the Liberal ideology.

The second wing of the intellectuals of middle class origin grouped itself into the SDF. This group was very different from the Fabians. It was a group of rebels, in revolt against the prevailing social order; at the same time it was a group which was endeavouring to join up with the mass movement rather than confining itself within the narrow walls of discussion clubs. The man who was most characteristic of this group was Henry Mayers Hyndman, the grandson of a large planter in British Guiana, son of an extremely wealthy merchant and related to a number of high officials in the colonial service—in short, the descendant of a family which was typical of a period when the aristocracy of birth and the aristocracy of wealth were merging. Hyndman tried his hand at a career in law, journalism and the civil service. After he began to study socialist ideas the fanaticism of an intellectual conscious of his middle class origins induced him to choose the most dogmatic version of this ideology. As soon as he accepted it he embarked energetically on revolutionary activities, trying to set up a mass movement with revolutionary socialist aims.

He was for a while successful in inflaming the enthusiasm of the masses but encountered some setbacks when he tried to keep this enthusiasm going at revolutionary pitch for a longer period. His campaign found hearers among the starving unemployed, driven to the ultimate edge of despair, but went unnoticed in those sections of the working class which had already emerged from the state of fragmentation and alienation. Both Hyndman's successes and his failures had an objective cause—his personal characteristics. It is, however, all the more interesting that these, which were essentially those of his entire group, in great measure limited his scope for action.[1]

1   Here are some descriptions of Hyndman by several of his contemporaries. 'Broad and powerful in physique, with features large and regular . . . eyes that betoken a faithful and devoted friend, but a dangerous and powerful enemy . . . a great heavy beard, and a fine shock of hair now tinged with the first grey.' (*Aberdeen Journal.*) Quelch wrote of him, 'It was at one of the public meetings held by the Association that I first met H. M. Hyndman; and I must say that I, as a Radical Republican, was not favourably impressed by his aristocratic manner and his style of dress . . . Later on, I met Hyndman again, the occasion being a visit Souther and I paid him one evening . . . and his evident disinterestedness and sincerity caused a considerable modification in my first prejudice.' (Quoted by Gould, *Hyndman*, pp. 124, 101–2.) Ben Tillett said of him, '. . . H. M. Hyndman, still remembered as a robust figure, the arrogant intellectual, the fierce exponent, possessing a mind forensic, exact and ruthless, with a patience and a capacity for details devastating to an opponent. He was in some ways our chief intellectual prize. He seemed to us a mental giant.' (*Memories and reflections*, p. 189.) And Eduard Bernstein commented, 'While he knew how to enlist recruits, he was less successful in holding them together.' (*My years of exile*, p. 255.)

Hyndman's protest was based mainly on intellectual grounds; but the same group of revolutionary socialist intellectuals contained many people, most of them writers and artists, whose social protest rested on emotional, and frequently on aesthetic, grounds. It was a feeling of revolt against the ugliness of the capitalist world of his day, with its trampling on art and beauty, which led William Morris—the 'dreamer born out of his due time'[1]—to make fiery speeches at street corners in the winter weather, in spite of his nearly sixty years and the rheumatic pains that afflicted him.[2] As Lethaby and Steele wrote after his death, 'Morris was a socialist because he rebelled against the capitalist system, which imposes uniformity on craftsmanship and treats the workman as a mere unit, and against uncontrolled competition, which sacrifices beauty to cheapness, solid work to seductive shams, and art to machinery'.[3] He objected as vigorously to the tyranny of collectivism as to that of capital. Morris's socialism had little in common with scientific socialism—it was rooted in his heart rather than in his head. When questioners at a Glasgow meeting asked him whether he accepted Marx's 'theory of value' he is reported to have answered: 'Political economy is not in my line and much of it appears to be dreary rubbish. But I am, I hope, a Socialist none the less . . . It is enough political economy for me to know that the idle rich class is rich and the working class is poor, and that the rich are rich because they rob the poor. That I know because I see it with my eyes.'[4]

Morris was not alone in raising this kind of aesthetically and emotionally motivated protest. Robert Blatchford, whose mother was an actress, was brought up in a rather obscure bohemian milieu, and his socialist convictions emerged from a combination of religious influences, the reading of Dickens and his own tender heart, which shuddered at the sight of barefoot children in the streets of London, of half-naked women heaving sacks of salt in the mines of Cheshire, and at the appalling slums of Manchester.[5] He was opposed to political organisations and political leaders—not any particular leaders but leaders as an institution—and warned the workers against 'this fatuous dependence on "leaders"'. He regarded himself as an 'adviser' of the masses, not a leader of them, since in his view the road to socialism required not so much an organised movement as the intellectual transformation of the masses.[6]

1   Lord Snell, *Life of Ramsay MacDonald*, pp. 110–11.
2   E. Meynell, *Portrait of William Morris*, Chapman, London, 1947, p. 173.
3   Appreciation of him by W. R. Lethaby and Robert Steele, after his death, in the *Quarterly Review*; also *ibid.*, p. 163.
4   Quoted by Snowden, *An autobiography*, pp. 62–3.
5   Blatchford, *My eighty years*, pp. 36 et seq.
6   Thompson, *Robert Blatchford*, pp. 53–4.

Apart from the personal motives which stirred such men as Hyndman, Morris and Blatchford to action and sacrifice, they represented to an equal degree the Utopian social philosophy which was so contrary to the nature of the British labour movement. They were therefore not a part of the mainstream of the movement, but a specific side product of an era of great flexibility and dynamic social change. The labour movement evolved independently of them, just as it evolved independently of the highly intellectual, armchair-socialist Fabians.

The figures typical of the elite of the labour movement of the period were different. These were the hard-headed, well balanced, practical men who were professional trade union officials, and the idealistic, somewhat romantic, grass-roots leaders of the new union movement and working class socialism. The first group was not peculiar to this period; such men could be found in both the preceding and the following ones. The second group, on the other hand, was a unique phenomenon, associated with the era when the movement spread to the masses, when the mass of workers awoke and when a political movement with a class base was born. This is why the individuals in the second group are most characteristic of the elite of the labour movement of the time. And it is also why a sociological analysis of the labour elite of the period can most aptly be summed up by delineating the characteristics of the leading personality in this second group, James Keir Hardie.

The son of a ship's carpenter, Keir Hardie was born in a mining area and by the age of six was working as a baker's boy, the only breadwinner in a family of ten. When he was thirteen years old he went down the mine for the first time, working twelve to fourteen hours a day. He had an innate love of knowledge, and after an exhausting day would stand in front of a bookshop window and teach himself to read from the titles of the books on display, but he was fifteen before he learned to write. Later it was much the same story as with Clynes, Thorne, Tillett and many others: night schools after work; books bought instead of food; reading the works of Burns, Carlyle and Henry George; the delight of discovering the beauty of words, and the arduous polishing of prose style; the first contributions to the local newspaper; and the rumours about the 'educated miner' which began to circulate among the miners. When he was twenty-one Keir Hardie was elected secretary of the Miners' Association in Ayrshire, and three years later he became its president. At meetings he expressed in a clear and intelligible form what the miners felt but could not say—and swiftly gained the respect and dispelled the suspicions of the tough old miners. Soon he was their acknowledged leader. He was only thirty years old when he appeared at the TUC as their representative.

On his first visit Hardie scandalised that respectable institution ruled by the Broadhursts and Howells. Thenceforward scandal was to accompany his every appearance on the TUC platform until the authority of the old elite was broken. Hardie's first step was to support an amendment to the executive's report on the activities of trade union MPs in Parliament. He pointed out: 'The amendment providing an eight-hour labour day in the mines was proposed, but was defeated, your secretary speaking and voting against it in the name of Congress.'[1] Two years later Hardie mounted a frontal attack on Broadhurst for owning some shares in a factory notorious for exploiting its workers (see p. 123), and for giving his support to the candidature as a Liberal MP of a manufacturer whose factory was equally notorious.[2] This was war to the death: Hardie was not one of those who would refrain from using any methods which he thought could assure victory for a principle.

In 1888 he was the first man in British history to stand for Parliament as an independent labour candidate, not associated with any of the existing bourgeois parties. He lost this contest, but four years later, at the age of thirty-five, he was elected MP for West Ham, becoming the first independent labour MP in Parliament.

Like his debut five years earlier at the TUC, Keir Hardie's first appearance in Parliament created a sensation and became a long-term source of scandal not only for the members of the 'best club in London' but also for the lobby correspondents. Hardie arrived at the Houses of Parliament in a two-horse cart drawn by his supporters and with a trumpeter on the box. He was wearing a cloth cap and tweed coat, in an institution in which top hats were *de rigueur* and members were shocked by the new Lib–Labs who wore bowlers.[3] This challenge to Parliamentary conventions was, however, only the bare beginning, for all Hardie's activities in the House of Commons went far beyond the framework of accepted Parliamentary *mores*. His electoral campaigns were more like crusades than political skirmishes. His speeches were indictments, his revolutionary plans were challenges aimed at middle class 'common sense', and his every utterance in Parliament reduced those who heard him to a state of rage mingled with terror. Hardie paid no regard to any Parliamentary ceremonial. He came to the House not to co-operate in legislating for society as it was but to unmask and denounce the hypocrisy and anti-social nature of the laws.

1 Report of the TUC, 1887, p. 22.
2 Report of the TUC, 1889, p. 22.
3 If Smillie's account is correct, Hardie intended to wear a hat on his first appearance in Parliament, but could not find it in the confusion caused by his enthusiastic supporters. When he realised, however, what an uproar his appearance in a cap had caused he decided as a matter of principle to wear it regularly: this was in order to avoid giving the impression that he was giving way in face of the criticisms of him for wearing a working man's cap. (Smillie, *My life for labour*, p. 99.)

He could see each issue only in class terms, and in contrast to most other labour members he did not vote with the Liberals, only against the party in power. Both parties were, in his view, what they were in fact—bourgeois parties. Thus he regarded it as his function to oppose whichever of them was ruling the working class at a given period.

Keir Hardie was not a politician nor a statesmen in the sense accepted by the bourgeois Parliamentary system. He did not fit into that system, in the same way as the revolutionary mass movement of labourers did not fit into it. In the lobbies of the House of Commons Hardie always moved on his own, a stranger to the middle class political world, in which he was the ambassador of a new and hostile power. His speeches were not in fact directed at this world, which they saw as absolutely perfect, whereas he regarded it as absolutely finished. When, later, Emrys Hughes was looking at the photographs of top-hatted Labour members entering Buckingham Palace at the royal summons on the formation of a new government, he asked Keir Hardie's daughter what her father would have done if he had lived seventy years to become the leader of a Labour government. Her answer was 'He would have sent for the king.'[1]

With the Labour group's rapid increase in size Keir Hardie suddenly became the leader of a considerable Parliamentary body. He was not particularly successful in this role, being no organiser in spite of having been in at the birth of both the ILP and the Labour Party. When it came to reaping the harvest which his labours had fully earned, better harvesters than he emerged. Hardie calmly and unhesitatingly handed over the whole administration to younger men, admitting openly that he disliked it and was not good at it; all administrative functions he regarded as a superfluous burden which might easily come into conflict with his conscience.

The setting up of a Labour group in Parliament was not an end in itself for Hardie, by contrast with many professional union leaders. As he wrote in *The Miner*,

> What difference will it make to me that I have a working man representing me in Parliament, if he is a dumb dog who dare not bark and will follow the leader under any circumstances? There is something even more desirable than the return of working men to Parliament and that is to give working men a definite programme to fight for when they get there and to warn them that if they haven't the courage to stand up in the House of Commons and say what they would say in a workers' meeting, they must make room for someone else who will.[2]

1 Hughes, *Keir Hardie*, p. 13.
2 Quoted by Hughes, *Keir Hardie*, p. 36.

This passage contains the whole conception of Parliamentary struggle and the role of a labour MP which was characteristic of the man.

His programme of political struggle was never clear or precise. The only definite element in it consisted not of its aims, nor even of its methods, but of its reaction to human problems. Keir Hardie was characterised by an all-embracing humanitarianism, which transformed all human suffering into a fiery protest against the unjust order of things. His 1910 electoral posters in Merthyr Tydfil bore the following lines[1] from William Morris and Burns:

> O why and for what are we waiting?
> While our brothers droop and die
> And on every wind of the heavens
> A wasted life goes by.
>
> Man's inhumanity to man
> Makes countless thousands mourn.

When he was speaking in the Commons on his motion concerning the 'socialist commonwealth' in 1901, Hardie said: 'We are called to you at the beginning of the twentieth century to decide upon the question propounded in the Sermon on the Mount as to whether or not we will worship God or Mammon.'[2] These words contain his whole political programme, his whole protest against the bourgeois order and also his tendency to hazy humanistic generalisations.

Hardie's life was not influenced by any considerations for his personal career, whether in terms of prestige or of wealth. In 1888 the Liberal George Trevelyan suggested that Hardie should withdraw his candidature in exchange for a safe seat without Liberal competition; he was also offered a salary of £300 a year. Hardie refused, although in actual fact he had no source of livelihood. Later his only source of income for many years was the salary of £150 paid him as leader of the ILP. From this he not only had to meet all his organisational expenses but also contributed to the publication of the *Labour Leader*, which did not cover its costs. In 1902 he told miners in Durham that if he were to die at that moment he would leave his wife debts so enormous that he was afraid even to think about them.

Hardie was something of a missionary or saint in character. He looked like a patriarch and his ascetic way of life and strongly emotional nature had left their mark on his face, gestures and manner of speaking. In appearance he was stocky, strongly and robustly built, with a long flowing beard and

1 Quoted by Hughes, *ibid.*, pp. 128–9.
2 Quoted from Frank Bealey, 'Keir Hardie and the Labour group,' II, *Parliamentary Affairs*, spring 1957.

frowning eyebrows. He could easily win over a working class audience and sweep his hearers away. The workers, who knew him, worshipped him, surrounding him with a cult which sometimes exceeded human attachment. This cult derived a religious tinge from the aura of self-sacrifice which surrounded Keir Hardie, the man who was subjected to insults and calumnies by the capitalist press, and treated with suspicion, if not hatred, by professional union leaders, who regarded him as a 'hot air merchant',[1] a dangerous dreamer and an unrealistic visionary.

The 'old man' was surrounded by a small but faithful band of people who resembled him and imitated his behaviour. Whereas Broadhurst had written of his meetings with the Prince of Wales in his memoirs in order to feed his vanity, it was Keir Hardie who figured in the Prince's role for Smillie and others. Smillie was to recall with emotion and pride how Hardie had waited by the door of a public house while he drank a tankard of beer, something which Hardie, as a militant teetotaller, detested.

Clynes wrote of Keir Hardie: 'For many years, mocked by the parasites he threatened, doubted by the workers he wished to help, flayed by the Press, excommunicated by the society church, feared by his contemporaries in the House, shunned by all who wished to remain respectable, this remarkable man went up and down Great Britain, fanning the Labour smoulderings to flame.'[2]

When the Labour Party began to build up an increasingly large administrative machinery and to be transformed from a militant organisation to an electioneering machine, Hardie simply faded out. He did not understand the new era, nor recognise the party which he had created and dreamed of in the administrative machine that was gaining power before his eyes. He watched with apprehension as his party showed less and less concern for principles and more and more for organisational efficiency, and as the commandment of fraternal love was violated by the pro-war vote. Shortly after his resignation he died.[3]

The party was not affected by his death because it had by then left him far behind. The militant, romantic youth of the new political movement had passed. Now the unification of the old movement and the new, the conciliation of the new movement by the old, were under way. The assimilation of the new trade union activists and the development of new, larger and more powerful administrative machinery for the Labour political movement were proceeding simultaneously. The era of a new

1 Page-Arnot, *The miners*, p. 111.
2 Clynes, *Memoirs*, 1, pp. 23–4.
3 Unless otherwise indicated the information about Keir Hardie is taken from E. Hughes, *Keir Hardie: some memories*, Johnson, London, 1939, and *idem*, *Keir Hardie*, 1956; also from *The book of the Labour Party*, III, London, 1925.

political elite, or a sociologically new category of trade union leaders, was beginning—men among whom Keir Hardie, the Utopian preacher, would have been decidedly out of place. The era of Ramsay MacDonald was at hand—the era of a new stabilisation of the labour movement in Britain, this time on a class basis.

James Keir Hardie was thus typical of the first phase of the period in which the mass labour movement evolved, a phase in which the movement was an expansive and dynamic force, destroying the old structures and setting up new ones only fortuitously and half-consciously. But this period also saw the beginning of new processes which were the seeds of the next period—that of the stabilisation of the total movement. These processes began and evolved as the mass movement consolidated itself, and the two sections of the labour movement perfected their forms and programmes. This was particularly so as the new movement became assimilated not, as formerly, into the economic structure but into the political structure of the country. At this time, as I have said, people of a new type came to the fore. Like the leaders of the old unions, they belonged to the category of administrators; but unlike those leaders, they also fitted into the category of politicians. Their rise signified the shifting of the centre of the labour movement from the economic to the political wing. It was a by-product of the movement's institutionalisation of class interests, not occupational interests as in the past—although in the British case those class interests were the sum and in a way the generalised extension of occupational interests. The real dominance of this new political oriented administrative elite did not begin until our next historical period, and will be dealt with in appropriate detail later. Nevertheless, the roots of this elite reach back to the period of the mass movement, and a picture of the elite-making processes of this period would be incomplete if one were to omit the name of James Ramsay MacDonald—a name of unparalleled importance in the history of the British labour movement.

Ramsay MacDonald was active over the two periods of history. Indeed, he formed the link that connected them. He was a politician and administrator on a scale that was understandable and normal only in the conditions of the later period. But at the same time he showed a disbelief in the possibilities of the labour movement strange in a man of outstanding perspicacity and political shrewdness, and a misunderstanding of the new role of the political movement of the working class in the British political system. This straddling of the two eras seems to explain the many superficially unintelligible inconsistencies and inner conflicts in the story of his life and his political profile. It is thus very important, when analysing MacDonald's place in the processes of the creation of an elite in the labour movement, not to forget that neither historical period could lay exclusive claim to him; he belonged simultaneously to two periods with different sociological characteristics.

Ramsay MacDonald was the complete antithesis of Keir Hardie, as the administrator is the antithesis of the agitator. One could build up a simplified profile of MacDonald by the simple means of listing the opposites of the traits that went to make up the profile of the latter. Keir Hardie's strength lay in denunciation, MacDonald's in affirmation. Hardie put his own convictions and the dictates of his own conscience above everything—including the party line, with which he was in conflict more than once. In so far as MacDonald had any lasting convictions of his own—which there are some reasons to doubt—he was always able to overcome them for the transient benefit of the party machine. Hardie never ceased to expose politics as such, regarding it as a dirty and unwholesome game which one was compelled to play only by necessity. MacDonald, on the other hand, regarded success in the political game as an end in itself, and politics and the intricacies of diplomacy as his element. Hardie had a straightforward mind, and he approached matters directly and sincerely. MacDonald, on the other hand, was well known for his casuistry, his deliberate confusion of simple matters and his tendency to rationalise motives that were not always rational. Hardie never acted from personal motives nor was he motivated by ambition. In MacDonald's case personal ambitions were among the most significant motivations and determinants of his political life.

MacDonald's youth differed hardly at all from the youth of other self-emancipated workers born in the second half of the nineteenth century. He was the son of an agricultural worker, whose family lived in profound poverty. By some miracle, and at extreme cost to himself, he managed to get himself educated and to attend night school. But he differed from others of the same age in that he was prepared to make sacrifices for a definite purpose—to escape from the intolerable confines of poverty, drudgery, starvation and social humiliation. He realised that the way of escape led through education, and deliberately set about preparing himself for a clerical job. He was never a manual labourer, nor did he learn any trade, but educated himself, according to a plan, for a white-collar occupation.

MacDonald was nineteen years old when he came to London to pluck the first fruits of his youthful self-denial. He began work as an office clerk for the ludicrously low starting salary of 12s 6d a week; later it was raised to 15s. In after years he recalled how he had learned to live on sixpence or sevenpence a day. He drank hot water instead of tea or coffee and bought vegetables from the market to make soup, which was his principal source of nourishment. But he also managed to continue his studies and dress himself in a modest but genteel style. He began to move in political circles and at the age of twenty-two became private secretary to Thomas Lough, a politician of radical–liberal tendencies. This work afforded him an extremely useful political training; at the same time it introduced him to the great world of politics which had long been a far-distant goal for him, and to a sphere in which one could advance infinitely higher than a clerk's position. At this time MacDonald's salary was £75 per annum—an extremely modest amount, but much higher than he would have received in an office.

It was probably during the course of his four years' work with Lough that he came to the conclusion that the Liberal Party did not offer sufficient scope for an ambitious young man of working class origins whose self-taught knowledge was broadly based but hardly systematic. There was too much competition from men with greater education and a better social background. In a party of labour the situation was completely different. An able and ambitious man of MacDonald's type could go as far as he wished and as far as the organisation which he was to help create could push him. So MacDonald wrote to Keir Hardie, announcing his willingness to work for the ILP. Hardie accepted, and Ramsay MacDonald took over the full-time post of party secretary—with Keir Hardie willingly shifting the burden of administration on to younger men's shoulders. In the same year he married Margaret Gladstone, a great-niece of Lord Kelvin and the daughter of a well known scientist. This happy marriage not only effected a complete change in his financial situation but also associated him with the political and intellectual elite of society. The importance of his marriage in MacDonald's life cannot be over-estimated—as all his biographers are agreed.[1] Its immediate consequence was that he could devote himself to party work for the sake, not of present financial, but of future gains, despite his ludicrously small salary, which started at twenty guineas per annum and was raised after five years to £25. Money was not the decisive factor to one who was both a far-sighted politician and a man of independent means.

Did Ramsay MacDonald link his fortunes with those of the ILP from ideological motives? Did his socialist beliefs contribute, at least in part, to the forming of that vital decision? The question is a very difficult one to answer. In any case, it is not of particular sociological relevance to know how far socialist ideology as a motive *per se* was combined in him with socialist ideology as a rationalisation of the entirely different motives of a man who with some reason saw the labour movement as a ladder leading comfortably towards advancement. MacDonald was a socialist in the sense intended by Sir William Harcourt when he said, 'We are all socialists

---

1   For example, Lord Elton, *Life of Ramsay MacDonald*, p. 79; H. H. Tiltman, *James Ramsay MacDonald*, Jarrold's, London, 1929, p. 44; A. P. Nicholson, *The real men in public life*, Collins, London, 1928, p. 36.

now.' In each of his two major theoretical works and in his day-to-day political dealings MacDonald's socialism emerged as a promised land, not an attainable one, portrayed only in attractive-sounding generalisations. MacNeill Weir has compared this kind of socialism with the landscapes of Turner in all their marvellous colours and magnificent indeterminacy. He was of the opinion that MacDonald's version of socialist ideology could be professed by anybody at all without any effort or even a feeling of awkwardness. MacDonald was neither a prophet nor even an agitator of socialism, as was Keir Hardie. His socialism was a respectable one, settled comfortably on the Parliamentary benches, always subordinated to considerations of political solidarity and the winning of respect among the middle class politicians. In his early years MacDonald's socialist sermons consisted basically of warnings against violent methods of action, while in his later years they generally amounted to nothing at all. His speeches were so insubstantial in content that, according to Raymond Postgate, his opponents could not even reproach him with lying or inconsistency, as they could with Lloyd George. They were never certain what his precise meaning was. Hubert Bland, the most radical of the Fabians, castigated MacDonald's attitude to socialist theory in the following terms: 'It seems that we are to work for socialism, fight for socialism, even die for it, but not, for God's sake, to define it.'

His attitude to socialism was only one of many exemplifications of MacDonald's general attitude to life. His set of basic political precepts consisted of an avoidance of sharp conflicts and all positions which could appear extreme from any angle, a deliberate accentuation of the ambiguities of his own attitudes and a simultaneous pandering to different and opposed viewpoints. This set of precepts was extremely useful, because at every important juncture it enabled him to juggle with the balance of forces in the party and also to manipulate it to his own advantage. It made it possible for him to gain the support of groupings whose support was entirely unexpected, usually by misleading them as to his real political intentions. MacDonald's well known opposition to the war, which was generally misinterpreted as an indication of his stability and strength of character, was also a masterpiece of this kind of diplomatic manipulation. MacDonald never actually shared the attitude adopted by the ILP to the first world war. He denounced the war when it began, but never joined those who actively opposed it. On the contrary, he said more than once that 'now we were in the war we must see it through'.[1] His opportunistic and ambivalent attitude enabled MacDonald to build up support for the post-war future from the two wings of the party, which were for the time being at each other's throats. The half-heartedness of his opposition to the

1   MacNeill Weir, *The tragedy of Ramsay MacDonald*, p. 76.

war enabled him to reach agreement with the group which supported it, while the actual fact of his opposition to it marked him as the leader of those anti-war elements whose numbers were, as he rightly foresaw, to grow rapidly as the initial transports of patriotism died down. Events developed as he had foreseen. In the 1922 election for the leadership of the Labour Parliamentary party MacDonald won the support of sizeable groups from both wings of the party in his contest with Clynes. His victory was decided by the votes of the party left, the Scottish militants from Clydeside. MacDonald had painstakingly gained their favour by writing ultra-left wing articles for the Glasgow *Forward* which were diametrically opposed in content and form to his speeches in Parliament. The socialist group voted for MacDonald in the deep conviction that he would give the party a push leftwards and reveal his tough character as an opponent of the imperialistic war. Before the election MacDonald talked in turn to all those whose views had any weight in the party, promising each one the fulfilment of their mutually conflicting demands. At a session of the Parliamentary party just before the elections took place, Clynes mentioned that the speaker had decided to divide the front bench of the Opposition between the Labour Party and the Liberals. At this MacDonald rose and protested against any sort of compromise with the Liberals, although as an old Parliamentarian he knew perfectly well that nothing could change the Speaker's decision. Moreover, it was his intention, if the Parliamentary party came to power, to make much greater compromises with the Liberals.

The left was, however, delighted with the attitude he had taken and cast its votes for him. MacDonald was to display a similiar facility for being all things to all men, a desire to meet all preferences, to compromise with all viewpoints of any importance or influence, when he drew up the list of his first government in 1924. At first sight this list seems a strange conglomeration of people representing heterogeneous milieux. Only when one begins to look for the forces and interests behind each name does the reason for selection become understandable, some having clearly been chosen as commanding strong support from the trade unions, other as controlling the party machinery, others still as being far out on the left or, again, as being well known right-wingers. Such a Cabinet was unlikely to be capable of effective action, but it was an excellent investment to increase MacDonald's power in the party. With such a Cabinet to his credit he had no need to fear opponents who sought to take over the party leadership.

MacDonald's control of the party was total. It was not only based on the strength of the administrative machine, which MacDonald operated with unrivalled skill; it had also an emotional component. A cult of MacDonald gradually developed in the party. Pictures of him hung in every party headquarters, and his appearance on party platforms was greeted by enthusiastic demonstrations. MacDonald himself was skilled at manipulating a crowd, and would adroitly arrange his public appearances so as to appear in the middle of general enthusiasm and bring the audience to a climax of emotional tension. His contemporaries went so far as to say that his existence was a great piece of good fortune for the Labour Party, and that without him it would not have achieved its position in politics. He had, it was also said, reared it from the cradle to political maturity, and given it new inspiration. Many and conflicting reasons were advanced for his vast authority over the party, but the real reason was that he happened to be at its head during the period when it was developing from a reforming group and becoming a part of the country's political elite. It was also attaining a level of social significance unintended by its creators, and one which was initially confusing to the less ambitious leaders. In the arena of party in-fighting MacDonald was the first man to play not only the ordinary trump cards of an established union secretary or a good party organiser but the trump card of the immense authority of a Prime Minister of Great Britain—a card of an entirely different order and dimension, taken from another plane of social relations. MacDonald's authority came not from the world of the party but from a wider world which the Labour Party had not until then dreamed of conquering. Supported by the powerful structure of the State, MacDonald was a giant in comparison with the remaining party leaders, with their traditional control of the unions or the party machine. Such authority was never achieved later by any labour leader, since it was the product of a unique historical era. MacDonald personified Labour's final advancement to the position of an alternative government, and the honour accorded to him was in part a superstitious veneration for the party's new position.

A man of the era to come, MacDonald must have felt superior to his comrades, who had been reared in the party's unambitious youth. Once he had achieved a clear field for himself in the party he never again glanced downwards or around himself, but concentrated his gaze upwards. Winston Churchill called him the greatest snob on earth. Having entrenched himself solidly as the creator of the party, he aspired to become the saviour of his country. MacDonald was tormented to the end of his days by an inferiority complex; he felt ashamed of his own obscure origins and the fact that his party had not yet achieved full acceptance. He therefore sought avidly and unceasingly for appreciation, or at least equal treatment, from those who determined the prevailing conventions of gentlemanly behaviour. As the years passed he increasingly tried to assume the airs of an English gentleman. He showed an excessive concern that all the customary privileges linked with the state offices which he filled should be observed, and performed with pleasure the role of the man of destiny and the leader of the nation. Just before the final rupture with the Labour Party, Snowden recalls how he told him, gleefully rubbing his hands, 'Yes, tomorrow every duchess in London will be wanting to kiss me!'[1] As time went by, MacDonald became less and less at ease in the company of party and union leaders. With his colleagues he was more and more peevish and insensitive, laying increasing stress on the distance between himself and them. He maintained informal relations only with that comic-opera *bon vivant*, J. R. Thomas, leader of the railwaymen—a bigger snob than any other trade union leader, who liked to address peers by their Christian names and clap them on the shoulder in public. MacDonald kept himself at a distance from all the others behind a barrier of chilly formality. He displayed definite ambitions to play a *Führer*-type role and considered the attitudes of Mussolini and Hitler as not entirely devoid of political merit. At the outset he disliked his rivals within the party, but later came simply to despise them. Gradually he also began to despise the party which had raised him to the political heights, and in 1931 finally left it to become Prime Minister of the coalition National Government.

Viewed superficially, this move may seem unexpected and inconsistent in so sober and calculating a politician. But even if this were applicable to MacDonald himself, it was certainly not applicable at that stage of the party's development. In the case of men like Attlee or Gaitskell, it would be ludicrous to suppose that either would have broken with the Labour Party in order to become Prime Minister. On the contrary, they would have been most likely to try and increase their own strength within the party, as the best means of attaining national office. With all his diplomatic talents, MacDonald never outgrew the complex induced by belonging to a minority party. The connection between the party structure and the highest national offices might, and indeed did, still seem to be accidental and transient, and the party structure too fragile for a man aiming at the highest office. The leadership of the Labour Party was already part of the Country's political elite, but the fact took a long time to penetrate the consciousness of its own contemporaries, even the most observant of them. As a result MacDonald, the man of the era after Burns, made the same mistake as Burns. He accepted national office while at the same time losing the support which had enabled him to obtain that office. Mac-Donald ended his days as a Conservative pensioner, as Burns had done as a Liberal one; and like Burns he was reviled and hated by his own party. It is a historical paradox that MacDonald, who began his party career by launching a new style and era of politics, ended that career with a move in

[1] Snowden, *An autobiography*, p. 957.

the style with which he had broken at the very outset. This personal inconsistency is an expression of historical consistency. The error and defeat of MacDonald were the final act in the political coming of age of the Labour Party.[1]

From that moment the phase of consolidation, which had been gaining strength gradually from the early post-war years, gained complete control. The party became one of the two political teams which competed for control of the country, while its elite became a component part of the political elite of capitalist Britain.

---

1 Unless otherwise indicated, the factual information about Ramsay MacDonald is taken from the following works: Lord Elton, *Life of Ramsay MacDonald*; MacNeill Weir, *The tragedy of Ramsay MacDonald*; H. H. Tiltman, *James Ramsay MacDonald*; Nicholson, *The real men in public life*; J. H. S. Reid, *The origins of the British Labour Party*, University of Minnesota Press, 1955; G. D. H. Cole, *British working class politics*; M. Cole, *Growing up into revolution*, Longmans, London, 1949; H. Dalton, *Call back yesterday*, Muller, London, 1953; *Beatrice Webb's diaries*; Hyndman, *Further reminiscences*; *Scottish socialists: a gallery of contemporary portraits*, Faber, London, 1931.

IV

The consolidation of
the labour movement
1924–55

Towards the end of the mass-movement period the labour movement attained a form and a social position which were not to undergo any qualitative changes in the ensuing period. Once the movement had mobilised and assimilated all the strata of the working class its sources of internal dynamism were exhausted and its flexibility gave way to conservatism and consolidation. During the period to which Part IV is devoted the labour movement slowly rigidified in the form which it had assumed as a consequence of the changes of the previous period.

This was not the first period of consolidation in the movement's history. A similar process had occurred in the third quarter of the nineteenth century, but the movement was then still one of skilled workers. In form, the two processes were extremely close—they were marked by the same external characteristics and displayed the same peculiarities. As regards their social content, however, the two processes differed greatly. They took place on a different scale, and the working class was in a different situation while each was going on. In Part IV I shall endeavour to elucidate the similarities and, above all, to point to the class differences between the two processes.

By way of introduction it should be stressed that the whole of this study is sociological in character. Its primary task is to grasp general social laws and trends, while the presentation of a chronology of historical events falls into a subsidiary place. Only by accepting such a methodological premise can one treat the period which I shall be analysing in Part IV as an integrated whole, fused together by the action of the same historical trends. For from a modern historian's viewpoint this period is far from uniform. One has only to recall the sudden radicalisation of the labour movement in Britain after the first world war and the Russian revolution, its subsequent partial pacification, the revival of radical elements after the great financial crisis and the Ramsay MacDonald era, and thereafter a new upsurge of conformism. The mass unemployment of the inter-war years and the large-scale conflicts in Europe caused some deviations in the basic direction in which the British labour movement was evolving. In spite of all these historical zig-zags, however, a sociological analysis indicates that the processes which were occurring in this tortuous manner were nevertheless taking a consistent direction. Hence the importance of this initial distinction between the viewpoint of the historian and that of the sociologist.

I

The structure of
the working class

The unification of the working class, which began considerably earlier, continued in this period as well, on an even larger scale than before. The changes which in the preceding period were in only a germinal stage are now being realised in full. The differences between the two poles of the labour hierarchy, the qualitative differences between occupations on the same hierarchical level, and the differences in qualifications between similar occupations in different branches of industry—all these are being erased. All the lines which half a century earlier divided the working class are becoming blurred. The occupational stratification of the working class has been losing more and more of its social importance, while its material and cultural consequences have also been slowly disappearing, giving way to an increasingly uniform status for the working class as a whole.

To be more precise, there has been a continued decrease in size in the two extreme sectors of the working class—the skilled (in its original sense) and the unskilled—in favour of a rapid growth in numbers of the group of occupationally unspecialised workers described as semi-skilled (or skilled in the new industrial sense). At the same time the distance between the two poles has been diminishing in terms of the degree of occupational training, and the amount of money and time invested in its acquisition, and also of wages, living standards, social position, and overall education and culture. At the top of the working class there remains only a small group of highly skilled workers, and even they are being squeezed out by a stratum which represents a new phenomenon in industry—that of technicians with a specialised formal technical education. The latter are now blending socially with the emerging white-collar stratum which is part of the constantly increasing administrative function in industry.

The fact that mechanisation has come to dominate heavy industry has led to the depreciation of craft skills and apprenticeships lasting for several years. Speed, intelligence, the ability to adapt efficiently—these are qualities far more sought after on the labour market than clearly defined, rigid, one-sided qualifications. Employers no longer hire their labour force 'raw' as they did a century ago. There is a socially accepted minimum standard. Workers are required to have a general knowledge of technical matters, a familiarity with the working of machines, and an ability to master the simple problems of operating them. There follows a short period of induction and training, lasting from a couple of days to a few weeks, after which the raw labour force is transformed into a work-force trained sufficiently to meet the demands of modern industry. Regardless of the operations which they perform, all the machines involved in different industries have become increasingly similar so far as their main controls are concerned. It has thus become more and more easy to transfer the labour force from one branch of production to another.[1] Statistics do not show the actual dimensions of this process, since many occupations continue, by virtue of tradition, to be included in the skilled category, usually because they are still called by the same names. From the sociological viewpoint, however, they have lost all the characteristics traditionally

Table 14

The proportion of skilled, semi-skilled and unskilled workers employed in the firms belonging to the Engineering and Allied Employers' National Federation (per cent)

| Year | Approximate percentage | | |
	Skilled	Semi-skilled	Unskilled
1914	60	20	20
1921	50	30	20
1926	40	45	15
1928	34	53	13
1933	32	57	11

Source M. L. Yates, *Wages and labour conditions in British engineering*, Macdonald & Evans, London, 1937, pp. 31–2.

linked with the 'skilled' category. Nonetheless, even though the statistics for the semi-skilled category include in principle only the new occupational categories of workers of medium skill, such as the undefined categories of 'machine operator' or 'assembler', they do bring out the tempo and direction of this process. By way of example, one may cite the statistics of employment in engineering works belonging to the Engineering and Allied Employers' National Federation (see table 14). This industry was a stronghold of the earlier type of skilled worker.

A similar process was also taking place in other branches of production, and its tempo and dimensions depended not so much on the differences

1   Cf, for example, R. L. Raimon, 'The indeterminateness of wages of semi-skilled workers, *Industrial and Labor Relations Review*, January 1953, 181–93.

between various industries as on the degree of mechanisation and automation in a given workplace. Much greater differences in the tempo and dimensions of the change could be noted between large and small establishments within the same industry than between establishments of the same size in different branches of industry.

Technological changes have led to a depreciation of the skilled trades, with a simultaneous increase in the value of the middle and lower levels of the occupational hierarchy. The consequence has been a far-reaching levelling out of wage ranges. Within the working class, wage rate differentials have become much smaller and the difference between even the lowest and the highest wage rates does not make for substantial difference in social position. Far more important social effects are produced by differences not derived from occupational stratification, but concerned with such matters as the number of people whom a wage-earner supports, the number of wage-earners in a family, the incidence of external events, and so on. From the first world war onwards, through all the economic crises, booms and recessions, there has been an inexorable trend for wage rises to favour women rather than men, and the less skilled rather than the more highly skilled. The highest increases have gone to those sectors of workers who were worst paid in the past.[1] Ferdynand Zweig writes:

> The premium on skill, as shown by the gap between the skilled man's rate and the labourer's rate, has declined since the turn of the century, and this may be regarded as a continuing trend. In the building industry the labourer before the first world war had 64 per cent of the craftsman's rate; in 1922, 75 per cent; from 1945 onwards, 80 per cent. In the engineering industry the premium for skill at the beginning of this century was 50 per cent, and it is now in the neighbourhood of 15 per cent. In the printing industry the gap between the craftsman's and labourer's wage before the first world war was 33 per cent, while now it is less than 20 per cent. The same trend can be noticed in the cotton industry.[2]

Another set of calculations made by Mark Abrams gives a similar result: it shows that before the first world war unskilled wages were about 60 per cent of skilled rates, while by 1919 they had moved up to 75 per cent.[3] Dudley Seers, in statistics going up to 1949, shows that the levelling out of wage rates was continuing with undiminished momentum in the period after the second world war.[4]

1 Cf, for example, A. Flanders, *Trade unions*, Hutchinson, London, 1952, p. 108.
2 F. Zweig, *The British worker*, Penguin Books, Harmondsworth, 1952, p. 67.
3 M. Abrams, *The condition of the British people, 1911–45*, Fabian Society, London, 1945, p. 82.
4 D. Seers, *The levelling of incomes since 1938*, Oxford Institute of Statistics, 1951, p. 58.

The evidence of the basic wage rate statistics is eloquent enough, but the levelling out of the social position of different sections of the working class has been even greater than the statistics just cited would imply. This is because additional factors have been at work, factors which have favoured the lower paid workers and undermined further the hitherto privileged position of the skilled workers.

First there is the fact that during this period not only did basic wages rise, but the prices of consumer goods increased. In such circumstances the movement of real wages is dependent not only on the relation between basic wages and the price index but also on the specific character of the typical family budgets of different groups; this is because increases in the prices of different goods and services take place at unequal rates. For this

Table 15

Cost of living indices (1938 = 100) according to household expenditure in 1938

Household expenditure in 1938 (£ p.a.)	Cost of living index			
	1946	1947	1948	1949
200	147	156	171	177
250	154	164	178	184
300	159	170	183	188
350	163	173	187	191
400	166	176	190	193
450	168	178	192	195
500	169	180	193	196

Source D. Seers, *The levelling of incomes since 1938*, Oxford Institute of Statistics, 1951, p. 58.

reason, as economic studies show, a dynamic rise in prices was less detrimental to the lower-paid workers. Families with budgets typical of the skilled worker suffered more from price increases than did families with budgets of the unskilled worker type. This proposition is borne out by statistics, even if one takes into account that the value of the calculations is lessened by the fact that the actual budgets of different strata were, as a consequence of the changes in the structure of prices and wages, subjected to dynamic structural changes. Thus it is impossible to capture the whole of the process in figures alone. Table 15 illustrates the basic trends in this process with the use of Seers' data.

Here it should be noted that table 15 covers a period after the second world war in which spending patterns were to a considerable extent standardised in many spheres; initially imposed by war-time rationing, these patterns had gradually become habitual. In spite of this circumstance, which undoubtedly counterbalanced differences in the tempo of change in various groups, the differential social effects of the years of inflation emerge quite clearly.

A second factor which has operated in a way similar to the first, especially in the post-war years, has been the nation-wide system of social services. In *British socialism* I argued that this system of social services has been much less influential than is often maintained in levelling out differences of income level between different classes in British society. Within the working class, however, the social services have undoubtedly helped to promote a still greater uniformity of social status among various strata of workers. The worst-paid strata have gained the most, since in the case of the highest-paid strata the total of benefits actually received has rarely reached the level of contributions and deductions made on their account. As a result, after deducting taxes and contributions towards social benefits and adding the money value of the benefits actually received, it emerges that the difference between the highest and lowest wage rates is even less than would appear from the basic wage rate statistics, or even from tables of real wages, which take into account the differences between strata in the cost of living indices.

In addition, one must take into account the wide range of social benefits and services provided by the welfare State,[1] which have played an increasing role in working class budgets, pushing wage differentials into second place. In Seebohm Rowntree's third enquiry into the economic situation of the working class population of York, in 1950, he attempted to reconstruct the situation which would have existed in York in that year had social services and benefits remained at the same level as in 1936. The results are shown in table 16.

Rowntree classified working class families according to their actual material circumstances, so that economic categories are not directly correlated with occupational ones. The decisive weight is given to factors unconnected with occupation, such as the number of children, the illness or death of the main wage-earner and so on. Nevertheless, the table brings out the aspect which concerns us here, namely that the system of social benefits has exerted its greatest effect on the strata which was economically most in need and has helped to narrow the gap between the lowest-paid workers and the better-off strata.

A third factor which has been working in the same direction as the other

1   Cf, for example, M. P. Hall, *The social services of modern England*, Routledge & Kegan Paul, London, 1952.

Table 16

Effect on families of all the welfare measures, taken together

Economic class	Actual situation in 1950	Situation in 1950 if welfare measures had been identical with those in force in 1936
	Families per cent	*Families per cent*
A (lowest)	0·41	6·62
B	4·23	18·11
C	19·40	14·32
D	17·38	13·32
E (highest)	58·58	47·63

Source B. Seebohm Rowntree and G. R. Lavers, *Poverty and the welfare State*, Longmans, London, 1951, p. 40.

two is the full employment which has existed in Britain since the end of the second world war. Another way of describing full employment would be the existence of a dynamic balance between supply and demand on the labour market. In earlier periods skilled workers enjoyed a better bargaining position than unskilled workers in conflicts with employers. The former were not so easily exchanged or replaced as a 'raw' labour force, and thus benefited from the employers' fear of losing their most valuable workers. In normal circumstances, when a considerable reservoir of unemployed existed, the employers could freeze the wages of the less skilled workers, of whom there was a surplus on the labour market, to make up for their wage concessions to the skilled workers whom they particularly wished to attract. A situation of full employment would, on the other hand, operate to the benefit of the less skilled workers, improving their position compared with that of skilled men, in conflicts with the employers.

The point here is that the most highly qualified workers, who are also the most highly specialised, have as a rule invested considerable time and money in their skills. It is thus a relatively difficult matter for them to change their occupation, or to move from one factory to another or to another branch of industry. They are 'tied to the job'[1]—permanently restricted to a particular kind of work. If they lose their job they cannot, as can for instance a machine operator, easily find equally suitable work in another factory or even in another industry. Their position, in a dispute with

1   F. Zweig, *Labour life and poverty*, Gollancz, London, 1949, p. 84.

an employer, can therefore be more vulnerable than that of the unskilled, and still more vulnerable than that of the semi-skilled. The two latter categories of worker can move fairly freely to other jobs, factories and industries, and find suitable work anywhere.

Hence in conditions of full employment the situation is very nearly reversed. The employer is bound to feel even more apprehensive about losing that part of his labour force which has general technical qualifications than the part whose mobility is hampered by its own highly specialised skills. (Again, however, this is only a general trend, with numerous exceptions, e.g. jobs in rapidly expanding industries where the relevant skills are still in short supply.) Obviously the unskilled and semi-skilled have benefited from this situation. As a result of the high turnover of the labour force in the general sectors, the wage rates of workers with medium technical skills in a number of occupations and industries have tended to average out, and this average has in turn moved towards the wage levels of the skilled workers who are tied permanently to a single trade and do not benefit from this effect of full employment. There is a considerable body of statistical data which indicates clearly that, given the generally large degree of horizontal mobility among working groups in Britain, particularly among young people entering industry in a period of full employment,[1] the average change-over of occupation and industries among highly skilled workers has been much lower than among the rest [2] The result is obvious—there has been an unremitting pressure on the labour market to raise the wages of the semi-skilled towards the levels of the highly skilled.

The increasing standardisation of the economic situation of the working class has meant a considerable reduction in, though not a total removal of, the most blatant symptoms of poverty. For the reasons mentioned above, there has been a levelling out of living standards within the working class, and also a rise in the lowest level of living standards. To put it more precisely, there has been a decrease in the percentage of people earning less than the amount needed for the barest physical needs. In the 1890s, it should be realised, about 40 per cent of the working class population of London and York lived below that level. For later periods one can turn to the enquiries made by Bristol University, under the direction of Herbert Tout, and Seebohm Rowntree's unique socio-economic study of York repeated three times over a half a century. The Bristol University team found that in 1957 about 11 per cent of the working class population of

1   T. Ferguson and J. Cunnison, *The young wage-earner*, Oxford University Press, London, 1951, pp. 37–8.
2   Cf, for example, M. Jefferys, *Mobility in the labour market*, Routledge & Kegan Paul, London, 1954, pp. 76–7.

Bristol (this corresponds to Rowntree's class A) lived well below the minimum, with another 21 per cent (Rowntree's class B) living on its margin,
in constant danger of falling below it—a total of about 32 per cent in all.[1]
Rowntree's figures for the working class population of York in 1936 show
that 14·2 per cent of the population fell into class A and another 16·9 per
cent into class B—again making a total of almost 32 per cent.[2] The improvement in the workers' material circumstances, by comparison with the end
of the nineteenth century was thus quantitative rather than qualitative. It
may be noted that both Tout's enquiry and Rowntree's second study were
carried out during an inter-war period of particularly intense poverty
—the country was still experiencing the painful after-effects of economic
crisis, and was succumbing to an immense wave of chronic unemployment. A considerable part of the poverty of the time was due to unemployment of the main bread winner, or else to the still unhealed wounds
inflicted on individual families in the worst years of the economic crisis,
years which had been even harsher than the years of depression and the
sluggish alternation of half-hearted industrial expansion and recession
which followed it.

A basic change occurred during the second world war and afterwards,
with the rapid shrinkage of the section of the working class population
which was living in poverty. This was due to the compensatory effect of the
social and welfare services, and the shift in the wage structure which I have
already mentioned. In 1950 Seebohm Rowntree and G. R. Lavers found
only 0·37 (individuals, not families) in York who fell into class A, and 2·40
per cent who fell into class B—together a total of less than 3 per cent of the
working class population.[3] This was a minute total, qualitatively quite
different from the total for these classes in earlier years.[4]

The data concerning the changing causes of poverty in different periods
provide the necessary corrections for the fluctuations caused by economic
booms and recessions and make explicit the long-run trend that has
persisted throughout the ups and downs of the development curve.
Table 17 combines the analyses of Tout and Rowntree relating to the
causes of poverty. Table 17 suggests that in 1950 the great majority of
cases of poverty were the result either of inadequate old age pensions or of

---

1 H. Tout, *The standard of living in Bristol*, Arrowsmith, London, 1938, pp. 25–6.
2 B. Seebohm Rowntree, *Poverty and progress*, Longmans, London, 1941, pp. 31–2.
3 Rowntree and Lavers, *Poverty and the welfare State*, p. 31.
4 Since this book was written and published in Poland new studies have appeared;
   using new definitions, criteria and indices, they have arrived at conclusions widely
   different from those of Rowntree's last work. By far the most significant and cogent
   appear to be the data presented by Brian Able Smith and Peter Townsend (*The poor
   and the poorest*, Bell, London, 1965). Rowntree's series nevertheless retains its value
   as indicating the real trend in distributions measured by unchanging scales.

Table 17

The causes of poverty among the working class population of Bristol and York

	Percentage of families living in poverty		
Causes	Bristol	York	
	1937	1936	1950
Breadwinner unemployed	32·0	28·6	–
Inadequate earnings	27·8	42·3	1·0
Old age	15·2	14·7	68·1
No main bread-winner	13·3	7·8	6·4
Sickness or incapacity	9·0	4·1	21·3
Other	2·7	2·5	3·2

Note   In 1899 52 per cent of the workers of York were living in poverty because of inadequate wages in spite of being in regular employment. This completely dwarfs the figure of 2·3 per cent for those whose poverty was caused by unemployment at that time.

Source   H. Tout, *The standard of living in Bristol*, Arrowsmith, London, 1938, p. 46; Rowntree and Lavers, *Poverty and the welfare State*, p. 35.

inadequate sickness benefits—i.e. of factors which could in principle be dealt with by changes in social legislation. On the other hand, the part played by excessively low wages as a cause of poverty in working class families was decreasing consistently. By 1950 it had disappeared almost entirely from the list of causes of poverty as a consequence of virtually full employment, and also of upward adjustments in unemployment benefits.

With all their well publicised limitations the institutions of the welfare State helped to create a new feeling of security in the event of sickness and the disastrous consequences which it had formerly brought on working class families. People who in former years had called a doctor only to a deathbed now began to get regular medical attention, including preventive medicine. Though still far from being adequate, family allowances mitigated to a considerable extent the burdens of a large family. (According to Tout, the percentage breakdown by size of family of all families living below the minimum standard was: families with one child, 6·5 per cent; families with two children, 11·1 per cent; families with three children, 24·8 per cent; families with four or more children, 51·3 per cent.)[1] Old

1   *The standard of living in Bristol*, p. 38.

age pensions and unemployment benefits were on a modest level but still gave a hitherto unknown measure of security in the face of the greatest misfortunes that could befall the manual worker—old age and the loss of one's job. Last, but not least, this security, however partial, was institutionally guaranteed by society, something which gave the working class a vested interest in the existing social order, embodied in the capitalist State.

There were improvements in other sectors as well. The slums began to disappear slowly from the cities of Britain, making way for new housing units and blocks of flats put up by local councils. In 1922 the percentage of the population living over-crowded at a rate of over two persons to a room was 43·3 per cent in Scotland, and 14 per cent in England (29·9 per cent in the mining districts of Northumberland and Durham). By 1931 the figures for the same areas were: Scotland, 35 per cent; England, 10 per cent; Northumberland and Durham, 20·2 per cent.[1] Britain is probably the country with the best housing conditions in Europe. The gradual improvement of housing standards promoted cultural development among the working class population. The advent of cheap, convenient public transport, and media for mass recreation such as the cinema, radio and television, further helped to raise the working man's standard of living in contrast to that of his predecessors a century or even half a century back.

Socio-economic changes have also tended to lessen the gap in living standards between the working class and the rest of the population. Britain is of course still a capitalist country and the traditional bases of power have not been undermined despite the introduction of all kinds of equalising measures, operative, as they are, in a secondary sphere of effects. It is, however, chiefly the status of the upper middle class which has remained intact; the economic strength of the 'middle' middle class and the lower middle class have been declining, and the frontiers between them and the working class are today far less distinct than they were a half century ago. Moreover, a change has been taking place in the internal stratification of the middle class itself which has also helped to modify the relations between classes—this in spite of the fact that a basic social division still exists and is also expressed in differences of economic situation.

In 1938 the average budgets of working class and middle class families differed sharply, according to Seers' calculations. It cost £1 2s 7d a week to keep one person in the average working class family, but the corresponding middle class figure was £4 17s 9d (this last average, of course, covers the far higher amounts spent in upper middle class families).[2] A middle class

1   Abrams, *The condition of the British people*, pp. 45–6.
2   D. Seers, *Changes in the cost of living and the distribution of incomes since 1938*, Oxford Institute of Statistics, 1949, p. 8.

family spent between four and seven times as much as a working class family on food and household goods; seven to ten times more on clothing and footwear; ten to fourteen times more on services; fourteen to twenty times more on travel and luxury goods; and twenty to thirty times more on alcohol.[1] These figures show that at the end of the inter-war period there was still a gulf between the standard of living of the working class and that of the capitalist classes as a whole. But the everyday political attitudes of the masses are shaped not by a theoretical consideration of statistical averages but by everyday experience in its most accessible form. In this

Table 18

Distribution of pre-tax and post-tax income in Britain, 1938 and 1947

	1938		1947	
Type of income	*Before tax*	*After tax*	*Before tax*	*After tax*
Rent, interest				
and profits	37·9	33·4	36·5	29·6
Salaries	21·6	22·8	17·4	17·7
Wages	33·7	36·3	35·8	40·3
HM Forces' pay	1·5	1·7	3·4	3·9
Social income	5·2	5·8	6·9	8·5

Source D. Seers, *Changes in the cost of living and the distribution of incomes since 1938,* Oxford Institute of Statistics, 1949, p. 8.

connection, one development had a considerable impact. Certain categories of manual worker (skilled labourers and artisans, coal hewers, engine drivers, etc) were now not only better paid than many white-collar workers with technical qualifications, but even better paid than some low-earning sectors of the professions. Meanwhile such traditional middle class occupations as teaching and the lower ranks of the civil service were right at the bottom of the table.[2]

The average statistics for the classes thus form a veritable class mosaic. As regards income, at least some strata of the two basic classes have be-

1 Abrams' figures are different. According to him the average weekly budget of a working class family in 1937–8 was £4 5s 1d, that of a middle class family £8 12s 1d. (*The condition of the British people,* p. 87.) Seers' enquiries were, however, much more detailed, and his concept of the middle class closer to actuality.

2 C. F. G. Masterman, *England after war,* Hodder & Stoughton, London, 1922, p. 71.

come interlaced, and the blurring not so much of differences as of boundaries between the classes which began in the previous period has progressed still further. This trend was strengthened by the graduated income tax introduced after the war. The new system did not destroy the power of the upper middle class but struck mainly at middle class groups with moderate and low incomes, pushing them down to the economic level of the better-off strata of the working class. The operation of this tax is shown in table 18, which is based on Seers' statistics.

Over the same period the after-tax total of income received under the heading 'Rent, interest and profits' decreased by 15 per cent, while working class wages, after deduction of tax, increased by 18 per cent.[1] This important change could not be deprived of its significance by the fact that in the previous decade sources of income of a capitalist type had again begun to increase their share of the overall national income, nor by the fact, to which I shall return later, that in the official statistics the heading 'Salaries' covers a considerable portion of the income of the middle class. On the other hand, the economic effects of this change were intensified by the fact that, while there was an overall rise in the cost of living, the typical budget of a middle class family rose even more rapidly. Taking 1938 as 100, the average cost of living index had risen to between 190 and 191 by 1949; for the middle class, however, it was 201-2, for the upper middle class as high as 213, while for a working class family it was only 181-2.[2]

The way in which the national income is divided reveals beyond all doubt the capitalist nature of British society. In 1955 according to the official statistics on national income and expenditure, 61,000 persons had an annual income of over £5,000, while just under 16 million had an income of less than £500 per annum. Of the estates on which death duty was paid in 1954-55, 682 were valued at over £100,000 each. But such statistics are inadequate to describe inter-class relations: in particular they do not cover the very significant changes within the middle class, changes which had a profound effect on the objective and subjective position of the working class within society as a whole.

The fact is that the new period of evolution in British industry has not only brought greater uniformity to the occupational structure of the working class, but has also led to a further increase in the numbers employed in distribution, office work and the professions. According to Abrams, the number of people in non-manual, predominantly white-collar occupations, excluding public administration and teachers, rose from

1   *Ibid.*, p. 64.
2   Seers, *The levelling of incomes*, pp. 10-11, 21.

1,043,000 in 1911 to 2,213,000 in 1931; that is to say, by 112 per cent.[1] On the basis of the 1951 census figures Cole estimated that of every 100 persons gainfully employed in Britain sixty were manual workers,[2] while nearly one-third consisted of employers, high-level administrators, managers, farmers, shopkeepers, professional supervisors, clerks and typists.[3] The tempo of the change in the proportion between the numbers of manual workers and those in the various 'middle class' occupational categories is illustrated in table 19, based on data collected by A. L. Bowley.

Table 19

The numerical increases in the 'middle classes' and the working class in Britain, 1881–1931

Period	Percentage rise over the preceding period		Percentage rise over the 1881 figures	
	Middle classes	Working class	Middle classes	Working class
1881–91	23	11	23	11
1891–1901	23	10	55	22
1901–11	24	9	92	33
1911–21	10	4	111	39
1921–31	12	7	137	49

Source A. L. Bowley, Wages and income in the United Kingdom since 1860, Cambridge University Press, 1937, p. 136.

Table 19 should be seen in the context of the proliferation of office jobs among the middle classes. The social type of the bourgeoisie was changing. The stratum of those who combined the functions of manufacturer, owner and managing director was branching out into numerous groupings distributed up and down the managerial ladder. To a considerable extent, the stratification of the new middle class became occupationally based,

1 There is a striking similarity between these results and some contemporary statistics of social structure in US society. These show that in 1940 the percentage of manual workers was about 55 per cent, as against 25 per cent of persons working in the new middle class of office workers, sales people, salaried professional and technical and managerial personnel. These changes are perhaps further advanced in the United States than in Britain. (C. Wright Mills, The new men of power, Harcourt Brace, New York, 1948, p. 275.)

2 Abrams, The condition of the British people, p. 67.

3 Cole, Studies in class structure, p. 184.

and the class hierarchy was overshadowed by the bureaucratic hierarchy, both in public and in private. The middle classes have become increasingly managerial in character. They have taken over academic and administrative posts, and have even established themselves comfortably in the new civil service departments set up to administer the welfare State.[1] But the new bureaucratic and administrative hierarchy has not helped the middle classes only. It has also provided a mechanism of upward social mobility for the more ambitious and talented individuals in the working class.

Professor Burn has compared the contemporary social structure of Britain to a 'moving staircase which carries upwards everyone on it but yet provides opportunity for the man in a hurry to get to the top first'.[2] The simile is a good one—the new structure of the economy has greatly increased vertical mobility and has effectively creamed off the most active and talented elements of the working class, thus going a considerable way to meet the ambitions of individuals for advancement and those of working class parents who desire advancement for their children.

Real social mobility has, of course, nothing to do with fairy tales about individuals who go from rags to riches. This latter type of advancement is rarely if ever encountered in real life; moreover, instances of the much more modest phenomenon of a worker managing to become the owner of his own small workshop are extremely infrequent. The virtual closing of this door to advancement is reflected in the working class consciousness. In the mid-nineteenth century the more ambitious workers dreamed of using their savings to start up their own workshop, with the prospect of becoming a capitalist in the nineteenth century sense. Now, however, such an ambition is rarely encountered. The ambition to 'set up on one's own' has today been almost entirely replaced by aspirations to managerial posts, technical or administrative, although these are generally not for oneself but for one's children.[3] Most workers do look up to those who have 'got out of the pit',[4] but the objects of their esteem are chiefly the white-collar workers who are engaged in 'clean' work, who wear the uniform of the middle class and partake to a small extent of the prestige vested in it. The pressure of the active section of the working class to seek advancement on an individual basis has found an outlet in the bureaucratic and administrative machinery of contemporary capitalist industry. It has

---

1   R. Lewis and A. Maude, *Professional people*, Phoenix House, London, 1952, p. 35; *idem*, *The English middle classes*, p. 277; N. A. Smith, 'Theory and practice of the welfare State', *Political Quarterly*, October–December 1951, p. 369.

2   *Quarterly Review*, July 1946, p. 300.

3   J. E. Floud, 'Educational opportunity and social mobility' in *The year book of education*, Evans Bros., London, 1950, p. 119.

4   Cf, for example, Massey, *Portrait of a mining town*, p. 36.

proved no mean outlet, since the administrative and technical hierarchy, while it is in actuality divided by a number of class boundaries, is also a single whole from top to bottom, connected by numerous channels of internal mobility.

A number of social scientists who have studied vertical social mobility in Britain in recent decades are agreed about its relatively high incidence. In 1928 Morris Ginsberg found that about twelve out of every 100 persons employed in occupations typical of the managerial and technical levels came from working class families, whereas in occupations typical of the lowest levels in these categories, forty out of 100 were of working class origins.[1] G. T. Saunders showed that in 1930 about seventeen out of every 100 children of skilled workers, and about sixteen out of every 100 children of semi-skilled workers, had attained various levels of the administrative and white-collar hierarchy.[2] Finally, a post-war enquiry by D. V. Glass and J. R. Hall[3] indicated that about 23 per cent of the sons of skilled workers and 14 per cent of the sons of semi-skilled workers had moved upwards into the administrative and professional categories and thus into the middle classes. These various estimates differ from one another, as is to be expected with the findings of studies carried out in different areas at different periods and using different methods of enquiry and different criteria of ranking. But in every case the findings are of the same numerical order and they indicate with certainty that intergenerational mobility has assumed considerable dimensions in recent decades.

It would be hard to overrate the significance of this new mechanism of vertical social mobility. I have already drawn attention to the collective advancement of the working class in terms of its socio-economic status. Now we also find a relatively broad channel for the advancement of individuals between classes, a channel which in principle meets the actual demands for such advancement. These two kinds of advancement have in principle absorbed the whole social pressure towards vertical mobility. As a result they have decreased the social tension which could have arisen within the working class as a result of artificial barriers blocking group and individual mobility. They have in effect produced not only conformist attitudes towards the existing social order but also a conservative attitude to prevailing socio-economic relationships and the existing political structure. The setting up of new channels of inter-class mobility

1   M. Ginsberg, 'Interchange between social classes', *Economic Journal*, December 1929, pp. 560, 564.
2   C. T. Saunders, 'A study of occupational mobility', *Economic Journal*, June 1931, p. 231.
3   D. V. Glass and J. R. Hall, *Social mobility in Great Britain*, Routledge & Kegan Paul London, 1954, p. 183.

not broad enough to satisfy the standards of equality but sufficiently broad to meet practical requirements has weakened the mechanisms which might have shifted the class conflict from the economic sphere to that of social relations and politics. The blurring of differences in socio-economic status between the two classes has prevented an accumulation of social protest within a class, while the breaking down of the barriers which hold the most able individuals of working class origin back from advancement has averted the setting up of a potential nonconformist elite. Both meta-morphoses have taken place within the structure of capitalist society and have been effected and guaranteed by that structure. This means that in the period under discussion we are dealing not only with the emergence of the working class from its former state of social marginality and estrange-ment, but also with its conversion to a conservative defence of the existing social order, which is seen as a basically reliable mechanism for satisfying group and individual aspirations. The technical and administrative machinery affords a channel through which potential leaders of a social protest movement can move upwards and out of the foci of dissent. By the same token, the ideology and social values of the ruling class, along with its aspirations and images of social advancement, are spreading downwards. This machinery affects not only those who have gained the privilege of climbing the ladder but also their families, kin and acquaintances, the ever wider circles of those who dream of and hope for a similar career for their own children. In Glasgow Ferguson and Cunnison found that amongst school-leavers the number of boys who wished to take up office work exceeded fathers working in offices by three to one.[1] Such dreams can, moreover, be realised. White-collar work is a focus for the aspirations of the more ambitious workers' sons; it thus channels their claims to advance-ment in a way that is both useful and safe for the capitalist social structure.

Individual mobility between the generations has in part also helped to solve the problems of individual mobility within a single generation. An educational system which prepares its products to perform technical and administrative functions picks out—or at least, should pick out—all the talented children of working class families before they enter the factories. If this system works efficiently—and in spite of numerous deficiencies it does in fact work increasingly well—the pressure towards advancement within the factory population should be greatly reduced, as those who are most geared to individual advancement can satisfy their ambitions in another way. An increasing number of studies have shown that, although the possibilities of advancement for factory workers are very small, owing to the minimal wage differentials and the reservation of super-visory positions for persons with supervisory training, very few individuals

1   *The young wage-earner*, pp. 9–10.

seek promotion even within this modest framework. It is thus extremely difficult to fill a foreman's job.[1] Some trade unions take a strong line on the principle of promotion and upgrading according to seniority, not merit.[2] This is a principle which, along with that of 'jobs for the boys', also reflects the negligible part played by vertical mobility within the factory in solving the problem in its total dimension. Mobility between the generations defuses the source of the frustration which could be generated on the shop floor as a result of (a) the educational barrier raised between the work force and the technical/administrative supervisors, and (b) the increasing socio-economic levelling out of different manual jobs which were formerly far apart in the occupational hierarchy.

For these reasons, it is necessary to take a closer look at the British educational system as the basic instrument of inter-generational mobility.

With the steady rise in the number of lucrative and socially profitable jobs to which entrance is reserved for those with formal educational qualifications, more and more parents have come to regard the educational system as a 'social lever'.[3] School and university reports and examination certificates have become the most important means for enabling individuals to enter the higher levels of the social hierarchy. It must be remembered that this is an important upgrading of the social role of the educational system, compared with its function even half a century earlier. Each successive educational reform has helped to perfect this system, making it into a centrifuge to skim off the cream of the lower classes and assimilate them into the existing hierarchy of capitalist society. The educational system makes it possible to satisfy the ambitions of would-be leaders of a nonconformist labour movement within the present social structure. The school-leavers' path leads to the offices of large companies, to the lucrative liberal professions, or to civil service posts. The school is the fundamental instrument of individual mobility between the generations. (We are talking here of expectations. In fact, the excessive expectations aroused by educational promise may help to generate serious social disturbance in the light of endemic unemployment among graduates. But that is another story.)

In the early 1920s Kenneth Lindsay studied the workings of the English schools from the viewpoint of their social consequences. Even then, before the basic post-war reforms, he concluded that in the three areas studied— London, Warrington and Oxfordshire—the secondary schools were each lifting a small number of young people from manual to clerical and other

1 Cf, for example, T. Brennan, E. W. Cooney and H. Pollins, *Social change in south-west Wales*, Watts, London, 1954, pp. 70–2; Zweig, *The British worker*, p. 22.
2 *Nationalised industry: problems of promotion policy*, Acton Society Trust, London, 1951.
3 Floud, 'Educational opportunity and social mobility', p. 122.

occupations. Of the male school-leavers, 20 per cent went on to university, over 36 per cent went straight into clerical and commercial jobs and only 16·4 per cent went into industry. The latter percentage was far lower than the percentage of workers' sons in the secondary schools.[1] The schools were to function in this kind of way even more extensively in later years, as the system of scholarships and grants was developed and the network of State grammar schools was enlarged. The basic qualitative step was, however, taken after the second world war, when the Labour government

Table 20

The social origins of boys gaining entrance to grammar schools (per cent)

	South-west Hertfordshire			Middlesbrough		
Period	Middle class	Lower middle class	Work-ing class	Middle class	Lower middle class	Work-ing class
1884–1900	22	68	10	30	48	22
1904–18	30	55	15	22	38	40
1922–30	28	53	20	18	32	50
1934–38	20	63	18	15	33	52
1943	22	48	30	15	30	55
1950–53	22	38	40	20	30	50

Source J. E. Floud, A. H. Halsey and F. M. Martin, *Social class and educational opportunity*, Heinemann, London, 1956, pp. 21, 25.

carried out a complex reform of the educational system, with the State undertaking to meet the State scholar's university tuition fees, and even his maintenance costs, if the father's earnings did not exceed £500 per annum. The State also provided considerable assistance for students whose parents' income came to under £2,200 per annum.[2] This reform also contributed to the partial standardisation of the grammar school system, until then extremely complicated, and gave working class young people the chance of an ostensibly equal start—in fact there was soon a significant increase in their numbers in the grammar schools. Table 20 shows some statistics over a seventy-year period in the grammar schools in south-west Hertfordshire (Watford) and Middlesbrough.

1 K. Lindsay, *Social progress and educational waste*, Routledge, London, 1926, pp. 17–19.
2 Lewis and Maude, *Professional people*, pp. 234–5.

This statistical comparison between two regions differing in social composition shows up a certain by-product of the reform of the schools. In districts where the local middle class was poor and compelled to limit its ambitions for the education of its children the reform could actually increase the proportions of non-working class pupils. In general, however, the number of working class children in the grammar schools increased conspicuously in most areas.[1]

A growing number of working class families have begun to raise their sights beyond the grammar schools to the extent of aspiring to a university education for their children. In the study of south-west Hertfordshire and Middlesbrough already mentioned, Floud, Halsey and Martin carried out a survey of parents' preference for grammar schools, that is to say, the schools which, unlike the 'blind alley' secondary modern schools, make it possible for their successful pupils to go on to university. The results of the survey showed that in Hertfordshire 48 per cent of the parents who were skilled workers, and 43 per cent of the parents who were unskilled workers, preferred grammar schools for their children. In Middlesbrough the corresponding figures were 53 per cent and 48 per cent.[2]

The extension of the scholarship network also made it possible for the sons of workers to enter the public schools, whose fees had previously been prohibitive for children from the poorer strata. In the years before the first world war, when it cost the then enormous amount of £300 to send a boy to Eton (and only a little less for Harrow, Marlborough or Charterhouse),[3] these schools produced 'a race of well-bodied, well-mannered, well-meaning boys, keen at games, devoted to their school, ignorant of life, contemptuous of all outside the pale of their own caste,

---

1   This does not, of course, mean that young people of the working class really attained an equal start with their middle class age mates. To be sure of this, one has only to compare the 1950–53 statistics of the grammar schools above with those of the social origins of the boys who took the entrance examination for these schools. In Hertfordshire, 7 per cent of the boys were from the middle class, 26 per cent from the lower middle class and 67 per cent from working class families. The corresponding percentages for Middlesbrough were 5, 18 and 70. The general living conditions and cultural environment of the working class were still considerably lower than those prevailing in middle class and lower class milieux, and this worsened the chances of working men's sons in formally equal competitive examinations. Moreover, even with the State paying for the education of workers' sons, a boy's attendance at school meant that the family must for some years do without the earnings which he could have contributed to the family budget. (J. E. Floud, A. H. Halsey and F. M. Martin, *Social class and educational opportunity*, Heinemann, London, 1956, pp. 7–8.) This was an investment which not all working class families could afford, while some of those who could might not think it worthwhile.

2   Floud, Halsey and Martin, *Social class and educational opportunity*, p. 82.

3   A. Ponsonby, *The decline of aristocracy*, Unwin, London, 1912, p. 225.

uninterested in work, neither desiring nor revering knowledge'.[1] Since then access to the public schools has been granted to a limited number of lower middle and working class pupils, without undermining either the educational system that has traditionally prevailed in such schools or the snobbish attitudes which they inculcate in the minds of those boys who aspire to social advancement. The public schools have in principle remained the domain of the privileged strata, but they have also become a channel through which a certain section of working class youth is steered into the national political elite, including, *inter alia*, the highest administrative grade of the civil service.

To sum up, although the school system in Britain is still based to a considerable extent on preference and privilege, it has opened its gates sufficiently wide to allow potentially combustible nuclei of social energy to be off-loaded.

The way in which the educational system, as gradually reformed, has operated as a mechanism for individual social mobility between one generation and another for people of working class origin can be illustrated by the changes in the composition of the civil service. In the middle of the nineteenth century the latter was a classic example of a semi-feudal bailiwick of the aristocracy, and it was only in the second half of the century that it began unwillingly and rather grudgingly, to open its doors to the sons of middle class families. The reform of recruitment procedures which took place in the 1850s seriously undermined the system of patronage that had previously held sway, but the machinery of competitive examinations introduced by the reform created natural privileges for the sons of wealthy squires and industrialists, who had the large fortunes necessary to provide them with a university education. The system of competitive examinations has lasted until the present time and still favours the children of the privileged classes. Owing to the post-war educational reforms, however, it is no longer so one-sided in its operation as it was even half a century ago.

The number of government offices has grown steadily and rapidly over the last century. In 1797 there were 16,267 civil servants, while as late as 1851 there were still only 39,147. By 1901, however, the total was 116,413; in 1914, 280,900; in 1929, 311,000; in 1938, 422,000; and in 1955, 633,380.[2] As its numbers have increased the civil service has offered an ever wider range of careers for an ever increasing number of people. Simultaneously, there has, also, over the preceding decades been a rise in the percentage of

1 C. Norwood and A. H. Hope, *The higher education of boys in England*, Murray, London, 1909, p. 187.

2 H. Finer, *The British civil service*, Fabian Society, London, 1927, p. 14; E. N. Gladden, 'The British civil service in transition', *American Political Science Review*, April 1949, p. 338; F. Dunnil, *The civil service*, Allen & Unwin, London, 1956, pp. 219–20.

people of working class origin among the newly recruited civil servants. One is therefore reasonably justified in asserting that over the last hundred years the civil service has become one of the most important instruments of inter-generational mobility for the sons of workers. According to the calculations of R. K. Kelsall, in 1929 working men's sons formed only 7 per cent of the membership of the administrative class above the rank of Assistant Secretary. In 1939 the figure was 10 per cent and by 1950 17 per cent.[1] It would follow that the percentage of working class youngsters among the new intake into the administrative class should have been still higher and should have risen still more rapidly.

Obviously, the social composition of the civil service is still far from reflecting the social structure of British society, but all the same its function as a channel for syphoning off the more able individuals in the ranks of the working class has been growing. Moreover—and this is particularly significant in the present context—it has been growing despite the retention of the system of recruitment which gives preference to people with a university education. L. N. Helsby found that, of fifty-two candidates accepted from the administrative class in 1953, twenty-six were graduates of Oxford, fifteen of Cambridge, five of London University, five of Scottish universities and one of the University of Nottingham. Twelve of the total were, however, the sons of manual labourers, and seven of these twelve were graduates of Oxford or Cambridge.[2] Since the 1944 Education Act began to produce results only in 1953, it could be expected that in later years even larger numbers of working class children would start flowing through the once elitist and exclusive universities and through the net of competitive examinations into the upper levels of the civil service. It would appear quite improbable, given the retention of capitalist class divisions, that the percentage of workers' sons in the total class of higher civil servants could be as high as the percentage of workers in the society as a whole. But this is not important from the viewpoint of individual social mobility. Seen from this angle, the civil service has been performing and will probably continue to an increasing extent to perform a role as one of the most important mechanisms for achieving that inter-generational mobility of individuals which is one of the most important reasons for the growth of conservative attitudes in the British working class.

Another reason for this same phenomenon has probably been the gradual transformation that has taken place in industrial relations. Over the last century these have undergone a profound evolution. In the first half of

1   R. K. Kelsall, 'The social background of the higher civil service', *Political Quarterly*, October–December 1954, p. 335.
2   L. N. Helsby, 'Recruitment to the civil service', *Political Quarterly*, October–December 1954, pp. 330–1.

the nineteenth century they were based on the absolute dictatorship of the employer, whose power was exercised with total hostility towards the workers, and with the undisguised objective of maximum exploitation. In the twentieth century, however, there was an increasing tendency to treat the labour force as partners in production. An influential factor here was the steady growth of trade union power, mainly in consequence of the shift from a local and occupational base to a country-wide and class base to which I have already referred. While the principle of industrial partnership may not always find expression in reality, it is formally expressed in the administrative methods employed by managements. The changes have obviously not gone, nor can they go, so far as to give working groups a

Table 21

Elements in management–labour relations in 598 large firms

	Percentage of firms		
Nature of activity	*In practice*	*Never operated*	*Dis- continued*
Joint consultation	73	20	7
Co-partnership	2	98	Negli- gible
Profit sharing	29	68	2
Training for adults	38	62	–
Training for juveniles	71	29	–
Training for promotion	27	72	1
Clear statement of conditions of employment	97	3	–
Specialised welfare activities	*Operate*	*Do not operate*	*Did not reply*
Medical:			
Clinical	62	38	–
After-care	35	65	–
Canteen	72	28	–
Recreational:			
Sports	77	23	–
Social	75	25	–
Cultural	24	39	36

Source W. Robson-Brown and N. A. Howell-Everson, *Industrial democracy at work*, Pitman, London, 1950, pp. *9 et seq.*

genuine influence on the direction of production. Nevertheless, there are fewer and fewer industrial establishments in Britain which can hope to achieve their production targets without maintaining at least formal links between management and labour force based on agreements and joint consultation. Today industrial relations constitute a separate field of study with their own widely ranging body of specialised literature. There is not room here to deal with this important subject as it deserves, so I shall simply refer to the results of certain studies rather than the detailed analyses, for which readers are referred to the copious specialist literature.

W. Robson-Brown and N. A. Howell-Everson investigated certain aspects of management–labour relations in 598 large British firms, 'particularly in the fields of joint consultation, co-partnership, profit sharing, general welfare development and education'. Some of their findings are shown in table 21. Many studies have shown that the application of these modern methods of organising industrial relations eases the processes of conciliation and tempers the external manifestations of the conflict of interests between employers and workers. Moreover, it has been shown to promote higher productivity and therefore higher profits far more effectively than primitive methods of naked exploitation which evoke social protest.[1] Different researchers have attributed special importance

1   The majority of employers are well aware of the importance of many elements of industrial relations techniques for this purpose. This fact is illustrated in the accompanying table, which is also based on the work of W. Robson-Brown and N. A. Howell-Everson. (*Industrial democracy at work*, Pitman, London, 1950, pp. 11–14.)

Management views on the influence of joint consultation and welfare activities (per cent)

(a) *Influence of joint consultations (about 440 firms)*

	Favourable	No influence	Unfavourable
Output (quantity or quality)	50	50	–
General morale	86	14	–
Works discipline	67	33	–
Absenteeism	48	52	–
Personnel turnover	26	74	–
Reduction of internal friction	91	9	–

(b) *Influence of welfare activities (about 480 firms)*

	Favourable	Unfavourable	No influence
Output	28	–	72
Morale	70	–	30
Management–labour relations	84	–	16
Absenteeism	32	–	68
Personnel turnover	40	–	60

to particular aspects of industrial relations, principally in the sphere of management–labour relations. For instance, George B. Baldwin, in considering the functions of joint consultation, lays stress on the fact that it gives the rank-and-file workers a feeling of fuller participation in the affairs of their enterprise and 'improves the respect which union leaders and managers have for each other'.[1] Robson-Brown and Howell-Everson maintain that consultations have the function of 'making provision for ventilation of legitimate criticism through regular channels'.[2] There can be no doubt that the widespread use of measures to improve industrial relations has been an important factor in promoting the trend towards conservatism in the working class, and the diffusion of conformist attitudes towards the existing social and economic system, with a consequent restriction of the expansionist tendency of the labour movement. 'Modern' industrial relations techniques are one of the most important factors in promoting vertical class mobility and raising the socio-economic status of the working class as a whole.

To sum up, it may be said that in the period under discussion mechanisms evolved in Britain to promote social class mobility and individual mobility between generations. At the same time there was a certain curtailing of individual intragenerational mobility, if we consider the social system without taking the labour movement into account. These mechanisms for the promotion of individual mobility between one generation and another did nevertheless directly reduce the social demand for individual mobility within the same generation. Moreover, the working class as a whole won a recognised position within the capitalist social system and, in terms of the prevailing middle class hierarchies of social values, accepted both the system and its ideological superstructure. The emergent working class hitched its ambitions to the social systems as it stood and in general adopted an increasingly conservative outlook, imbued with a desire to preserve the *status quo*, which guaranteed such measures for satisfying social aspirations as were confined within the framework of the capitalist economic and political structure.

The degree to which the working class has become integrated into the hierarchy of capitalist society is shown by the fact that it looks at its own social position through the lens of middle class values. The working class has adopted, almost *in toto*, middle class stereotypes, ambitions and criteria of human worth.

T. H. Pear has distinguished between two types of class and class privilege in Britain: the 'opportunity class' and the 'snob class'. He considers

1 G. B. Baldwin, *Beyond nationalization*, Harvard University Press, Cambridge Mass., 1955, p. 96.
2 Robson-Brown and Howell-Everson, *Industrial democracy at work*, p. 77.

that the privileges of the 'snob class' are, in the British situation, derived from a social prestige that is general, not functional, independent of personal qualities and services but based on titles, money and education.[1] Many writers, including Lewis and Maude,[2] have pointed out that in Britain, by contrast with many other capitalist countries, among them the United States, wealth is still subordinate to social status in the class hierarchy—or, at least, 'the effects of the one are modified and often neutralised for a time by the other'. The validity of this proposition has been demonstrated in the history of the relations between the aristocracy and the middle class. At the present time, when these relations have lost their dynamic quality and receded into the background the application of the proposition has shifted to a different social area.

In contemporary Britain status is determined not only by family background and property but also by the position which one occupies in the economic and political functional hierarchy. Wealth and birth have not ceased to determine social status and prestige, but they have lost their monopoly in this regard. Birth and wealth are still an asset in making one's way up the occupational and functional ladder, but the rung which one reaches on that ladder does make up for a lack of advancement on the two remaining ladders. It is a substitute for class flexibility, which has been reduced to nil by the ossification of the two other hierarchies. All three ladders lead to the heights of British society, to the ruling class, to the economic and political elite which has the greatest say in making decisions of social importance. At the top they lead together into a single ruling class, in which the political and financial elites perform side by side and merge into one another. There is a similar coming together at the middle levels of the ladders. One may liken the hierarchy of birth and that of wealth to two buildings with windows at the different storeys but with no doors or stairways inside, while the functional hierarchy resembles scaffolding between the two buildings. It is easier to get out of the windows at various levels of the scaffolding than to make the arduous climb up the crossbars of the scaffolding itself. But the scaffolding does allow people to move to different floors of both buildings, something which would otherwise be impossible. The uppermost floors of the two buildings and the top platform of the scaffolding form a single level. The people on it have got there either from the top storeys of one of the buildings or from the lower levels of the scaffolding via the appropriate rungs. Once they have arrived, however, they can move fairly freely between the two storeys of the building

1 T. H. Pear, 'Psychological aspects of English social stratification', *Bulletin of the John Rylands Library*, May–June 1942, pp. 351–2.
2 Lewis and Maude, *Professional people*, p. 20.

and the highest platform of the scaffolding, without much regard to the route by which they got there.

I have already shown that there has been a great improvement in the socio-economic status and social prestige of the working class as a whole. But in general, with only a few exceptions, the working class in its manual occupations is still found as a stratum on the bottom levels of the two build-ings and the scaffolding just mentioned. The introduction of mobility between the floors has not after all transposed the levels of the different floors. Moreover, it has not broken down their traditional separateness. None the less, the fact that there is a means of climbing higher makes those who live on the ground floor take a different view of the residents on higher ones, and of the distance between them. This process is also facilitated by the greater ease with which ideas can be exchanged. We must assume that the social status of the stratum and the index of the social mobility of individual members are not quantities which are unrelated to each other. The contemporary class position of the working population cannot be treated in abstraction from the mechanisms even of individual mobility between or within generations.

It is because of these mechanisms that the social frontiers between the class of manual labourers and the lowest levels of the occupational and functional hierarchy have been almost completely blurred. At the end of the nineteenth century Charles Boots described manual labourers and clerical workers as two completely separate classes, almost castes, living in isolation from each other and not entering into social relations, still less marital ones. If a worker's son passed into the non-manual stratum, at however low a level, it meant a complete break with his own class, a feeling of shame at his origin and a desire to efface all traces of it. A similar gulf divided manual labourers from shop assistants. The latter regarded them-selves as linked by class culture and ideals with the 'enlightened' classes. They endeavoured to imitate those classes in their behaviour and way of life, rejecting trade unionism as unworthy of their social position although they too earned their living as hired labour.[1] In the twentieth century the

---

1   The cartoons of Jack Dodsworth in the periodical *The Shop Assistant* at the beginning
    of the twentieth century are more characteristic of this viewpoint than any official
    statements. In one of these a smartly dressed young man with a set of golf clubs
    is shown standing at a shop door. He is asking the assistant behind the counter to
    come out and take a break. The latter answers gloomily that a cigar is his only
    break. Another cartoon shows a shop assistant standing behind the counter and
    dreaming of golf, tennis and yachting. Both cartoons, like many other of the same
    type, were part of the shop assistants' campaign to get legislation enforcing earlier
    closing hours.
       The first trade unions of clerical workers (the Railway Clerks' Association, the
    National Association of Local Government Officers, the Post Office Workers'

clerical stratum did not cease to feel an affinity for the middle class style of life and middle class attitudes; but it did shed its caste-like character almost completely. The intensification of inter-generational contacts between the stratum of manual labourers and the lowest non-manual stratum has, in consequence, led to a blurring of the social barriers which divided them.

Because there has been a relatively high incidence of individual mobility from one generation to another, a large number of families have ceased to be integral cells of a single class. Within the same family may be found manual labourer grades, office workers, professionals, party politicians and others. What was formerly a considerable range of differentiation in the occupational hierarchy no longer involves, as once it did, the break-up of the family. Instead, it involves the break-up of the family as a class unit. Marriages between the clerical and manual strata are frequent and have ceased to be regarded as *mésalliances*. The loss of the caste-like divisions and the general blurring of class barriers at this level are confirmed by the fact—on which many researchers' findings agree—that inter-generational vertical social mobility works both ways—i.e. while the offspring of manual labourers have been passing into the white-collar stratum, there has also been a movement from the white-collar stratum into skilled manual jobs. This latter movement is regarded as something quite normal, which does not offend class sensibilities. The indistinctness of class frontiers at the bottom of the non-manual occupational and functional hierarchy, combined with the internal continuity of the hierarchy, has had a considerable influence in changing the working class consciousness; it has also helped that class to accommodate itself to the norms of middle class consciousness and has contributed to the blurring of the feeling of class distinctiveness.

Such processes are well illustrated by enquiries into 'subjective class position' or self-ranking. In 1948 a British Institute of Public Opinion survey showed that 47 per cent of respondents regarded themselves as belonging to the middle class, and only 46 per cent as belonging to the working class.[1] In 1952 a Gallup Poll survey produced similar results: 49 per cent of respondents regarded themselves as middle class and 46 per cent as working class.[2] 46 per cent was much lower than the actual

Union and the National Union of Clerks) were set up only in the twentieth century. Before the first world war, moreover, they were only in their formative stage and had very few members. (*British trade unionism*, ed. J. Kuczynski, PEP, London, 1943, p. 14.) It was only the economic crisis of the post-war years and the change in relationships between the clerical stratum and the working class which accelerated the development of the clerical trade unions.

1 Cole, *Studies in class structure*, p. 79.
2 Maude, 'The Conservative Party and the changing class structure', *Political Quarterly*, April–June 1953, p. 169.

proportion of manual workers in the population, even if one leaves out of account the close connection between the bottom levels of the administrative and technical hierarchy and manual workers.

In the consciousness of the British working class, belonging to the middle class has been linked to an ever-increasing degree with status, not wealth. Accordingly, a high estimate of one's own social position is linked with a hope of advancement in terms of status rather than wealth. A typical instance of this transformation has been the change in the pattern of savings. In the 1950s over half the population had a bank or savings account, but the workers who saved did not view the saving of money as an end in itself—their objectives were entirely practical, as, for instance, a holiday, the purchase of certain consumer goods, and so on.[1]

I have already tried to show that there is a close link between the solution of the problem of all three types of vertical social mobility, and the appeasing of the working class as a whole, along with the smothering of its nonconformist attitudes towards the prevailing social structure. This process is expressed externally in the disappearance of feelings of frustration, the negligible amount of class antipathy towards other social strata, the absence of envy over the privileges of other strata and in an increasing lack of interest in political matters. A very small section of the working class has become more actively interested in politics, but the political interests of the great majority are entirely satisfied by their participation in the Parliamentary elections every five years. Political problems are rarely discussed in private conversation. Working class people read newspapers for other than political reasons, and even the Labour Party's own newspaper, the *Daily Herald*, devoted little space to political questions.

The proportion of active socialists among British workers is small. The majority will say, 'I'm not a socialist, I'm Labour.' Many of the minority who declare themselves to be socialist define socialism in terms of higher wages, shorter hours, better working conditions, and they regard trade union activity as the core of socialist action.[1] They thus deprive socialist ideology of its traditional nonconformist colouring, and do not set it up against the existing social structure or the prevailing hierarchy of social values. In consequence, the impulses towards social dissent, which never disappear entirely, and which from time to time make themselves felt in the form of unofficial strikes, do not, despite their spontaneous quality step outside the framework of the social system, nor even assume a political character.

The various processes described in this chapter have led to a running down of the dynamic nonconformism of the working class. If the working

1   *Small savings*, Fabian Tracts, Fabian Society, London, 1943, p. 4; Zweig, *The British worker*, p. 169.

class has not actually become established on the socio-economic status level which it has already reached, it has, at all events, accepted the contemporary hierarchy of which this level is a part. One can also note the consolidation of the mechanisms of individual mobility combined with an acceptance of the structure within which those mechanisms function, and of the criteria of mobility itself.

2

The structure of the
labour movement

During the period under review the evolution of the structure of the
labour movement, like that of the structure of the working class, was
influenced by the same factors and on the whole evolved in the same
direction as in the preceding period. The trends outlined in Part III have
continued to operate, but in this latter period they have led to their logical
conclusions, so that the phase of the development of mass movement
has become that of consolidation.

Over recent decades, therefore, we have seen an increase in the numbers
of unionised workers—both absolutely and in proportion to the size of
the working population and the population as a whole.[1] If one excludes
the years after the first world war, the increase in the numbers of trade
union members can be shown as an ascending curve. The only feature to
disturb its balance was the premature and over-rapid expansion of union
membership in the period when the working masses were subject to radical influences due to the first world war and the Russian revolution. This
expansion was so explosive that the machinery of the trade unions was
unable to assimilate all the newcomers with sufficient speed. When the
emotional tensions decreased, the associational links which it had created
were not replaced by more stable bureaucratic links. Thus the first blow
struck by the depression caused the number of trade union members to
fall dramatically to a level at which the existing trade union structure was
in a position to absorb them. The period immediately after the General
Strike saw the end of this exodus. Thereafter the total again began to climb,
this time slowly but steadily and consistently, since it moved on a parallel
with the growth of the trade unions' structural capacity to absorb new
members.

In 1891 only 3·9 per cent of the population of the United Kingdom belonged to a trade union, but by 1947 this percentage had risen to 18·22, or
43·46 per cent of the working population.[2] On the other hand, in the United
States at approximately the same time trade unionists constituted only

---

1 *Yearbook of the International Free Trade Union Movement, 1957–58*, London, 1957,
   p. 252.
2 J. D. M. Bell, *The strength of trade unionism in Scotland*, University of Glasgow (Department of Social and Economic Research) occasional papers No. 4, McNaughtan &
   Gowanlock, Glasgow, 1950, pp. 6, 12.

Table 22

Membership of TUC-affiliated trade unions

Year	Number of members
1868	118,367
1900	1,250,000
1910	1,647,715
1920	6,505,482
1930	3,744,320
1939	4,669,186
1945	6,575,654
1950	7,883,555
1955	8,106,958

Note According to the *Ministry of Labour Gazette*, the number of trade unionists belonging to all unions in Britain, including those not affiliated to the TUC, was 9,235,000 by 1950.

Source *Ministry of Labour Gazette*, November 1951.

34·4 per cent of the working population,[1] and the proportion was far lower in the majority of other capitalist countries. During this period the British trade unions reached what is, in terms of a sociological analysis, the final stage of their expansion. Their influence extended to all the strata of the working population and further growth could be only quantitative, not qualitative. Thus the further evolution of the trade union structure has taken the form of a slow and partial adaptation. There were no perceptible social forces which could give rise to speedier or more profound changes. A state of affairs in which a structure is capable of only quantitative growth, and has lost its inner capacity for change, is a state of consolidation. In this case the state was all the more stable because there were no social strata outside the labour movement whose entry into it could lead to renewed clashes between opposed forces and trends, such as might shake the movement out of its ossified state, destroy the established union structure and necessitate its total reconstruction in a revolutionary way.

The last stratum to be absorbed by the labour movement was that of the salaried employees working in the massive administrative and technical structure created by the modern economy. The spread of trade unionism among this stratum occurred during the period now under consideration. In 1941 unions such as the National Amalgamated Union of Life Assurance Workers, the Guild of Insurance Officials, the Bank Officers'

1 Wright Mills, *The new men of power*, p. 53.

Guild, the Clerical and Administrative Workers' Union and the National Association of Theatrical and Ciné Employees, etc, has a total membership of about 140,000. This was not quite 10 per cent of the overall number of white-collar workers, and was thus a good deal less than the corresponding percentage of manual workers belonging to trade unions.[1] After the second world war, however, as the assimilation of the different strata of workers and the social unification of manual and white-collar workers proceeded through family ties and the convergence of socio-economic status levels, the percentage of white-collar trade unionists rose rapidly, in line with the increasing integration between the trade unions representing wage-earners and salary-earners.

The assimilation of the supervisory and technical stratum was not, however, the only change in the social composition of the trade union movement in this period. In considering the structure of the union movement one cannot disregard the influence exerted by changes in the occupational structure of the working class, particularly the standardisation of the jobs of semi-skilled workers, something that was linked with the blurring of divisions between different skills and branches of industry. This process could not take place without a conflict with the structural principle of the trade union movement, which was based on the institutionalisation of occupational interests and therefore on the assumption that these interests were distinct, like the occupational skills themselves.

Obviously, the skilled unions were the least prepared for the task of absorbing workers from the new branches of industry and for the new occupational structure. Despite the overall growth of industry and the number of workers employed, their recruitment grew consistently smaller. Their capacity to attract new members was decreasing even more rapidly because joining this type of union meant being confined willy-nilly to a specific kind of craft job; even if such a union achieved its maximum potential membership, it would still seriously limit its members economic opportunities by comparison with the giant general unions, with their unlimited potential for expansion. But even the industrial unions were not ideally adapted to the new conditions of the occupational structure. Possible exceptions might be found in the comparatively isolated communities of the mining towns and the stratum of agricultural labourers, whose migration into industry had more or less ended, at least in so far as mass migration was concerned. In the case of the railwaymen the situation was less clear, since although the railways were a distinct entity and the railway companies' labour turnover was exceptionally low, there were numerous jobs on the fringe of the railway service whose labour force could move between the railways and other branches of the economy

1 Kuczynski, *British trade unionism*, pp. 31–2.

with relative ease. In the remaining sectors of manufacturing industry and transport, however, the transformation in the occupational structure of the preceding period had sapped the foundations on which not only the craft but also the industrial unions had been built.

The only type of union actually to profit from the metamorphosis in the occupational structure was the general unions, which were by definition concerned with any specific occupational industrial divisions. Not only did such unions emerge unscathed from the changes of the preceding period, they also experienced at this time a stormy phase of development and growth. In 1913 their membership was 13·7 per cent of the total membership of unions affiliated to the TUC, and in 1923 14·3 per cent. By 1939 the percentage had risen to 19·6 and in 1947 it was 24·2. In the period that followed, their membership grew much faster than that of other unions.[1] The increase in numbers came from the recruitment of new members to existing branches in particular industrial concentrations, and also from the setting up of new branches in areas which had yet not been reached by any trade unions or in which only other types of union existed. Another way of increasing their membership was by absorbing separate union structures in their entirety. For instance, the Transport and General Workers' Union by 1922 comprised eighteen formerly separate unions; during the period 1923–39 it absorbed another twenty-nine and in 1940–47 an additional eleven, including the important Government Civil Employees' Association.[2] As one looks through the list of newly incorporated unions it is hard to discover any kind of occupational or industrial connection. The reason is that the general unions are organised on a class level, and their basic conception involves a negation of all other more specific divisions between strata. A single trade union organisation covers London dockers, tinplate workers from South Wales, colliery surfacemen from Yorkshire, steel workers from Sheffield, cement workers from the Thames valley, gasworkers, steel toy makers, doubling mill workers, brick makers, polishers and grinders, metal workers, glass bottle makers, etc.[3] No occupational limitations determine the direction in which the general unions should expand and no barriers between different industries curb their expansion. By 1938 the National Union of General and Municipal Workers had 18,000 members in the textile industry, 43,500 in building and construction, 40,500 in heavy engineering, 7,500 in the manufacturing of claystone, brick, etc, 28,000 in mining, 146,000 in municipal service, and so on.[4]

1   Bell, *Industrial unionism*, p. 16.
2   Flanders, *Trade unions*, pp. 31–2.
3   H. A. Clegg, *General union*, Blackwell, Oxford, 1954, pp. 3–4.
4   *Ibid.*, pp. 32 *et seq.*

Since then the composition of the union has become even more hetero-geneous and its social base has moved very far from the original one.

In Part III I referred to the beginnings of the general unions, as associa-tions of predominantly unskilled workers, organising the pariahs of the contemporary industrial scene against the existing trade union movement. This no longer applies. It would still be an exaggeration to assert that there is no longer any difference in social composition between the general and the craft unions. In the latter the percentage of skilled workers is propor-tionately higher than in the former; moreover, unskilled workers are still not accepted as members by many craft unions. But at the present time no type of union has a monopoly of any level of occupational gradation and workers at different levels of skill are associated in various proportions in every type of trade union structure. The differences between the various types of union have therefore largely ceased to correspond to hierarchical differences between occupations. Meanwhile the extent to which the majority of the working population of Britain today—semi-skilled workers, machine operators of all kinds, assembly workers and similar categories—are recruited by the unions depends exclusively on the unions' organisa-tional flexibility and absorptive potential. In consequence, it is hard to withstand the impression that the traditional classifications all too often invoked in studies of the British labour movement, classifications based on an occupational gradation, are completely outdated and need to be radically revised. The structure of the trade union movement still remains rather heterogeneous. Nevertheless, if one excludes a fringe of numerous but small-scale, locally based craft unions, which possess little influence, the basic core of the most important unions is growing increasingly similar, considered in terms of structure, and they can be placed in different structural categories more by virtue of their traditions and origin than be-cause of their actual position at the present time.

The explanation is that the period under consideration has seen not only an overall increase in the power of the general unions, but also profound changes in the structure of those unions which, for reasons of historical continuity, are still often defined as craft unions in a sense approximating to the conception of a craft union of the times of Allan and Applegarth. Only organisational continuity could justify this glaring anachronism. The original Amalgamated Society of Engineers and its descendant, the Amalgamated Engineering Union of more recent times, are profoundly dissimilar as structure. This dissimilarity is decisive so far as the contem-porary pattern of the union movement is concerned, since those craft unions which have not passed through a similar transformation have seen their importance in the union movement decline steeply as a result of the downgrading of the stratum of craftsmen within the working class, and

are now more or less on its fringes. The great change in the social significance of the unions, and the strong current of social and political advancement which has borne the movement upward in the economic and national
hierarchy, have been proceeding independently of them and without their
participation. Alongside the general unions an active part in this evolution
has been taken only by those craft unions which have ceased to be craft
unions in the traditional sense and have let themselves be influenced by
the prevailing trends of structural evolution.

This trend has been leading towards a kind of federation of unions,[1]
which would result in the destruction of the most important structural
principle of the craft unions—the institutionalisation of occupational
interests. The broadening of the occupational base has paved the way for
interests which extend beyond the framework of occupation or locality.
The union, in fact, becomes an all-embracing union, a type of structure
which can be attained as well by encompassing a number of different
occupations as by paying no regard to them. Recent decades have produced
continual amalgamations between unions traditionally ranked as general
unions. But the Amalgamated Engineering Union, traditionally regarded
as a craft union, was created in 1920 by a merger between craft unions
only—the Amalgamated Society of Engineers, Steam Engine Makers,
Toolmakers, Machine Workers, Smiths and Tinkers, Brass Finishers and
many others.[2] Since that time it has absorbed more and more unions,
and today it is the equivalent in size and power of the classic general unions,
while most of its former fellow craft unions have lost ground in the ranks
of the union movement. Similarly, the Boilermakers' Union, the Weavers'
Association and others are today craft unions only in name—in reality they
are multi-occupational associations.[3]

1   H. Tracey, *Trade unionism: its origins, growth and role in modern industry*, Labour
     Party Educational Series, London, 1952, p. 29.
2   Cole, *Organised labour*, p. 85.
3   Here again, as in other cases, the tendency of craft unions to evolve towards multi-
     occupational associations is not an exclusively British trait. In the United States in
     1951 there were still ten craft-type unions, as compared with 132 intermediate,
     multi-occupational or general unions. (Stephanski, 'The structure of the American
     labor movement', pp. 44–6.) The craft unions were gradually transforming them-
     selves into multi-occupational unions, initially by means of federations and later
     by amalgamations leading to structural uniformity. (Brooks, *When labor organizes*,
     pp. 32–3.) It is difficult to give an exact statistical presentation of this process because
     American sociologists accept different criteria for the division between types of
     union, based on differing conceptual categories. For instance, Hoxie does not dis-
     tinguish multi-occupational unions at all, while Glocker introduces the concept
     'amalgamation of related trades', which in turn is divided up by Saposs and Davison
     into as many as three categories: 'multiple craft unions', 'trade unions' and 'semi-
     industrial unions'. (R. F. Hoxie, *Trade unionism in the United States*, Appleton,

In spite of their growing intensity, these trends have not led to the development of a more uniform structure in the trade union movement. Moreover, it is very improbable that any such uniform structure could evolve spontaneously amidst the powerful influences and interaction of the wide variety of specific factors which prevail in Britain. In 1946 there were still 162 unions with a membership of less than one hundred persons each,[1] while at the end of 1950 about 400 had fewer than 1,000 members, and over 650 fewer than 25,000 members each.[2] So the union movement is seemingly fragmented to a very high degree, and it is difficult amid this variegated mosaic of structures to ascertain with certainty whether a uniform integrative trend is at work. But if we consider that fifty, or 7 per cent, of the total number of unions which existed in Britain in 1951 made up 84·4 per cent of the average number of trade unionists in the country, and fifteen unions, each with a membership of over 100,000, represented 69·6 per cent of the total affiliated membership of the TUC[3]—then our conclusions become more intelligible. In the engineering, foundry and vehicle building industries twenty-seven unions were still active in 1955.

New York, 1917; T. W. Glocker, 'Amalgamation of related trades in American unions' in *Trade unionism and labor problems*, ed. by J. R. Commons, Ginn, Boston, Mass., 1921; D. J. Saposs and S. Davison, *Structure of AFL unions*, Washington, D.C., 1939.) The classification of Saposs and Davison is the more recent but seems less useful than that introduced by Glocker. It is excessively specific because it tends to attach too much importance to inner structural details. This probably makes it useful for highly specialised enquiries into union structure, but it is inconvenient from a sociological viewpoint, because it splits up elements which, though they assume various forms, follow a homogeneous trend, and so makes it difficult to grasp the most important sociological regularities. In France the economic and political consolidation of the trade union movement which the new economic circumstances made essential was achieved in a different way than in Britain. The movement had sprung chiefly not from craft unions but from industrial *syndicats*, and its structure was much more homogeneous. The content of this process was, from the sociological viewpoint, identical with the emergence of the British general unions, but even more consistent; it found expression in the steadily growing role of the *bourses du travail*, which united different *syndicats* on a local departmental basis and in practice acted as organisational units of the trade union movement. (H. A. Marquand *et al.*, *Organised labour in four continents*, Longmans, London, 1939, pp. 4 *et seq.*)

1 Kuczynski, *British trade unionism*, p. 8.
2 These figures are based on data from the Ministry of Labour, which differed considerably from those of the TUC. This was partly because the Ministry was counting as independent entities 186 unions which the TUC's statistics showed as grouped in thirteen federations. Another reason was that a good number of unions, especially the small ones, were not at that time affiliated to the TUC. Flanders, *Trade unions*, pp. 24–5.)
3 General Labourers' National Council and National Transport Workers' Federation, *Report of special conference on amalgamation*, pp. 2–6, 27.

The corresponding figure for textiles was twenty-one; for building, nineteen; in the iron, steel and minor metal trades, seventeen; in glass, pottery, food, chemicals, etc, fifteen; and among non-manual workers, fourteen.[1] These figures seem to suggest a degree of decentralisation and fragmentation in the trade union movement; in fact they conceal the decisive superiority of several large unions, superior not only in size of membership but also in the influence they can exert on the future of the movement and on its place in social life. In Britain the present, and probably the future as well, belongs to the general, multi-occupational unions.[2]

The process of amalgamation among the unions and the tremendous growth in their membership has gone hand in hand with a further development of union functions. Collective bargaining and joint consultation have become increasingly prominent activities. On the economic plane the unions have not become friendly societies, as happened with the 'new model' unions of the third quarter of the nineteenth century, nor organs of class warfare, aimed at the political transformation of existing society, as was the case with the labourers' unions at the turn of the nineteenth and twentieth centuries. Instead they have become an instrument for negotiating with the employers for better wages and working conditions. They have come to resemble institutions like building societies, whose members, in return for their contributions, can look forward to assured profits which they could not hope to obtain by investing their modest capital as individuals. To meet this new and paramount task the unions have gradually evolved strong and permanent negotiating machinery, employing full-time specialists with financial and industrial expertise. In contrast to the union delegates who were convened on an *ad hoc* basis for negotiation with individual employers or a group of employers in the days of the 'new model' unions, these are professional units, specially organised and trained, with staffs of salaried experts and the most up-to-date clerical and administrative facilities.

The social advancement which the trade union organisation has experi-

---

1 *Yearbook of the International Free Trade Union Movement, 1957–58*, p. 272.

2 It must be admitted that the trend towards unification which has arisen from occupational standardisation has been accompanied by a considerable increase in inter-union conflicts. These conflicts most frequently arise because the large unions aspire to establish an organisational monopoly within a given industry, area or occupational group. (H. A. Turner, 'Trade union organisation', *Political Quarterly*, January–March 1956, pp. 63–4.) They do not, however, work against the general trend to unification, but are a manifestation of it, as it proceeds in many centres and along many channels simultaneously. The TUC has attempted many times to prevent such conflicts, but without success, a fact which once more attests to the strength of the trend towards unification. (Cf, for example, General Council of the TUC, *Final report on trade union structure and closer unity*, London, 1946.)

enced over this period is reflected in the development of collective bargaining and joint consultation over the last half-century. Even local and individual disputes are as a rule settled at national level, to cover a whole industry or even an entire industrial sector. Union leaders meet for discussions, not with individual employers or those who are in charge of a single industrial complex, but with the directors of employers' associations. Negotiations are conducted at the elite level of British economic life, within a three-cornered group—the union leaders, the employers' leaders and the relevant Ministry. Today union activities are carried on at a level which was unattainable for the old unions, considering their size at the time and the narrow interests which they represented. Since the time of Mundella the negotiating and conciliation function has always been carried out by the unions to some degree. In its contemporary form, however, it is an unprecedented phenomenon, the manifestation of a qualitatively new phase in the evolution of the union movement and of the movement's qualitatively new social role.

In the years between 1920 and 1938 the Industrial Court acted as arbitrator in 1,669 cases of industrial disputes; 315 settlements were reached with the aid of single arbitrators, and 1,999 conciliation settlements were reached under the Ministry of Labour's auspices.[1] In the years 1940–49 (i.e. over a period only half as long as the previous one), 1,645 disputes were settled by the National Arbitration Tribunal, 107 by the Industrial Court, 125 by single arbitrators, forty-nine by the existing Joint Industrial Councils, ninety-six by the intervention of the Minister of Labour, and 1,539 with the assistance of industrial relations officials of the Ministry of Labour's conciliation services. The statistics for the war years show that the number of settlements reached through the various kinds of conciliation and arbitration machinery show no tendency towards fundamental change. It may be said that in the period after the second world war the trade unions' bargaining machinery reached the stage of consolidation; its basic organisational outlines were drawn, and it had achieved general social recognition.[2]

1   Flanders, *Trade unions*, pp. 96–9.
2   The consolidation of the bargaining machinery has been reinforced by the fact that some time ago it reached a stage of development in which its settlements constituted a function of the actual disposition of class forces in industry and of the economic situation, and not particular characteristics of the structure of the apparatus itself. Proof of this can be found by comparing the results of the operations of the negotiating machinery with the results of strikes. Ducksoo Chang has estimated that during the period 1919–32 the Industrial Court found in favour of the employers in 35 per cent of cases, in favour of the workers in 22 per cent, and reached a compromise solution in 43 per cent of cases. During the same period strike action ended with victory for the employers in 35 per cent of cases, for the workers in 23 per cent

At the top of the joint negotiating machinery for each industry stand the Joint Industrial Councils, representing employers' associations and trade unions. Before the second world war there were fifty-five. By 1946 their number had risen to 111 and in 1950 there were 130. Some trade unions which have retained their occupational or local separateness have set up federations in order to meet the need to participate in these councils. An example is the Amalgamated Association of Operative Cotton Spinners and Twiners.[1] It should be stressed that the functioning of the bargaining machinery is not dependent on changes of government, but is an established part of the country's economic life, accepted by both sides and both political parties.[2]

The stability of the bargaining machinery, and the high esteem in which it is held by the nation at large, show how far the trade union movement has advanced in recent decades. This machinery has set the union leaderships on the heights of the economic hierarchy; it is the main motive force of their advancement to the highest rungs of the ladder of social prestige and authority. Thus the unions are always ready to put up a fierce defence of their negotiating and arbitration function, and to jettison other principles of the union code for its real or apparent benefit. During the London bus strike of 1958 a representative of the National Union of Railwaymen, to which workers on the Underground belong, refused to call the latter out in sympathy with the busmen. The reason he gave was that the excellent negotiating machinery set up by the railwaymen could not be put at risk by the uncertainties of strike action. In this sense the negotiating machinery today plays the peace-keeping role which in the nineteenth century was performed by the insurance functions of the unions. A century of achievements by the union movement has been capitalised in the form of the negotiating machinery, and this has imposed a policy of moderation and restraint in industrial conflicts. Though the number of disputes in British industry has by no means decreased only a small percentage of them have led to strike action in the analysed period. Table 23 contrasts the intensity of strike action in periods with similar social and economic features.

Not only has the number of strikes been decreasing; they have also been getting much less bitter, have been fought less viciously by both sides, and

of cases, and in a compromise settlement in 42 per cent of cases. (*British methods of industrial peace*, Columbia University Press, New York, 1936, pp. 167–8.) The virtual coincidence of these two sets of figures shows that both methods of settling industrial disputes reflect to an equal degree the actual power relations between the partners in the conflict. One may ask whether this coincidence would persist if, for some reason, there were not threat of a strike to influence the decisions of the arbitration body.

1 Rayner, *The story of trade unionism*, p. 70.
2 Williams, *Magnificent journey*, p. 428.

Table 23

Number of working days lost in Britain during industrial disputes (annual
average in millions of days)

	Pre-war years		Post-war years	
	Year	Number	Year	Number
	1910–14	16·1	1919–23	35·6
	1934–39	1·8	1946–50	1·9

Source Comparative labor movements, ed. W. Galenson, Prentice-Hall,
New York, 1952, p. 65.

have tended to last a shorter time. In 1911 only 47·1 per cent of all strikes
lasted for less than a week, but in 1930 the percentage was 60·2 per cent
and by 1947 it had reached 87·3 per cent.[1] The existence of a close connection between the negotiating machinery and efficient union organisation
on the one side and the decrease in the number of strikes and their violence
is confirmed by the fact that the lowest incidence of strikes has been found
in those branches of production whose workers are particularly well
organised and whose trade organisations have a particularly stable social
status. This observation, which is significant in the British case, coincides
with data drawn from a number of other countries.[2] Notwithstanding
superficial appearances and easy generalisations, a decrease in the incidence
of strikes is clearly not a consequence of the development of negotiating
machinery. Each phenomenon affects the other, but there is not causal
connection either way. Both of them represent to an identical degree the
interconnected results of the changes that have taken place in the social
situation of the working class and the labour movement.

In the contemporary phase of development of the British trade union
movement, the conflict between workers and employers has been geared
into the normal machinery which makes the capitalist economy work. The
co-partners in this economy are employers' associations on the one side
and, on the other, workers' associations which resemble the former in type.
In quite a number of cases the course of strikes has been determined not so
much by the logic of traditional conflict patterns as by the survival value of
the unions' institutional framework. In this connection it is instructive to
look at the course of the London bus strike in May–June 1958. The efforts

1 K. G. C. Knowles, Strikes, Blackwell, Oxford, 1952, p. 74.
2 M. Ross and D. Irwin, 'Strike experience in five countries', Industrial and Labor
   Relations Review, April 1951, pp. 328 et seq.

of the employers, represented by the chairman of the London Transport Executive, Sir John Elliott, were directed less at stopping the strike and defeating the strikers than at finding a solution to the conflict which would save the face of Frank Cousins, general secretary of the Transport and General Workers' Union. No endeavours by the union leaders could prevent the strike, because the workers bluntly refused to accept the decision of the industrial court, with its differential treatment of different groups of busmen. In these circumstances any proposal that the strikers should capitulate would have weakened the union's influence among the workers. It was even possible that a second, more militant union would be set up as a rival. The employers therefore concentrated on a search for face-saving escape clauses for the union leaders and emphasised all along that whatever the outcome of the strike no one would be victimised. In general it was stressed that to judge an industrial dispute in terms of victory or defeat was obviously anachronistic in an era of co-operation between unions and employers, co-operation aimed at achieving greater efficiency in the particular branch of industry whose direction they shared.

The extent to which the unions and the machinery of negotiation and arbitration created by them have become an integral part of the capitalist economic system in Britain is indicated by the support shown for the union movement by employers in all branches of industry and by the fact that the unions are taken into account in all the employers' plans and calculations. The employers see the existence of the unions as the surest guarantee of industrial peace—this is why they are interested in ensuring that as many of their workers as possible should belong to trade unions and be subjected to union discipline and moderating influences.[1]

On the union side, as the movement's social base has become broader and its organisational level has changed, and hence its potential role, the unions have begun to have aspirations which extend beyond activities concerned with negotiations and arbitration, even at the key points of the

[1] Here are two very characteristic instances of this viewpoint. On 8 October 1919 Lord Northcliffe declared, 'Every skilled worker belongs to a union and his employers want him to ... I believe that the labour unions make for smoother relations. Without labour unions our strike last week [the rail strike] would have been a civil war. It was the control of the men by their leaders which made it a peaceful struggle.' (Quoted by Knowles, 'Strikes', p. 74.) Seebohm Rowntree reported how, during his second survey in York, he found the following announcement on some factory walls: 'We have been informed that a number of employees would like to know what is the attitude of the directors to Trade Unions. While recognising that it is entirely a matter for the employee's own judgment as to whether he shall or shall not join a Trade Union, the opinion of the directors is that it is desirable in the interests of the Company and its employees that the latter shall be suitably organised, and that membership of a Trade Union is, in the general case, desirable.' (*Poverty and progress*, p. 205.)

economy. In their study of collective bargaining Frederick Harbison and John Coleman distinguish a series of stages in the development of this function, depending on the extent to which the union is accepted by management and the extent to which its leadership feels dependent on the employers for achievement of its objectives. They see the highest phase of this function's development as co-operation between unions and employers to solve production problems and eliminate obstacles interfering with greater efficiency, a co-operation which is based on the assumption of both parties' equal responsibility.[1] If we employ such a classification then it must be admitted that on the whole the position of the union movement in the British economy has over the decades been entering the latter phase. The unions are becoming partners not only at conference tables where wages and working conditions are discussed, i.e. questions which are directly linked with the interests of various sections of the working class; they are also involved in more general questions concerned with the management of economic policy in spheres whose connection with shop-floor interests is not so immediately evident. The transition to this phase of activity is a necessary consequence of the fact that the movement has climbed to the highest level of the national economy in a manner characteristic of its past history.[2]

Involvement in consultations relating to production management is not

1   F. H. Harbison and J. R. Coleman, *Goal and strategy in collective bargaining*, Harper, New York, 1951, pp. 119, 89–90.

2   As early as 1925 Walter Citrine, who was at that time secretary of the TUC General Council, an exceptionally far-sighted union politician and one of the pioneers of the new phase of union development, wrote, 'The third course is for the Trade Union Movement to say boldly that not only is it concerned with the prosperity of industry, but that it is going to have a voice as to the way industry is carried on, so that it can influence the new developments that are taking place. The ultimate policy of the movement can find more use for an efficient industry than for a derelict one, and the unions can use their power to promote and guide the scientific reorganisation of industry as well as to obtain material advantages for that reorganisation'. (Quoted by Marquand, *Organised labour in four continents*, p. 160.) From 1925 onwards the policy of the unions was consciously, and on the whole consistently, directed towards the 'third course' mentioned by Citrine. Up to the outbreak of war in 1939 the trade unions were pressing for the extension of the scope of the problems about whose settlement they might be consulted. Even before the war, there was an increase in the number of high-level mixed joint committees on which the trade unions were represented. After the outbreak of war there was a considerable extension of the powers and influence of such committees, and the unions were allowed to participate in the management of industry and in all economic matters associated with the conduct of the war. (J. Price, 'The trade unions and the war', *Fabian Quarterly*, Autumn 1941, p. 32.) Not only were these war-time acquisitions not withdrawn when the immediate reason for them was past; on the contrary, after the war they were extended and fortified still further.

the ultimate extension of union influence. Questions concerning the social status of employees, promotion policies, and the whole range of socio-psychological relations in industry have loomed increasingly large in their activities. So have general problems of national social security, health, education and planning.[1] The trade unions are well represented on the bodies which direct all these aspects of social life. In this way the union movement is finally being absorbed in the existing economic and political structure, and is becoming an indispensable mechanism in the functioning of present-day capitalist society.[2] The trade unions have finally transformed themselves from protest unionism into administrative unionism, and although this transformation is most apparent in the nationalised industries, it is by no means confined to them.

The new functions of the unions have made new demands on their organisational structure. Never before in British trade union history has there been such an emphasis on executive and administrative efficiency, something to which even the matter of union funds is subordinated. It is executive and administrative efficiency which determines to what extent union machinery can exploit the opportunities made available by the new status which the movement has achieved.[3] Among these opportunities I have in mind both the further raising of the socio-economic status of a particular group of trade unionists, and also the enlargement of the channels of individual intragenerational mobility for active trade union workers. In this sense—contrary to the almost universal interpretation placed on it by sociologists—the extension of the trade union machinery is neither a morbid perversion of the unions' voluntary functions, nor even an imposition paid in return for the successes of an organisation whose membership is increasing. Instead it is a realisation of basic union functions in the same sense as are negotiating and arbitration or insurance schemes. At their present stage of evolution, the trade unions are carrying out two interconnected and equally important tasks, and it would be pointless to ask whether the function of raising the status of their members is more or less important than that of clearing a path for union leaders as individuals to the highest positions in the highest social brackets. In the same way that the scope of measures intended to solve industrial conflict is ultimately a function of the pressure of the overall membership towards improving the socio-economic status of their structure, it should be assumed that, in the final analysis, the extension of the unions' full-time staff, at least at the

1 *Nationalised industry; the future of the unions*, Acton Society Trust, London, 1951, p. 23; J. I. Roper, *Trade unionism and the new social order*, Workers' Educational Association, London, 1942, p. 17.
2 Baldwin, *Beyond nationalization*, p. 51.
3 Roper, *Trade unionism and the new social order*, p. 13.

present stage of development, is ultimately not the result of the internal peculiarities of bureaucracy as such, but a function of the pressure of the union elite towards individual advancement within a single generation. One should remember that in Britain the machinery of the labour organisations is the only contemporary large-scale channel of intragenerational upward mobility for individual workers. Moreover, it constitutes an essential and extremely important addition to the mechanism of inter-generational upward mobility for individuals which has already been described. This means that one must reject the traditional view, proposed by Michels, of the growth of full-time union hierarchies as a perversion of the democratic 'nature' of trade unions. At the same time it is necessary to analyse this phenomenon in terms of its role in the overall process of solving the problem of social mobility for the working class and its elite within the framework of capitalist society and inside the boundaries of the institutions and value hierarchies set up by that society.

The work of the trade union movement in its present phase is carried out simultaneously at the very top of both the trade union hierarchy and the economic hierarchy as a whole. So it is not surprising that as the activities of various unions expand there is a far more rapid increase in the number of professional officials and in the complexity of organisational machinery at national headquarters than occurs at the lower levels of district and local branches. Since the steep rise in membership of the National Union of General and Municipal Workers, for example, the organisation of the district offices has hardly changed, except for the addition here and there of one or two full-time posts, even though the increase in numbers has made itself felt chiefly at district level. There have, however, been fundamental changes at head office, which has grown greatly both in size and function. From a set-up with half a dozen national officers and a small staff of clerical workers, it has developed into a considerable organisation comprising some thirteen industrial and administrative departments.[1] The *Souvenir history* published by the union on the occasion of its fortieth anniversary showed on its final page, with unintentional symbolism, the drawing of a large office block captioned 'Where we want to go. Drawing of projected new head offices, to be named Thorne House.'[2] One may add that, although Thorne was greatly averse to offices and administrative work, the existence of this staff of high-status officials, not all of them of working class birth or background, is not less a result of the endeavours of Thorne's generation than is the social advancement of the former labourers as a social stratum.

The process of centralising union administration entered its final phase

1   Clegg, *General union*, p. 67.
2   *Souvenir history of the National Union of General and Municipal Workers.*

in the 1920s, when such administration was recognised as a locus of full-time professional activity. Plans were put into effect to train professional administrative staff, and at the same time the principle of restricting the powers of the regional bodies extending those of head office was openly accepted.[1]

Such a process involves consequences which are very important from a sociological viewpoint, in that the associational function of the trade union movement is diminished. The unions once performed an important role in cementing different sectors of the working class as they emerged from their fragmented unorganised state on the occupational and later also on the class level. Today, however, they no longer deserve to be called organisations which produce effective social bonds. Prominent in the list of union functions is the promotion of two kinds of social mobility—that of the stratum and that of the individual—with a resulting extension of the sections which are involved in this function. The remaining functions and the institutional machinery associated with them are shrinking and gradually disappearing.

One should probably look to this phenomenon for the basic reason behind the growing autocracy of the union leaders, which is usually ascribed —again following Michels—to their abandonment, under the influence of necessity, of the ideologies and policies which they accepted in the past and in which their rank-and-file membership still believe. History shows that as union organisations become established, and the importance and prestige of their functions are recognised by the prevailing social order, union officials become increasingly attached to the structure within which and on behalf of which they are working. There have been cases of officials betraying their union in some way, or exploiting their position for personal advancement outside the union, but only in the early days of trade unions, when their status in society was not yet established and when in any case union officials had yet to become fully aware of that status. On the contrary, leaders of the trade unions of today, at least in Britain, aim to meet, as far as is possible, the socio-economic interests and demands of the workers they represent. Rank-and-file support, even in the most passive form, is the basis of the unions' status and cannot therefore be treated lightly. Hence autocratic tendencies of the union leaders are not, and certainly do not have to be, equated with a conflict of interests and policies between the upper and lower levels of the organisation.

There is, on the other hand, a weighty reason for the increasingly autocratic trend among union leaders. With the disintegration of the associational function of the union, the leaders are left facing a scattered rank and file which lacks an articulate voice. For the leaders have at their

1   A. W. Petch, *Trade union administration*, TUC, London, 1929, pp. 5, 20–2.

disposal every kind of modern means of mass communication, while the rank-and-file membership has not. It is the leaders who edit and circulate the union publications, interpret union policy and record union achievements, prepare reports on union activities and draft the texts of union decisions. They, and only they, can make sure that candidates for high union office become sufficiently popular to pass through the net of formal representative democracy. These union elites gather in their hands all the organisational threads which lead from headquarters to each district, and through the district office to each branch separately, without linking the various branches to one another. This monopoly of communications is the basis of the growing autocracy of the leadership and of the steadily growing concentration of every kind of decision-making in headquarters offices. Yet this autocracy must not be interpreted in terms of the ideals of direct democracy, which are inadequate for the functions which are nowadays performed by the union movement. For it does not—or, at least, should not—mean that the union leaders are carrying out a policy that is at variance with the ideals of the rank-and-file members. In the first place, it is increasingly difficult in the contemporary situation of the trade union movement to talk about the ideals of the rank-and-file members, since they seldom as a general rule express their interests in a separate form. Second, the consensus between union policy and the economic interests of the masses is in the long run accomplished by means of mechanisms entirely different from the traditional model of direct majority democracy.

The passivity of the rank-and-file trade unionists has been described and analysed at length in the sociological literature. It would appear to be a natural and inevitable manifestation of the unions' new status and functions. In which sphere could the members take an active part? Which of the two major functions performed by the unions at the present day requires the active co-operation of the ordinary card-holding members for its realisation? If this phenomenon of apathy is viewed in terms, not of the ideals of direct democracy, but of the reality of the unions' actual functions, it hardly seems to be in conflict with the functional prerequisites of the union organisations. Joseph Goldstein, who made an extremely interesting analysis of the internal structure of the Transport and General Workers' Union, believed that the apathy among the rank-and-file members which he noted in this union was due to the breakdown of democratic principles.[1] His explanation seems a simplistic one, since it would be unwise to assume that a more scrupulous application of formal democratic principles might stimulate union members to take a more active part either in negotiations with the leaders of sectors of industry, or in opening up a path for the trade

1   J. Goldstein, *The government of British trade unions*, Allen & Unwin, London, 1952, p. 60.

union elite into the economic elite of the country. The Webbs have already pointed out, from their observations of the unions of their own period, that the mass of union members display activity in the life of the unions only during the brief periods of strike action; otherwise, they behave towards their organisation as towards 'a mere benefit club in the management of which they do not wish to take part'.[1] Since the Webbs' day this observation has been confirmed and reformulated far more forcefully on many occasions.[2] The reason is that the unions have developed in a direction in which occasions calling for active participation by rank-and-file members have been reduced to a minimum. On the other hand, new functions have appeared which existed only in embryo at the time of the Webbs' studies. These functions require even less active interests from the rank and file than the receipt of benefits. Alarmist comments about apathy among union members are derived, it would appear, not from any analysis of the actual functions of the trade unions today but rather from the contrast between union structure and democratic ideals. Moral and ideological considerations apart, we should admit that apathy, being only one of the many symptoms of the recurring disintegration of associational bonds and the reversion to rank-and-file amorphousness, is a normal outcome of the evolution through which the unions have passed in recent decades. Statistical evidence of dwindling activity in local branches[3] would seem to indicate a definite trend of development within the large general and near-general unions—a trend for the central brain to develop in all directions, while the regional organisations shrivel into more or less vestigial bodies with a very simplified role in union life. Thus any criterion of the apathy of rank-and-file members is meaningful only in so far as it is linked with a broadly conceived critique of the whole pattern of general unions and their functions. To censure indifference while accepting the pattern would seem to be a *contradicto in adjecto*.

Cole considered that

> trade unionism is in fact becoming in a good many industries more and more a business movement and less and less a democratic fellowship of

---

1 S. and B. Webb, *History of trade unionism*, p. 465.

2 Cf, for example, N. Baru, *British trade unionism*, Gollancz. London, 1947, p. 136; I. Mikardo, 'Trade unions in a full employment economy' in *New Fabian essays*, Turnstile Press, London, 1932, pp. 157–8.

3 In one union branch which Goldstein studied in the years 1942–49 the average attendance at union meetings fell from 7 to 3 per cent. An average of 37 per cent of union members participated in electing representatives to the central executive council, and in 1945 the union secretary was elected by the votes of 22·2 per cent of members. (*The government of British trade unions*, pp. 197, 100–102.) A similarly apathetic attitude is frequently described in studies of other unions, especially the large general ones with no specific occupational basis.

workers who are in close touch one with another through the meetings and discussions of the branch. Politically, the average trade unionist who pays his political dues to his trade union gets out of it no real sense of belonging to a democratic political movement. He pays, and that is all—.[1]

As a result, to quote C. Wright Mills, 'democracy within the unions . . . is usually a democracy of machine politics imposed upon a mass of apathetic members'.[2] The union leadership's interest in the rank and file is confined to financial reports.[3] A considerable majority of the union members interviewed by Goldstein gave a negative answer when asked whether they believed they could help in settling problems of trade union policy.[4]

It is worth noting that the metamorphosis in union functions and internal relations has run parallel with a change in the motivations for joining a union. The decision to join has become less and less an ideological act. The unions are an integral part of the establishment, a part of the existing and accepted social structure. Joining one does not necessarily involve any political implications or indicate a definite attitude towards social questions and the social order. Among ordinary workers it may be that the decision is most frequently motivated by working class tradition and a feeling of irrational working class kinship, but it is also the result of rational considerations, such as the wish to invest in a profitable enterprise. In some cases joining a union is a necessity. Some unions require all workers in a given area or trade to become members. The reason they give is that the benefits derived from union activities are available to an equal degree for all workers, whether they belong to the union or not. In other cases a union card is evidence that one has the required skills, and is thus a condition of getting the job one seeks. In many cases, therefore, the trade unions have basically ceased to be voluntary associations and their membership dues have in reality become a kind of unavoidable tax, paid to a powerful and demanding protector, who is armed with sanctions. In such circumstances joining a union is almost a perfunctory decision involving no commitment.

The same symptoms are just as clearly visible in the second political section of the British labour movement—the Labour Party. During the period under discussion Labour has become a mass party in the full sense of the term. Its membership has passed six million, although about five-sixths of the overall number are members by virtue of their membership of trade unions. What is most important, however, is that the party has at

1 G. D. H. Cole, 'The Labour Party and the trade unions', *Political Quarterly*, January–March 1953, p. 34.
2 Wright Mills, *The new men of power*, pp. 63–4.
3 Petch, *Trade union administration*, p. 7.
4 Goldstein, *The government of British trade unions*, p. 238.

last ceased to be a political superstructure for the trade unions and has set itself up as a separate autonomous entity. The Labour Party is a separate structure in spite of the fact that its independent grass-roots organisations are still, and will probably remain, insignificant in size by contrast with the masses of members acquired via the trade unions. It is a separate structure because its apex reaches up to the country's political elite. Its upper echelon is one of the two alternative teams in the national political power elite; it is separate from the union leadership, which is part of the economic power elite. The party organisation services and ministers to this team, supporting it at the heights of the political hierarchy and also bringing in fresh reinforcements. The Labour Party's real emancipation from the unions occurred not when it introduced individual membership and set up its own local organisations but when the party elite became the official opposition and a possible alternative government. That was the moment when the party gained an independent foothold in the political power structure and in consequence ceased to be dependent on the favours of the trade union organisation. Thus in spite of the very considerable organisational integration between the Labour Party and the trade unions (the very special significance of which shall be discussed later) the party is a separate and independent organisation, in sociological terms, and it should be analysed as such.

The establishment of the Labour Party as a separate organisational structure has been accompanied by a metamorphosis in its class characteristics at each of the three levels on which the characteristics of a class-based party can be considered. These are related to the social composition of its elite, the class composition of its supporters (whether party members or voters), and the mutual relationships between party policy and the interests of various classes and social strata. At all three levels the Labour Party has ceased to be a purely working class party. In composition, its elite is today a social mosaic. Among its members, and still more among those who vote for it, are to be found people from a wide range of classes and social strata. Finally, there are elements in its policies which are linked with very differing, sometimes even opposed, interests. As I shall be discussing the changes within the Labour Party elite separately, I propose to concentrate here on the two remaining levels of the party's class characteristics.

So far as the class composition of Labour's rank-and-file supporters is concerned, the historical turning point came when a large section of working class voters began to support it, while voters from the remaining strata focused on the Conservative Party. Labour thus became a genuine alternative ruling party. During the first twenty years of its existence the party could virtually count only on the votes of trade union members, but from the 1920s onwards an increasing percentage of middle class voters supported Labour candidates. Samuel Beer has pointed out that the London Labour Party could not win an election without some support from the middle class.[1] The Labour Party began to win elections because it became one of two competing and mutually complementary organisations in the country's political system, organisations which were shaping the British power elite. Gradually Labour has ceased to be a class party in the strict sense and has become a national one. According to G. Elton's definition, a national party is one which (*a*) seeks the support of more than one class, interest group or section of the nation; (*b*) is not sectional in its policy; and (*c*) is not sectional in structure.[2] If we accept this definition we can accept that the Labour Party is a national party.

Various surveys of Labour supporters have shown that while the highest percentage, both absolute and relative, of Labour voters is drawn from the working class, the party has many supporters in other strata of the population; furthermore, it has not monopoly among the working class. The bastions of its support are still the great urban centres with the largest concentrations of working class population, while the areas which it has most difficulty in winning are still the agricultural districts, which remain the stronghold of the Conservative Party. But neither of these two types of area with differing population structures is homogeneous in its political sympathies. Instead, each contains a considerable group of political dissidents. Moreover, analysis of a series of general election results shows that the difference between the degree of support gained in the cities and that gained in other areas is not great and even shows a tendency to decrease (see table 24).

In 1945 Labour Party candidates polled their highest votes in areas with large concentrations of working class population. Such were South Wales (66·2 per cent of the vote); Northumberland and Durham (60·5 per cent), the West Riding (57·1 per cent), the east Midlands (53·7 per cent), greater London (52·8 per cent), the west Midlands (52·6 per cent) and Glasgow and west central Scotland (50·2 per cent). However, Labour also won a substantial proportion of votes in areas with virtually no industrial centres. In the northern rural belt the total was 39 per cent, and in the West Country 34·5 per cent.[3] Yet the fact that the percentage of Labour votes in the urban areas was relatively low by comparison with the working class

1 S. H. Beer, 'Great Britain: from governing elite to organised mass parties', in *Modern political parties*, ed. S. Neumann, University of Chicago Press, 1956, p. 49.
2 'The future of the Labour Party' in 'The future of the political parties: a symposium'. *Political Quarterly*, January–March 1932, p. 54.
3 Association for Planning and Regional Reconstruction, *Political opinion*, ed. H. W. Durant, Allen & Unwin, London, 1949, p. 10.

Table 24

Labour Party strength in urban areas in the period 1924–50

Areas	Percentage of votes for Labour in:			
	1924	1935	1945	1950
London	39·0	43·4	56·3	51·0
Fourteen big cities [a]	38·3	38·2	50·4	49·2
Intermediate [b]	38·0	42·9	52·9	48·6
Small towns [c]	37·3	41·0	51·9	47·4
Total urban	38·0	41·3	52·3	48·6
National	33·0	47·9	48·0	46·3

Notes [a] Over 230,000 population.
　　　 [b] Over 111,000 population.
　　　 [c] Over 60,000 population.
Source S. J. Eldersveld, 'Patterns of urban dominance' in J. K. Pollock
et al., British election studies, 1950, Wahr, Michigan, 1951, p. 85.

concentration, and relatively high in the non-industrial areas, would indicate that the party's supporters are drawn from diverse classes. The
impression is confirmed by surveys carried out among voters during the
general elections of 1945 and 1950.[1] The most detailed analysis for the 1945
election was carried out under the direction of Henry Durant, Director of
the British Institute of Public Opinion (see table 25).

Thus the supporters of the Labour Party include not only an obvious
majority of workers and a good number of white-collar workers—the intellectual section of the working class in the modern sense of this term—but
also a sizeable minority of professionals. In addition Labour gained the
support of just over one-fifth of shopkeepers, small businessmen and
farmers, most of them probably from the lower middle class sector of
British employers. Taken as a whole, therefore, all strata of society contributed to the Labour vote, though obviously not in the same proportions.
Moreover, this division of political sympathies was not the result of a
particular electoral campaign, or of differing standpoints on particular
aspects of national policy over which the elections were being fought.
Changing political trends, which, because of English electoral law, can
easily cause large scale swings in the distribution of seats among the parties,

1 H. G. Nicholas, The British general election of 1950, Macmillan, London, 1951, p. 303;
Political opinion, pp. 6 et seq.

Table 25

Analysis of voting in the general election of 1945 by various occupational groups

| Occupational group | Percentage voting for | | | |
	Labour	Conser- vative and Nat. Lib.	Liberal	Other
Professions	26	60	12	2
Salaried clerical employees	30	53	16	1
Proprietors of shop or business; farmers	21	71	8	–
Weekly wages: factory, heavy industry, transport, miners	77	15	6	2
Agricultural workers, excluding farmers	53	34	11	2
Weekly wages, all others	55	35	8	2

do not generally lead to any major changes in the distribution of votes. The bulk of the voters hold fixed political views, which are often inherited, and they do not allow their voting decisions to be influenced by fluctuations in political trends. According to Dr Henry Durant, the percentage of voters who had ever changed their voting preference was, until 1945, barely 20 per cent. Of this 20 per cent, however, it must be remembered that a large proportion were Liberal supporters, who in most electoral areas had no candidate of their own, so that they faced the alternative of not voting at all or of voting for the candidate of another party.[1] Even in such situations, the voting patterns of Liberal sympathisers on the whole remained constant. In 1950 a *Daily Mail* survey showed that in areas where there was no Liberal candidate 40 per cent of Liberal sympathisers would vote Conservative. A more detailed survey by the British Institute of Public Opinion showed that in such cases 42·5 per cent of potential Liberal votes would go to the Conservative Party and 22·5 per cent to Labour, while 35 per cent of people would abstain from voting.[2] This shows the small-scale proportions of the floating vote, and the stability of the political division between the two major sectors of the political power elite. D. E. Butler has pointed out

1   H. Pollins, 'The significance of the campaign in general elections', *Political Studies*, October 1953, p. 209.
2   T. B. Jenkin, 'The British general election of 1950' in J. K. Pollock *et al.*, *British election studies*, Wahr, Michigan, 1950, p. 17.

that a simple-majority, single-ballot electoral system can often create the impression of apparent gains and losses in political support which do not really exist. The great swings in voting sympathy in the election years of 1945, 1950 and 1951 were an illusion, resulting from the distribution of seats; so far as voting patterns were concerned, the swing ranged only between one and two per cent of the electorate.[1]

The division of assets between the two largest political parties has, as the above data show, been carried out on a permanent basis. Moreover, the dividing line cuts across all the strata of society in a way which is to some extent reminiscent of the class composition of the voters who support the two principal American political parties. The Labour Party's links with trade union movement help to conceal the similarity of social content between the British and American political parties. Their origins were undoubtedly different, but from the contemporary angle the differences in sociological type between the British and the American parties are founded largely upon differences in their respective political machinery. It should be stressed that the complexity of the class composition of Labour supporters finds its counterpart in the composition of the local branches of the Labour Party. In many areas which lack large trade union organisations, the membership of the party's branches is recruited almost entirely from the middle classes.[2] In the majority of local branches, moreover, the percentage of members not drawn from the milieu of the manual workers is large—perhaps larger than the corresponding percentage among Labour supporters in general. Thus, at the level of the class composition of the masses of its supporters, the working class character of the Labour Party, which was so decisively manifest four or more decades ago, has been considerably reduced. As would befit one of the two competitors in the political power elite, it has become a focus for many elements drawn from various social classes. In this respect Labour is very different from the Conservative Party, just as the Labour elite, as part of the country's political elite, is essentially different from the Conservative elite. I shall, however, be discussing this question at more length in the final chapter. Here I am concerned only to point to certain basic trends in the development of the Labour elite, trends linked closely with the changes occurring in the class composition of the party's supporters.

The transformation in the class composition of the Labour Party elite emerged in the composition of the Parliamentary party elected in 1922. By contrast with earlier Labour Parliamentary parties, which were composed almost exclusively of trade union candidates and professional union

---

1 D. H. E. Butler, *The electoral system in Britain*, Clarendon Press, Oxford, 1953, p. 202.
2 H. J. Hanham, 'The local organisation of the British Labour Party', *Western Political Quarterly*, June 1956, p. 383.

officials of working class origins, the total of 140 Labour members in 1922 included fifty who came from outside trade union circles. Among them were doctors and lawyers, and such experienced professional politicians of middle class origins as Trevelyan, Lees-Smith, Arthur Ponsonby, Roden Buxton, Noel Buxton and E. D. Morel, all of them former members of the Liberal Party.[1] This was only the beginning of a process which steadily gained in strength over the years that followed, except for a short transitional period of shock after MacDonald and his associates went over to the Conservatives (one of the results of which was a loss of confidence in the party's intellectuals). The changing composition of the Parliamentary Labour Party is illustrated in table 26.

Table 26

The participation of trade unionists in the Parliamentary Labour Party, 1918–45

		Number of trade unionists	
Election year	Total number of Labour members	Actual	Percentage of Labour MPs
1918	57	49	86
1922	142	87	61
1923	191	101	59
1924	151	88	58
1929	288	115	40
1931	46	32	70
1935	152	80	51
1945	393	117	30

There is every reason to believe that the process illustrated in table 26 is irreversible and linear, although it will probably never lead to the complete elimination of trade unionists from the elite of the Labour Party, unless some additional factors emerge which are absent at the present time. In any case, the contribution of non-working class elements to the party elite has been increasing for several decades and will probably continue to do so, even though it has already brought about a major reshuffling of forces within the elite. This contribution has been growing because the party's new functions since it became an alternative government have demanded

1   Snowden, *An autobiography*, II, pp. 371–2.

other types of qualifications and abilities than those which are in general possessed even by people who have come to the top in the field of trade union activities. It has also been growing because association with the Labour Party has not only ceased to mean a loss of social standing for people from strata traditionally higher than the working class in the social hierarchy; on the contrary, it has come to be of value to such people in their ascent to the heights of the contemporary social hierarchy. The Labour Party is useful to them because there is much less competition within it for those who aspire to climb than there is in the Conservative Party. The bulk of middle class professionals overshadow the professional union officials in precisely those qualifications which are required for a political career. Hence, on the one hand, the demand for more powerful Labour Party machinery for the professional politicians from the middle classes; and, on the other, the supply which meets that demand with interest.[1] I should like to stress that the pattern described above is of a statistical nature and cannot be used to interpret individual cases. The motivations which have led different members of the privileged classes to join what only yesterday was the party of the underprivileged, have probably been influenced by ideological intellectual considerations and expressed in moral terms. It is, however, enough to set the extremely rare cases of individual professionals who joined the party at the beginning of the twentieth century against the large influx of middle class professionals since the 1920s to see that some broader pattern has been operating over and above the rationalised motives of individuals. As a result, Labour is ceasing to be a class-based party at the level of the social composition of its ruling elite as well.

A similar trend has also been evident over the period under discussion at the level of the relation between party policy and the interests of different social classes and social strata.

H. L. Beales voiced a view generally held by students of British political life when he wrote that 'party programmes are very difficult to distinguish one from the other nowadays'.[2] Snowden observed that Labour,

1   In the history of the labour elite one can find numerous instances of such a coincidence of demand and supply, not only in statistical terms but even in cases involving one and the same person. A characteristic example was that of William Allan Jowitt, Lord Chancellor in Attlee's government. When he was Prime Minister Ramsay MacDonald asked Jowitt to move over to the Labour Party, since it was unable to fill the legal posts in the government. Jowitt, who had lost his seat, like most of his fellow Liberal MPs stood as a Labour candidate and won. Immediately after his victory he was appointed Attorney-General and a year later became a peer on MacDonald's recommendation. (M. Goldsmith, *Who's who in the Attlee team*, Muse Arts, London, 1945, p. 25.) This is not to say that in every case demand and supply was concentrated so blatantly in the history of one individual.

2   H. L. Beales, 'The Labour Party in its social context', *Political Quarterly*, January–March 1953, pp. 97–8.

which had started as a party of social protest, a foreign body in the Parliamentary system, had become 'an ordinary political party, with little to distinguish it from the quality of other parties.[1]

The programmes of both parties are indeed very similar. Moreover, notwithstanding the sharp battles which are fought during elections and in Parliamentary debates, they fall within the same general conceptual framework and are based on acceptance of the same social system and on all the basic assumptions of that system's political and economic structure. The clashes between Liberals and Conservatives were, after all, pretty fierce even at the beginning of the twentieth century, when their class composition was fairly similar and they were expressing similar class interests.

The spheres of influence of the Labour and Conservative parties of the 1950s cover the same social strata, although not in the same proportions. They also express two variants of reformist conservatism or conservative reformism in their attitudes towards the same social system. They differ in their attitudes to the speed with which the desired reforms should be carried out; they differ somewhat in the elements which they would aim to conserve; but they do not differ in their attitude to the problems of conservatism and reform as such. As the pressure of working class social protest diminished, once this class escaped from its former state of alienation and achieved substantial socio-economic improvement, and as the pressure of the labour movement opened up a path for individual social mobility for the working class population leading to the peaks of the social hierarchy, the Labour Party naturally began to adopt a conservative attitude towards the structure and the social hierarchy within which the advancement both of the workers as a class and of workers and their sons as individuals was being accomplished.

Like the Conservative Party, Labour has become a target for the activities of numerous pressure groups, not all of them working class. Whether it is in power or in opposition, the Labour Party is not only a party of the working class. Pressure groups approach it as a ruling or as an opposition party, without regard for its traditional ideological colouring or its class connections. Among the interest groups whose pressures have influenced the formulation of party policy one can easily find several of a decidedly reactionary nature.[2] This state of affairs has speeded still more the party's move towards a conservative adjustment to the British political system.[3]

1   Snowden, *An autobiography*, II, p. 1039.
2   Cf, for example, F. C. Newman, 'Reflections on money and party politics in Britain', *Parliamentary Affairs*, summer 1957, p. 314; S. Beer, 'Pressure groups and parties in Britain', *American Political Science Review*, March 1956, pp. 1–4.
3   In his analysis of the *rapprochement* of the two major political parties in terms of their

At all three possible levels of interpretation, therefore, the class character of the Labour Party has been subject, over the period under discussion, to changes tending in the same direction but has moved away from its working class base to a much broader social base, suited to its role in the two-party system of government. During its evolution Labour has absorbed differing proportions from all the social strata at various levels of the social hierarchy.

The party's change of social role over this period has also left its mark on its own internal structure, and particularly on the distribution of decision-making units within it.

A glance at the power relations between the various elements which go to make up the federated Labour Party seems at first to indicate that the party is now, as it was half a century ago, a docile tool in the hands of the trade union movement and that it therefore promotes only the political goals of that movement. In 1949, for instance, during the annual party conference, the sixty-nine unions controlled 4,782,000 votes, of which six largest unions had 3,130,000.[1] The 581 local party branches had a total of

party programmes, Maurice Duverger points to the part played in this by the British simple-majority, single-ballot electoral system. In Duverger's view this system works to eliminate a third political party and to impede the rise of a third candidate. It works this way not only technically—since the number of seats won by a small party does not match the number of votes received by it—but also psychologically—since electors regard a vote given to a small party as a wasted vote and are thus reluctant to support such a party. In consequence, there is, according to Duverger, no room for a Centre party. In the very society where there is no Centre party, however, the centre influences the whole of Parliamentary life. Both parties tend to standardise their programmes in an effort to gain the support of the centre. (*Political parties*, Methuen, London, 1954, pp. 225–6, 388.) In fact electoral campaigns of the two major parties have been aimed chiefly at the 10 per cent of floating voters from the intermediate strata. Both parties draw up their election programmes with one eye fixed firmly on the preferences of this intermediate 10 per cent. One may therefore agree that the factor indicated by Duverger has contributed somewhat to the move towards a political consensus between the Labour and Conservative parties. This factor does not, however, appear to act on its own, still less to determine the direction of the process which is taking place. It is the changes in class structure and inter-class relations that probably play a decisive role here—for they explain the stability of the British electoral system, which the Labour Party once sought to replace by proportional representation, only to desist after entering on a conservative phase of its evolution. Duverger himself has commented that a two-party system of the British type is possible only when the differences between the two rival parties relates merely to secondary goals and means, since the general political philosophy and the fundamental basis of the system are accepted by both sides. One can only agree unreservedly with his statement, but it also indicates the hierarchical reality in which electoral system is subordinated to the more basic factor of class relations.

1 These were: the Transport and General Workers' Union, the United Society of

only 851,000 votes between them, while all the remaining affiliated organisations together had only 62,000.[1] This division would in itself indicate that the trade union machine has a decisive voice in party policies and programmes. This impression is enhanced when one goes into the details of the official Labour Party budget. In 1950, for instance, the heading 'Revenue' covered the following items: from affiliated unions £124,000 for membership fees, £27,000 towards the party's development fund and £148,000 towards the general election fund—a total contribution of £229,000. The local branches, on the other hand, contributed barely £22,000 on all counts, or about fourteen times less.[2] Yet influence on party methods is in some sense proportionate to the extent of one's financial support, or rather of its financial dependence.

The impression as to the extent of union influence is not entirely false. To put it more precisely, it is not so much the unions as the union machines which can exert influence. It is highly doubtful whether this machinery enables the views of rank-and-file union members to be heard at the party forum, or whether the practice of affiliating their rank and file with the party makes the union particularly strong or active. Be that as it may, however, the men representing the unions have every reason to claim a right to exert considerable influence in all the matters which are important for the functioning of the party. This influence is shown first and foremost in the continuing presence of a relatively high percentage of union MPs within the Parliamentary Labour Party. I remarked above that this percentage has been decreasing steadily for a number of years. Even so, it remains relatively high in relation to the number of Parliamentary seats open to all comers. Under the conditions of contemporary political life, professionals with a politically useful academic background have far more chance of success than professional trade union officials qualified in other spheres of activity. If there were to be open competition, the proportion of trade union members would fall suddenly and drastically. That it is still of the order of one-third of the total is due only to the fact that the results of the competitive system are distorted by union influences working in a different direction. By way of return for providing the lion's share of the party's financial support and the lion's share of the support which the Parliamentary Labour Party receives at party conferences, the trade unions reserve almost all the safe seats for their own nominees. They finance these

Distributive and Allied Workers, the National Union of Railwaymen, the National Union of Mineworkers, the National Union of General and Municipal Workers and the Amalgamated Engineering Union.

1   Report of the Labour Party, 1949, pp. 105, 80–85.
2   R. T. McKenzie, 'A note on party finance', in *The British party system*, ed. S. D. Bailey, Hansard Society, London, 1953, p. 137.

constituency parties and put up their own candidates for them.[1] In a number of districts the Labour Party leadership has no say in the choice of Labour MPs, districts which are somewhat in the nature of twentieth century rotten boroughs or feudal domains of the unions which are strongest in them.

Given open, unfettered competition for seats, the unions' participation in the Parliamentary Labour Party would be much smaller than it is at present. On the other hand, were the only considerations financial contributions and the built-in division of votes at the annual conference, the unions' participation would be far higher than it is now and they would form a crushing majority of the Parliamentary Labour Party. The actual state of affairs is a consequence of the two opposed but counterbalancing trends. Moreover, it appears weighted to the disadvantage of the unions as a result of two additional factors. First, the relatively low salaries of MPs are not a particularly tempting incentive for the better paid, high-ranking union officials. Second, as the union leaders have advanced up into the power elite with the aid of their economic base, they have ceased to regard the political machinery as the only channel of individual advancement. Both factors have diminished the pressure of the trade union elite for a high allocation of Parliamentary seats and have thus on the whole worked in the same direction as open competition would have done.

Nonetheless, one should not confuse all these rather mechanical and external indications of the distribution of power within the Labour Party with the division of influence exerted on the taking of political decisions that are important for the party. In this sphere the Parliamentary Labour Party, led by a team of professional politicians, plays a role which far exceeds all the numerical and financial ratios of its independence. Party policy is formed as a result of the existence and functioning of a political organisation which is involved in a specific political system, and devoted to the task of winning or keeping within the framework of that system and in accordance with its rules and requirements. For this reason the party's strategy and political tactics are to an increasingly large extent the consequence of its present political function as a separate structure and to a decreasing extent the consequence of its history as the political superstructure of the trade union movement. The story of the Labour Party is the story of the struggle of the Parliamentary party against the restrictions imposed on it by its trade union connections.[2] It is simultaneously the

1 A. M. Potter, 'British party organisation', *Political Science Quarterly*, March 1951, p. 76.
2 A motion which was put forward by the Parliamentary Labour Party and passed by the House of Commons is a characteristic example of the outward symptoms of this struggle: '. . . it is inconsistent with the dignity of the House, with the duty of a

story of the gradual but consistent process by which the Parliamentary
Labour Party, and with it the Labour Party as a whole, has freed itself
from the shackles of its dependence on the trade union movement in two
spheres which are vital for the survival of the party. A number of scholars
have assembled a rich body of evidence to recreate the process of the union
organisations' gradual capitulation in the face of the growing independence
of the political section of the working class movement. They point out
how the effective dominance of the Parliamentary party—or, to be more
precise, of its leadership—grew up under the cover of the 'old forms' and
the old 'shibboleths', still widely held but no longer valid, about the key
political role of the trade unions; after the second world war even the
semblance of these was rejected long after they had lost any relevance or
actuality.[1] The process would appear to have been influenced by the fact
that the trade unions achieved an important place in the economic life
of the country, and were consequently able to participate in high-level
economic decisions after the Labour Party was founded and came to maturity. This has undoubtedly caused their interest in matters of policy at the
Parliamentary level to slacken: for the trade union movement's influence
on the management of the economy, and its leaders' participation in the
activities of the economic elite, are an established fact which is now no
longer dependent on swings of political favour, or on the identity of the
political party in power. Under these circumstances, unilateral links
between the unions and a particular party can only prevent them from
extracting all the potential advantages which could derive from their new
social role. Hence too the decreasing interest in the political activities of
the Labour Party and the increasing lack of correlation between the fortunes of the unions and the electoral success of the party. This does not
mean—and the point is an important one—that the unions' fortunes are
not dependent on the fact that such a party exists and that it might form a

Member to his constituents, and with the maintenance of the privilege of freedom
of speech, for any Member of this House to enter into contractual agreement with
an outside body, controlling or limiting the Member's complete independence and
freedom of action in Parliament or stipulating that he shall act in any way as the
representative of such outside body in regard to any matters to be transacted in
Parliament, the duty of a Member being to his constituents and to the country as a
whole, rather than to any particular section thereof'. (Quoted by D. G. Hitchner, 'The
Labour Government and the House of Commons', *Western Political Quarterly*,
September 1952, p. 439.) For all this motion's generalising nature and its sharp
warning to all MPs to avoid all outside connections, students of Labour Party
history will easily discern in it the overriding intention of its movers that trade
union links should take second place to loyalty to the Parliamentary Labour Party.
This kind of external connection has, after all, been of the greatest concern to the
Labour Party's political leadership.

1   Cf, for example, Hanham, 'The local organisation of the British Labour Party', p. 376.

government. The fact that such a party exists is a guarantee of the permanence of the unions' newly attained social position, and acts as a brake
on elements which seek to undermine their position. This factor has probably helped the Parliamentary Party's efforts to achieve political independence, by weakening the trade union machine's resistance to the process. One may risk the claim that the turn of the nineteenth and twentieth
centuries was the only period in which the idea of setting up a separate
political party of labour could have won the support of the union movement. If for some reason such a party had not been created at that time,
then the trade union movement of the 1930s, still less that of the 1940s and
1950s, would never have undertaken such an enterprise (in so far as reasoning of the 'if' type is justified at all, in view of the incalculable variety and
multiplicity of interacting variables). The unions' new social position and
the new channel of direct advancement for individuals to the trade union
elite in the economic sphere would have defused the social pressures which
once induced the union movement to support the idea of an independent
party of labour.

During the last half-century the structure of the Labour Party has
undergone considerable change. To cope with the tasks resulting from its
new political position the party has built up a broadly based permanent
staff of professional officials and administrators. The executive machinery
of the party has also adapted itself appropriately, with centralised decision-
making, a nomocratic structure of administration, a precisely defined
hierarchy and firm internal discipline. Labour headquarters has built up a
body of trained organisers, professional agents who are sent out to rein-
force the local organisations and who represent headquarters' policies
uncompromisingly. The filling of these posts is a matter of constant concern to the party leadership. This concern is necessary because the network
is still far from perfect. With salaries ranging from a minimum of £400 to
a maximum (in Grade I) of £550 per annum in 1954–55, it was extremely
difficult to find suitable candidates for this job, which required hard work
and a number of qualifications.[1] The full-time staff had increased and
continued to do so, exclusively for electoral work. The official instructions
to local agents stressed that it was their job to get as many votes as possible for the Labour candidate.[2] The same set of instructions gave the
winning of votes as the reason why the party needed to have its own policy
and listed in this connection the kind of auxiliary organisation needed by
the local agent.[3] In addition, the techniques which the agents were advised

1 Nicholas, *The British general election of 1950*, pp. 38–9, 28–9; Hanham, 'The local
organisation of the British Labour Party', pp. 379–80.
2 H. Croft, *The conduct of Parliamentary affairs*, Labour Party, London, 1949, p. 10.
3 The instructions stated that the agent staff should include the following: an elec-

to use reveal beyond any shadow of doubt the degree to which political issues were subordinated to the utilitarian function of winning votes.[1] The party machine developed and continues to develop more and more in the direction of an auxiliary organisation for the Parliamentary Labour Party, which it serves during the preparation and running of election campaigns. The machine's principal function is to guarantee that the Parliamentary Labour Party holds as many seats as possible. The policy which the machine carries out is not the highest goal; it is only a tool in the battle for votes. To perform these functions more efficiently, numerous research and publishing offices have come into being at party headquarters, making the latter completely independent not only of voluntary help from the trade unions but even of the Fabians. The Fabian Society has been relegated to the role of an auxiliary agency in the Party structure which should, in principle, carry out specific commissions for party headquarters and be paid an appropriate fee. It has become rather difficult for the Society to insist on playing the role of a socialist 'brains trust', an ideologically motivated political organisation aiming to exert a decisive influence on the evolution of the labour movement and to use its support to turn the scales in the political struggle inside this movement. The rule of the professional party machine, which is given over to the objectives of the electoral struggle, has become absolute.[2]

The real master inside the Labour Party is the Parliamentary Labour Party—the political elite of the labour movement, and the store of human resources from which the Labour component of the national political power elite is drawn. Over recent decades the PLP has been transformed into a compact and well disciplined body strictly subordinated to its leaders and enjoying full ascendancy over all extra-Parliamentary organisations within

tion clerk for Central Office, committee room clerks, meetings officer, women's clerk, financial clerk, typist, messengers, auxiliary officer, transport officer, Press officer, money man. This list reveals, on the one hand, the distance travelled by the party machine since the days when Clynes stumped up and down the country, collecting half a crown for several meetings in a single day. On the other hand, it is a blown-up, caricature-like view of the political party of William Adamson.

1 I cannot resist quoting the following passage, which deals with one of the most highly recommended techniques of vote-catching: 'The candidate (and his wife) should proceed in a motor-car slowly through a street while the bands of helpers knock at the doors and invite electors to see the candidate and ask him any questions. The electors are not likely to ask questions, but all the residents of that street will be discussing the candidate for the rest of the day. The candidate's car can pause for a moment or two while he greets the folk at the doors and around.' (*Ibid.*, p. 8.)

2 Potter, 'British party organisation', pp. 83, 85; A. Skeffington, 'The Fabian Society and the Labour Party', *Fabian Journal*, April 1954, p. 27; M. Cole, *Growing up into revolution*, p. 94.

the labour movement.[1] The history of the Labour Party is not only the history of its struggle to free itself from the restrictions imposed on it by the trade union movement but also that of the Parliamentary Labour Party's successful fight to gain control of such extra-Parliamentary institutions within the Labour Party as the executive, the annual delegates' conference and the party machine. This fight began in 1906, the first year in which a significant number of Labour MPs entered Parliament, and its beginnings were described in Part III. In the period now under consideration the struggle has grown even more intense as the PLP was transformed first into the official Opposition and later into a ruling party. Simultaneously it has led to the anticipated and inevitable outcome—the final triumph of the PLP based no longer only on the party machine but on new foundations of political power deriving from the national political structure.

In spite of the PLP's established supremacy over the extra-Parliamentary organisations, sporadic attempts to undermine it are made by the party executive or the annual delegate conferences. Such attempts have however, met with increasingly sharp and determined opposition from the PLP leadership.[2]

1 R. T. McKenzie, *British political parties*, Heinemann, London, 1955, p. 385; L. D. Epstein, 'Cohesion of British Parliamentary parties', *American Political Science Review*, June 1956, pp. 376–7; L. Lipson, 'The two-party system in British Politics', *American Political Science Review*, June 1953, p. 337; J. M. Burns, 'The Parliamentary Labour Party in Great Britain', *American Political Science Review*, December 1950, pp. 869–70.

2 An instance of this opposition was reported in connection with Ramsay MacDonald in the 1928 report of the Labour Party. He stated that 'as long as he held any position in the Parliamentary party—and he knew he could speak for his colleagues also—they were not going to take their instructions from any outside body unless they agreed with them'. (Report of the Labour Party, 1928, p. 174.) In 1937, replying to a resolution by Sidney Silverman (which read in part that 'this conference instructs the Parliamentary Labour Party to vote against . . .'), J. Walker said, 'I want to point out why the Executive cannot accept the resolution moved by Mr Silverman. It contains an instruction to the Parliamentary Party. I think I will get the full and unqualified support of my friend Mr Aneurin Bevan in this: that the Parliamentary Party reserves to itself the right to determine questions of procedure, so that the Conference in discussing a thing like this and putting it into a resolution would be doing something contrary to the constitutional procedure not only of Parliament but of the Party itself'. (Report of the Labour Party, 1937, p. 210.) Ten years later, when the Westmorland Divisional Labour Party moved a resolution for nationalising the nation's water supplies 'at once', Bevan replied, 'It is the function of conference to move a decision of principle but it must be left to the Parliamentary Party to decide Parliamentary priorities, because some things are more important than others'. (Quoted by H. G. Nicholas, 'The formulation of party policy' in Bailey, *The British party system*, p. 147.) In this connection, Ian Mikardo wrote in *Tribune*, 28 May 1948, 'with the Labour Party in governmental power, the Annual Conference as a policy-making institution is as dead as a dodo'. To this we might add

The contest between the PLP and the overall party organisation was not only an internal struggle for power. It had important consequences for the overall functions and structure of the Labour Party. As soon as the PLP gained a foothold on the topmost level of the political hierarchy and achieved supremacy within the Labour Party, the remaining party institutions were virtually reduced to the role of electoral agencies. This development has been pointed out by many analysts of Labour Party structure.[1]

that, if the Labour Party is not in power, no decisions made by any of the party institutions have any executive force. At the time of the well known quarrel between Attlee and Harold Laski, Attlee wrote to Winston Churchill on 2 July 1945, 'Neither by decision of the conference nor by any provision in the party constitution is the parliamentary Labour party answerable to or under the direction of the national executive committee. Within the programme adopted by the party conference, the parliamentary Labour party has complete discretion in its conduct of parliamentary business and in the attitude it should adopt to legislation tabled by other parties. The standing orders which govern its activities are drawn up and determined by the parliamentary party itself'. (Quoted by I. Bulmer-Thomas, *The party system in Great Britain*, Phoenix House, London, 1953, p. 192.) In his memoirs Snowden gave a clear account of the role of the party conferences: 'My experience of Conferences has taught me to attach very little importance to their resolutions. Of the hundreds of resolutions I have seen passed by Labour Conferences outlining a drastic programme of reform, I can hardly call to mind one which has had any practical result. Conferences will talk; let them talk. Governments, including Labour Governments, dispose of Conference resolutions. There is all the difference in the world between the licence and irresponsibility of a Conference and the position of a Government which has to face practical difficulties and knows that no government can move far ahead of public opinion. Nobody knows that better than members of the Labour Cabinet . . . Every four years the Party is presented with a new programme, while not one item in the old one has been carried into effect'. (*An autobiography*, 1, pp. 87–8.) In the early days of the Labour Party's existence there was a statutory limitation on the number of MPs who could be members of the party executive. As the PLP gained in strength, this restriction was simply disregarded; today the PLP leadership can count automatically on the executive's allegiance and, through its good offices, on annual conferences. In the years between 1943 and 1949, for instance, the PLP held approximately 55–59 per cent of Executive National Committee seats and votes. After 1950 it gained 66·7 per cent of seats. (B. Hennessy, 'Trade unions and the British Labour Party', *American Political Science Review*, December 1955, p. 1060.)

1   For example, R. T. McKenzie says that 'it should be evident that the mass organisation, the Labour Party, is primarily a vote-getting agency. Like the Conservative National Union it has, of course, certain additional functions . . . But it must be emphasized that the primary purpose of the Labour Party, like that of the National Union, is to secure the return of a parliamentary party in sufficient strength to form a Government'. (*British political parties*, first edn., p. 455.) G. D. H. Cole, commented, 'The local Labour Parties remained primarily electoral lackies, preoccupied with the winning of seats at national and local elections'. (*British working class politics*, p. 249.) In the instructions from the Labour Party executive to which reference has already been made there is a characteristic definition of political parties in Britain

The internal structure of the party had for a number of decades been evolving towards a situation in which overall political and organisational power was concentrated in the hands of a relatively small elite, while the grass-root organisations fell into decay. In certain respects this process was reminiscent of the phenomena already described in our analysis of the structure of the trade union movement—at least with regard to the structural factors which have produced these trends. Yet at the same time the process we are concerned with here differed from those phenomena primarily in that it could not go as far as could a similar process within the trade union structure. The reason is that the centralisation of power within the unions was connected with the takeover by headquarters of virtually all the important functions of the local organisations. In the case of the Labour Party, however, such a state of affairs cannot arise, since the local organisations must continue to get votes, something which Transport House cannot do for them. Yet in spite of this qualification one should stress two circumstances which help to restrict the role of the party's mass organisation. First, the local branches had come to limit their role almost exclusively to vote-getting. Their functions had become increasingly one-sided, and in reality only this single function remained of the many political organisational and publicity functions which were once the tasks of the local branches of the ILP. Second, this single remaining function had been passing more and more into the hands of professional party agents, who were delegated by and directly responsible to party headquarters. The local parties thus became auxiliaries to the agents appointed by headquarters. Both these circumstances conduced to the withering away of Labour's grass-roots organisations. Since the Parliamentary Labour Party had become established and the rough overall distribution of political sympathies within the electorate had become stabilised, the local organisations became increasingly insignificant. In safe seats, indeed, they had virtually no importance at all, because the choice of the candidate endorsed by the party was almost automatic, and required hardly any electoral activity. In short the Labour Party has become more and more an established mass organisation serving the electoral requirements of the elite. This description is, of course, schematic but it does indicate the predominant trend.

This trend has produced a steady increase in the power of the elite at one pole and a decrease in the active participation of rank-and-file party members at the other. No great inducement to active participation derived from the limited possibilities left to them for influencing developments within the party or from the tasks left to them to carry out, although party

as 'voluntary associations of like minded *electors*' [my italics]. (Croft, *The conduct of Parliamentary affairs*, p. 1.)

leaders often complained of the passivity of the rank-and-file and exhorted them to take a more responsible attitude to party affairs. Here one should point out that the criteria of membership in the Labour Party are extremely vague by comparison with other parties in the West, including the social democratic parties. In the Labour Party the distinction between the category of 'member' and that of 'voter' is extremely blurred, something which diminishes still further the active participation of rank-and-file party members. In the French socialist party (the SFIO) one member would bring in eleven voters, while in the German and Dutch parties the ratio would be roughly ten non-member voters to one member, in the Swiss and Norwegian three to one and in the Danish, Swedish and Austrian parties two to one. In the British Labour Party, however, there is an average of only one non-party voter to each party member—the lowest proportion among all the European social democratic parties.[1] In this connection it should be remembered that a considerable majority of Labour Party members belong to the party in more or less automatic fashion, as members of trade unions. The general atmosphere of passivity which prevails in the local trade union organisations is also reflected in the attitudes of the same people in the party organisations, from which they are even more cut off than they are from their trade unions. The involuntary nature of the membership of a large section of Labour rank and file was shown in 1927, when the system by which everyone belonging to a union automatically became a member of the party unless he applied in writing to opt out was reversed with union members having to 'opt in' for party membership by written application. Labour Party membership fell at once from 3·2 million to 2 million. In 1946 the original system was reintroduced, and overall membership jumped from 2·6 million to 4 million. In each case over a million trade unionists were not sufficiently concerned about their party affiliations to put pen to paper. The apathy of ordinary party members has also been illustrated by more direct indications drawn from surveys of various local organisations. For example, the studies of party organisations in Gorton, Manchester, by Donnison and Plowman in 1953 showed that in the preceding half-year period barely 19 per cent of members had attended even one meeting. Fifty per cent of members could not name any of their town councillors, only 17 per cent knew the names of all three Labour councillors, and nobody could name all four Cabinet Ministers who were the subject of enquiries in the questionnaire.[2] The survey produced one more interesting result. It appeared that the range of difference in political views, in so far as such views were defined at all,

1 Duverger, *Political parties*, p. 95.
2 D. V. Donnison and D. E. G. Plowman, 'The functions of local Labour Parties',
   Political Studies, June 1954, pp. 162–3.

was much greater within the Labour Party than amongst the Conservative rank and file. While 84 per cent of Conservative Party members gave the same answer to various political queries, the same applied to only 63 per cent of Labour members in Gorton and 57 per cent in the nearby town of Glossop.[1]

These figures seem to indicate that, in the same sort of way as with the trade unions, the party organisations have a minimal associational role. The limited, strictly electoral basis of the organisations conceals a considerable range of attitudes in all other spheres, and precludes both the need for and the possibility of securing a greater degree of unity in matters not concerned with elections. During the last four decades or so an increase in political activity among the rank and file has been noted only in times of crisis: one instance was the period immediately after the first world war, when the pressure of special external circumstances goaded the working class into a readiness for action which was lacking in normal periods.

To sum up, it may be said that during the decades under scrutiny both wings of the labour movement—the trade unions and the Labour Party—displayed all the phenomena which indicate a state of structural stabilisation. This stability was far deeper and more lasting than that manifested in the third quarter of the nineteenth century by the 'new model' unions. It would appear that the most important element in the present stabilisation is the function of the labour movement as a channel of vertical social mobility, complementing in the intragenerational sphere the channels of individual social mobility between the generations set up by the structure of modern economic capitalism. Another factor of stabilisation has been the rising socio-economic status of the working class as a whole, brought about both by changes in the structure of the economy and also by the achievements of the labour movement. For this reason it will not be inappropriate to end this chapter with an analysis of the role of the contemporary labour movement in Britain as a channel of individual mobility within a single generation.

From the viewpoint of social mobility the labour movement performs a twofold function. On the one hand it is concerned with raising or maintaining the socio-economic status of the working class as a whole—in the extended sense of the term. This function comprises activities concerned with wage levels, the length of the working day, employee welfare measures at work, management–labour relations, factory legislation, social security, and so on. On the other hand, the labour movement is concerned with security and advancement for individuals through the appropriate machinery, both from one generation to another and within a

[1] D. E. G. Plowman, 'Allegiance to political parties', *Political Studies*, October 1955, p. 226.

single generation. The former is pursued mainly by pressing for a more egalitarian educational system; the latter chiefly through the channels of advancement available within the labour movement. At the same time there is pressure to raise the social status and prestige of the occupations of trade union or party officials, so that promotion in the union or party hierarchy should also constitute an advancement on the general scale of status and prestige and should lead to key positions in the ruling economic and political elite of the country.

As regards the first function, the activities of the unions and the political organisation in the sphere of material well-being and national social services are well known and have been described frequently, both from the angle of its achievements and from that of its limitations. It is, however, worth while drawing attention to those elements in the rise in socio-economic status of the working class which derive from the actual increase of activity by the trade union movement, independently of results. I am referring here to the new kind of industrial relations achieved by the unions, not without the co-operation of members of the economic power elite; the new industrial relations are based on relatively wide powers for workers' representatives in many industrial matters. This factor, which is directly linked with the active operations of the labour organisations, has probably made an important contribution to the improvement of the workers' socio-economic status.

As for the second function, the new type of industrial relations has opened up a fairly wide field for individual upward mobility within a single generation. In conditions where the channel linking manual jobs with positions higher in the technical and supervisory machinery has become increasingly blocked, or works only between one generation and another, the new relationships in industry constitute an alternative mechanism of great efficiency. The Joint Councils and the large number of sub-committees which exist in thousands of industrial establishments of various sizes bring about half a million trade unionists together at the same table with management, and give them some feeling of having a voice in matters of economic consequence.[1] The entrance to the intragenerational channel of upward mobility, objective or subjective, is thus exceptionally wide, and on the whole adequate to satisfy ambitious individuals within the labour force. This does not make much difference to the living conditions of the unambitious worker, but he is impressed and feels his own worth enhanced by the fact that the political heights have been scaled by such men as 'the engine-driver [who] rose to the rank of Colonial Secretary, a starveling clerk [who] became Great Britain's Premier, a foundry

1   J. I. Roper, *Joint consultation and responsibility in modern industry*, Workers' Educational Association, Study Outlines No. 19, London, 1950, pp. 66–7.

hand [who] was changed to Foreign Secretary, the son of a Keighley weaver [who] was created Chancellor of the Exchequer, one miner [who] became Secretary for War and another Secretary of State for Scotland'.[1] The myth of the worker who becomes a Cabinet Minister has taken over from that of the shoe-black who made himself a millionaire.

The full-time union machinery in Britain is not particularly developed in comparison with, for instance, that in the United States. Moreover, as I have already pointed out many times, there are frequent signs of hardening arteries at the high levels of the trade union hierarchy, which impedes the upward mobility of the elite within the union movement and restricts the flow of new blood. In spite of this, and contrary to views frequently expressed, detailed studies have shown clearly that there is a relative balance between supply and demand in the British trade union set-up, taken as a whole; and furthermore that in many cases the number of union posts available exceeds the demand for them. For instance, the number of local branches in the National Union of General and Municipal Workers has been continually increasing, together with the average number of members in a branch; in consequence there has also been an increase in the number of posts available for branch secretaries, who are released from their ordinary jobs and paid out of union funds. H. A. Clegg wrote, 'There is not usually any difficulty in obtaining a place on the branch committee. Sometimes the difficulty is to find members who are willing to serve.'[2] The reasons for this state of affairs, noted by Clegg and others, are probably similar to those which make it difficult to find people willing to take on positions in the lower levels of technical supervision, i.e. the decreasing pressure to seek advancement following upon the rising status of the working population as a whole and the distracting effect of mechanisms for individual inter-generational mobility. In consequence, even the relatively modest size of the trade unions' organisational machinery is on the whole adequate to maintain a balance between the existing pressures towards upward mobility and the labour movement's ability to satisfy them (although there are naturally some exceptions). In this connection we should not forget that, in the vast majority of cases, the path to the highest levels of the trade union hierarchy, which now rank very high in the national hierarchy, starts at the lowest levels, where local branch officials are usually recruited, from whom in turn the headquarters staffs are drawn.

I have already referred to the social status attaching to the highest positions in the union hierarchy. Here it should be added that today these positions do not *per se* set the limits to the career of a trade union leader.

1   Clynes, *Memoirs*, I, p. 17.
2   Clegg, *General union*, p. 39.

Today the highest levels of the union hierarchy lead to the upper levels of other hierarchies—to Parliament and Ministerial posts or, on a considerably wider range, to the many joint advisory and other similar committees, where the economic elite is to be found.[1] Positions in the central advisory and consultative committees provide a platform on which the trade union elite is brought together with the other elements of the economic power elite, those which direct the capitalist economy of the country.

1   Roper, in *Joint consultation*, gives a list of the committees of which union representatives are members, which includes the following:

   1   *General committees*

       The National Joint Advisory Council (attached to the Minister of Labour)
       The Central Joint Advisory Committee (attached to the Minister of Supply)
       The Central Joint Advisory Committee (attached to the Minister of Fuel and
           Power)
       Committee on Building Materials and Process
       Central Price Regulation Committee
       Service Departments' Committee on Manpower Economy
       National Insurance Advisory Committee
       Colonial Labour Advisory Committee
       Colonial Economic and Development Council
       Economic Planning Board.

   2   *Specialised Industrial Committees*

       Civil Aviation Consultation Board
       Iron and Steel Board
       Shipbuilding Advisory Council
       Railways Joint Consultative Council
       Mines Consultative Council
       Building Trade National Consultative Council
       Agricultural Machinery Advisory Council
       British Transport Joint Council
       National Coal Board Consultative Council
       Post Office and Civil Service Whitley Council
       Building Trade Joint Council
       National Maritime Board
       National Dock and Labour Board
       Printing Trade Joint Council.

(Kuczynski, *British trade unionism*, pp. 114 *et seq.*; Roper, *Joint consultation*, pp. 17–18.) Even wider prospects of advancement for the trade union vanguard are offered by the nationalisation of various branches of the economy. In 1950, after a round of nationalisation by the Labour government, the national boards of the newly State-owned branches of industry contained nine full-time directors and seven part-time members drawn from the trade union movement. The salaries for full-time directors were high, ranging from £3,500 to £5,000 per annum, and their status equalled that of directors of the largest industrial groups. (*Nationalised industry: the men on the boards*, pp. 6–14.)

After outlining the opportunities offered by the trade union movement, one should add those which are available through the political section of the labour movement. Both kinds of opportunity are, after all, inter-connected—in contrast to the position in the United States, the functioning of the union machinery as a channel into the economic elite is closely dependent on the power of the Labour Party. The latter gives a substantial section of prominent trade union leaders the possibility of obtaining public or political posts which carry considerable prestige and a high social status. Here also the supply of posts frequently exceeds the demand—the present leaders of the Labour Party have difficulty in finding enough trade union MPs to fill an adequate proportion of places in the shadow Cabinet, although—as we shall see later—it is extremely important for the function-ing of the party to maintain the proper proportions.

To sum up, we find a link between the lowest levels of the hierarchy of the labour movement and the highest levels of the hierarchy of economic and political power. The connecting channel grows narrower towards the top but is wide at the bottom; and in consequence of the gradual extension of means for individual mobility between one generation and the next it satisfies existing needs in principle. The same situation has worked to neutralise one of the most important factors which promote conflict and nonconformist attitudes. Those who could form a potential elite to lead a nonconformist movement are successfully assimilated by the existing social hierarchy, based on the capitalist socio-economic system. The state of equilibrium between the movement's machinery for advancement and working class pressures to move upwards, which has been achieved within the existing social order, is the basis of the growing consolidation and conservatism of the movement and the reason for its lost dynamism.

To quote Gordon Lewis, the labour movement, which was revolutionary in origin, has finally produced what is simply a welfare State in which, as with the middle classes after 1832, a working class elite has been admitted into the ranks of a selective governing group.[1]

1   'The present condition of British political parties', p. 235.

3

The structure of the elite
of the labour movement

The period of consolidation with which we are concerned in Part IV has seen the further evolution and logical development of the same trends which were operating in the previous historical period. This period of consolidation was the outcome of the growth of a mass movement, preceded by the articulation of the class on an occupational basis and the social legitimisation of the role of trade unionist which we noted during the period in which the union movement grew to maturity.

The same also applies to the evolution of the elite of the movement. During the period we are now concerned with the same trends can be found in this evolution as were observed in the previous period—but expressed in a more complete and determined manner. We have the creation of the occupation of trade union official, a setting up of its own administration hierarchy; the bureaucratisation of that occupation; the creation of a separate and fairly independent elite within the political labour movement; and the extension of the class base of the elite. The new feature in the present period, a feature which makes this phase a distinct one in the history of the labour elite, is the final transformation of that elite into an integral part of the overall economic and political power elite of British society.

The union movement's need for consolidation and continuity has been intensified by the increasingly complex tasks which it is performing. In response to this need, the movement's elite has continued to evolve in the same direction as before, transforming itself into a team of prudent, sober and solid businessmen, concerned with the needs of the organisations which they lead and avoiding Utopian notions which could endanger their principal task, that of preserving the unity of the trade union machinery. The typical union leader has been moving further and further away from the models of the leaders of the new unionism at the end of the nineteenth century. He is not, however, returning to the model of the leadership of the old movement in the third quarter of that century. Like the generation of Allan and Applegarth, the new leaders belong to the category of administrators. One of them, Norman McKillop, wrote that he had often wondered

> why the imaginative fiction writer so often depicts the old-time—and not seldom the modern—trade union leader as a lank, cadaverous, burning-eyed, shrieking caricature of a human being, whose hand is against everyone

in authority, who spews hatred, and in whose vocabulary the main word is 'no'. Nothing could be further from the real picture. Nothing could be more repellent to the fellows with whom I've been in close contact for over three decades.[1]

Like other leaders of this category, the trade union leader of today is successful if he is not of a different calibre from the rank-and-file members of his union; if he is not an unusual individual but an ordinary man with the traits of an ordinary man, somewhat enhanced. He should think in such a way that the men whom he leads get the impression that his thinking runs on similar lines to theirs, but is somewhat more penetrating. Yet ordinary traits which are enhanced cease to be ordinary, although they continue to appear so. The elite possesses qualifications which the average member of a trade union organisation does not and cannot possess. Yet they are at the same time qualifications of a similar type to his own and therefore intelligible to him. This is a characteristic of the category of administrators as a whole. But in the case of the post-war union leadership it was more clearly evident than in the day of Allan and Applegarth. For the new generation had to apply the qualities of sober judgment, prudence, common sense and business instinct to problems that are much more large-scale and complex than anything which faced Broadhurst or Howell, Odger, or Coulson.

The post-war elite of the union movement was the creation of the union structure, which determined its form and characteristics. As it has become more established the trade union movement has increasingly shaped its elite in its own image. This is not just a figure of speech. Today the movement has a monopoly of the acquisition of the skills which are essential if one is to reach a leading position within it. The personality of a member of the union elite is not formed outside the movement or independently of it. It is rather rare to encounter cases like those which were so frequent half a century ago, in which an individual with a strong character and a ready-made capacity for leadership would, by virtue of his personal qualities, take over the still flexible union structure. Today the future trade union leader usually enters the union apparatus as an apprentice, just as the future manager of a private firm often starts as one of the many junior clerks in a large office. The aspirant to union leadership has to pass through a tough training school at the grass roots of the trade union machine. He has to face the usual phases of apprenticeship and when this ends gradually acquire traits which cannot be acquired in any other way, but which are an essential condition if he is to reach the heights of a trade union career. The personality of a member of the union elite is shaped

1 McKillop, *The lighted flame*, p. 31.

at the lower and middle levels of the trade union hierarchy.[1] The road to
the top runs through the strictly hierarchical machinery of professional
trade union officials. In this sense one can state that the trade union
machinery, in the present phase of its development, possesses the monopoly
of skills, having become their exclusive distributor. The genetic dependence
of the elite on the structure of the movement has never been so great
nor—it may even be said—so complete. In this respect we can note an
entirely new phase of evolution in the history of the British labour movement. In the present stage of consolidation the union movement has continued to recreate its elite in the same form, following consistently cultivated models, while the consolidation of the union machinery is a guarantee
of the continuity of elite characteristics.

A number of writers have noted that this union monopoly is instinctively
protected by the suspicious attitude with which the milieu of full-time trade
union officials regards those active unionists who have more than average
education. The trade union organisation is opposed to any transformation
of the union elite into an elite of education. Such an elite would automatically owe its privileged position to factors outside the structure of the
movement, even though its social position would be determined in its
essence by the monopoly of skills and would remove from the union
organisation its decisive role of regulating the turnover of the trade union
elite. The trade union machinery is still the domain of individual intragenerational upward mobility. It provides the way to a career for workers
who show special abilities of the kind needed to produce qualified trade
union leaders but lack the formal education which would enable them to
make a career in the outside world, such as would afford their children
the chance of advancement. This characteristic of the British trade union
movement is exceptionally long-lasting and difficult to undermine, for
reasons which include the fact that the movement has its political branch,
the Labour Party, which provides an outlet for workers with qualifications
based on education.[2]

To sum up, the men at the head of the trade union movement today
form a rather compact and homogeneous social group, linked by a common social status, uniform origins and similar career opportunities.

1   B. C. Roberts, *Trade union government and administration in Great Britain*, Bell, London,
    1956, p. 303.
2   It is worth noting that in the United States, where there is no party of labour and
    thus no broad channel of political advancement for people of working class origin,
    the setting up of the CIO in the 1930s undermined the monopoly of skills main-
    tained within the AFL gerontocracy. The latter, like today's British trade unions,
    looked askance at well educated candidates for jobs in the union administration.
    The CIO, in contrast, based its hierarchical ladder on achievement. (Wright Mills,
    The new men of power, pp. 68–73.)

Almost all the union leaders have been recruited from working class families. Almost every one of them has done manual work, although over a very short period in comparison with their predecessors half a century ago. Hardly any of them have much education. In practice virtually all of them have reached their high positions in the unions and in society by climbing step by step up the successive rungs of the official trade union hierarchy. These shared traits determine their community of interests, views and general attitudes. On the other hand, the nature of these common characteristics determines the union leaders' exceptional attachments to the system which served as a ladder for their ascent and now functions as a structure on which they base the high social status they have attained. It is not true that the specific interests of the group of leaders could collide in any way with those of the organisations they lead. On the contrary, the union leaders have no other means of increasing their own power than by reinforcing the organisations at whose head they stand—just as the directors of a large industrial or financial combine can show concern for their own position only by seeking to ensure the prosperity of the firm of which they are in charge. In this way the identity of interests is almost automatically regulated. This mechanism operates much more efficiently than democratic control of the administration by rank-and-file workers. As Allen rightly comments, 'Trade union officials who can regularly announce wage increases need fear nothing from recalcitrant rank-and-file members.'[1] Union leaders strengthen their personal power by increasing the benefits rank-and-file members derive from belonging to the organisation. The size of the dividend is a justification of the efficiency of the leaders, but it is also the basis of the power of the machinery they are in charge of.

The kinship between this type of work and social ties leads to links between union leaders and leaders in the world of industry and commerce who meet and work together in everyday life. Lees Smith has perceived an elusive similarity between a meeting of professional trade union officials and a conference of management representatives; he pointed out that in recent years friendly relationships have evolved between union leaders and managers of private industry. Today men from what were once two opposing camps often call each other by their first names and maintain contacts which are not solely official.[2] The union structure has not only produced a homogeneous social group of union leaders but has brought the latter closer to those who occupy key positions at the top of the business hierarchy. The two differing components of the economic

1 Allen, *Power in trade unions*, p. 21.
2 H. B. Lees Smith, *Trade unionism*, Christian Social Union pamphlet No. 9, p. 11.

power elite come together on the basis of their organisational and administrative links. Similarities of organisational structure and personal dependence have created an atmosphere of mutual understanding between
the two contracting parties at the negotiating table and have taught them
to use a common language. This circumstance has reinforced still further
the need for amicable joint conciliation machinery between the employers
and the labour organisations. The union elite's all-round dependence on the
consolidation of the union machinery has caused it to feel a far-reaching
loyalty towards the trade union organisation. The well-being of the organisation, conceived of in terms of the administration's efficiency, takes first
place in every deliberation. Obtaining better conditions for the sale of their
members' labour is the only way to strengthen the unions.

Nonetheless the security and stability of the organisation constitute
the principal care and concern of the average union leader.[1] One can cite
many contemporary instances to bear out the assertion that the function
of getting more for the union's members retreats into second place at
moments of crisis: the permanent task is the continuing consolidation of
the organisation. The greatest trade union leaders of this period, like
Ernest Bevin, were distinguished by the fact that they put the solidarity
of the organisation higher than the outcome of any specific dispute over
wages; they were ruthless in their endeavours to inculcate the union
organisations with an ironclad solidarity and the draconian methods of an
absolute hierarchical discipline.[2] In pursuit of this goal the union elite has
made use of the model evolved in private business administration. Their
efforts have been directed to creating a climate in union offices which
would resemble atmosphere of concentration and purposefulness which
prevails in commercial and industrial administrations. The printers'
leader, G. Isaacs, who finally pushed his union on to a modern course,
firmly insisted that his subordinates should wear starched collars and ties.[3]
Trade union officials seek to resemble office workers and their superiors
in business administration in dress as well as other matters.

The resemblance is not confined to outward appearance, nor even to
ways of thinking and looking at social reality and the functions which are
performed in both milieux. An unusual similarity may also be noted in
the lives of those who aspire to a career in union administration or in
business. In both cases these careers are in all basic features white-collar
ones. They lead from one office to another, from lower clerical positions
to higher ones—strictly following an established, rigid bureaucracy. In

1   Harbison and Coleman, *Goal and strategy in collective bargaining*, p. 13; A. M. Ross,
    Trade union wage policy, University of California Press, Berkeley, 1948, p. 43.
2   Williams, *Ernest Bevin*, p. 114.
3   Eastwood, *George Isaacs*, p. 69.

both cases the same kinds of traits are a help or a hindrance in one's career. Speed or promotion depends on obedience to superiors and an ability to demonstrate one's own lack of personal opinions and ideas. What counts are the qualities needed for desk work. Any other qualities are a hindrance to promotion, as is any kind of originality. The resemblance between the machinery of promotion has in both cases produced—at least in the majority of cases—the same defensive reactions, and favours the development of particular traits of character and the disappearance of others in both groups. It has become increasingly hard to distinguish between professional trade union officials and the general run of white-collar and administrative workers.[1]

The majority of the leading trade union figures in recent decades have reached the top by successive steps of the administrative hierarchy. In the Transport and General Workers' Union, Ben Tillett, the leader of the masses, was succeeded by Ernest Bevin. Bevin, a mineral-water rounds-man in his youth, became a union official at a very early age, starting low down but rising steadily to higher posts. His active participation in numerous successful negotiations and arbitration settlements attracted considerable attention, and each successive achievement gave him a boost upwards. Simultaneously he proceeded on a systematic and long-term basis to create inside the union's headquarters staff something in the nature of a personal entourage—a team of full-time officials whom he selected from the rank-and-file workers, trained and treated with special favour. In periods of normal trade union work the members of this team, who were completely his men, carried out his orders obediently; at moments of crisis they provided him with unfailing support in his struggle with active or potential competitors. Bevin was the first in this union to blaze a trail from the post of assistant general secretary[2] to that of general secretary. His successors

1 What difference is there between the account of the machinery for promotion in the NUMGW described by H. A. Clegg and that of the same machinery in any large private office? 'Promotion from the office staff [to the post of union secretary] is also a fairly natural method of selection. The members of the staff must join the union and are, therefore, eligible. They acquire a wide knowledge of the union and its activities from their work, and the district secretary and committees have ample opportunity to form an estimate of their qualities. On their side, capable and ambitious members of the staff are likely to regard such promotion as the only means of "getting on" in their job. Officers selected in this way are unlikely to have direct experience of industry, and their promotion is frequently criticized on these grounds. The reply is that today a considerable part of the work of a trade union officer is administrative, and for that they have been better trained than the lay member, and that many of those promoted in this way have quickly picked up sufficient knowledge about industrial conditions and industrial processes to become capable negotiators'. (Clegg, *General union*, p. 78.)

2 Unlike the general secretary, his assistant is not elected: he is a full-time official, a

had the easier task of following in his footsteps. When Bevin went into
politics his place was filled by Arthur Deakin, who had been his assistant.
Deakin was followed by Frank Cousins, a trade union official for over
thirty years, and formerly Deakin's assistant. Another prominent trade
union leader of the post-war period, J. G. Baty, joined the Associated
Society of Locomotive Enginemen and Firemen at the age of seventeen.
At twenty he became a union official and moved upwards from branch to
district and thence to headquarters. When he was thirty-eight he became
general secretary of the union (1947), after which he returned to a key job
on the full-time headquarters staff. A similar course was followed by Isaacs
and many other leading figures in the post-war union movement. In
general, V. L. Allen estimates that out of sixty-eight known cases in which
assistant general secretaries contested elections to fill vacancies for the
position of general secretary there were only six cases of defeat.[1] Of the
general secretaries elected before 1920, 11 per cent had been assistant
general secretaries; but after 1920, as Allen's survey of forty-eight key
unions shows, up to 50 per cent of general secretaries were being drawn
from these posts. Furthermore, as many as 61 per cent went on to some sort
of administrative post at union headquarters.[2] Allen cites as typical the
career of G. B. Thorneycroft, of the Transport Salaried Staffs' Association.
He became general secretary after working as a personal clerk to the general
secretary, minute clerk to the executive council, chief clerk, LNER secretary,
senior assistant secretary and assistant general secretary.[3]

Senior trade union posts assure an extremely enduring social position
to those who hold them. The well-being of the union organisation—in
terms of both continuity and financial stability, as well as prestige—requires
that those who are in charge of it should have their terms of office extended
for as long as possible. Accordingly, there is also a tendency for those in the
top posts, with their high status, to remain in them as long as they can.
The outcome of these two factors is that in the majority of unions the
election of a general secretary is in practice final, while in some it is even
formally so. This means that, once elected, the general secretary remains
in office for as long as he gives satisfaction—in practice, for as long as he
himself wishes. In many cases union rules make no provision for removing
the general secretary, but the rules are not the real point here. Regardless
of them and any rules about periodic re-election procedures, general
secretaries do not on the whole relinquish their positions until they reach

  specialist in administration who is supposed to assure the operational continuity of
  the union machinery despite the changes of general secretary.
1 Allen, *Power in trade unions*, p. 202.
2 *Ibid.*, pp. 271 et seq.
3 *Ibid.*, p. 209.

pensionable age or move up into some sort of political post. Allen[1] writes that of 128 general secretaries belonging to twenty-four trade unions whose constitutions provide for periodic elections, an incumbent was defeated on only two occasions. The first was the work of Applegarth in 1862 and the second occurred in 1913. In eighty-six unions, however, with a total membership comprising 73·88 per cent of all TUC-affiliated unions, the constitutions do not provide for such elections. In the case of both categories of union the results have been similar. Re-election processes are in the majority of cases simply a formality, with nobody standing against the existing general secretary.[2]

The value of a union leader's position is not measured only in terms of the attributes of his position in the union machinery. During the period under consideration the trade union movement, together with the entire labour movement in Britain, has made an important leap forward in its evolution; and today its leadership occupies a high position in the social scale. The higher rungs of the union ladder lead to top political positions and to lucrative, prestigious jobs on high-powered mixed committees. They may also entitle those concerned to the highest honours—the titles and orders to which the average Briton responds so eagerly and which, in Britain as in no other capitalist country, have always vied with material wealth as determinants of the social prestige and even status of individuals. Isaacs wrote, 'I little thought when—as a boy with my father—I stood for hours to see Queen Victoria during the Diamond Jubilee celebrations, that when the next Queen came to the Throne I would be a Privy Councillor.'[3] Clynes saw in the Labour government of 1924 'the first fruits of that harvest for which Labour prophets and workers had toiled together throughout the past century'.[4] The distance covered by the labour movement was now measured not merely in terms of higher wages and more humane working conditions in the factories, nor even of education for the workers' children, but in terms of that form of advancement which was most conspicuous and most directly affected trade union

1　*Ibid.*, pp. 216–7.
2　This situation is not characteristic only of Britain. In a study of 2,307 cases of elections for high offices in unions in the United States, there was only one candidate in 76·8 per cent of the cases. (P. Taft, *The structure and government of labor unions*, Harvard University Press, Cambridge, Mass., 1954, p. 33.) Another study showed that in 764 elections in seven large unions over the years 1910–41 there was no opposition candidate in 83 per cent of cases. (Wright Mills, *The new men of power*, p. 64.) G. L. Berry was union president for over fifty years; William Mahon, William Hutchinson, D. B. Robertson, Sidney Hillman and others all stayed in office as union presidents for 25–30 years, without being called to face an electoral contest on a single occasion during that period.
3　Eastwood, *George Isaacs*, p. 218.
4　Clynes, *Memoirs*, I, p. 147.

officials: the sudden elevation to the political elite, the road to the heights of government and court, and the new and alluring style of life involved. When Arthur Henderson became a member of the Cabinet for the first time, in 1915, Beatrice Webb asked him what most impressed him about being a Cabinet Minister. He replied 'The number of things I used to have to do for myself which other people now do for me.'[1] But this was some time ago, when the period of consolidation had hardly begun. Today the special features of Ministerial office would not come as any surprise to the average trade union leader. To hold such an office is entirely within the scope of his lifetime plans and ambitions. It emerges clearly and precisely as a possible crown to his career and a fulfilment of his own aspirations for advancement.

The outrage with which the trade union movement greeted Burns' appointment to the government was quickly forgotten. Before twenty years had passed the majority of union leaders had come to regard a Ministerial post as a deserved distinction, almost as their rightful due. An increasing number of trade unionists became convinced that 'no Cabinet would be complete without them'.[2] When Ramsay MacDonald formed his first government in 1924 he had to increase the size of his Cabinet from fourteen to twenty because some influential union leaders refused to accept Ministerial posts which would not give them a place in the Cabinet.[3] After he had drawn up the final list of his second Cabinet in 1929 MacDonald complained to Dalton, 'It has been terrible. I have had people in here weeping and even fainting.'[4] Labour Cabinets have, as a rule, contained more members than Tory ones. A government post was the only outlet for the aspirations of the trade union and party elites, so that the pressures in that direction were exceptionally strong.

Some trade union leaders have rapturously absorbed the delights of the great world in which they suddenly found themselves living. There were some who favoured the style of life symbolised by J. R. Thomas, the railwaymen's leader, whom the cartoonist Lowe called the 'First Lord of the Boiled Shirt'.[5] This *bon vivant* and sybarite quickly made his way into aristocratic circles, where with disarming self-assurance he talked about peers and other titled notables without scruple or shame by their christian names, played the rough diamond and deliberately cultivated his lower class accent.[6] Thomas grasped with both hands the opportunities of a gay

1   Dalton, *Call back yesterday*, p. 147.
2   Smillie, *My life for labour*, p. 304.
3   *Beatrice Webb's diaries*, p. 263.
4   Dalton, *Call back yesterday*, p. 217.
5   Macneil Weir, *The tragedy of Ramsay MacDonald*, p. 265.
6   Nicholson, *The real men in public life*, p. 214.

life which were offered him. Others among his trade union colleagues celebrated their own private victories rather less boisterously; but in general, with few exceptions, they did not deny themselves the major and minor pleasures which their new social position conferred on them.

The negative, nonconformist attitude to the established hierarchy of social honours, based traditionally on class privileges and derived from them, was replaced by respectful acceptance and a decidedly conformist attitude towards that hierarchy from the moment it was opened up to trade union leaders as well. By accepting titles and honours from the Sovereign the union elite tacitly pledged itself to collaboration in the continuance and perpetuation of the system of privileges. In 1907 Randal Cremer was offered and accepted a knighthood, and in 1917 Shackleton also became a knight. In 1931 their example was followed by James Sexton, Ben Turner and Robert Young. This was only the beginning. In the years following the second world war, each New Year Honours List has included the names of a number of trade union leaders.[1] Men who were once factory workers prefix their names with the title of 'Sir', which sounds well in Anglo-Saxon ears, and immediately feel more secure at the top of the traditional social hierarchy. It is characteristic of the same process that while in 1935 Labour was still asking the electorate for a mandate to abolish the House of Lords, by 1945 it was stating merely that it would not tolerate obstruction from the upper House.[2] There was nothing surprising about this change, since a sizeable group of labour leaders had entered the upper House, where they shared the highest honours with the descendants of ancient families. Even those who showed personal modesty (Snowden, for instance, said, 'a peerage had no attraction for me'[3]) wrote glowing descriptions in their memoirs of the ceremony of introducing new members to the Chamber which was once reserved only for the most distinguished families.

The trade union elite has now attained complete and unrestricted access to all the honours and titles which are conferred by the country's system of social privilege. The aspirations of those individuals who are socially mobile within a single generation are also satisfied in this way. The elite working class activists make their way into the ranks of power and prestige supported by the strength of the trade union structure. To the ascendancy of prestige and status over wealth which has always prevailed in Britain one should probably attribute the significant fact that, although trade

---

1   V. L. Allen, 'The ethics of trade union leaders', *British Journal of Sociology*, December, 1956.
2   Hitchner, 'The Labour government and the House of Lords', *Western Political Quarterly*, December 1948, p. 426.
3   *An autobiography*, II, p. 1001.

union officials are paid considerably less than administrators in corresponding positions in private industry, there is little pressure to raise their
salaries to levels which would correspond to the social value of the qualifications which they possess and which are demanded of them. Many find
social recognition and an open door to social honours a recompense for the
prospect of relatively low pay.[1]

The new opportunities for advancement provided by the Labour
movement have not only influenced the fortunes of the union elite. They
have changed the structure of the elite of the labour movement as a whole,
and have considerably modified its social composition.

As has been said before, 1922 was the crucial year in the history of the
Labour Party. For the first time the Parliamentary Labour Party contained
not only professional trade unionists and a few 'declassed' socialists of
lower middle class origin but also individuals from upper middle and upper
class circles, including men who could be regarded as professional politicians. The party's new position as the official Opposition, and an alternative
government in a capitalist State, required leaders of a new type. The figure
of Ramsay MacDonald was to become a model for the party politicians of
the future—specialists in political manoeuvres and diplomacy. The party
also needed experts with specialised qualifications in economics, finance,
military matters and law. Such people could not be found among full-
time union officials. It was necessary to recruit them from non-working
class circles, from those with a university education, and from professions
such as the law, journalism and economics. On the other hand, an effective
bait for considerable sections of the middle classes was provided by the rise
in status of the working class, the respectability which it had acquired in
terms of the categories accepted by the ruling class, and the opportunities
which it now offered for a political career. The majority of the Conserva-

---

1   It is characteristic that in the United States, where the role of status in social life is
    minimal compared with Britain, and prestige is generally a function of material
    affluence, while union leaders receive no social privileges by virtue of their functions
    (O. W. Phelps, 'Community recognition of union leaders', *Industrial and Labor
    Relations Review*, April 1954, p. 432), social advancement in the unions is measured
    not by the awarding of social honours but by the amassing of a fortune. This is the
    source in part of the plague of labour racketeering (Seidman, *Labor czars*, p. 282),
    and also of the widespread corruption and betrayal of trade union interests for
    personal gain in the American labour movement (in Britain trade union and per-
    sonal interests are indivisible). This is the reason for the extremely high salaries
    drawn by American union leaders: for instance, $50,000 per annum for Lewis,
    $40,000 for Petrillo, $30,000 for Tobin, $20,000 for Murray, without including the
    many thousands of dollars drawn by them for personal expenses. (Wright Mills,
    The new men of power, p. 100.) For the American trade union leader, unlike his
    British colleague, the movement affords a mechanism for hoisting him up by
    means of making money.

tive leadership is drawn from people whose social position, usually a high one, is not owed to the party (i.e. they may be members of the economic elite, the descendants of eminent families, and so on). The members of the Labour Party elite, on the other hand, owe their elite status to their party function, or hope to achieve it by means of that function. Their jobs and their social position outside the party are in most cases too low to serve as a springboard for advancement to the heights of the political hierarchy. It is not, however, only people from a working class background who make their way up into the political elite by means of party functions.

The road taken by professionals from the middle classes differs from that followed by the trade unionists who have climbed doggedly rung by rung up the administrative ladder. Biographies of the intellectual nucleus of the Labour Party leadership show that in general the professional politicians do not serve an apprenticeship in insignificant party posts. It is no accident that the lower levels of the administrative network in the Labour Party are considerably less developed than those in the trade union movement. Professional politicians, those who finally reach a really high level in the party hierarchy, generally move directly into high party posts. Their credentials for this are not their previous services, rendered to the party in day-to-day work, nor an impeccable administrative career within the party, but high qualifications in specialised fields of political importance. They have usually joined the ranks of the Parliamentary Labour Party without having performed any party functions. Their promotion to the front bench also depends on the extent of their Parliamentary expertise, not on the support of the administrative machinery or on administrative service. They have not, however, joined the party, as the Fabians did at the turn of the century, to fertilise it with ideas thought up in an exclusive and select circle of intellectuals. Instead they have enlisted in the service of a solid and compact party machine, receiving in return opportunities for a personal career.

The first leader of the party who originated from this social group was Clement Attlee. He came from a typical English middle class family which was moving up the social scale. His grandfather was a miller and corn merchant, who left his highly successful business to two of his sons, set another two up as the owners of large breweries, put the fifth into the Church after sending him to university, and established the sixth in a firm of solicitors. This last was Clement Attlee's father, an extremely able lawyer, who rapidly increased the capital which he inherited and made a considerable fortune. In 1906 he was elected president of the Incorporated Law Society. Some years before that he had bought Comarques, a large, late seventeenth century property built by a Huguenot captain of that name. There 'they lived in modest middle class comfort.' One of the governesses of Clement's sisters was a Miss Hutchinson, who had previously been governess in the household of Lord Randolph Churchill. Attlee has described the attitude which he acquired at home. 'I was . . . a Conservative . . . The "gentlemanly party" was to me far preferable . . . I thought then that quite definitely only gentlemen were fit to govern. I believed in the legend of the white man's burden . . . The well-to-do were for the most part where they were because of their virtue.'

Attlee's biographer, Roy Jenkins, had little doubt that his change of political orientation was influenced by the Liberal victory in 1906 and the consequent emergence of a sizeable labour group in Parliament. The fact is that Attlee was far from holding any ideas of a socialist persuasion when, after qualifying at the Bar, he became interested in and later manager of Haileybury House, a settlement in Limehouse supported by his own old school. Attlee was profoundly influenced by the poverty which he saw all round him in the East End of London and expressed his concern in articles which he sent to labour journals. Nevertheless, to quote his biographers, there was 'nothing of the professional rebel' in Attlee. He differed fundamentally from the nineteenth century middle class militants who had denounced and attacked the class of their origin from the working class camp. His political viewpoint may be presented as a desire to maintain the middle class style of life, which he considered the best and the best suited to his compatriots, but also to extend it to those who lacked it. His moral indignation was rooted in the fact that not everyone in Britain could benefit from the blessings of bourgeois civilisation. His ideology was therefore one of philanthropic middle class style, elevated to the level of socialism. It was totally opposed in origin and values to the ideological views of Hyndman and other revolutionary intellectuals from a middle class background.

At the same time Attlee was building up a strong power base for his future political career. In the working class citadel of the East End he acquired a host of supporters, and gradually advanced to the leadership of the local party organisation, which guaranteed him a Parliamentary seat in the future. He was building up a strong position in one of the four major Labour Party strongholds, and could therefore look forward not only to a seat in Parliament but also to the support of an important party centre, which would be of tremendous help to him in his Parliamentary career. Thereafter, developments were relatively straightforward. Attlee was a calm, level-headed man who did not antagonise any of the rival groups within the Labour Party but was on equally good terms with all. His statements were carefully moderated so as to offend nobody. In the years following the crisis over MacDonald, Attlee was to emerge as the only one capable of obtaining the support of all the groupings and factions inside the party. He was thus something of a stop-gap leader, but once at the head of the party he displayed abilities and qualities which observers had not suspected him of possessing. He proved to be a highly efficient organiser and a consummate politician, a clever diplomat and a tough administrator. In the outcome he was transformed from a stop-gap leader into a genuine one, firmly seated in the saddle and gathering all the reins of party influence in his hands. For his whole period of office as leader of the Labour Party he had in effect no rivals.[1]

The career of Attlee's successor, Hugh Gaitskell, virtually duplicated that of Attlee, but in a greatly accelerated tempo and accentuated form. Moreover, the process went further in his case. Like Attlee, Gaitskell came from a well-to-do middle class family. He took a degree in economics and gradually became an expert in economic matters and a popular lecturer at the London School of Economics. There he frequented Labour intellectual circles, but was only loosely involved with the party and did no active work in it. His political career started almost accidentally when, after the outbreak of the second world war, at the suggestion of a former colleague at the university, Hugh Dalton, he went to work in the Ministry of Economic Warfare set up by Churchill's coalition government. For most of the war he was Dalton's right-hand man at the Ministry, and later, on Dalton's advice, decided to leave the civil service and go into politics.

In 1945 he was elected MP for Leeds South and within months he was a Junior Minister and by 1947 he became Minister of Fuel and Power. A man who only a few years earlier was entirely unknown in the political arena was moving rapidly to the heights of the party hierarchy, on the basis of a civil service and Parliamentary career, without even any of the emotional motifs still apparent in the biography of Attlee. Gaitskell had the same qualities and diplomatic talents which made his predecessors successful, and after Attlee's retirement he emerged as the only person capable of securing the support of the most influential groups within the party. After he became leader, Gaitskell also showed himself a master of the art of directing the party machine. He won the support of all the influential circles within the party in turn by means of compromise and a share of party posts. (He was able to emerge victorious—not only unscathed but in fact climbing to further heights of power and influence—from the dramatic crisis of 1960. Having succeeded, as the only politician of sufficient status to be able to do it, in uniting all factions of the party, Gaitskell seemed to have reached the summit of his career when he died in 1963.)

Attlee and Gaitskell were, in their time, examples of the sizeable group of professionals who have been joining the Labour Party, where they got

1   The information about Attlee is drawn mainly from his own memoirs and Roy Jenkins' biography *Mr Attlee*, Heinemann, London, 1948.

on much more easily than the trade union leaders and also much more easily than those from the same class origins as themselves who set out to make a career in the Conservative Party. This was the course pursued by Hugh Dalton, the son of the tutor of King George V, who later became canon of St George's Chapel, Windsor. After the first world war he decided not to go back to the Bar. 'I had lost my barrister's wig and forgotten nearly all my law. It would, I thought, be a slow and speculative business . . .'[1] Instead he opted for a political career, and made rapid progress within the Labour Party. A similar path was followed by another scion of a wealthy middle class family, Stafford Cripps, Labour's 'wonder child'. His party career advanced by leaps and bounds punctuated only by gaps due to left-wing deviations.

The professionals are not the only group who have moved in to fill leading positions in the Labour Party. In 1945–50 the Parliamentary Labour Party included at least twenty-four MPs with important City connections. John Diamond, a figure of some influence in the party, had been a director of sixteen large companies.[2] Most of the middle class activists, however, were drawn from rather less well-to-do strata than those in the Conservative Party.

A relatively small group in the Labour Party of this period consisted of intellectuals of the type of Maxton, who harked back to the Keir Hardie tradition, which had now receded into the background. When it was discovered that he was using *Das Kapital* as a textbook for his class on citizenship 'the class was brought to a sudden end . . . by the authorities'. Later he was jailed for disseminating anti-war propaganda. He failed in his first attempt to enter Parliament but during his campaign won his victorious Liberal opponent over to the Labour Party. Like Lansbury, he called the Prime Minister of the day a murderer in the House of Commons. Every speech he made in the House created a sensation. After MacDonald's betrayal he took the ILP out of the Labour Party, making the confident assertion that within five years he would win a Parliamentary majority for the ILP. He was greatly loved by the Scottish workers—the section of the British working class which remained under-privileged and militant for the longest period. He was not, however, the proper kind of politician for a party which had become one of two alternating teams of administrators in a capitalist State.[3] But neither was he typical of the professional and other non-working class elements which were entering the Labour Party during that period.

1   Dalton, *Call back yesterday*, p. 103.
2   'Cross-bencher', 'The proletariat of Westminster', *Sunday Express*, 1948–49.
3   The information about Maxton is drawn mainly from J. MacNair, *James Maxton*, Allen & Unwin, London, 1955.

As the facilities for individual mobility between the generations developed, the composition of the group of professionals inside the Labour Party has ceased to be uniform in terms of social origin. The intellectuals of middle class beliefs and origins at the head of the party have been joined by a considerable group of working class intellectuals, people of working class origins who have, by means of the educational system, entered occupations which qualify them for this stratum. This group has not generally gone through any trade union training and has joined the party leadership without the backing of union connections. MacDonald's second Cabinet contained several men of this type—Will Graham, Arthur Greenwood, George Lansbury, Tom Johnston—workers by origin but not trade unionists, working class intellectuals who entered the Labour movement's elite simply by virtue of their party political activities. Because of this group and that of the trade unionists the social composition of the Labour Party elite differs from that of the elites of other British parties, despite the overall trend for the groups to become socially closer.

In general, however, regardless of social origins, the fact that both parties in Parliament operate within the framework of the same social system, on the basis of their acceptance of the same, constitutional, principles, has led to the gradual creation of a type of professional politician which is common to both parties. Such a politician derives his livelihood mainly from his political activities, regarding politics as his lifetime profession and the only road for his personal advancement. In Parliament, where all MPs are 'honourable', all lawyers 'learned' and all peers 'noble',[1] two MPs of different parties have, as Robert de Jouvenal expresses it, more in common with each other than an MP has with an ordinary member of his own party. The group of professional politicians which holds the key positions within the national power elite maintains its internal political divisions but is becoming increasingly homogeneous in terms of the approved scales of values, ideas about the social good, views on methods of realising political goals and, lastly, an ability to understand one another's differing viewpoints.[2] There have in the history of British politics been close and cordial friendships like the one which grew up between the leaders of the two rival parties, Winston Churchill and Clement Attlee. There is also the well known mutual respect which existed between Lord Halifax and Ernest Bevin.[3] Such relations are found *en masse* at lower levels. The barriers that once divided the professional middle class Parliamentarian from the uneducated working class MP have been broken down once for all. Thus Conservative and Labour MPs, while they are

1 W. I. Jennings, *Parliament*, Cambridge University Press, 1948, p. 19.
2 Finer, *The British civil service*, p. 9.
3 T. Evans, *Strange fighters, we British*, Hale, London, 1941, pp. 95 *et seq.*

divided during debates by the inextinguishable professional antagonism which exists between government and opposition, are coming to form a single unit whenever Parliamentary procedure does not prevent them.[1]

Elsewhere[2] I have given a statistical description of the changing composition of the Labour Party elite in terms of social origin, education and first job after leaving school. I studied the biographies of seventy-seven leading figures in the Labour Party over the last three decades [i.e. up to 1955]. These included Cabinet Ministers, front benchers, members of the Labour Party executive and chief whips. Twenty-seven of these were in

Table 27

Class origins of the Labour Party elite (per cent)

Categories	1925	1950	Percentage change
Working class	68	34	− 34
Lower middle class (white-collar, minor officials, small shopkeepers, Nonconformist clergy)	37	26	+ 19
Middle class	7	16	+ 9
Intelligentsia (professional)	7	18	+ 11
Landowners	11	6	− 5

positions of leadership in 1925, i.e. approximately in the period of the first Labour government; the remaining fifty occupied key positions in 1950, i.e. during the government of Clement Attlee. One group is roughly linked with the beginning of the period of stabilisation, the other with its later phase. Table 27 presents the comparative statistics.

Here one should note the considerable decrease in the proportion of individuals of working class origin and the great increase in the number of individuals from the lower middle and professional classes. In table 28 the most striking feature is undoubtedly the increase in the proportion of

1   This process is made much easier than in the United States (though not as much as in France or Italy) by the fact that in Britain there is the tradition of a career politician, an MP who is not a businessman but a professional politician. Whereas 61 per cent of those who held Cabinet office in the United States over the period 1889–1949 were businessmen, only 29 per cent of Cabinet Ministers in Britain in the years 1886–1950 belonged to this category, and the percentage is probably even lower now. The remainder are individuals whose hopes of making a career can be linked only with their activity in politics. (H. D. Lasswell, D. Lerner and C. E. Rothwell, *The comparative study of elites*, Stanford University Press, 1952, p. 30.)

2   Z. Bauman, 'The evolution of the elite of the English labour movement', *Studia socjologiczno-polityczne*, No. 1, 1958.

Table 28

The Labour Party elite: occupational status immediately after leaving school (per cent)

Categories	1925	1950	Percentage change
Manual labour	52	26	− 26
White-collar and clerical	26	18	− 8
Professional	11	44	+ 33
Commercial and industrial	11	12	+ 1

individuals who started off immediately in a variety of non-manual occupations, without spending a single year in a factory or mine. The large number in this group suggests that it must also have contained a certain number of people from a working class background. In this connection one is reminded once again of the operation of the administrative and managerial ladder of social mobility.

It is also worth recalling a fact which emerges from the biographies, i.e. that, of those members of the elite in 1950 whose first job after leaving school had been in a factory or mine, a considerable majority had not stayed there for more than five to eight years. Those in the earlier elite group who had been manual workers had remained in this category far longer. Generally, their advancement had proceeded slowly and laboriously via the unions, and they had attained their positions of leadership only late in life. Workers who have moved up into the elite in recent times have done so much more quickly than their predecessors.

There are some instructive data in table 29, which endeavours to present statistically not only a social profile of the elite but also the changes which occurred over these twenty-five years in the machinery for recruiting new members. I should point out that this table does not indicate that 36 per cent of the leading party figures in 1950 never performed any union or party functions at the lower or middle levels before they were elevated to the highest grouping in the party hierarchy. They were selected for the latter because of their expert qualifications and level of education, and because of experience gained outside the party, in business, the law and so on.

These statistics show that the features which made the Labour elite different from the elite of other political parties are gradually becoming blurred. The trend has been for the characteristics of the different elites to become standardised. There is an increasing number of people in the Labour elite whose origins are not working class; of people with an educa-

Table 29

The Labour Party elite: determinants of membership (per cent)

Category	1925	1950	Percentage change
Voluntary work for the party or union	23	–	− 23
Work in the party organisation	34	46	+ 12
Expert qualifications (economics, financial, legal)	4	18	+ 14
Election to Parliament prior to getting a party post	11	8	− 3
Political activity outside the party machine	28	28	–

tional background typical of the ruling class; and of people who, even though they come from a working class background, have either never done manual work or have done it for a rather shorter period. To be a professional requires a specialist training which has to begin early. To enter political life as an amateur is difficult for people whose occupations are remote from it, and does not produce satisfactory results.

Many statistical surveys of the composition of successive Parliamentary Labour Parties have shown the same trend at work, but to a somewhat lesser degree. The smaller and the closer to the top the elite group which we are analysing, the more obvious becomes the preponderance of professional politicians. This trend is, however, also evident in the statistics for the Parliamentary Labour Party as a whole. The Labour MPs elected in 1951 included thirty-three journalists and 103 representatives of the liberal professions, of whom forty were lawyers, and 122 people with a university education, of whom fifty-two had previously been educated at a public school.[1] In the 1955 Parliament 43.5 per cent of Labour MPs were from the liberal professions and another 20 per cent came from a white-collar background. Very few MPs in that Parliament had ever been manual workers. Most of the MPs who had once done such work were born before 1900. These were men of the type of Tom Williams or Wilfred Paling, miners who had become MPs in 1922, or David Mort, a steelworker in his youth who from 1915 onwards held various trade union posts. Only a few of the younger MPs had ever been manual workers.

The influx of professionals into the Labour Party elite is a necessary and

1 D. H. E. Butler, *The British general election of 1951*, Macmillan, London, 1952, pp. 39, 41.

indispensable process. It does, however, bring up the problem of relationships between the two branches of the Labour elite, particularly with regard to the party's performance of its function as a mechanism for individual advancement for the most ambitious and talented individuals from working class circles. In actual fact, professionals have a decided superiority over trade union functionaries as regards the skills required by a professional politician at the present time. Viewed in abstraction, we could postulate a situation in which the group of professionals would compete with and totally eliminate the group of trade unionists. But this could be done only in the abstract. In real life it is not only political skills which are a criterion in the selection of the Labour elite. Unlike the majority of socialist parties in Europe, the Labour Party's structure is a composite one, based on the affiliation of the trade unions. As a consequence, the trade union functionaries draw support from an independent organisational structure outside the party. They use this support to put up an effective opposition to the group of professionals, who have only their qualifications behind them. This possession of an independent source of power gives them an even chance, and makes up for the handicap of being less well qualified. The structure of a social democratic party such as the Labour Party appears to prevent it from ceasing to function as a mechanism for individual advancement for leaders of working class origins. Each leader of the Labour Party, if he wishes to succeed as a leader must, when forming his Cabinet, consider carefully not only the candidates' qualifications but also their organisational background and their influence on particular groups within the party. As a result, the Labour Party continues to perform the task of guiding the working class elite into the ranks of the political power elite, and thereby, *inter alia*, maintains its ties with the mass labour organisations. This state of affairs makes it highly improbable, one may suppose, that the group of professional politicians will take over the Labour Party completely in the immediate future. This supposition is supported by the fact that, owing to the changes in the status of the trade union movement, the pressure towards advancement by the union elite of the Labour Party has moderated considerably, and can thus be met at a decreasing cost. For some time to come Labour Prime Ministers are likely to have serious difficulty, not in finding enough government posts for the trade unionists, but in finding trade unionists who wish to take up government posts.

The historical period covered by our model analysis ends around 1955. By that date the labour movement in Britain seemed to have developed into a fully equilibrated system, with all three elements—class composition organisational model and psycho-social profile of the elite—well matched to meet the system's many functions.

The labour movement is not, however, a self-sufficient system whose historical contingencies can be satisfactorily derived from its inherent dynamics alone. It is an integral unit of a larger social system and its internal equilibration can—without any visible change—turn into a dynamising and revolutionary factor. The changing status of Britain, with the tensions resulting therefrom, is one of the factors which can, for instance, transform the unions' bargaining machinery, perfectly adjusted to an expanding economy dominating world markets, into a defensive weapon, causing both an increasing systematic resistance and an awareness of the inadequacy of the unions' armament. That is why our diagnosis, however analytically sound, bears little predictive value. There are still plenty of open ends left. The coming epoch may bring defensive efforts to resist the inroads made against the status the labour movement has achieved. But it could also bring a submissive but reluctant retreat to an inferior status—as well as a new upsurge of the old militant and radical spirit in strata where it has for long been regarded as an extinct volcano.

Nor is it easy to predict which course will be taken by the Labour Party —hitherto the political wing of the movement. The party has long since outgrown the too tight-fitting gown of political representation of the working class trade union organisation. Thanks to the logic of the British parliamentary and electoral system, it has become, and is likely to remain in the forseeable future, one of the two large 'national parties', forced to cater for many different tastes and appentencies. Old stereotypes die hard, and quite a few Labour politicians may still think of the party in terms of ideological and organisational unity while in fact operating in a setting that in many ways bears a striking resemblance to the variegated, loosely knit tissue of, say, the Democrats in America. It may happen, equally, that the trade unions, suddenly radicalised, may in their turn find the over-stretched, discoloured political gown of the party too ample for their more narrowly pointed class politics. The first trend seems more probable, since the wind of reform which once filled Labour's sails spent itself when the vessel reached the haven of the 'welfare State', and since both the unions and the State have arrived at a stage in their mutual adjustment where they can cope with an impressively wide range of issues without exactly bringing passions to the boil, and without necessarily invoking political action. But then, human history is notorious for its insidious defiance of probabilities.

Conclusion

In this study I have tried to investigate the dependences which link the evolution of the working class with that of the labour movement and the group at the head of that movement. I have attempted to identify the objective causes which lead a class or particular strata of it to develop an interest in maintaining and strengthening the existing pattern of social forces and the accepted rules of the political game. It is known that social developments of this type have been exceptionally strong and enduring in the case of the British labour movement. For that reason this movement lends itself extremely well to the kind of analysis undertaken here.

We can now draw attention to some more general conclusions which emerge from the present analysis.

1. In the course of my analysis of the evolution of the structure of the labour movement in Britain I distinguished two analytically extreme states which seemed likely to be heuristically useful: (*a*) the state of dynamism, characterised by flexibility of organisational forms and a great qualitative absorptive capacity in the movement (i.e. the capacity to assimilate new, hitherto unorganised strata of the working class; strata with specific, so far unrepresented interests); and (*b*) the state of stabilisation, characterised by an increasing rigidity of organisational forms and an absorptive ability that is only quantitative (i.e. the ability to absorb only more members who belong to strata already taken in by the organisation). By using these two extreme types of structural state one can represent the history of the British labour movement as in the accompanying diagram. Points A and C indicate

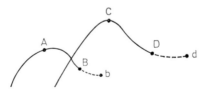

the states of maximum dynamism of the skilled workers' movements and the new unionism, while the curves B–b and D–d indicate the states of stabilisation achieved at different levels of the structural evolution of the movement.

2. The movement's states of dynamism were accompanied by non-conformist attitudes among the members of the stratum that was being taken in by the movement. The term 'nonconformist attitude' is, however, usually applied too loosely, and it seems that one should distinguish two different attitudes: (i) nonconformism with regard to the prevailing social structure and its associated hierarchy of values; and (ii) nonconformism with regard to the division of the resources which rank high on that values hierarchy, combined with acceptance of the actual hierarchy and the social

structure which supports it. The second attitude (ii) was characteristic of the period of dynamism experienced by the trade union movement of a relatively small stratum, while the first one emerged when the movement represented the overall interests of the working class as a whole.

States of stabilisation have been accompanied by a third attitude: (iii) acceptance of both the hierarchy of prevailing values and their distribution. Here one must stress most emphatically that all three attitudes are of a somewhat simplistic 'ideal type' nature. For instance, at the present time the third attitude is a trend and not an empirical generalisation on the trade union movement in Britain.

In the history of the British trade union movement the evolution of the attitudes which accompanied the transition from a state of dynamism to a state of stabilisation could be expressed by the sequence (ii) → (iii) in the case of the movement which institutionalised the interests of a stratum, and (i) → (ii) → (iii) in the case of the movement which institutionalised the interests of a class.

3. The factors operative in achieving the ultimate accommodation of the labour movement in the socio-political system were: (*a*) the raising of the lowest socio-economic status sufficiently to allow various strata of the working class, or the working class as a whole, to extricate itself from its state of marginality and estrangement while confirming its aspirations towards individual upward mobility within the limits set by the existing capitalist social structure; (*b*) the construction and functioning of adequate channels for individual mobility from one generation to another and within a single generation; in Britain these were provided by the educational system, the bureaucratic and administrative hierarchy, and the advancement of the professional trade union official up the dominant scale of social prestige. In other words, the harmonisation of class relations was furthered by the fact that although the essential differences in the socioeconomic positions and prestige of the classes and strata were maintained, the boundaries which divided them were more or less blurred and the lowest limit of the whole hierarchy was raised. Both these factors reached a point of maximum influence twice in the course of a century. The scale of this influence was defined by the class content of the stage reached by the movement, as shown in points A and C of the diagram above.

4. Another important factor which helped to determine the peaceful direction taken by the trade union movement was the typically British circumstance that occupational interests were activated before class interests had a chance of becoming articulated. This made it possible for the labour movement to be absorbed by the capitalist political and economic structure with sufficient gradualness to make a correspondingly gradual adaptation of this structure possible. The same circumstance led to the

eventual articulation of class interests in the form of the sum of occupational interests; this circumstance was largely responsible for giving the structure of the movement its specific form and made possible a swift transition from attitude (i) to attitude (ii).

5. An analysis of the history of the British labour movement enables one to confirm the existence of strict dependences between the structure and the social position of the class, the structure of the movement and the structure of the elite. The structure of the movement was at every period the expression of the existing position of stratum or class interests and their mutual relations; meanwhile it was itself also an important factor in articulating these interests and helping to crystallise the structure of its social base. On the other hand, the composition, mechanism of recruitment and social characteristics of the movement's elite were always closely linked with the structure of the movement and its social position. The actual emergence of the elite as a definite stratum in the movement was conditional upon the attainment by the movement of a stage of development in which its leaders required qualifications other than those possessed by its members by virtue of the work which they performed, and in which the social position conferred by a leading post in the movement was higher than that which potential candidates for such posts derived from their social connections outside the movement.

It can be said that the line of historical development and maturing of the British labour movement has been governed by a double dialectic: that of situation and its ideological assessment (which is a two-pronged term, and thus preferable to the somewhat misleading, one-directional term 'definition'), and that of the organisational framework and psycho-social processes. The frequently discussed 'gradualness' (for some authors synonymous with peacefulness) of this movement's evolution consisted, it would seem, in the fact that neither pole of the two paradigms would reach a dangerously intensive dynamic without the second having been set on a corresponding change. In the first case, the mutual adjustment of the situation and the ideological formula employed was never undermined to the extent of rendering the existing assessment useless as an explanatory and guiding device. In the second case, substantial new changes in the scale of psycho-social processes were never brought about before the organisational structure previously developed was able to absorb and mould them. Although entirely spontaneous, the perfect working of the two dialectics brings to mind an ingenious and well planned long-range defensive strategy of the socio-political system.

I prefer to discuss the issue in terms of dialectics instead of cause and effect. There is not much to be learned from the periodically resurrected

argument of 'situation generating a matching ideology' versus 'definitions creating the situation'. What seems to be significant is the fact that
nothing important happens in human history unless the two analytically
separable deterministic chains of 'situation' and its 'ideological assessment'
meet, i.e. unless an available ideology renders a privately or collectively
experienced situation intelligible to the actors and does it in a way which
makes the ideologically reshaped aims of the actors feasible. The relation
is dialectical and not deterministic, since the compatibility of a situation
with an ideology within reach happens to be an after-effect of this ideology
as it was operative at an earlier phase; at least to the same extent as the
selection of an ideology from those which are available is a function of the
form taken by the situation. On the face of it, the Turners and the Tilletts
rebelled against the *Weltanschauung* of the Applegarths and the Odgers.
In fact their revolt was rendered possible by the historical fact that the
ideology of the Applegarths and the Odgers 'worked'. 'Cutting the other's
cloth to one's own measure' is an activity which operates dialectically in
both directions. The position in Britain was that the labour movement
seemingly embodied the quality ascribed by Marx to whole formations:
it never set itself targets which it was still too immature (or lacked the
reserves) to reach.

The same quality seems to be clearly discernible in the realm of the
second paradigm as well—that of organisational framework and psycho-
social processes. It happened that the size of the spontaneous movements
was always tailored to the measure of the absorptive capacities of the already established organisations—which were, in their turn, adjusted to the
movements of a preceding epoch. That is why the continuity in organisational evolution was virtually never interrupted and shattered. A well
rooted organisation, though setting action patterns and establishing
stereotypes, somehow indirectly regulated the course of events without
actually dominating them.

And there is still the third kind of dialectics, which has provided the focal
issue of the study: the dialectics of the historical destiny of a class, the
structure of its movement and the socio-psychological profile of its elite.
None of these three units, though analytically separate, has played an
independent, much less a determining role in pushing the labour movement through the bends and traps of its historical itinerary. They may be
better conceived as three nodes of a triangle of interacting forces, but even
this diagrammatical presentation portrays only an approximation of the
truth. In fact, the actual meaning of each of the three elements at every
single moment is definable solely in terms of the other two elements and
the momentum of their dynamics. This is why comprehending the history
of a large historical movement defeats any attempt to force dialectical

phenomena into an unyielding pattern of cause and effect, whether 'objectively' or 'subjectively' interpreted. Neither unit is 'decisive' and 'determining' in itself; each opens up a bundle of options, and only through the interaction of all units does one option become the historical reality.

Index

compiled by Janina Bauman